Complete A+ Guide to IT Hardware and Software Lab Manual

A CompTIA A+ Core 1 (220-1001) & CompTIA A+ Core 2 (220-1002) Lab Manual

EIGHTH EDITION

CHERYL A. SCHMIDT

FLORIDA STATE COLLEGE AT JACKSONVILLE

PEARSON IT
CERTIFICATION

Complete A+ Guide to IT Hardware and Software Lab Manual, Eighth Edition

Copyright © 2020 by Pearson Education, Inc.

ISBN-13: 978-0-13-538019-2
ISBN-10: 0-13-538019-7

Library of Congress Control Number: 2019930936

3 2021

Trademarks

All terms mentioned in this book that are known to be trademarks or service marks have been appropriately capitalized. Pearson IT Certification cannot attest to the accuracy of this information. Use of a term in this book should not be regarded as affecting the validity of any trademark or service mark.

Warning and Disclaimer

Every effort has been made to make this book as complete and as accurate as possible, but no warranty or fitness is implied. The information provided is on an "as is" basis. The author and the publisher shall have neither liability nor responsibility to any person or entity with respect to any loss or damages arising from the information contained in this book.

Special Sales

For information about buying this title in bulk quantities, or for special sales opportunities (which may include electronic versions; custom cover designs; and content particular to your business, training goals, marketing focus, or branding interests), please contact our corporate sales department at corpsales@pearsoned.com or (800) 382-3419.

For government sales inquiries, please contact governmentsales@pearsoned.com.

For questions about sales outside the U.S., please contact intlcs@pearson.com.

Editor-in-Chief
Mark Taub

Executive Editor
Mary Beth Ray

Senior Editor
James Manly

Development Editor
Ellie C. Bru

Managing Editor
Sandra Schroeder

Project Editor
Mandie Frank

Proofreader
Debbie Williams

Technical Editor and Contributors
Chris Crayton
Jeff Burns
Melodie Schmidt
Karl Schmidt
Elizabeth Drake

Publishing Coordinator
Cindy Teeters

Cover Designer
Chuti Prasertsith

Compositor
Tricia Bronkella

Art Production
Justin Ache
Katherine Martin
Marc Durrence
Amanda McIntosh
KC Frick
Vived Graphics

Photographers
Raina Durrence
George Nichols

Contents at a Glance

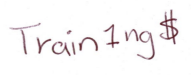

Contents

About the Author

Cheryl Schmidt is a professor of Network Engineering Technology at Florida State College at Jacksonville. Prior to joining the faculty ranks, she oversaw the LAN and PC support for the college and other organizations. She started her career as an electronics technician in the U.S. Navy. She teaches computer repair and various networking topics, including CCNA, network management, and network design. She has published other works with Pearson, including *IP Telephony Using CallManager Express* and *Routing and Switching in the Enterprise Lab Guide*.

Cheryl has won awards for teaching and technology, including Outstanding Faculty of the Year, Innovative Teacher of the Year, Cisco Networking Academy Instructor Excellence Award, and Cisco Networking Academy Stand Out Instructor. She has presented at U.S. and international conferences. Cheryl keeps busy maintaining her technical certifications and teaching but also loves to travel, hike, do all types of puzzles, and read.

Dedication

A Note to Instructors:

I was a teacher long before I had the title professor. Sharing what I know has always been as natural as walking to me, but sitting still to write what I know is not as natural, so composing this text has always been one of my greatest challenges. Thank you so much for choosing this text. I thank you for sharing your knowledge and experience with your students. Your dedication to education is what makes the student experience so valuable.

A Note to Students:

Writing a textbook is really different from teaching class. I have said for years that my students are like my children, except that I don't have to pay to send them through college. I am happy to claim any of you who have this text. I wish that I could be in each classroom with you as you start your IT career. How exciting!

Another thing that I tell my students is that I am not an expert. IT support is an ever-changing field and I have been in it since PCs started being used. You have to be excited about the never-ending changes to be good in this field. You can never stop learning or you will not be very good any more. I offer one important piece of advice:

> Consistent, high-quality service boils down to two equally important things: caring and competence.
> —Chip R. Bell and Ron Zemke

I dedicate this book to you. I can help you with the competence piece, but you are going to have to work on the caring part. Do not ever forget that there are people behind those machines that you love to repair. Taking care of people is as important as taking care of the computers.

Acknowledgments

I am so thankful for the support of my family during the production of this book. My husband, Karl, daughters, Raina and Karalina, and son-in-law, Marc, were such a source of inspiration and encouragement. My grandsons, Gavin, Riley, Logan, and Liam, and my granddaughter, Brie, are a constant source of wonderment for me. They were a shining light at the end of some very long days. Thanks to my mother, Barbara Cansler, who taught me to love words and my brother Jeff Cansler for just listening. Thanks to my walking buddy, Kellie, for the miles of letting me work through knotty sections. Thanks to my colleagues, adjuncts, and students at my college who offered numerous valuable suggestions for improvement and testing the new material. Thanks to my colleagues Pamela Brauda and David Singletary for just letting me rant. Finally, I want to thank my personal technical team, Justin Ache, Raina Durrence, Marc Durrence, and Jeff Burns.

Many thanks are also due the folks at Pearson. The professionalism and support given during this edition was stellar. Thank you so much, Pearson team, especially Eleanor Bru, Mary Beth Ray, Kitty Wilson, Mandie Frank, and my favorite technical reviewer/hatchet man, Chris Crayton. A special thanks to Mary Beth Ray, my executive editor and juggler extraordinaire. I hope all of you can see the results of your contributions. I thank the whole team so much for your conscientious efforts.

Finally, thank you to the students who have taken the time to share their recommendations for improvement. You are the reason I write this book each time. Please send me any ideas and comments you may have. I love hearing from you and of your successes. I may be reached at cheryl.schmidt@fscj.edu.

Credits

Figure Number	Attribution/Credit Line
Lab 13-1	George Nichols
Lab 13-2	George Nichols
Lab 13-3	George Nichols
Lab 13-4	George Nichols
Lab 13-5	George Nichols

Cover credit: PopTika/Shutterstock

We Want to Hear from You!

As the reader of this book, *you* are our most important critic and commentator. We value your opinion and want to know what we're doing right, what we could do better, what areas you'd like to see us publish in, and any other words of wisdom you're willing to pass our way.

We welcome your comments. You can email or write to let us know what you did or didn't like about this book—as well as what we can do to make our books better.

Please note that we cannot help you with technical problems related to the topic of this book.

When you write, please be sure to include this book's title and author as well as your name and email address. We will carefully review your comments and share them with the author and editors who worked on the book.

Email: community@informit.com

Introduction

Complete A+ Guide to IT Hardware and Software, eighth edition, is a textbook that corresponds with this lab manual intended for one or more courses geared toward CompTIA A+ Certification and computer repair. The textbook covers all the material needed for the CompTIA A+ Core 1 (220-1001) and CompTIA A+ Core 2 (220-1002) exams. The textbook is written so that it is easy to read and understand, with concepts presented in building-block fashion. The book focuses on hardware, software, mobile devices, virtualization, basic networking, and security.

Some of the best features of the book include the coverage of difficult subjects in a step-by-step manner, carefully developed graphics that illustrate concepts, photographs that demonstrate various technologies, reinforcement questions, critical thinking skills, soft skills, and hands-on exercises at the end of each chapter. Also, this book is written by a teacher who understands the value of a textbook from someone who has been in IT her entire career.

This Lab Manual contains more than 140 labs that enable you to link theory to practical experience.

What's New in the Eighth Edition?

This textbook update has been revised to include more coverage of hardware, mobile devices, and troubleshooting. There are also new sections on managed/unmanaged switches, VLANs, cloud-based network controllers, IoT device configuration, Active Directory settings, common documentation, and scripting. The following are a few of the many new features of this edition:

> This book conforms with the latest CompTIA A+ exam requirements, including those of the CompTIA A+ Core 1 (220-1001) and CompTIA A+ Core 2 (220-1002) exams.
> Chapter 2 now includes network cabling basics.
> The video chapter has been removed as the certification exam includes only Windows configuration of video, which is covered in Chapter 16.
> Chapter 12 now includes all virtualization and cloud technologies information.
> Chapter 13 includes IoT device configuration.
> The operating system–related chapters have been rearranged. Chapter 14 is an introduction to operating systems and Windows basics. Chapter 15 contains the command prompt and scripting sections. Chapter 16 contains the bulk of the information on configuring and supporting Windows 7, 8, and 10. Chapter 17 is still the macOS and Linux chapter.
> Chapters 1 through 9 focus on hardware. Chapter 10 covers mobile devices. Chapter 11 is on computer design and serves as a troubleshooting review. Chapter 12 covers Internet connectivity, virtualization, and cloud computing. Chapter 13 dives into networking. Chapters 14 through 17 cover operating systems. Chapter 18 handles security concepts. Finally, Chapter 19 contains operational procedures. Appendix A provides an introduction to subnetting.
> The book has always been filled with graphics and photos, but even more have been added to target those naturally drawn to the IT field. This edition is full color.
> There are questions at the end of each chapter, and even more questions are available in the test bank available from the Pearson Instructor Resource Center.

Organization of the Text

The text is organized to allow thorough coverage of all topics and also to be a flexible teaching tool. It is not necessary to cover all the chapters, nor do the chapters have to be covered in order. The labs in this manual correspond to these topic areas.

> **Chapter 1** provides an introduction to IT and careers that need the information in this book. It identifies computer parts. Chapter 1 does not have a specific soft skills section, as do the other chapters. Instead, it focuses on common technician qualities that are explored in greater detail in the soft skills sections of later chapters. Finally, Chapter 1 has a great introduction to using Notepad, the Windows Snipping Tool, and Internet search techniques.

> **Chapter 2** is about connecting things to the computer and port identification. Details are provided on video, USB, and sound ports. The soft skills section is on using appropriate titles.

> **Chapter 3** details components, features, and concepts related to motherboards, including processors, caches, expansion slots, and chipsets. Active listening skills are the focus of the soft skills section.

> **Chapter 4** deals with system configuration basics. BIOS options, UEFI BIOS, and system resources are key topics. The soft skills section covers the importance of doing one thing at a time when replacing components.

> **Chapter 5** steps through how to disassemble and reassemble a computer. Tools, ESD, EMI, and preventive maintenance are discussed. Subsequent chapters also include preventive maintenance topics. Basic electronics and computer power concepts are also included in this chapter. The soft skills section involves written communication.

> **Chapter 6** covers memory installation, preparation, and troubleshooting. The importance of teamwork is emphasized as the soft skill.

> **Chapter 7** deals with storage devices, including PATA, SATA SCSI, SAS, and SSDs. RAID is also covered. Phone communication skills are covered in the soft skills section of this chapter.

> **Chapter 8** covers multimedia devices, including optical drives, sound cards, cameras, scanners, and speakers. The chapter ends with a section on having a positive, proactive attitude.

> **Chapter 9** provides details on printers. A discussion of work ethics finishes the chapter.

> **Chapter 10** is on mobile devices, including details on mobile device operating systems, configuration, backup, security, and troubleshooting. The soft skills section takes a brief foray into professional appearance.

> **Chapter 11** covers computer design. Not only are the specialized computers and components needed within the types of systems covered, but computer subsystem design is also included. Because design and troubleshooting are high on the academic learning progression, the chapter also includes a review of troubleshooting, including logic, error codes, and troubleshooting flowcharts. The soft skills section provides recommendations for dealing with irate customers.

> **Chapter 12** handles Internet connectivity, virtualization, and cloud technologies. Internet browser configuration is covered, along with the soft skill of mentoring

> **Chapter 13** introduces networking. Basic concepts, terminology, and exercises make this chapter a favorite. The introduction to subnetting has been moved to an appendix. The focus of the soft skills section is being proactive instead of reactive.

> **Chapter 14** provides an introduction to operating systems in general and discusses basic differences between the Windows versions and how to function in the various Windows environments. The soft skills section includes tips on how to stay current in this fast-paced field.

> **Chapter 15** is a new introduction to scripting and includes how to function from the command prompt and the basics of scripting in Python, JavaScript, shell scripting, VBScript, batch files, and PowerShell. The soft skills section discusses looking at a problem from the user's perspective and being more empathetic.

> **Chapter 16** covers Windows 7, 8, and 10. Details include how to install, configure, and troubleshoot the environment. Avoiding burnout is the soft skill discussed in this chapter.

> **Chapter 17** discusses the basics of macOS and Linux. It provides a basic introduction to these two environments to help a technician become familiar with the environment and a few tools. The soft skills section talks about being humble.

> **Chapter 18** describes computer, mobile device, and network security. The soft skills section is on building customer trust.

> **Chapter 19** guides the student through operational procedures such as workplace safety, recycling, disposal, a review of power protection, change management, and communication skills.

1 Introduction to the World of IT Labs

Lab 1.1 Getting Started in Windows 7

Objective: To be able to use Windows 7 to locate and launch applications

Parts: Windows 7 computer

Procedure: Complete the following procedure and answer the accompanying questions.

1. Power on the computer and log in. You may need to contact an instructor or a student assistant for the user ID and password.

2. Click the *Start* button in the bottom-left corner of the screen. The Start button is used to launch applications and utilities, search for files and other computers, obtain help, and add/remove hardware and software. The Start button menu is configurable, as shown in a later lab. Lab Figure 1.1 shows a sample Windows 7 Start button menu.

Start button

LAB FIGURE 1.1   Windows 7 Start button

3. The left panel of the Start button window contains a list of commonly used applications. An item that has an arrow to the right of the name has a submenu that contains recently used application files that can be accessed by holding the pointer over the right arrow and clicking on the filename in the right panel. A recently used file does not have to be used. You can simply click the name of the application, and it will open.

    List one application found in the left panel of the Start button menu.

    _____

4. There are several other ways to access applications from the Start button menu, especially if it is not shown in the left panel. Explore one way by clicking on the *All Programs* link at the bottom. The All Programs Start button option contains applications and folders that contain other applications. Notice the scrollbar on the right (see Lab Figure 1.2); it enables you to scroll through the installed applications.

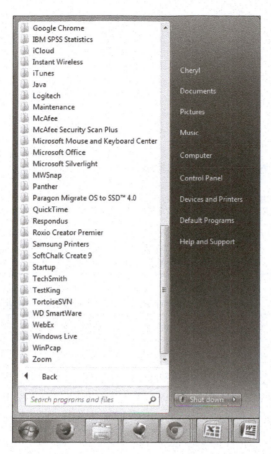

LAB FIGURE 1.2   Windows 7 All Programs menu

What is the name of the last All Programs application or folder shown on your computer?

_____

5.   Examine the available applications located throughout the list.

     Which application do you think you might use the most?

_____

6.   To access an application within a folder, you must first click on the folder and then click on the application. Locate and select the *Accessories* folder.

     List three applications found in the Accessories folder.

_____

_____

_____

7.   Another way of accessing applications is through the *Search programs and files* textbox, accessed from the Start button. Click on the *Start* button, and right above the Start button you can see this textbox. Click once inside the textbox and start typing the word `note`. At the top of the screen you see a couple of programs that have the word "note" in them.

     List one application found using the keyword "note."

_____

8.   Click on the *Notepad* application at the top of the list. The Notepad application opens.

9.   Notice the three buttons in the top-right corner. These three buttons, which are common in windows, are shown in Lab Figure 1.3. Lab Table 1.1 details the purpose of these buttons.

LAB FIGURE 1.3   Windows 7 window buttons

LAB TABLE 1.1   Windows top-right window buttons

Button	Purpose
Minimize (straight line)	Keeps the program running but removes it from being active on the screen. Use the Alt+Tab buttons to re-access the app.
Maximize/Restore Down (rectangle)	Used to make the window that holds the app full screen (maximize) or, if you size the window, restore it to its default size.
Close (X)	Used to close an app.

10. Click on the far-right close button to close Notepad.

11. Use the *Search programs and files* textbox to locate and launch the *Calculator* application.

   Which three menu items are available with the Calculator application?

   _____

12. Whenever you use an application, the open application icon appears on the Windows 7 taskbar, at the bottom of the screen. The taskbar is customizable, and this skill is taught later in the book. Notice that a small calculator icon appears on the taskbar. Click on an icon, and the corresponding application appears on the desktop.

13. Minimize the Calculator application by clicking on the *Minimize* button (straight line) in the top-right corner. Notice that the calculator is still loaded, as indicated by the icon on the taskbar.

14. Use the *All Programs* Start button item to locate the *Sticky Notes* application accessory. Remember that you must first access the Accessories folder to locate the applications within that folder. Notice that the Sticky Notes application icon is on the taskbar.

15. An easy way to move between applications is by using the Alt+Tab keys. Hold down the Alt key. While keeping that key held down, tap once on the Tab key. A window with all open applications appears. While keeping the Alt key depressed and tapping the Tab key once, the cursor cycles through the open applications. When it highlights the application you want to re-access, let the Alt and Tab keys go. Use the Alt and Tab keys to re-access the Calculator application.

Instructor initials: _____

16. Close the Calculator application by clicking the *Close* button.

17. Click on the *Sticky Notes* application icon on the taskbar. Close the Sticky Notes application by clicking the *Close* button.

18. Easily access the Windows 7 Start button menu at any time by pressing the Windows key (⊞).

Lab 1.2 Getting Started in Windows 8

Objective: To be able to use Windows 8.x to locate and launch applications and locate control panels used in future labs

Parts: Windows 8 or 8.1 computer

Procedure: Complete the following procedure and answer the accompanying questions.

1. Power on the computer. Windows 8 was designed for mobile (touch) devices, so the Windows 8 desktop is different from previous Windows versions. However, some people bought computers and laptops that did not have touch monitors. The method used to unlock a Windows desktop depends on the type of computer you have:

    - **Touch screen**—Press your finger on the screen and move upward.

    - **Desktop computer**—Press any key and release, click the mouse anywhere, click the mouse near the bottom of the screen, or hold the mouse button down while moving the cursor upward.

    - **Laptop**—Press any key and release, click the mouse anywhere, hold down the left trackpad section or button, or move the cursor upward.

2. Type the password. Contact the instructor or lab assistant if the password is unknown.

    Note: Anywhere in this lab when the direction is to "click" something, if a touchscreen is available, you can tap with your finger instead.

3. The Windows Start screen appears. Lab Figure 1.4 shows a sample Windows Start screen. You can press the Windows key (⊞) at any time to bring up the Start screen. You can also point at the bottom-left corner of the screen until a small Start screen display appears so you can click on it.

LAB FIGURE 1.4   Windows 8 Start screen

4. The Start screen has the user listed in the upper-right corner. This icon can be used to lock the computer and sign out of the user account.

    What user account is being used to do this lab?

    _____

5.   The Start screen also contains tiles. Tiles are used to access apps, such as the current news, weather, or traditional applications, such as a web browser or word processing software. Tiles are rectangular or square and fill the Start screen. Use the scrollbar at the bottom of the screen to access the tiles to the right.

What is the name of the last app shown on the right?

_____

6.   Examine the available tiles.

Which app do you think you might use the most frequently?

_____

7.   Parts of the Start screen that are not immediately evident are the charms. Charms are little icons that are used to quickly access apps. The charms that appear depend on the manufacturer and are software dependent. The charms seen from the Start screen commonly include charms to perform a search and access some common Windows settings. Lab Figure 1.5 shows an example of Windows 8 Start screen charms.

LAB FIGURE 1.5   Windows 8 Start screen charms

8.   Access the Start screen charms by pointing to the bottom-right corner of the screen. Click the *Search* charm. Lab Figure 1.6 shows an example of the menu that appears.

LAB FIGURE 1.6   Windows 8 Search Apps window

9.   The options below the Search text window are selectable items to designate where you want to search. When learning to configure, maintain, and repair Windows, you will commonly use the default selection, Apps. In the Search textbox, type notepad and *do not* press ⏎Enter. Notice that the Notepad application appears to the left.

10. Click once on the *Notepad* app. The Notepad app opens.

11. Notice the three buttons in the top-right corner (refer to Lab Figure 1.3 in Lab 1.1). Lab Table 1.1 (also in Lab 1.1) details the purpose of each of these buttons.

12. Click on the far-right *Close* button to close Notepad.

13. Sometimes the application you need is not one you remember. When you click on the Search charm, all apps display in the left panel, and you can use the scrollbar at the bottom of the screen to search through them. When you find the app you want, click it to open it.

14. Access the *Search* charm. Do not type in the Search charm textbox. Instead, access it by clicking one time in the panel to the left, where all apps display. Locate the Sticky Notes app by scrolling through the apps. Open the *Sticky Notes* app.

     Which symbol is in the top-left corner of the Sticky Notes app?

     _____

15. Close the Sticky Notes app by selecting the *Close* button.

16. There are several ways to access the traditional Windows desktop. One way is to access the Desktop tile from the Start screen. Use one of the methods described to access the *Desktop* tile from the Start screen.

     What happened when you clicked or tapped the Desktop tile from the Start screen?

     _____

Instructor initials: _____

17. Re-access the Windows 8 Start screen by pressing the Windows key (⊞), clicking the *Windows* icon in the bottom-left corner, if available, or pointing the mouse to the bottom-left corner of the screen and clicking on the small *Start* screen that appears.

Lab 1.3 Getting Started in Windows 10

Objective: To be able to use Windows 10 to locate and launch applications and locate control panels used in future labs

Parts: Windows 10 computer

Procedure: Complete the following procedure and answer the accompanying questions.

1. Power on the computer. The method used to unlock a Windows desktop depends on the type of computer you have.

    - **Touch screen**—Press your finger on the screen and move upward.

    - **Desktop computer**—Press any key and release, click the mouse anywhere, click the mouse near the bottom of the screen, or hold the mouse button down while moving the cursor upward.

    - **Laptop**—Press any key and release, click the mouse anywhere, hold down the left trackpad section or button, or move the cursor upward.

2. Type the password. Contact the instructor or lab assistant if the password is unknown.

    Note: Anywhere in this lab when the direction is to "click" something, if a touchscreen is available, you can tap with your finger instead.

3. Windows 10 was designed for both traditional desktop and mobile (touch) devices. The Windows 10 desktop is different from previous Windows versions; it is a mixture of Windows 7 and Windows 8, as shown in Lab Figure 1.7. You can press the ▦ key on the keyboard at any time to bring up the Start menu.

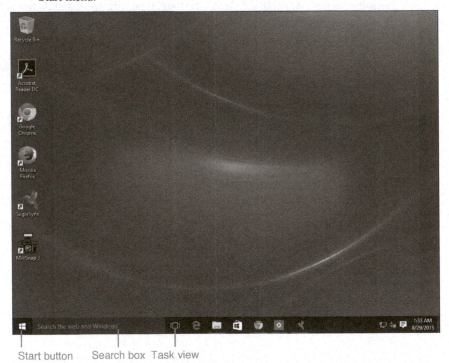

LAB FIGURE 1.7   Windows 10 desktop

4. Notice the *Windows* icon in the left corner; this is the Windows 10 version of the Start button. Click on the *Start* button to access the tiled apps much as you would in the Windows 8 Start screen, as shown in Lab Figure 1.8.

LAB FIGURE 1.8   Windows 10 Start button

5.   Again click the *Windows* icon (Start button) in the lower-left corner to return to the desktop. The desktop has a new look to it along the bottom. The Start button is different. The text area to the immediate right of the Start button used to be in the Start button menu or part of the charms in Windows 8. In Windows 10, there is an area for the icons of the most commonly used applications, and to the far right is the notification area.

List one icon of a commonly used application that is on your desktop.

_____

6.   Click the *Start* button. Locate and select the *All apps* option. Scroll through the options. Notice that the list contains both applications and folders.

7.   Locate and select the *Windows Accessories* folder to expand it. Locate and select the *Notepad* app to launch it.

What is the name of the last menu item shown on the far right inside the Notepad app?

_____

8.   Notice the three buttons in the top-right corner in the Notepad window (refer to Lab Figure 1.3 in Lab 1.1 to see them). Lab Table 1.1 (also in Lab 1.1) details the purpose of each of these buttons. Click the *Minimize* button (straight line). Notice that the application icon displays at the bottom of the screen in the taskbar as a small blue spiral notebook.

9.   Click on the *Notepad* application icon at the bottom of the screen. The Notepad application opens on the screen. Click the *Close* button (X) to close the application.

10. Another way to locate and launch an app is by using the *Search the web and Windows* textbox. Click once inside this textbox and type the word note but do not press ↵Enter. Notice that the Notepad desktop app is listed at the top of the screen. The Sticky Notes app also appears.

List one other app that is shown that has the letters "note" in its name.

_____

_____

Note: When you have two or more applications open in Windows 10, you can hold down the Alt key and press the Tab⇆ key to cycle through any open applications. Windows 10 has a Task View icon on the taskbar that serves the same purpose. Refer to Lab Figure 1.7 to see that useful icon.

11. Select and launch the *Sticky Notes* app. The Sticky Notes app opens.

    What symbol is in the top-left corner of the Sticky Notes app?

    _____

12. Close the *Sticky Notes* app.

13. Click on the *Start* button in the bottom-left corner. Click in the tiled apps area. Launch one of the apps by clicking on a tile.

    Which app did you choose?

    _____

Instructor initials: _____

14. Close the application by clicking the *Close* button.

Lab 1.4 Using a Search Engine

Objective: To use Google to effectively search for information

Parts: Windows 7, 8, or 10 computer with Internet access

Procedure: Complete the following procedure and answer the accompanying questions.

1. Power on the computer. Log in or unlock the screen.

2. **Windows 7 users**—Click on the *Start* button in the bottom-left corner, select *All Programs*, and then select a web browser.

   Windows 8 users—Access and launch a browser app such as Windows Explorer, Google Chrome, or Mozilla Firefox from the Windows start screen. If one is not readily visible, click on the Windows icon (⊞) in the bottom-left corner to get a customized view of the applications. (On a mobile device, this may be a Windows symbol that you touch on the front side of the device to access these apps. You can then click the ⊡ that is inside the circle in the bottom left to view all apps and pick a browser app from there.)

   Windows 10 users—Access and launch a browser app such as Microsoft Edge, Microsoft Internet Explorer, Google Chrome, or Mozilla Firefox from the Windows start screen. If one is not readily visible, click *All apps* and scroll through the list to locate a browser app. Click on the browser app name to launch it.

3. In the browser window, type the following: `www.google.com`

   If a computer user has a Dell Windows 10 computer that the user complains is slow to boot, what search terms would you put in the browser window? List at least three.

   _____

4. In the search textbox, type the following: `Windows 10 computer problems`

   Approximately how many results list at the top of the screen under the menu?

   _____

5. Change the search criteria to `Windows 10 computer problem` (removing the *s* from problems).

   Approximately how many results list at the top of the screen under the menu?

   _____

6. Go into the first three problems by clicking on the first title line. To return to the search results, click the *Back* arrow (⟵).

   Do any of the problems have anything to do with slow booting?

   _____

7. In the search textbox, type the following: `Windows 10 slow boot`

Access the first result by clicking on the title line.

What was the resolution given in the resulting web link?

_____

_____

8. Sometimes computer resolutions contain links to software that might not be free after so many days and may contain malware or a virus. Only click on a link or use software tools from trustworthy vendors. Return to the search criteria by clicking on the *Back* arrow (⬅) or retyping `www.google.com` in the search textbox. Now change the search to the `Microsoft Windows 10 slow boot`. Look at the number of results listed and then access the first result.

Approximately how many results are available?

_____

Access the first result by clicking on the title line.

What was the resolution given?

_____

_____

_____

Do you think that this might be a good solution for the person who owns the Dell computer?
[Yes | No | I have no idea]

_____

9. Now add the word *Dell* to the search criteria, searching for the following: `Microsoft Windows 10 Dell slow boot`

Approximately how many results are available?

_____

Access the first result by clicking on the title line.

What resolution was given?

_____

Lab 1.5 Performing a Screen Capture with Snipping Tool

Objective: To use the Microsoft Windows Snipping Tool to effectively capture information

Parts: Windows 7, 8, or 10 computer with the Snipping Tool application

Procedure: Complete the following procedure and answer the accompanying questions. If you are not familiar with launching an application, complete Lab 1.1, 1.2, or 1.3 before doing this lab.

1. Power on the computer. Log in or unlock the screen.

2. Access a web browser. Leave it on the screen.

3. Many times when you are solving a problem, performing a task, or helping someone else, a picture is worth a thousand words. Locate and launch the Snipping Tool by expanding Windows Accessories or searching using the Windows Search textbox. The Snipping Tool application starts, as shown in Lab Figure 1.9, with a small window opening.

LAB FIGURE 1.9 Snipping Tool application window

4.   The Snipping Tool enables you to capture everything that shows on the screen (full-screen snip), a particular window that is open on the screen (window snip), a particular section of the screen that could be captured in a rectangle (rectangular snip), a particular part of the screen that is odd shaped, or simply an icon or a symbol. Click the ▼ beside the *New* menu option. Four options display. The default one has a ⦿ beside it.

5.   Click on the *Options* (*Tools > Options*) menu item. One particular option that you can select by clicking inside a box is the *Ink color* drop-down menu to select an ink color along with the related option of *Show selection ink after snips are captured* option. This feature automatically creates a box around whatever information is captured. Do not select it yet. Click *Cancel*.

6.   Ensure that the browser window is not taking up the entire desktop area. You can use the Maximize/ Restore Down button located in the top-right corner to size the window (refer to Lab Figure 1.3 and Lab Table 1.1 in Lab 1.1 for information on the buttons that are in the top-right corner).

7.   In the Snipping Tool window, click the ▼ beside the *New* menu option and select *Full-screen Snip*. The Snipping Tool application captures whatever is on the screen. If that is not what you want to capture and you only want to capture the search textbox, click *New*, and the Snipping Tool reverts to the small window.

8.   Click on the ▼ beside *New* again and select *Window Snip*. With a window snip, you must take the additional step of clicking on the window that you want. Click anywhere in the browser window.

     What information is shown inside the Snipping Tool window?

     _____

9.   Pretend this still is not what you wanted because it is too big, and you want to just capture the search textbox. Click the *Minimize* button (the button to the left of the Maximize/Restore Down button you used before).

10. Re-access the browser window by clicking anywhere on it. In the address bar of the browser window, type **www.pearson.com** in the textbox at the top of the screen but do not press the ↵Enter key.

11. With the browser window open, re-access the Snipping Tool by clicking on the *Snipping Tool* icon located in the taskbar (the icon showing scissors within a red circle) at the bottom of the screen. If the taskbar is not there, which may be the case on a Window 8 computer, hold down the Alt key and, while continuing to hold it down, press Tab⇄. The currently running programs appear. Press the Tab⇄ key again until the Snipping Tool is selected. Let go of both keys, and the Snipping Tool application window appears on the screen. Ensure that the Snipping Tool application window is on a part of the desktop by itself (not on top of the browser window). In order to move a window, you can click on the top part of the Snipping Tool window and, while continuing to hold down the mouse or touchpad, drag the window to a different part of the screen.

12. Click the *New* menu option and select *Rectangular Snip*. The screen appears grayed out. This is normal. A crosshairs symbol (which looks like a plus symbol) appears on the screen. Move the screen cursor (which, in turn, moves the crosshairs symbol) to the top part of the browser window, which contains the search textbox. Click and drag the crosshairs until it captures the part of the browser window that shows www.pearson.com.

     List one instance in which you think an IT person might use the rectangular snip option.

     _____

13. After taking a screen capture, the Snipping Tool window has more menu options available. Click the *File* menu option.

     Which four menu options are available?

     _____

14. Click the *Edit* menu option. This option can be used to select *Copy* so you can simply paste into an email or word processing document. Select the *Tools* menu item. Point to the *Pen* option and select *Blue Pen* from the menu. Use the pen to circle the words *pearson.com*.

15. Access the *Tools* menu item again and select the *Highlighter* option. Highlight *www*.

Instructor initials: _____

16. Close the Snipping Tool window by clicking on the *Close* button, which is located to the immediate right of the Maximize/Restore Down button. The Close button is in the top right of the Snipping Tool application window and has an X on the icon.

17. When asked if you want to save the snipped document, click *No*.

Lab 1.6 Creating a Text File

Objective: To use the various applications and apps to create a text file

Parts: Windows 7, 8, or 10 computer

Procedure: Complete the following procedure and answer the accompanying questions. If you are not familiar with launching an application, complete Lab 1.1, 1.2, or 1.3 before doing this lab.

1. Power on the computer. Log in or unlock the screen.

2. Locate and launch the *Notepad* application. The Notepad application starts, as shown in Lab Figure 1.10.

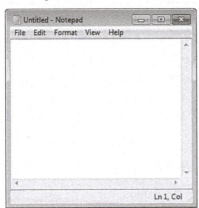

LAB FIGURE 1.10   Notepad application

Which five menu options are available?

_____

Which menu options do you think would be used to automatically insert the date and time?

_____

3. Notepad can be used to document problems on a computer that does not have a word processing app loaded, a working word processing app, or that has other issues. It can also be used for scripting, which is covered in Chapter 15, "Introduction to Scripting." Both Microsoft Notepad and WordPad ship with the Windows operating system. Notepad does not have as many capabilities as WordPad. One of the things you can do with Notepad is insert the date and time into the document. Click the *Edit* menu item to see the full Edit menu, as shown in Lab Figure 1.11.

LAB FIGURE 1.11   Notepad Edit menu

4. Notice the words on the left and the corresponding keystrokes to the right. This means, for example, that you can either use the mouse to access the *Edit* menu and then select *Time/Date*, or you can simply press the F5 key to do the same thing. Click away from the Edit menu so you can try the keyboard shortcut. Click inside the blank *Notepad* window. Now press the F5 key.

5. Click the *View > Status bar* menu option.

   What did this option do?

   _____

   _____

6. Click the *View > Status bar* menu option again and notice that there is now a checkmark by the Status bar option, indicating that this option is enabled.

7. Notepad allows a few font modifications. To bold the date and time, click the *Format > Font* menu option to see the options, as shown in Lab Figure 1.12.

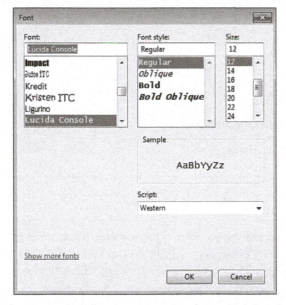

LAB FIGURE 1.12   Notepad Font dialog box

What is the default font (the font that is selected and highlighted by default)?

_____

What are the names of the first and last font types? Use your mouse and the scrollbar to see the fonts.

_____

8. Click the *Bold* option in the Font style section. Click the *OK* button to return to the Notepad window. Your date and time should have turned bold. Redo steps 7 and 8 if the words are not boldfaced.

    On your own, add the following message to the Notepad document. Ensure that you use the Verdana Regular 12 font type and size:

    Replaced display and tested. User confirms that the problem is solved.

9. Click the *Help* > *View Help* menu option.

    Which help topic would be of most interest to you?

    _____

10. Close the Help window by clicking on the *X* in the upper-right corner.

11. A header is a part of a document that might not appear on the screen, but when the document is printed, the information inside the header prints at the top of the page. A footer is at the bottom of the document. To insert a header and a footer in Notepad, click on the *File* > *Page Setup* option. Note that when you change the information in the header and footer, that information stays there for the current Notepad document and future documents as well.

    Use Help to determine what the &f, the default setting for the header, and Page &p, the default setting for the footer, mean. Document your findings.

    _____

    _____

12. Close the *Help* window.

    Instructor initials: _____

    _____

    _____

13. To save the document, click *File* > *Save As*. A window with several options appears, as shown in Lab Figure 1.13.

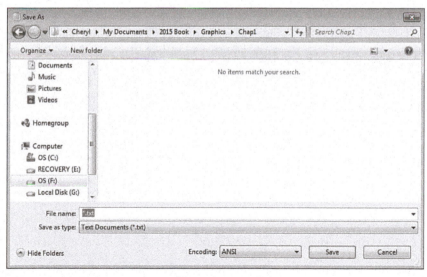

LAB FIGURE 1.13   Notepad Save As menu

14. When saving a file, you want to give it an appropriate name by entering it in the *File name* textbox. Start typing **documentation** in this textbox and notice how it automatically replaces the highlighted *.txt name. Do not press ⏎Enter yet.

15. The current location is shown at the top of the screen. To change this location and save it onto a flash drive, for example, you must first select your flash drive from the left window. Note that drive letters change depending on the system. In Lab Figure 1.13, the flash drive is G:. Click the *Documents* option in the left window. If any folders are on the drive, they appear. Click the *Cancel* button.

16. In the Notepad window, click the *Close* button (the button with a red X in the top-right corner). What message appears?

    _____

17. Click the *Don't Save* button.

2 Connectivity Labs

Lab 2.1 Identifying Ports

Objective: To identify various computer ports correctly

Parts: Computer ports, either built into a specific computer or as separate adapters

Procedure:

1. Contact your instructor for a computer on which to work or to obtain adapters.

2. Identify the computer port(s) given to you by the instructor. In Lab Table 2.1, fill in the connector type, number of pins, and port type. Note that you may have to refer to information in the book or on the Internet.

LAB TABLE 2.1   Connector identification

Connector type (D-shell, DIN, etc.)	Number of pins	Port purpose (video, USB, NIC, etc.)
1.		
2.		
3.		
4.		
5.		
6.		
7.		
8.		
9.		
10.		

Lab 2.2 Identifying Devices/Ports

Objective: To identify various computer ports correctly based on the type of connected device

Parts: Computer that has devices connected

Procedure:

1. Contact your instructor for a computer on which to work.

2. Ensure that the computer is powered off.

3. Use the same process on each device connected to the computer: (1) Identify one item attached to the computer. Trace its cable to a port. In Lab Table 2.2, write the name of the device on the first row. (2) On the same row in the second column, identify all ports that the device could possibly use to attach to the computer. (3) Disconnect the device from the port. On the same row in the third column, identify the port to which the device actually attaches. (4) Repeat steps 1–3 for all devices connected to the computer.

   Note: You may have to refer to information in the book or on the Internet.

LAB TABLE 2.2   Port Identification

Device attached	Ports that possibly could have this device attached	Remove device and identify the port the device actually connects to. Reattach device when finished.

3

On the Motherboard Labs

Lab 3.1 Using Windows to Discover Processor Information

Objective: To identify various computer features, such as the type of processor being used, processor socket, and additional expansion ports

Parts: Computer with Windows 7, 8, or 10

Procedure: Complete the following procedure and answer the accompanying questions.

Note: If you do not remember how to locate an application, please refer to Lab 1.1 for Windows 7, Lab 1.2 for Windows 8, or Lab 1.3 for Windows 10.

1. Boot the computer and log in.

   In Windows 7, access *Windows Explorer* through *All Programs > Search programs and files.*

   In Windows 8, access *File Explorer* by using the *Search* function or a desktop tile.

   In Windows 10, access *File Explorer* by using the *Search the web and Windows* search textbox or through the *Start* button.

2. Right-click on the computer in the far left panel. This is commonly shown as *Computer* or *This PC*. Select *Properties*. Use the information displayed to answer the following questions.

   Which processor is used?

   _____

   How much RAM is installed?

   _____

3. Click on the *Device Manager* link in the left panel. From the top menu, select *View > Devices by type.*

4. If only one line displays in the *Computer* category, expand the information by clicking on the icon to the left of the computer name.

   Is the computer a 32- or 64-bit computer?

   _____

5. Expand the *Processors* category.

   How many CPUs are listed?

   _____

6. Expand the *System devices* category.

List any expansion slot types shown.

_____

7. Close all windows.

Lab 3.2 Identifying Processor Speed, Processor Socket, and Ports

Objective: To identify various computer features, such as the type of processor, processor socket, and additional expansion ports

Parts: Computer with Internet access

Procedure: Complete the following procedure and answer the accompanying questions.

1. Boot the computer.

2. Use *Windows Explorer/File Explorer* and the *Computer* or *This PC* properties to determine the processor type and speed.

Write down the processor type and speed.

_____

3. Power off the computer and unplug the power cable. Open or remove the cover. Locate the processor.

Which type of processor socket is on the motherboard? If you are unsure, use the Internet as a resource. Use some of the search skills described in Chapter 1, "Introduction to the World of IT." Write down the processor socket type.

_____

Which model of processors can go into this type of socket?

_____

List the type of cooling that is used for the processor.

_____

4. Look at the back of the computer, where the ports are located. List every port located on the computer and one device that could connect to the port. Document your findings using Lab Table 3.1. Add more lines as needed.

LAB TABLE 3.1   Activity for computer ports

Port	No. of ports	Device that commonly connects to the port

5. Locate a picture of a SCSI connector on the Internet. Document the URL for the site where you find this image. Note that the SCSI connector is on the A+ certification.

_____

6. Using the Internet, locate one vendor that makes a motherboard that supports the Intel Z170 chipset. Provide the name/model of the motherboard and the URL where you found this information.

_____

4 Introduction to Configuration Labs

Lab 4.1 Determining the Configuration Method

Objective: To determine which configuration method a computer uses

Parts: A computer and Internet access

Procedure: Complete the following procedure and answer the accompanying questions.

1. Open the computer and look at the motherboard. Note that you may have to use the computer model number and the Internet to do research for parts of this lab or to answer some of the questions. Verify any information found on the Internet with what you see in the computer.

    Document (write down) the location, name, and purpose of every motherboard jumper.

    _____

    _____

2. Locate the motherboard battery and document the battery type.

    What type of battery is installed?

    _____

    What is an advantage of having a battery that keeps CMOS information?

    _____

    _____

    How can you tell the purpose of a jumper(s)?

    _____

    _____

    What is one of the first indications that a battery is failing?

    _____

    _____

What is the keystroke(s) required to access the Setup program?

_____

Lab 4.2 Examining BIOS/UEFI Options

Objective: To examine BIOS/UEFI features

Parts: A computer

Note: Internet access may be required.

Procedure: Complete the following procedure and answer the accompanying questions.

1.   Power on the computer and watch the screen closely for directions for how to access the BIOS/UEFI. Press the appropriate key before the operating system boots. Note that you may have to restart the computer or power it down and then power it back on in order to access the BIOS/UEFI. This may take several tries. You may also be required to research the computer brand and model on the Internet to determine which keystroke is required.

      Which keystroke is required to access BIOS/UEFI?

      _____

2.   Examine the main menu.

      List at least three main menu options.

      _____

      Which keystroke(s) allow(s) you to save settings and exit BIOS/UEFI?

      _____

3.   Explore various menus in order to answer the following questions.

      List the boot devices in the order in which they are currently configured through BIOS/UEFI.

      First boot device: _____

      Second boot device: _____

      Third boot device: _____

      _____

      On which menu screen can you set a power-on password?

      _____

      List the options you can set for any integrated motherboard port.

      _____

      The BIOS/UEFI enables which type of monitoring? Select all that apply and add any that are not listed. [power | fan | CPU | HDD (hard disk drive) | temperature]

      What diagnostics, if any, are available through BIOS/UEFI?

      _____

      Which power saving options, if any, are available through BIOS/UEFI?

      _____

      Through which menu option is virtualization support enabled or disabled?

      _____

      Which tool would a technician use for troubleshooting?

      _____

      Which setting(s) would you choose to make the computer boot faster?

      _____

      _____

      _____

What is the BIOS/UEFI version?

_____

Which keystroke(s) allow(s) you to exit BIOS/UEFI without saving any changes?

_____

4. Using whatever keystroke(s) you documented in the last question of step 3, exit BIOS/UEFI without saving any changes.

Lab 4.3 Accessing BIOS/UEFI Through Windows 8 or 10

Objective: To access BIOS/UEFI through the operating system

Parts: A working Windows 8 or 10 computer

Note: Refer to Lab 1.2 or Lab 1.3 for directions on basic Windows 8 or 10 usage.

Procedure: Complete the following procedure and answer the accompanying questions.

1. Power on the computer and log in as required.

2. With newer devices that have fast-booting hard drives, accessing BIOS/UEFI setup is challenging. Windows 8 and 10 support accessing BIOS/UEFI through Windows, but not all vendors add this support:

    Windows 8: Point to the upper-right corner of the screen or access *Settings > Change PC Settings* link > *Update and Recovery > Recovery > Restart Now* button > *Troubleshoot > Advanced Options > UEFI Firmware Settings > Restart* button

    Windows 10: Access *Settings > Update and Security > Recovery > Restart Now* button > *Troubleshoot > Advanced Options > UEFI Firmware Settings* or *Startup Settings > Restart* button

    Describe a situation where you think a technician would use this technique?

    _____

    What BIOS/UEFI options are available on the main screen?

    _____

    What option or keystroke(s) allow(s) you to exit BIOS/UEFI?

    _____

3. Using whatever keystroke(s) you documented in the last question of step 2, exit BIOS/UEFI without changing any settings.

Lab 4.4 Configuring System Resources Through the Setup Program

Objective: To access the system resources through the Setup program

Parts: A computer

Procedure: Complete the following procedure and answer the accompanying questions.

1. Power on the computer.

2. Press the appropriate key(s) to enter the Setup program.

3. Go through the various menus or icons until you find an interrupt (IRQ) setting for a particular device or port.

    Write the device or port and the associated IRQ in the space below.

IRQ	Device or port

Why do different devices generally not have the same interrupt?

_____

4.   Go through the various menus or icons until you find an I/O address setting for a particular device or port.

Write the device or port in the space provided, along with the associated I/O address.

I/O address	Device or port

Why must each device and port have a separate and unique I/O address?

How do I/O addresses, interrupts, and memory addresses get assigned to an installed adapter?

What is the best source for viewing interrupts, I/O addresses, and memory addresses that have been assigned?

5.   Exit the Setup program.

6.   Go to Device Manager and determine whether the information collected in steps 3 and 4 is the same.

Instructor initials: _____

Lab 4.5 Examining System Resources by Using Windows

Objective: To be able to view and access system resources by using Windows

Parts: A computer with Windows loaded

Procedure: Complete the following procedure and answer the accompanying questions.

1.   Power on the computer and verify that Windows loads. Log on to the computer, using the user ID and password provided by the instructor or lab assistant.

2.   Locate and access *Device Manager*. If necessary, refer to Lab 1.1 (Windows 7), Lab 1.2 (Windows 8), or Lab 1.3 (Windows 10) for basic Windows usage.

3.   Click the *View* menu option and select *Resources by Type.*   *Interrupt request (IRQ)*

Which types of system resources are shown?   *Direct memory access (DMA), input/output (IO), memory*

4.   Click the *plus sign* (or arrow) or *Interrupt Request (IRQ)* to expand the section.

Scroll through the list to determine whether there are any interrupts in use by multiple devices (the same number used by two things)? If so, list one.

What device, if any, is using IRQ8?   *System CMOS/real time clock*

Is this the standard IRQ for this device?   *yes ?*

Instructor initials: _____

5.   Collapse the *Interrupt Request (IRQ)* section. Expand the *Input/Output (IO)* section.

What is the first I/O address range listed for the first occurrence of the Direct Memory Access controller?   *[00... - ..oF]*

6.   Collapse the *Input/Output (IO)* section. Expand the *Direct Memory Access (DMA)* section.

Are any DMA channels being used? If so, list them.

none?

7.   Collapse the *Direct Memory Access (DMA)* section. Expand the *Interrupt Request (IRQ)* section again. Click to select any device listed in the *Interrupt Request (IRQ)* section. Move your mouse slowly over the icons at the top until you locate the *Update Driver Software* icon. When the mouse is moved slowly enough, a description of the icon appears.

In what position is the Update Driver Software icon located? [first | last | second | third from the right | answer not listed]

8.   Move your mouse slowly over the icons at the top until you locate (but do not click!) the *Uninstall* icon. Now locate the *Disable* icon. Both options can be used to troubleshoot problem devices.

In what situation do you think a technician would use either option?

Unistall no longer needed, disable

9.   From the main menu, select *View > Devices by Type*. Expand any section and select a particular device. Select the *Action* menu item and select *Properties*. The *Properties* window opens. The General tab shows you the status of the device and whether it is working properly.

What device was chosen?

Audio inputs + outputs

What is the status of the device?

10. Click the *Driver* tab, which shows information about the device driver.

What device driver version is being used by the device chosen?

What other important button is found on this tab that you think might be used if a device is not performing exactly as expected?

11. Click the *Resources* tab, which shows what system resources a particular device is using.

What resources are being used?

What message displays in the conflicting *device list* section?

Is the *Use automatic settings* checkbox enabled?

Instructor initials: _____

12. Click the *Cancel* button to return to Device Manager. Close the Device Manager window.

Lab 4.6 Becoming Familiar with Device Drivers

Objective: To become familiar with finding a driver, driver information, and the current driver version

Parts: A computer with access to the Internet

Procedure: Use the Internet and a computer to answer the following questions.

1.   A customer is looking to upgrade to Windows 10. She has a Creative Labs Sound Blaster Z PCIe sound card installed.

Is there a device driver for this card that the customer can use if she decides to upgrade? Provide the URL where you find the answer.

yes.

support. creative. com

2.   What is the latest device driver version for a Gigabyte Video card GV-R523D3-1GL video adapter for a Windows 7 64-bit computer? Also provide the URL where you find this information.

AMD Driver

drivers. guide

3.   What are the device driver version and date for any USB root hub on the computer?

4.   Locate a USB Enhanced Host Controller in Device Manager. Use the Driver tab and update the driver if possible. Record your results.

5.   What is the latest Windows driver revision for a StarTech PCIe 1000 Mbps fiber network card that has the part number PEX1000SFP2?

Instructor initials: _____

5

Disassembly and Power Labs

Lab 5.1 Performing Maintenance on an Antistatic Wrist Strap

Objective:	To understand how to care for and properly use an antistatic wrist strap
Parts:	Antistatic wrist strap
	Computer chassis
	Multimeter
Note:	Electrostatic discharge (ESD) has great potential to harm the electronic components inside a computer. Given this fact, it is vitally important that you practice proper ESD precautions when working inside a computer case. One tool you can use to prevent ESD is an antistatic wrist strap. This tool channels any static electricity from your body to the computer's chassis, where it is dissipated safely.
Procedure:	Complete the following procedure and answer the questions.

1. Examine the wrist strap for any obvious defects, such as worn or broken straps, loose grounding lead attachments, or dirt or grease buildup.

2. If necessary, remove any dirt or grease buildup from the wrist strap, paying close attention to the electrical contact points, such as the wrist contact point, the ground lead attachment point, and the computer chassis attachment clip. Use denatured alcohol to clean these contact points.

3. If possible, use a multimeter to check continuity between the wrist contact point and the computer chassis attachment clip. A reading of zero ohms of resistance indicates a good electrical pathway.

   How many volts of static electricity does it take to harm a computer's electrical components?

   _____

4. Adjust the wrist strap so it fits snugly yet comfortably around your wrist. Ensure that the wrist contact is in direct contact with your skin, with no clothing, hair, and so on in the way.

5. Attach the ground lead to the wrist strap and ensure that it snaps securely into place.

6. Attach the computer chassis attachment clip to a clean metal attachment point on the computer chassis.

7. Any static electricity generated or attracted by your body will now be channeled through the antistatic wrist strap to the computer chassis, where it will be safely dissipated.

How many volts will an ESD be before you will feel anything?

_____

Should you use an antistatic wrist strap when working inside a CRT monitor or laser printer high-voltage power supply? Why or why not?

_____

_____

_____

Instructor initials: _____

Lab 5.2 Disassembling and Reassembling a Computer

Objective: To disassemble and reassemble a computer correctly

Parts: A computer to disassemble

                  A toolkit

                  An antistatic wrist strap (if possible)

Note: Observe proper ESD handling procedures when disassembling and reassembling a computer.

Procedure: Complete the following procedure and answer the accompanying questions.

1. Gather the tools needed to disassemble the computer.

2. Clear as much workspace as possible around the computer.

3. Power on the computer.

Why is it important to power on the computer before you begin?

_____

External Cables

4. Turn off the computer and all peripherals. Remove the power cable from the wall outlet and then remove the power cord from the computer.

5. Note where the monitor cable plugs into the back of the computer. Disconnect the monitor, including the power cord, and move it to a safe place. Take appropriate notes.

6. Remove all external cables from the back of the computer. Take notes about the location of each cable. Move the peripheral devices to a safe place.

Did the mouse cable connect to a PS/2 or USB port?

_____

Computer Case Side Access or Removal

7. If possible, remove one or both sides of the case. This is usually the most difficult step in disassembly, especially if the computer is one that has not been seen before. Diagram the screw locations. Keep the cover screws separated from other screws. An egg carton or a container with small compartments makes an excellent screw holder. Label each compartment and reuse the container. Otherwise, open the case as directed by the manufacturer.

Adapter and Internal Cable Placement

8. Make notes or draw the placement of each adapter in the expansion slots.

9. On your notes, draw the internal cable connections before removing any adapters or cables from the computer. Make notes regarding how and where the cable connects to the adapter. Do not forget to include cables that connect to the motherboard or to the computer case.

List some ways to determine the correct orientation for an adapter or a cable.

_____

_____

Internal Cable Removal

10. Remove all internal cables. Some cables have connectors with locking tabs. Release any locking tabs before disconnecting the cable. Make appropriate notes regarding the cable connections. Some students find that labeling cables and the associated connectors makes reassembly easier, but good notes usually suffice.

Warning: Do not pull on a cable; use the pull tab, if available, or use the cable connector to pull out the cable.

Adapter Removal

11. Start with the left side of the computer (as you look at the front of the computer) and locate the left-most adapter.

12. If applicable, remove the screw or retaining bracket that holds the adapter to the case. Place the screw in a separate, secure location away from the other screws that were already removed. Make notes about where the screw goes or any other notes that will help you when reassembling the computer.

13. Remove the adapter from the computer.

Why must you be careful not to touch the gold contacts at the bottom of each adapter?

_____

14. Remove the remaining adapters in the system by repeating steps 11–13. Take notes regarding screw locations, jumpers, switches, and so forth for each adapter.

Drives

15. Remove all power connections to drives, such as hard drives, optical drives, and so on. Note the placement of each drive and each cable, as well as any reminders needed for reassembly.

16. Remove any screws holding the drives in place. Make notes about where the screws go. Keep these screws separate from any previously removed screws.

17. Remove all drives.

Why must you be careful when handling a mechanical hard drive?

_____

What would you do differently when handling an SSD than when handling a SATA hard drive?

_____

_____

Power Supply

18. Before performing this step, ensure that the power cord is removed from the wall outlet and the computer. Remove the connectors that connect the power supply to the motherboard.

19. Take very good notes here so you will be able to insert the connectors correctly when reassembling.

20. Remove the power supply.

What is the purpose of the power supply?

_____

LAB 5

Motherboard

21. Make note of any motherboard switches or jumpers and indicate whether the switch position is on or off. What is the importance of documenting switches and jumpers on the motherboard?

_____

22. Remove any remaining connectors. Take appropriate notes.

23. Remove any screws that hold the motherboard to the case. Place these screws in a different location from the other screws removed from the system. Write any notes pertaining to the motherboard screws. Look for retaining clips or tabs that hold the motherboard into the case.

24. Remove the motherboard. Make notes pertaining to the motherboard removal. The computer case should be empty after you complete this step.

Instructor initials: _____

Reassembly

25. Reassemble the computer by reversing the steps for disassembly. Pay particular attention to cable orientation when reinstalling cables. Before reconnecting a cable, ensure that the cable and the connectors are correctly oriented and aligned before pushing the cable firmly in place. Refer to your notes and install the motherboard in the computer case and reconnect all motherboard connections and screws.

26. Install the power supply by attaching all screws that hold the power supply in the case. Reattach the power connectors to the motherboard. Refer to your notes.

27. Install all drives by attaching screws, cables, and power connectors. Refer to your notes. Attach any cables that connect the drive to the motherboard.

28. Install all adapters. Attach all cables from the adapter to the connecting device. Replace any retaining clips or screws that hold adapters in place. Refer to your notes and diagrams.

29. Connect any external connectors to the computer. Refer to your notes, when necessary.

30. Replace the computer cover. Ensure that slot covers are replaced and that the drives and the front cover are aligned properly. Ensure that all covers are installed properly.

31. Reinstall the computer power cable.

32. Once the computer is reassembled, power on all external peripherals and the computer. A chassis intrusion error message might appear. This just indicates that the cover was removed. Did the computer power on with POST error codes? If so, recheck all diagrams, switches, and cabling. Also, check a similar computer model that still works to see whether you made a diagramming error. The most likely problem is with a cable connection or with a part that is not seated properly in its socket.

Instructor initials: _____

Lab 5.3 Determining Amps and Wattage

Objective: To determine the correct capacity and wattage of a power supply

Parts: Power supply

                  Internet access (as needed)

Procedure: Complete the following procedure and answer the accompanying questions.

1. Locate the documentation stenciled on the power supply, if possible.

2. Use the Internet to find documentation about the power supply on the manufacturer's website. Use the information you find on the power supply or the website to answer the following questions.

   How many amps is the power supply rated for at 5 volts?

_____

   How many amps is the power supply rated for at 12 volts?

_____

How many +12 V rails does the power supply have?

_____

What is the maximum rated output power of the power supply, in watts?

_____

Instructor initials: _____

Lab 5.4 Performing a Continuity Check

Objective: To perform a continuity check on a cable and find any broken wires

Parts: Multimeter

                 Cable and pin-out diagram

Procedure: Complete the following procedure and answer the accompanying questions.

1.   Obtain a meter, a cable, and a pin-out diagram from your instructor.

2.   Set the meter to ohms.

3.   Power on the meter.

4.   Lay the cable horizontally in front of you. The connector on the left is referred to as Connector A. The connector on the right is referred to as Connector B.

5.   Determine the number of pins on the cable connector. On a sheet of paper, write numbers vertically down the left side of the paper, ensuring that there is a number for each connector pin. At the top of the numbers, write **Connector A** as the heading. Create a corresponding set of identical numbers vertically on the right side of the paper. (See step 5 of Lab 5.5 for an example of how to set up this table.)

6.   Check the continuity of each wire. Document your findings by placing a check mark beside each pin number that has a good continuity check.

     Which meter setting did you use to check continuity, and which meter symbol is used for this setting?

_____

7.   Power off the meter and return all supplies to the instructor.

Instructor initials: _____

Lab 5.5 Drawing a Pin-Out Diagram

Objective: To draw a pin-out diagram using a working cable

Parts: Multimeter

                 Good cable

Procedure: Complete the following procedure and perform the accompanying activities.

1.   Obtain a meter and a good cable from your instructor.

2.   Set the meter to ohms.

Instructor initials: _____

3.   Power on the meter.

4.   Lay the cable horizontally in front of you. The connector on the left is referred to as Connector A. The connector on the right is referred to as Connector B.

5.   Touch one meter lead to Connector A's pin 1. Touch the other meter lead to every Connector B pin. Notice when the meter shows zero resistance, indicating a connection.

Using the table that follows, draw a line from Connector A's pin 1 to any Connector B pins that show zero resistance. Add more pin numbers as needed to the table or use a separate piece of paper. Remember that all pins do not have to be used in the connector. There are no review questions; however, there is a connector table that contains connection lines.

Connector A	Connector B
❑ 1	❑ 1
❑ 2	❑ 2
❑ 3	❑ 3
❑ 4	❑ 4
❑ 5	❑ 5
❑ 6	❑ 6
❑ 7	❑ 7
❑ 8	❑ 8
❑ 9	❑ 9
❑ 10	❑ 10
❑ 11	❑ 11
❑ 12	❑ 12
❑ 13	❑ 13
❑ 14	❑ 14
❑ 15	❑ 15

6.   Power off the meter.

Instructor initials: _____

7.   Return all supplies to the instructor.

Lab 5.6 Checking a Fuse

Objective: To determine whether a fuse is good

Parts: Multimeter

Fuse

Procedure: Complete the following procedure and answer the accompanying questions.

1.   Obtain a meter and a fuse from your instructor.

2.   Look at the fuse and determine its amp rating.

What is the amperage rating of the fuse?

_____

3.   Set the meter to ohms.

Instructor initials: _____

4.   Power on the meter.

5.   Connect one meter lead to one end of the fuse. Connect the other meter lead to the opposite end.

6. Look at the resistance reading on the meter.

    What is the resistance reading?

    _____

    Is the fuse good?

    _____

7. Power off the meter.

Instructor initials: _____

8. Return all materials to the instructor.

Lab 5.7 Using a Multimeter

Objective: To check voltage and resistance levels using a multimeter

Parts: Multimeter

                AA, AAA, C, D, or 9-volt battery

                Extended paperclip or wire

Caution: Keep both hands behind the protective rings on the meter handles. See Figures 5.25
                and 5.26.

Procedure: Complete the following procedure and perform the accompanying activities.

1. All voltage inside the computer is DC voltage (except for some parts inside the power supply). Learn-
    ing how to measure DC voltage is important for a technician. The best place to start is with a battery.
    Obtain a battery. Look carefully at the battery and determine where the positive end or connector is
    located (it usually has a + [plus] symbol nearby) and where the negative end or connector is located.

    Why is it important to locate positive and negative on a battery?

    _____

2. Look carefully at the battery and determine the voltage rating.

    Document your findings.

    _____

3. Place the battery on a flat surface. If the battery is an AA, AAA, C, or D battery, place the battery so
    that the positive side (the side with a nodule) points toward your right side. If the battery is a 9-volt
    battery, place the battery so that the connectors are facing you and the positive connector (the smaller
    connector) is on your right side.

4. If the meter has leads that attach, attach the black meter lead to the appropriate port (colored black or
    labeled COM). Attach the red meter lead to the positive port, marked with a plus sign (+).

5. Turn on the meter. Set the meter so that it is measuring VDC (DC voltage). This might involve manu-
    ally rotating a dial and/or pushing a button. Note that some meters can autodetect the setting, but
    most require this configuration.

    Document what you did to configure the meter for VDC.

    _____

    What indication, if any, did the meter show in the meter window that VDC is being measured?

    _____

6. Hold the meter leads so that the black lead is in your left hand and the red lead is in your right hand.
    Ensure that your hands are behind the protective ring on the meter handle. Refer to Figures 5.25 and
    5.26 in the textbook if you are unsure.

LAB 5

7.   Place the black meter lead to the negative side (left side or left connector). Also touch the red meter lead to the positive side (right side or right connector) of the battery.

Make a note of the meter reading.

_____

Based on your findings, is the battery good (usable in an electronic device)?

_____

8.   Now reverse the meter leads, placing the black lead to the positive side and the red lead to the negative side.

Record your findings.

_____

What was different from the original meter reading?

_____

Instructor initials: _____

9.   Perform this voltage check on any other batteries given to you by the instructor or lab assistant.

10. Straighten a paperclip or obtain a wire. Place the paperclip or wire on a flat surface.

11. Change the meter so that it reads ohms. This is normally shown by the omega symbol (Ω).

While having the meter leads up in the air (not touching each other), what does the meter display?

_____

12. Touch the meter leads together to make a complete circuit or path.

What does the meter display now?

_____

13. Touch one meter lead to one end of the paperclip or wire and touch the other meter lead to the opposite paperclip or wire end. Sometimes it is easier to just lay the meter lead on top of the wire, close to the end.

What is the meter reading?

_____

14. Some meters have the ability to make a sound when a wire is good. This is frequently shown on the meter as a sound wave. If your meter has this ability, configure the meter and redo the test. You can see how much easier this would be than trying to hold your meter leads straight and watch the meter.

Instructor initials: _____

15. Power off the meter. Disconnect the leads as necessary. Return all parts to the appropriate locations.

Lab 5.8 Checking Wall Outlet and Power Cord AC Voltage

Objective: To check the voltage from a wall outlet and through a power cord

Parts: Multimeter

                Computer power cord

Caution: Exercise extreme caution when working with AC voltages!

Procedure: Complete the following procedure and perform the accompanying activities.

1.   Set the multimeter to AC VOLTAGE. (Refer to the meter's manual if you are unsure about this setting.)

Warning: Using a current or resistance setting could destroy the meter.

2.   Power on the multimeter. Locate an AC power outlet. Refer to Lab Figure 5.1 for the power connections.

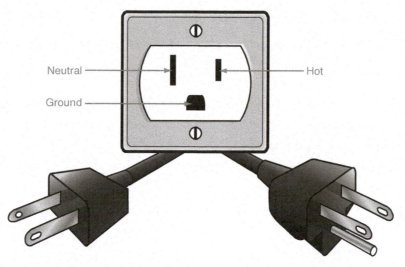

Neutral Hot

Ground

LAB FIGURE 5.1 AC outlet

3. Insert the meter's black lead into the round (ground) AC outlet plug.

4. Insert the meter's red lead into the smaller flat (hot) AC outlet plug. The meter reading should be around 120 volts. Use Lab Table 5.1 to record the reading.

5. Move the meter's red lead into the larger flat (neutral) AC outlet plug. The meter reading should be 0 volts. Use Lab Table 5.1 to record the reading.

LAB TABLE 5.1 Wall outlet AC checks

Connection	Expected voltage	Actual voltage
GND to hot	120 VAC	
GND to neutral	0 VAC	
Hot to neutral	120 VAC	

6. Remove both leads from the wall outlet.

7. Insert the meter's black lead into the smaller flat (hot) AC outlet plug.

8. Insert the meter's red lead into the larger flat (neutral) AC outlet plug. The meter reading should be around 120 volts. Use Lab Table 5.1 to record the reading.

9. Plug the computer power cord into the AC wall outlet that was checked using steps 3 through 8.

10. Verify that the other end of the power cord is not plugged into the computer.

11. Perform the same checks you performed in steps 3 through 8, except this time check the power cord end that plugs into the computer. Use Lab Table 5.2 to record the reading.

LAB TABLE 5.2 Power cord AC checks

Connection	Expected voltage	Actual voltage
GND to hot	120 VAC	
GND to neutral	0 VAC	
Hot to neutral	120 VAC	

12. If the voltage through the power cord is correct, power off the meter. Notify the instructor of any incorrect voltages.

Instructor initials: _____

Lab 5.9 Checking Device DC Voltage

Objective: To check the power supply voltages sent to various devices

Parts: Multimeter

                 Computer

Procedure: Complete the following procedure and perform the accompanying activities.

1.   Set the multimeter to DC VOLTAGE. (Refer to the meter's manual if unsure about the setting.)

2.   Power on the multimeter.

3.   Power off the computer.

4.   Remove the computer case.

5.   Locate a Molex or Berg power connector. If one is not available, disconnect a power connector from a device.

6.   Power on the computer.

7.   Check the +5 volt DC output from the power supply by placing the meter's *black* lead in (if the connector is a Molex) or on (if the connector is a Berg) one of the grounds* (a black wire). Place the meter's *red* lead on the +5 volt wire (normally a red wire) in or on the connector. Consult Lab Figure 5.2 for the layout of the Molex and Berg power supply connections. Lab Figure 5.2 also contains a table with the acceptable voltage levels.

     *Use and check both ground connections (black wires going into the connector); do not check all the voltages using only one ground connection.

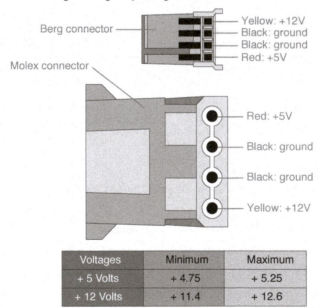

Voltages	Minimum	Maximum
+ 5 Volts	+ 4.75	+ 5.25
+ 12 Volts	+ 11.4	+ 12.6

LAB FIGURE 5.2   Molex and Berg power connectors

Write the voltage level found for the +5 volt wire in Lab Table 5.3.

LAB TABLE 5.3   +5 volt check

Voltage being checked	Voltage found
+5 volts	

8. Check the +12 volt DC output by placing the meter's *black* lead in (if the connector is a Molex) or on (if the connector is a Berg) one of the grounds. Place the meter's *red* lead on the +12 volt wire in or on the connector. See Lab Figure 5.2 for the layout of the Molex and Berg power supply connections. The figure also contains a table with acceptable voltage levels. Write the voltage level found or the +12 volt wire in Lab Table 5.4.

LAB TABLE 5.4   +12 volt check

Voltage being checked	Voltage found
+12 volts	

9. Notify the instructor of any voltages that are out of the acceptable range.

10. Power off the meter.

Instructor initials: _____

11. Power off the computer.

Lab 5.10 Using a Power Supply Tester

Objective: To check voltage levels using a power supply tester

Parts: Power supply tester

                 Working computer

Caution: Be sure you have the connector firmly attached to the power supply tester before applying power to the computer.

Procedure: Complete the following procedure and perform the accompanying activities.

1. Power on the computer and ensure that it works and boots to the operating system.

2. Power off the computer.

3. Access the interior of the computer. Remove the 24-pin motherboard power connector (the largest connector that goes from the power supply to the motherboard).

4. Attach the 24-pin motherboard power connector to the power supply tester.

   Note: All voltage inside the computer is DC voltage (except for some parts inside the power supply, of course).

5. Power on the computer. The LCD output should show each voltage level and/or give you an indication of whether the power output is okay. This varies between power supply testers.

   Does it appear that the power provided to the motherboard is accurate according to the power supply tester's output? [Yes | No]

   What indication do you have on the power supply tester about the power going to the motherboard connector?

   _____

6. Power off the computer. Remove the 24-pin motherboard power connector from the power supply tester and reattach it firmly into the motherboard.

7. Attach a SATA power connector to the power supply tester. Note that you may not have an available one and may have to remove it from the optical drive or hard drive.

LAB 5

8. Power on the computer. The SATA connector provides +12 V, +5 V, and +3.3 V to an internal SATA device. The power supply tester should provide some indication of whether these voltage levels are within acceptable ranges.

    Does it appear that the power provided to an internal SATA device is accurate according to the power supply tester's output? [Yes | No]

    What indication do you have on the power supply tester about the power going to the SATA power connector?

    _____

9. Power off the computer.

10. Detach the SATA power connector from the power supply tester and reattach it, if necessary.

11. Power on the computer and ensure that all devices are accessible and that the computer still boots.

Instructor initials: _____

12. Either using the instructions printed on the power supply tester or documentation found on the Internet, determine how the power supply tester indicates an abnormal voltage level.

    What indication do you have on the power supply tester that a particular power supply voltage is not within an acceptable voltage range?

    _____

Lab 5.11 Understanding the Windows 7 Power Options

Objective: To be able to control power options via the BIOS/UEFI and Windows 7

Parts: Computer with Windows 7 loaded

Procedure: Complete the following procedure and answer the accompanying questions.

1. Power on the computer and ensure that it boots properly before taking any further steps.

2. Reboot the computer and access BIOS/UEFI Setup.

    List the BIOS/UEFI options related to power management.

    _____

    Can ACPI be disabled via the BIOS/UEFI?

    _____

3. Exit the BIOS/UEFI Setup program without saving any settings. Boot to Windows 7.

4. Access the current power settings by selecting *Start > Control Panel > System and Security > Power Options*.

    What power plan is currently configured?

    _____

5. Select the *Create a Power Plan* link on the left. Type a unique name in the *Plan Name* textbox. Click *Next*.

6. Use the *Turn Off the Display* drop-down menu to select a time. Use the *Put the Computer to Sleep* drop-down menu to select a time for the computer to go into reduced power mode. Note that on a laptop computer, there will be two columns of choices: *On Battery* and *Plugged In*.

    Which global ACPI state do you think this would assign? Look back through the chapter to review.

    _____

7. Click the *Create* button. Notice that your new plan appears in the list of preferred plans. Also notice that the *Show Additional Plans* reveal arrow might be in the center of the window on the right if someone has hidden the additional plans. Click *Show Additional Plans*, and other plans are revealed.

8. Click the *Change Plan Settings* link under or beside the plan you just created. Select the *Change Advanced Power Settings* link.

   List at least three devices for which you can have power controlled through this Control Panel.

   _____

9. Expand the USB settings, if possible, and the *USB Selective Suspend* setting.

   What is the current USB Selective Suspend setting?

   _____

10. Expand the *Processor Power Management* setting, if possible.

    What is the minimum processor state?

    _____

    What is the maximum processor state?

    _____

11. Expand the *Multimedia* settings, if possible.

    What setting or settings are configured with this option?

    _____

12. Click the *Cancel* button to return to the Change Settings window. Click the *Cancel* button again. Show the instructor or lab assistant your settings.

Instructor initials: _____

13. To delete a power plan you created (the default ones cannot be deleted), select the radio button for the original power plan. Refer to step 4, if necessary. Under the plan you created, select the *Change Settings for the Plan* link. Select the *Delete This Plan* link and click *OK*. The plan should be removed from the power options list. Show the instructor or lab assistant that the plan has been deleted.

Instructor initials: _____

Lab 5.12 Understanding the Windows 8/10 Power Options

Objective: To be able to control power options via BIOS/UEFI and Windows 8/10

Parts: Computer with Windows 8 or 10 loaded

Procedure: Complete the following procedure and answer the accompanying questions.

1. Power on the computer and ensure that it boots properly before taking any further steps.

2. Reboot the computer and access BIOS Setup.

   List the BIOS/UEFI options related to power management.

   _____

   _____

   _____

   _____

   _____

   Can ACPI be disabled via BIOS/UEFI?

   _____

3. Exit the BIOS/UEFI Setup program without saving any settings. Boot to Windows.

4. Access the current power settings by using the Power Options section of the Control Panel.

   What is the current power plan?

   _____

5. Select the *Create a Power Plan* link on the left. Type a unique name in the *Plan Name* textbox. Click *Next*.

6.   Use the various options to select specific power plans. Not all platforms have all options, but document your settings in Lab Table 5.5.

LAB TABLE 5.5   Power plan options

Option	Minutes selected
Display	
Display brightness (mobile devices)	
Computer sleep	

7.   When you are finished configuring, click the *Create* button. Notice that your new plan appears in the list of preferred plans. Also notice that the *Show Additional Plans* reveal arrow might be in the center of the window on the right if someone has hidden the additional plans. Click *Show Additional Plans*, and other plans are revealed.

What global ACPI state do you think this would assign? Look back through the chapter to review.

_____

8.   Click the *Change Plan Settings* link under or beside the plan you just created. Select the *Change Advanced Power Settings* link.

List at least three devices for which you can have power controlled through this section of the Control Panel.

_____

Instructor initials: _____

9.   If available and possible, expand the USB settings and the *USB Selective Suspend* setting.

What is the current USB Selective Suspend setting?

_____

10.   Expand the *Processor Power Management* setting, if possible.

What is the minimum processor state?

_____

11.   Expand the *Desktop Background Settings > Slide Show* setting, if possible.

What setting or settings are configured with this option?

_____

12.   Click the *Cancel* button to return to the Change Settings window. Click the *Cancel* button again.

13.   To delete a power plan you created (the default ones cannot be deleted), select the radio button for the original power plan. Refer to step 4, if necessary. Under the plan you created, select the *Change Plan Settings* link. Select the *Delete This Plan* link and click *OK*. The plan should be removed from the power options list.

6 Memory Labs

Lab 6.1 Examining Memory Resources Using Device Manager in Windows 7/8

Objective: To be able to view memory resources currently being used by Windows 7 or 8

Parts: A computer with Windows 7 or 8 installed and rights to use Device Manager

Procedure: Complete the following procedure and answer the accompanying questions.

1. Power on the computer and verify that Windows loads. Log on to Windows using the known user ID and password or one provided by the instructor or lab assistant.

2. Access the *System and Security* Control Panel. Under the *System* section, select the *Device Manager* link.

3. Click the *View* menu option and select *Resources by Type*. Expand the *Memory* section by clicking the arrow beside the option.

   Which memory addresses are used by the system board?

   _____

4. Right-click the first memory address shown and select *Properties*.

   What tabs are shown in the window?

   _____

5. Select the *Resources* tab. All memory resources used by the first device or option are shown.

   Can the motherboard memory resources be changed using the Resources tab options? [Yes | No]

6. Close the *Device Manager* window.

Lab 6.2 Examining Memory Resources Using Device Manager in Windows 10

Objective: To be able to view memory resources currently being used by Windows 10

Parts: A computer with Windows 10 installed and rights to use Device Manager

Procedure: Complete the following procedure and answer the accompanying questions.

1.   Power on the computer and verify that Windows loads. Log on to Windows using the known user ID and password or one provided by the instructor or lab assistant.

2.   From the *Start* button in the *Search the Web and Windows* textbox, type `device` and click the *Device Manager* Control Panel link from the resulting list.

3.   Click the *View* menu option and select *Resources by Type*. Expand the *Memory* section by clicking the arrow beside the option.

    Which memory addresses are used by the system board?

    _____

4.   Right-click the first memory address shown and select *Properties*.

    What tabs are shown in the window?

    _____

5.   Select the *Resources* tab. All memory resources used by the first device or option are shown.

    Can the motherboard memory resources be changed using the Resources tab options? [Yes | No]

6.   Close the *Device Manager* window.

Lab 6.3 Using the System Information Tool in Windows 7 to View Memory

Objective: To be able to view memory resources currently being used by Windows 7

Parts: A computer with Windows 7 installed and rights to use the System Information Tool

Procedure: Complete the following procedure and answer the accompanying questions.

1.   Access the *System and Security* Control Panel. Select the *System* link.

2.   On the bottom-left side, select the *Performance Information and Tools* link.

3.   From the left panel, select the *Advanced Tools* link.

4.   Select the *View Advanced System Details in System Information* link. Note that an alternate way to do this is to type `msinfo32` in the *Search Programs and Files* textbox and press ⏎Enter.

    How much physical RAM is installed?

    _____

    How much physical RAM is available?

    _____

    How much total virtual memory does the machine have?

    _____

    How much available virtual memory does the machine have?

    _____

    What are the location and size of the page file?

    _____

5.   Close the *System Information* window.

Lab 6.4 Using the System Information Tool in Windows 8/10 to View Memory

Objective: To be able to view memory resources currently being used by Windows 8/10

Parts: A computer with Windows 8 or 10 installed and rights to use the System Information Tool

Procedure: Complete the following procedure and answer the accompanying questions.

1.   Windows 8 and Windows 10 make it harder to get to the System Information tool than previous versions of Windows, but you can still use a command to access it. In the search textbox, type **msinfo32** and press ⏎Enter.

How much physical RAM is installed?

_____

How much physical RAM is available?

_____

How much total virtual memory does the machine have?

_____

How much available virtual memory does the machine have?

_____

What are the location and size of the page file?

_____

2.   Close the *System Information* window.

Lab 6.5 Using Windows 7 Task Manager to View Memory

Objective: To be able to use the Task Manager tool to view memory resources currently being used by Windows 7

Parts: A computer with Windows 7 installed and rights to use Task Manager

Procedure: Complete the following procedure and answer the accompanying questions.

1.   After logging on to a Windows 7 computer, press the Ctrl+Alt+Del keys and select the *Start Task Manager* link.

2.   Access the *Performance* tab.

What percentage of the CPU is being used?

_____

What is the significance of the number shown next to Threads?

_____

Is the total amount of physical memory RAM, cache memory (virtual memory), or both?

_____

How much RAM is available?

_____

3.   Click the *Resource Monitor* button and select the *Overview* tab.

What is the percentage of used physical memory?

_____

4.   Expand the *Memory* section.

List three executable (.exe) files running in memory.

_____

5.   Open an application such as the Calculator accessory. Locate the application in the *Memory* section.

How many kilobytes are shown for the application in the Commit column?

_____

How many kilobytes are shown for the application in the Working Set column?

_____

How many kilobytes are shown for the application in the Shareable column?

_____

How many kilobytes are shown for the application in the Private column?

_____

6.   Select the *Memory* tab.

How much memory is reserved for hardware, if any?

_____

7.   Hold the mouse pointer over the colored bar portion of physical memory that represents the amount of memory *In Use*. A description of this portion of the bar appears.

What is the exact purpose of the *In Use* section?

_____

8.   Hold the mouse pointer over the colored bar that shows how the *Standby* portion of physical memory is being used.

What is the exact purpose of the *Standby* section?

_____

Determine the exact purpose of the Free section. Document your findings.

_____

9.   Close the *System Resource Monitor* window and the application window you opened to learn about the System Resource Monitor. Close the *Task Manager* window.

Lab 6.6 Using Windows 8/10 Task Manager to View Memory

Objective: To be able to use the Task Manager tool to view memory resources currently being used by Windows 8 or 10

Parts: A computer with Windows 8 or 10 installed and rights to use Task Manager

Procedure: Complete the following procedure and answer the accompanying questions.

1.   After logging on to a Windows 8/10 computer, search for and select the *Task Manager* tool.

2.   Access the *Performance* tab.

What percentage of the CPU is being used?

_____

How much RAM is available?

_____

How many RAM slots are used?

_____

What speed of memory modules is used?

_____

3.   Click the *Open Resource Monitor* link and select the *Overview* tab.

What is the percentage of used physical memory?

_____

4. Expand the *Memory* section.

    List three executable (.exe) files running in memory.

    _____

5. Open an application such as the Calculator accessory. Locate the application in the *Memory* section.

    How many kilobytes are shown for the application in the *Commit* column?

    _____

    How many kilobytes are shown for the application in the *Working Set* column?

    _____

    How many kilobytes are shown for the application in the *Shareable* column?

    _____

    How many kilobytes are shown for the application in the *Private* column?

    _____

6. Select the *Memory* tab.

    How much memory is reserved for hardware, if any?

    _____

7. Hold the mouse pointer over the colored bar portion of physical memory that represents the amount of memory *In Use*. A description of this portion of the bar appears.

    What is the exact purpose of the *In Use* section?

    _____

8. Hold the mouse pointer over the colored bar that shows how the *Standby* portion of physical memory is being used.

    What is the exact purpose of the *Standby* section?

    _____

    Determine the exact purpose of the *Free* section. Document your findings.

    _____

9. Close the *System Resource Monitor* window. Close the *Task Manager* window.

Lab 6.7 Installing RAM

Objective: To be able to install RAM

Parts: A computer or motherboard

                 RAM that matches the computer or motherboard

Procedure: Complete the following procedure and answer the accompanying questions.

1. If using a computer, open the side to see how many expansion slots are available.

2. Ask your instructor or lab assistant if dual- or triple-channeling is required.

    Do you need to plan for dual- or triple-channeling?

    _____

3. Determine the capacity of the chips that go in each bank. Document what chip(s) and what memory slot you plan to use in the space provided. Use motherboard documentation or information provided by the instructor or lab assistant. Draw a diagram if needed.

    Document your memory installation plan.

    _____

    _____

4.   Ensure that the memory slot(s) where you are going to install the DIMM(s) has/have the retaining tabs pushed outward away from the memory slot. Using the DIMM(s) provided, use antistatic procedures and insert the DIMM into the expansion slot, aligning the notch on the DIMM with the notch on the memory slot. Press downward, using even pressure, until the DIMM is firmly into the memory slot and the retaining tabs are firmly clasped into the DIMM. Note: Do not force the DIMM into the slot. Check the notch alignment again.

5.   Power on the computer. Note that you may receive a BIOS/UEFI error. This is normal when you have just changed the configuration. You may be required to go into BIOS and confirm the amount of memory installed.

Did you get a BIOS/UEFI error or beep? [Yes | No]

6.   Ensure that the machine boots properly and the operating system loads if a computer is being used.

Is the memory installed correctly? [Yes | No]

Instructor initials: _____

7.   Power off the computer. Remove the memory. Power on the computer and ensure that it boots without any errors.

Is the working again? (Just write "not applicable" if you were just using a motherboard.)

_____

7 Storage Devices Labs

Lab 7.1 Installing a Second PATA Hard Drive and Creating Two Volumes

Objective: To be able to install, configure, and manage a second hard drive using the Windows 7, 8, or 10 Disk Management console

Parts: Windows 7, 8, or 10 computer with an available PATA connection on the motherboard or an available PATA cable connection on an existing PATA connection to the motherboard

     Power connector

Procedure: Complete the following procedure and answer the accompanying questions.

Notes: Use proper antistatic and gentle handling procedures when dealing with hard drives.

     You must be a user who has administrator rights to configure hard drives.

     If an optical drive is installed, it can be replaced with the new hard drive to perform this lab.

1. Power on the computer and log in.

2. There are several ways to get to the window used to manage hard drives. Practice using all of them:

   (a) Click the *Start* button, type `compmgmt.msc` in the Search box, and press `⏎Enter`.

   (b) In Windows Explorer/File Explorer, right-click *Computer* (Windows 7) or *This PC* (Windows 8/10) and select *Manage*.

   (c) Access the *Administrative Tools* Control Panel > *Computer Management*.

3. In the console tree shown in the left pane, select the *Disk Management* option. Note that the Disk Management tool can also be directly accessed by using the `diskmgmt.msc` command. The disks and volumes already installed in the computer display in a graphical manner on the right.

4. Right-click the drive partition labeled C: and select *Properties*.

   Which type of file system is being used? [FAT16 | FAT32 | exFAT | NTFS]

   What is the drive number shown in the right panel? [0 | 1 | 2 | 3]

   What is the amount of free space?

5. Shut down the computer and remove the power cord.

6. Access the interior of the computer. Locate an available PATA port on the motherboard or an available PATA cable connector. Determine which port this is by looking at the motherboard's labeling or by using documentation.

    Are you using a PATA port that has nothing attached or an available PATA cable connector that has another device attached?

    _____

7. If another device is installed on the same cable, remove the drive and determine whether it uses cable select or master/slave jumpers. Handle the drive carefully. If you removed a PATA device to check the drive settings, reinstall it into the machine and reconnect the power and data cables.

    If this is the only device that will connect to a motherboard PATA port, connect the PATA cable to the motherboard.

    If another device is present, does the device use the cable select, master, or slave jumper? If you are not using a cable that has another device present, choose not applicable as the answer.
    [cable select | master | slave | _____ (different setting) | not applicable]

    If a PATA port that has nothing attached is being used, which motherboard PATA port is being used? If you are installing the drive as a second device on the same cable, choose not applicable as the answer.
    [primary | secondary | tertiary | quaternary | not applicable]

8. On the hard drive given to you by the instructor, configure the drive to the appropriate setting: cable select, master, or slave. Mount the drive, attach the data cable, and attach a power cable.

    Which drive setting did you choose?
    [cable select | master | slave | _____ (different setting) | not applicable]

9. Reinstall the computer power cord and power on the computer.

10. Using previously described procedures, open the *Disk Management* tool. Locate the drive in the bottom section of the window. If you are unsure about which drive is to be partitioned, contact the instructor or lab assistant.

    Note that the drive you were given may have been partitioned already and assigned a drive letter. If the drive was already partitioned and a drive letter has been assigned, locate the drive in the bottom window and right-click the partition. Select *Delete Volume* and click *Yes*. Also note that you may have to delete multiple partitions.

    If the drive shows the status as *Invalid* in the bottom section (left side), right-click the drive in that left section and select the *Convert to Basic Disk* option.

    At this point, the drive should show all space as unallocated.

    Was the drive already partitioned? [Yes | No]

    Was the drive already assigned a drive letter? [Yes | No]

11. Right-click the new drive you just installed and select *New Simple Volume*. The New Simple Volume Wizard appears. Click *Next*.

    What is the difference between a simple volume and a spanned volume?

    _____

    What is the minimum number of drives required to create a striped volume?

    _____

12. Enter a partition size that is less than 32 GB and still leaves room on the hard drive. Notice that the partition size is shown in megabytes. Click *Next*.

    Which partition size did you choose?

    _____

13. Select a drive letter (normally, this is the next drive letter available; take note of all the options) and then click *Next*.

How many drive letters are available as options?

_____

Which file systems are supported when you use this tool?

_____

Are any file systems supported by Windows that are not shown? If so, what are they?

_____

14. Select the *NTFS* option. Assign a volume label that is constructed from a couple letters from each lab partner's last name. Note that there is a 32-character maximum for NTFS partitions. Select (enable) the *Perform a Quick Format* checkbox and click *Next*. Click the *Finish* button.

How can you tell from the information in the Disk Management window whether a partition is NTFS or another file system?

_____

15. In the Disk Management window, right-click the free space for the drive you installed. Using the same process, create an NTFS simple volume, add a unique volume label, and perform a quick format.

Instructor initials: _____

Lab 7.2 Installing a Second SATA Hard Drive and Creating Two Volumes

Objective: To be able to install, configure, and manage a second hard drive using the Windows 7, 8, or 10 Disk Management console

Parts: Windows 7, 8, or 10 computer with an available SATA connection on the motherboard

               Power connector

Procedure: Complete the following procedure and answer the accompanying questions.

Notes: Use proper antistatic and gentle handling procedures when dealing with hard drives.

               You must be a user who has administrator rights to configure hard drives.

1. Power on the computer and log in.

2. There are several ways to get to the window used to manage hard drives. Practice using all of them:

    (a) Click the *Start* button, type **compmgmt.msc** in the Search box, and press ⏎Enter.

    (b) In Windows Explorer/File Explorer, right-click *Computer* (Windows 7)/*This PC* (Windows 8/10) and select *Manage*.

    (c) Access the *Administrative Tools* section of the Control Panel > *Computer Management*.

3. In the console tree shown in the left pane, select the *Disk Management* option. Note that the *Disk Management* tool can also be directly accessed by using the diskmgmt.msc command. The disks and volumes already installed in the computer display in a graphical manner on the right.

4. Right-click the drive partition labeled C: and select *Properties*.

Which type of file system is being used? [FAT16 | FAT32 | exFAT | NTFS]

What is the drive number shown in the right panel? [0 | 1 | 2 | 3]

What is the amount of free space?

_____

5. Shut down the computer and remove the power cord.

LAB 7

6. Access the interior of the computer. Locate an available SATA port on the motherboard. Determine which port this is by looking at motherboard labeling or by using documentation.

    Which SATA port should you use to install the second hard drive?

    _____

7. Power off the computer and access System BIOS/UEFI. If you do not know what keystroke is used to access BIOS/UEFI, watch the boot screen. If you still cannot tell, research the computer model on the Internet.

    Which keystroke did you use to access BIOS/UEFI?

    _____

8. Access the section of BIOS that controls the SATA port. The section you must enter varies from computer to computer. Make notes about where you went to get there in the question below. Ensure that the SATA port you located and identified in step 6 is enabled.

    Was the port enabled in BIOS already, or did you have to enable it?

    [already enabled | I had to enable it]

    Document the BIOS steps you took to ensure that the SATA port was enabled.

    _____

9. Save the BIOS/UEFI settings if changes were made.

10. Note that if you power on the computer with nothing attached to the SATA port, you may get an error message. That is okay because the drive has not been installed yet. Power down the computer, remove the power cord, and access the interior of the computer.

11. Mount the SATA hard drive in an available drive bay, attach the SATA data cable, and attach the hard drive power connector to the drive.

12. Reinstall the computer power cord and power on the computer.

13. Using previously described procedures, open the *Disk Management* tool. Locate the drive in the bottom section of the window. If you are unsure which drive is to be partitioned, contact the instructor or lab assistant.

    Note that the drive you were given may have been partitioned already and assigned a drive letter. If the drive was already partitioned and a drive letter has been assigned, locate the drive in the bottom window and right-click the volume. Select *Delete Volume* and click *Yes*. Also note that you may have to delete multiple volumes.

    If the drive shows the status as *Invalid* in the bottom section (left side), right-click the drive in that left section and select the *Convert to Basic Disk* option.

    At this point, the drive should show all space as unallocated.

    Was the drive already partitioned? [Yes | No]

    Was the drive already assigned a drive letter? [Yes | No]

14. Right-click the new drive you just installed and select *New Simple Volume*. The New Simple Volume Wizard appears. Click *Next*.

    What is the difference between a simple volume and a spanned volume?

    _____

    What is the minimum number of drives required to create a striped volume?

    _____

15. Enter a partition size that is less than 32 GB and still leaves room on the hard drive. Notice that the partition size is shown in megabytes. Click *Next*.

    Which partition size did you choose?

    _____

16. Select a drive letter (normally, this is the next drive letter available; take note of all the options) and then click *Next*.

   How many drive letters are available as options?

   _____

   Which file systems are supported when you use this tool?

   _____

   Are there any file systems supported by Windows that are not shown? If so, what are they?

   _____

17. Select the *NTFS* option. Assign a volume label that is constructed from a couple letters from each lab partner's last name. Note that there is a 32-character maximum for NTFS partitions. Select (enable) the *Perform a Quick Format* checkbox and click *Next*. Click the *Finish* button.

   How can you tell from the information in the Disk Management window whether a partition is NTFS or another file system?

   _____

18. In the Disk Management window, right-click the free space for the drive you installed. Using the same process, create an NTFS simple volume, add a unique volume label, and perform a quick format.

Instructor initials: _____

Lab 7.3 Installing an External Hard Drive and Creating Two Volumes

Objective: To be able to install, configure, and manage a second hard drive using the Windows 7, 8, or 10 Disk Management console

Parts: Windows 7, 8, or 10 computer with an available external connection

Procedure: Complete the following procedure and answer the accompanying questions.

Notes: Use proper antistatic and gentle handling procedures when dealing with hard drives.

                You must be a user who has administrator rights to configure hard drives.

1. Power on the computer and log in.

2. There are several ways to get to the window used to manage hard drives. Practice using all of them:

   (a) Click the *Start* button, type `compmgmt.msc` in the Search box, and press ⏎Enter.

   (b) In Windows Explorer/File Explorer, right-click *Computer* (Windows 7)/*This PC* (Windows 8/10) and select *Manage*.

   (c) Access the *Administrative Tools* section of the Control Panel > *Computer Management*.

3. In the console tree shown in the left pane, select the *Disk Management* option. Note that the *Disk Management* tool can also be directly accessed using the `diskmgmt.msc` command. The disks and volumes already installed in the computer display in a graphical manner on the right.

4. Right-click the drive partition labeled `C:` and select *Properties*.

   What type of file system is being used?
   [FAT16 I FAT32 I exFAT I NTFS]

   Which is the drive number shown in the right panel? [0 I 1 I 2 I 3]

   What is the amount of free space?

   _____

5. Locate an available external port that can be used for the hard drive provided.

   Which type of external port did you identify?
   [USB I eSATA I IEEE 1394 I Other (please identify: _____)]

LAB 7

6. Attach the external drive to the identified external port. Attach an external power brick/cord if necessary. Turn on power to the drive if necessary. The system should install the proper drivers and allow the drive to be recognized by the operating system.

7. Using previously described procedures, open the *Disk Management* tool. Locate the drive in the bottom section of the window. If you are unsure which drive is to be partitioned, contact the instructor or lab assistant.

8. Note that the drive you were given may have been partitioned already and assigned a drive letter. If the drive was already partitioned and a drive letter assigned, locate the drive in the bottom window and right-click the volume. Select *Delete Volume* and click *Yes*. Also note that you may have to delete multiple volumes.

9. If the drive shows the status as *Invalid* in the bottom section (left side), right-click the drive in that left section and select the *Convert to Basic Disk* option.

    At this point, the drive should show all space as unallocated.

    Was the drive already partitioned? [Yes | No]

    Was the drive already assigned a drive letter? [Yes | No]

10. Right-click the new drive you just installed and select *New Simple Volume*. The New Simple Volume Wizard appears. Click *Next*.

    What is the difference between a simple volume and a spanned volume?

    _____

    What is the minimum number of drives required to create a striped volume?

    _____

11. Enter a partition size that is less than 32 GB and still leaves room on the hard drive. Notice that the partition size is shown in megabytes. Click *Next*.

    What partition size did you choose?

    _____

12. Select a drive letter (normally, this is the next drive letter available; take note of all the options) and then click *Next*.

    How many drive letters are available as options?

    _____

    Which file systems are supported when you use this tool?

    _____

    Are there any file systems supported by Windows that are not shown? If so, what are they?

    _____

    _____

13. Select the *NTFS* option. Assign a volume label that is constructed from a couple letters from each lab partner's last name. Note that there is a 32-character maximum for NTFS partitions. Select (enable) the *Perform a Quick Format* checkbox and click *Next*. Click the *Finish* button.

    How can you tell from the information in the Disk Management window whether a partition is NTFS or another file system?

    _____

14. In the Disk Management window, right-click the free space for the drive you installed. Using the same process, create an NTFS simple volume, add a unique volume label, and perform a quick format.

    Instructor initials: _____

Lab 7.4 Installing a PATA/SATA Hard Drive with the Windows 7/8/10 Disk Management Tool, diskpart, and convert

Objective:	To be able to configure and manage a hard drive using the Windows 7, 8, or 10 Disk Management console
Parts:	Windows 7, 8, or 10 computer with an available PATA connection on the motherboard, an available PATA cable connection, motherboard SATA port, USB port, or eSATA port
	Internal or external PATA or SATA hard drive
	Available power connector for an internal hard drive
Procedure:	Complete the following procedure and answer the accompanying questions.
Notes:	Use proper antistatic and gentle handling procedures when dealing with hard drives.
	You must be a user who has administrator rights to configure hard drives.
	If an optical drive is installed, it can be replaced by the new hard drive to perform this lab.

1. Power on the computer and log in.

2. There are several ways to get to the window used to manage hard drives. Practice using all of them:

    (a) Click the *Start* button, type **compmgmt.msc** in the Search box, and press ⏎Enter.

    (b) In Windows Explorer/File Explorer, right-click *Computer* (Windows 7)/*This PC* (Windows 8/10) and select *Manage*.

    (c) Access the *Administrative Tools* Control Panel > *Computer Management*.

3. In the console tree shown in the left pane, select the *Disk Management* option. Note that the *Disk Management* tool can also be directly accessed by using the diskmgmt.msc command. The disks and volumes already installed in the computer display in a graphical manner on the right.

4. Right-click the drive partition labeled C: and select *Properties*.

    What type of file system is being used? [FAT16 | FAT32 | exFAT | NTFS]

    _____

    What is the total capacity of the drive?

    _____

    What is the amount of free space?

    _____

5. Shut down the computer and remove the power cord.

    Note: Three sections follow. Use the appropriate section, depending on whether you are installing an internal PATA, internal SATA, or external drive. Proceed to step 9 when you are finished with your respective section.

PATA Installation (Use This Section Only if a PATA Drive Is Being Installed)

6. Access the interior of the computer. Locate an available IDE PATA port on the motherboard or an available PATA cable connector. Determine which port this is by looking at motherboard labeling or by using documentation.

7. Determine whether the other device on the same cable (if installed) uses cable select or master/slave jumpers by removing the drive and examining it. Handle the drive carefully. If you removed a PATA device to check the drive settings, reinstall it into the machine and reconnect the power and data cables.

    If a PATA drive is being installed, is there a second device on the same cable? [Yes | No]

    If so, does the device use the cable select, master, or slave jumper?

    _____

LAB 7

8. On the hard drive given to you by the instructor, configure the drive to the appropriate setting: cable select, master, or slave. Mount the drive, attach the data cable, and attach a power cable. Reinstall the computer power cord and power on the computer.

SATA Installation (Use This Section Only if a SATA Drive Is Being Installed)

6. Access the interior of the computer. Locate an available motherboard SATA port. Determine which port this is by looking at motherboard labeling or by using documentation.

   If a SATA drive is being installed, which SATA port will be used for the new drive?

   _____

7. Mount the hard drive (provided by the instructor or lab assistant). Attach the data cable and attach a power cable.

8. Reinstall the computer power cord and power on the computer. Enter BIOS/UEFI Setup and ensure that the SATA port is enabled and the drive is recognized.

External Drive Installation (Use This Section Only if an External Hard Drive Is Being Installed)

6. Locate an available port to be used.

7. Attach the power cord to the drive, if necessary. Attach the drive to the appropriate port. Optionally, power on the drive. If the drive does not have a power switch, it is powered by the port.

   Which type of port is being used for the new drive?

   _____

8. Power on the computer. Install device drivers if required.

For All Drive Types

9. Using previously described procedures, open the *Disk Management* tool. Locate the drive in the bottom section of the window. If you are unsure about which drive is to be partitioned, contact the instructor or lab assistant.

   Note that the drive you were given may have been partitioned already and assigned a drive letter. If the drive was already partitioned and a drive letter assigned, locate the drive in the bottom window and right-click the partition. Select *Delete Volume* and click *Yes*. Also note that you may have to delete multiple partitions.

   If the drive shows the status as *Invalid* in the bottom section (left side), right-click the drive in that left section and select the *Convert to Basic Disk* option. At this point, the drive should show all space as unallocated.

   Was the drive already partitioned? [Yes | No]

   Was the drive already assigned a drive letter? [Yes | No]

10. Right-click the new drive you just installed and select *New Simple Volume*. The New Simple Volume Wizard appears. Click *Next*.

    What is the difference between a simple volume and a spanned volume?

    _____

    What is the minimum number of drives required to create a striped volume?

    _____

11. Enter a partition size that is less than 32 GB and still leaves room on the hard drive. Notice that the partition size is shown in megabytes. Click *Next*.

    What partition size did you choose?

    _____

12. Select a drive letter (normally, this is the next drive letter available; take note of all the options) and then click *Next*.

How many drive letters are available as options?

_____

What file systems are supported when you use this tool?

_____

Are there any file systems supported by Windows that are not shown? If so, what are they?

_____

_____

13. Select the *FAT32* option. Assign a volume label that is constructed from a couple letters from each lab partner's last name. Note that there is an 11-character maximum for FAT32 partitions and a 32-character maximum for NTFS partitions. Select (enable) the *Perform a Quick Format* checkbox and click *Next*. Click the *Finish* button.

How can you tell from the information in the Disk Management window whether a partition is FAT32 or NTFS?

_____

14. In the Disk Management window, right-click in the unallocated drive space on the drive you just installed and select *New Simple Volume*. The New Simple Volume Wizard appears. Click *Next*.

15. Select a partition size less than 32 GB but that still leaves some space on the drive. Click *Next*.

What amount of space did you choose for the logical drive size?

_____

16. Accept the default drive letter assignment and click *Next*.

17. Change the file system type to FAT32.

18. Make the volume label a unique name.

Write the volume label chosen.

_____

19. Select (enable) the *Perform a Quick Format* checkbox. Click *Next*, review the settings, and click *Finish*.

20. In the Disk Management window, right-click the free space for the drive you installed. Using the same process, create an NTFS simple volume (but leave some space on the drive), add a unique volume label, and perform a quick format.

Instructor initials: _____

21. You can change a FAT16 or FAT32 partition to the NTFS file system by using the `convert` command at a command prompt. After a partition is changed, you cannot go back to a previous file system type. Also, data is preserved (but should be backed up before the conversion, just in case of problems). Look to the left of the colored sections to see the disk number assigned (Disk 0, Disk 1, and so on).

In the Disk Management console, which disk number is used for the newly installed drive? [0 | 1 | 2 | 3]

Write the drive letter of the first FAT32 primary partition on the newly installed drive. Note that this drive letter will be used in the coming steps.

_____

Write the volume label used for the first FAT32 partition. This label is case sensitive, so write it carefully.

_____

22. Windows 7: Click the *Start* button. Locate the *Command Prompt* menu option. Normally, it is located in Accessories. Right-click the *Command Prompt* menu option and select *Run as Administrator*. Click *Yes*.

    Windows 8/10: Type **command** in the *Search* textbox > right-click on *Command Prompt* > select *Run as Administrator*.

23. Type **convert /?** to see a list of options. These options tell you what to type as an option after the convert command.

    Which option is used to run convert in verbose mode?

    _____

    Which option is used to convert a volume to the NTFS file system?

    _____

24. Type **convert x: /fs:ntfs** (where x: is the drive letter you wrote in step 21). For example, if the drive letter written in step 21 is d:, type convert d: /fs:ntfs. Notice the space between the drive letter and /fs:ntfs. /fs:ntfs is used to convert the existing file system (exFAT, FAT16, or FAT32) to NTFS. You are prompted for the volume label for the drive. Enter the volume label you documented in step 21 and press ⏎Enter. Do not forget that the volume label is case sensitive. The partition is converted and can never be returned to a previous type of file system, such as FAT32, unless the drive is reformatted.

Instructor initials: _____

25. Use the same process to convert the second FAT32 partition to NTFS. Look up the volume label and the drive letter before starting. Close the command prompt window. Have the Disk Management Window open to verify the file system.

26. Close the command prompt window. In the *Disk Management* window, right-click the last partition on the newly installed hard drive.

27. Select the *Shrink Volume* option. Reduce the amount of hard drive space and click *Shrink*.

    What was the result in the Disk Management console?

    _____

28. Right-click the second partition on the newly installed drive. Select *Extend Volume*. A wizard appears. Click *Next*. Use the maximum space available on the same drive and click *Next* and then *Finish*.

    What message appears?

    _____

    _____

    According to the information in the dialog box, do you think changing this volume to a dynamic disk will matter?

    _____

    _____

29. Click *No* and return to the Disk Management console. Review the disks and determine the disk number and drive letter of the boot volume.

    Write the disk number of the boot volume. [0 | 1 | 2 | 3]

    Write the drive letter of the partition that holds the boot volume.

    _____

30. Right-click the second partition of the newly installed drive and select *Delete Volume*. Click *Yes*.

31. Partitions can be created from the Disk Management console, and they can also be created by using the diskpart command utility. Open another command prompt window.

32. At the command prompt, type **diskpart** and press ⏎Enter. You may have to click *Yes* to allow access to the tool.

    How does the prompt change?

    _____

33. Type **help** and press ⏎Enter. Use the **help** command to determine which commands are available.

    Which command is used to make a new volume?

    _____

    Which command can be used to assign a drive letter to a drive partition?

    _____

34. Type **create ?** and press ⏎Enter.

    Which two options can be used with **create**?

    _____

35. Type **create partition ?** and press ⏎Enter.

    What types of partitions can be created?

    _____

36. Press the ⬆ key once. The same command appears. Use the ⬅Backspace key and replace the question mark with the word **primary** so the command reads **create partition primary**. Press ⏎Enter.

    What does the feedback say?

    _____

    Based on what you see in Help, what command do you think would be used to select a drive?

    _____

37. Type **select disk x** (where *x* is the disk number documented in step 21) and press ⏎Enter. A prompt says the disk is selected.

38. Retype the **create partition primary** command or press the ⬆ key until that command appears. Press ⏎Enter.

39. Look back to the Disk Management console and notice that the part of the drive previously marked as free space is now a partition.

40. At the command prompt, type **detail disk** and press ⏎Enter to see the partition you just created.

    Based on the command output, what drive letters are currently used?

    _____

41. At the command prompt, type **assign** and press ⏎Enter.

    Look in the Disk Management console window to determine what drive letter was assigned. Write the drive letter.

    _____

    What volume label, if any, was assigned?

    _____

42. (Skip this step if on a Windows 7 computer.) On a Windows 8/10 machine, when you are prompted to apply high-level formatting to the drive, click *Cancel* and then *OK*.

43. On all versions of Windows computers, at the command prompt type **exit** and press ⏎Enter to leave the **diskpart** utility.

44. Type **help** at the command prompt and press ⏎Enter to look for a command to help with the high-level formatting of the drive. The commands scroll quickly, so type **help | more** and press ⏎Enter. (The ⎸ keystroke is made by holding down the ⬆Shift key and pressing the key above the ⏎Enter key.) One page at a time is shown. Press the Spacebar once to see the next page of commands.

45. The next step requires you to fill in the following parameters. Let's review those here and then you must replace the italicized part of the command with values when you get to the section of this step that tells you to "Type the command…".:

    x:—the drive letter documented in step 41.

    /v:name—where *name* is a unique volume name with up to 32 characters.

    /fs:ntfs—to tell the system to use the NTFS file system. (Other options could be /fs:fat, /fs:fat32, or /fs:exfat, but this lab uses NTFS.)

    /q—to do a quick format.

    Type the command **format x: /fs:ntfs /v:name /q** and press ⏎Enter. An example of this command is format *x:* /fs:ntfs /v:Goofy /q. Remember that *x* is the drive letter documented in step 41.

    Note: If you get a message that the arguments are not valid, you did not exit the diskpart utility and did not do steps 42, 43, and 45. Go back and do them. When asked to proceed, press Ⓨ and then press ⏎Enter.

46. View the results in the Disk Management console. The last partition should be a partition that has a drive letter, that has a volume name assigned, and that uses the NTFS file system.

47. Using whatever method you like, copy one file to each of the three partitions you have created. Call the instructor over and show the instructor the three files and the Disk Management console. Do not proceed unless you have completed these parameters.

Instructor initials: _____

48. Close the command prompt window.

49. Starting with the partition on the far right in the Disk Management console for the newly installed drive, right-click each partition and delete each volume. Call the instructor over when the drive shows as one block (black bar across the top) of unpartitioned hard drive space.

Instructor initials: _____

50. Shut down the computer. Remove the computer power cord. Remove the data cable from the newly installed hard drive. Remove the power cord from the newly installed hard drive (optional on the external drive). Remove the hard drive. If necessary, reinstall the optical drive, data cable, and power cord. Reinstall the computer cover and power cord.

51. Boot the computer. Open *Windows Explorer* (Windows 7)/*File Explorer* (Windows 8/10) and select *Computer* (Windows 7)/*This PC* (Windows 8/10). Ensure that the optical drive is recognized. If it is not, redo step 50.

52. Show the instructor the optical drive in the Windows Explorer/File Explorer window and give the hard drive and any cable back to the instructor/lab assistant.

Instructor initials: _____

Lab 7.5 Striping and Spanning Using Windows

Objective:	To be able to configure and manage a striped volume or a spanned volume on a hard drive using the Windows Disk Management console
Parts:	Windows computer
	Motherboard or adapter that supports RAID 0
	Two IDE PATA or SATA hard drives
Procedure:	Complete the following procedure and answer the accompanying questions.
Notes:	Use proper antistatic and gentle handling procedures when dealing with hard drives.
	You must be a user who has administrator rights to configure hard drives.
	This lab assumes that you can install and configure two or more SATA or PATA hard drives so that they are recognized in the Disk Management console.

1.   Power on the computer and log in. Select the *Disk Management* option from the Computer Management console. The two newly installed hard drives should be visible in the Disk Management console. Initialize the drives, if necessary, by right-clicking each one of them and selecting *Initialize Disk*.

     What disk numbers are assigned to the newly installed hard drives?

     _____

2.   In the Disk Management console, right-click in the unallocated space of the newly installed drive with the lowest-numbered disk. Select *New Spanned Volume*. A wizard appears. Click *Next*.

3.   Select the second drive number written as the answer in step 1 in the Available pane and click *Add* to move the drive to the Selected pane. At least two drives should be listed in the Selected pane. Click *Next*.

4.   Select a drive letter to assign to the spanned volume. Click *Next*.

5.   Select *NTFS* from the drop-down menu and add a volume label. Select (enable) the *Perform a Quick Format* checkbox. Click *Next*. Click *Finish*.

6.   When a message appears to convert a basic disk to a dynamic disk, click *Yes*. Verify that the spanned volume appears.

     When using the Disk Management tool, how can you tell which two drives are a spanned volume?

     _____

     _____

7.   Show the instructor the spanned volume.

Instructor initials: _____

8.   Use Windows Explorer/File Explorer to view the drive letters assigned and the total capacity of each of the two drives.

     What drive letter was assigned to the spanned volume?

     _____

     What is the total capacity of the spanned volume?

     _____

     Which RAID level is spanning, if any?

     _____

9.   In the Disk Management console, right-click in the newly created spanned volume space and select *Shrink Volume*. Select a smaller amount of space in the *Enter the Amount of Space to Shrink in MB* textbox.

     How does the Disk Management tool change?

     _____

     _____

     _____

10. Show the instructor the shrunken volume.

Instructor initials: _____

11. In the Disk Management console, right-click in the spanned volume and select *Delete Volume*. When asked if you are sure, click *Yes*.

12. To create a striped volume from within the Disk Management console, right-click the lowest-numbered disk of the two newly installed drives and select *New Striped Volume*.

13. In the Available pane, select the second newly installed disk and click the *Add* button to move the drive to the Selected pane. Click *Next*.

14. Select a drive letter or leave the default. Click *Next*.

15. Leave the default system as NTFS and select (enable) the *Perform a Quick Format* checkbox. Click *Next*. Click *Finish*. Click *Yes*.

    How do the disks appear differently than the spanned volumes in the Disk Management console?

    _____

16. Open Windows Explorer or File Explorer.

    How many drive letters are assigned to a RAID 0 configuration?

    _____

17. Copy a file to the RAID 0 drive. Show the instructor the file and the Disk Management console.

    Instructor initials: _____

18. Right-click in the healthy volume space of either RAID 0 drive.

    Can a RAID 0 volume be shrunk? [Yes | No]

19. Select the *Delete Volume* option. Click *Yes*. Show the instructor the unallocated space.

    Instructor initials: _____

20. Power down the computer, remove the power cord, and remove the two newly installed drives.

21. Power on the computer and, if necessary, return the BIOS/UEFI settings to the original configuration. Ensure that the computer boots normally. Show the instructor that the computer boots normally.

    Instructor initials: _____

Lab 7.6 Windows 7 Hard Disk Tools

Objective: To be able to use the tools provided with Windows 7 to manage the hard disk drive

Parts: Windows 7 computer and administrator rights

Procedure: Complete the following procedure and answer the accompanying questions.

Notes: The defragmentation and Error-checking (Check Now) process can take more than 60 minutes on large hard drives.

1. Power on the computer and log on using a user ID and password that has administrator rights.

2. Click the *Start* button > *All Programs* > *Accessories* > *System Tools* > *Disk Cleanup*.

3. The Disk Cleanup window appears. Ensure that *only* the following checkboxes are checked (enabled) for the purposes of this lab:

   Temporary Internet Files

   Recycle Bin

   Temporary Files

   Game Statistics Files (if available)

   Click the *OK* button.

4. When prompted if you are sure, click the *Delete Files* button.

   List at least two related topics that are available from the Help and Support Center when getting help on the topic of disk cleanup.

   _____

   _____

5. Using Windows Explorer, right-click on the hard disk drive letter to check for errors. Select *Properties*.

6. Click the *Tools* tab. In the Error-checking section, click the *Check Now* button.

7. For any files and folders that have problems, you can either select *Automatically Fix File System Errors* or you can just have the check performed with a generated report at the end. A more thorough disk check can be done by using *Scan For and Attempt Recovery of Bad Sectors*. This disk check locates and attempts repair on physical hard disk sections and can take a very long time. The most comprehensive check is to check for both file errors and physical problems on the hard disk surface with the *Automatically Fix File System Errors* and *Scan for and Attempt Recovery of Bad Sectors*.

   For this exercise, deselect (disable) *Automatically Fix File System Errors*. Note that the *Scan For and Attempt Recovery of Bad Sectors* checkbox is automatically disabled (not checked). Click *Start*.

   What message appears when the scan is complete?

   _____

   _____

Instructor initials: _____

8. Click the *Close* button.

9. Either return to the hard drive *Properties* window and select *Defragment Now* or click the *Start* button > *All Programs* > *Accessories* > *System Tools* > *Disk Defragmenter*.

10. Select a particular drive to use. Click *Analyze Disk*.

    In the Windows Explorer Properties window General tab, what percentage of free space is shown for the drive?

    _____

    In the Disk Defragmenter window, select the *Tell Me More About Disk Defragmenter* link. What does Windows 7 Help say about using the computer during the defragmentation routine?

    _____

11. In the Disk Defragmenter window, click the *Defragment Disk* button.

    What would be the determining factor for you in recommending how often a particular computer user should make use of this tool?

    _____

    _____

    List one more recommendation that you would make to a user regarding this tool.

    _____

    _____

    _____

    _____

    _____

12. If class time is an issue, click the *Stop Operation* button. Click the *Close* button. Close the hard drive *Properties* window.

LAB 7

Lab 7.7 Windows 8/10 Hard Disk Tools

Objective: To be able to use the tools provided with Windows 8 or 10 to manage the hard disk drive

Parts: Windows 8 or 10 computer and administrator rights

Procedure: Complete the following procedure and answer the accompanying questions.

Notes: The defragmentation and Error-checking (Check Now) process can take more than 60 minutes on large hard drives.

1. Power on the computer and log on using a user ID and password that has administrator rights.

2. Open *Windows File Explorer*. Locate the *C:* drive in the left pane. You may have to expand *This PC*. Right-click on the C: drive and select *Properties*.

    On the General tab, what is the name of the volume?

    _____

    What is the drive capacity?

    _____

    What does the option *Allow Files on This Drive to Have Contents Indexed in Addition to File Properties* do?

    _____

3. Click *Disk Cleanup*. The Disk Cleanup window appears. Ensure that *only* the following checkboxes are checked (enabled) for purposes of this lab:

    Temporary Internet Files

    Recycle Bin

    Temporary Files

    Game Statistics Files (if available)

    Click the *OK* button. When prompted if you are sure, click the *Delete Files* button.

    What message, if any, is given to you at the end of the process?

    _____

4. Access the Disk Cleanup window again. Select the *Clean Up System Files* option. The Disk Cleanup window appears, and the related file sections are automatically checked. Click any one of the options that has an enabled (checked) checkbox. Click on the option itself (not the checkbox). Click *View Files*.

    If no files appear, then (1) you might be viewing an option that takes up no hard drive space. If you think this the case, return to the *View Files* window, select another checked option, and click *View Files* again; or (2) enable the viewing of files by clicking on the *View* menu option > *Options* down arrow > *Change Folder and Search Options* > *View* tab > enable (click on) *Show Hidden Files, Folders, and Drives* > disable (ensure the option is unchecked) *Hide Protected Operating System Files (Recommended)* > *Yes* (to the warning prompt) > *OK*. The files that are to be deleted appear.

5. Close the window. Return to the Disk Cleanup window. Click *OK* to delete unused system files. Click *Delete Files*. When finished, access the Disk Cleanup window again by clicking on *Disk Cleanup*.

6. Select the *More Options* tab. You may have to click on the *Clean Up System Files* option again to access this tab.

    What are the two sections shown in the window that allow for more disk cleanup?

    _____

    What do you think would be a disadvantage to using the Clean Up button for Programs and Features?

    _____

    _____

7. Click *Cancel*. Click the *Tools* tab. Note that the Tools tab contains two tools: *Error-checking* and *Optimize and Defragment Drive*.

8. Click *Check*. Click *Scan Drive*.

    What message appears?

    _____

9. Click *Close*. Click on *Optimize*.

    What percentage of the C: drive is fragmented? ____%

    Is scheduled optimization turned on or off so that drives are automatically optimized? [on | off]

10. Click on *Analyze*.

    Did the percentage of fragmented drive space change? [yes | no]

11. Click on *Optimize*. Click on *Close* when the process is done.

    In the corporate environment, do you think that any of these processes are done on a regular basis? Explain your answer.

    _____

Lab 7.8 Windows 8/10 Storage Spaces

Objective: To be able to use the tools provided with Windows 8 or 10 to manage the hard disk drive

Parts: Windows 8 or 10 computer and administrator rights

              One or more of the following already installed and accessible through Windows Disk Management tool: internal hard drive, external hard drive, SSD, or SSHD

Procedure: Complete the following procedure and answer the accompanying questions.

1. Power on the computer and log on using a user ID and password that has administrator rights.

2. Access the *Storage Spaces* Control Panel.

3. Select the *Create a New Pool and Storage Space* link > click *Yes* if asked permission to continue.

4. Enable (click in the checkbox to select) the drive(s) to be used > *Create Pool* button.

5. In the resulting window, name the storage space, optionally select a drive letter and file system, and select the resiliency type.

    What resiliency types are available? (Choose all that apply.)
    [simple | complex | extended | parity | no parity | two-way mirror | three-way mirror]

    What resiliency type is the default?
    [simple | complex | extended | parity | no parity | two-way mirror | three-way mirror]

    What file systems are available?

    _____

6. Select the pool size.

7. Select *Create Storage Space*. The storage space appears in File Explorer.

    Which drive letter did you choose?

    _____

Instructor initials: _____

8. To remove a storage space, access the *Storage Spaces* Control Panel again.

9. Locate the Storage Space > *Change Settings* > *Delete Pool* link located on the right side > *Delete Storage Space* button.

8

Multimedia Devices Labs

Lab 8.1 Managing Sound and Optical Drives in Windows

Objective: To be able to use the tools provided with Windows to manage sound devices and optical media drives

Parts: A computer with Windows 7, 8, or 10 loaded, with an optical drive installed, and that has Internet access

Procedure: Complete the following procedure and answer the accompanying questions.

Note: Parts of this lab may be completed differently depending on the hardware installed and the version of Windows installed.

1. Power on the computer and log in to Windows 7, 8, or 10.

2. Access the *Sound* Control Panel.

   Which tabs are shown in the window?

   _____

   Which device is the default playback device?

   _____

3. With the default playback device selected, click the *Configure* button.

   Which audio channels are available?

   _____

4. Click the *Test* button.

   What was the result?

   _____

5. Click the *Cancel* button and ensure that the *Playback* tab is selected. Click *Properties*. The Speakers Properties window opens.

   What jack information is displayed?

   _____

6. Click *Properties*.

   What is the device status?

   _____

7. Select the *Driver* tab.

   What is the driver version?

   _____

   What is the purpose of the Roll Back Driver button?

   _____

   Can the audio be disabled from this window?

   _____

8. Click *Cancel*. On the *Speakers Properties* window, click the *Advanced* tab.

   How many bits are used for sampling?

   _____

   What is the frequency response?

   _____

9. Click *Cancel*. Select the *Recording* tab.

   What is the default recording device?

   _____

10. Select the *Sounds* tab. In the *Program* (Windows 7)/*Program Events* (Windows 8/10) window, select any task that has a speaker icon to the left of it. Listening to these sounds is an easy way to check for issues without having to download a sound file. Click *Test*.

    Did sound emit? [Yes | No]

11. Select the *Sound Scheme* drop-down menu.

    What options are available?

    _____

    What is the checkbox used for in this section?

    _____

12. Click *Cancel*. Close the Control Panel window.

13. Open *Windows Explorer (Windows 7)/File Explorer (*Windows 8/10) and select *Computer* (Windows 7)/*This PC* (Windows 8/10) from the left panel. In the right panel, right-click the optical drive. Notice the *Eject* option, which can be used to eject a stuck disc.

14. Point to the *Share With* option and select *Advanced Sharing*. The optical drive *Properties* window opens. The *Sharing* tab allows you to share a disc with others.

15. If you closed the optical drive *Properties* window, go back into it and select the *Hardware* tab. In the *All Disk Drives:* window, select the optical drive. Click *Properties*.

    What is the device status?

    _____

16. In the *Properties* window, select the *DVD Region* tab if a DVD drive is installed.

What is the DVD region code? Write *Not applicable* as your answer if a CD drive is installed.

_____

17. Select the *Driver* tab.

Which version of the driver is installed?

_____

What is the date of the driver?

_____

18. Use the Internet to determine whether a newer device driver is available. Show this driver to the instructor or lab assistant.

Instructor initials: _____

19. In the device's *Properties* window, click *Cancel.*

20. In the original optical drive *Properties* window, select the *Customize* tab.

What types of things can be customized from this tab?

_____

21. Click the *Cancel* button. Close the *Windows Explorer* (Windows 7)/*File Explorer* (Windows 8/10) window.

Lab 8.2 Installing an Optical Drive

Objective: To install, configure, and test an optical drive

Parts: A computer with Windows loaded

An antistatic wrist strap or glove

An optical drive with accompanying cable and mounting equipment, if necessary

Procedure: Complete the following procedure and answer the accompanying questions.

1. Obtain an optical drive designated by the instructor or student assistant.

Which type of drive is this? [CD-ROM I CD-R I CD-RW I DVD-R I DVD+R I DVD±RW I DVD-R DL I DVD+R DL I BD-R I BD-RE]

List the drive manufacturer and model number.

_____

If possible, determine whether a driver is available and list the website on which you located this information.

_____

Which type of interface does the optical drive use? [PATA IDE I SATA I SCSI I Parallel I USB]

2. Power off the computer, remove the power cord, open the computer, and determine whether a cable and interface are available to install the drive. If not, obtain them from the lab supplies area, instructor, or lab assistant.

3. Configure the drive as necessary for the type of interface being used.

Which drive settings did you select, if any?

_____

4. If appropriate, install the drive into the computer and attach power.

5. If an external device is being installed, a device driver may need to be installed at this point. Always refer to the device installation instructions. Whether the drive is internal or external, attach the correct interface cable to the drive.

LAB 8

6. Power on the computer, load a device driver (if necessary), and ensure that the operating system recognizes the drive. Troubleshoot as necessary until the drive works.

    Which tests did you perform to ensure that the drive works?

    _____

7. Tell the instructor when the drive is successfully installed.

    Instructor initials: _____

8. Remove the drive and reinstall the computer cover. Power on the computer and ensure that BIOS/UEFI errors do not appear.

    Instructor initials: _____

Lab 8.3 Using DirectX for Diagnostics in Windows 7, 8, or 10

Objective: To be able to use the DirectX tool provided with Windows 7, 8, or 10

Parts: A computer with Windows 7, 8, or 10 loaded and with administrator rights and Internet access

Procedure: Complete the following procedure and answer the accompanying questions.

Note: This lab may be completed differently depending on the equipment installed and the Windows version and service pack.

1. Power on the computer and log in to Windows 7.

2. Click the *Start* button and in the *Search Programs and Files* textbox, type **dxdiag** and press ⏎Enter or select the dxdiag link. The DirectX tool may ask you if you want to check that the drivers are digitally signed and/or to allow an Internet connection for an update. Click *Yes*.

    After the tool is shown and the System tab is displayed, which DirectX version is running?

    _____

    How much RAM is installed in the computer?

    _____

    What is the size of the page file?

    _____

    How much of the page file is currently used?

    _____

3. Click the *Next Page* button. The next tab displays.

    What notes, if any, appear on the tab?

    _____

4. Ensure that you are on the *Display* tab.

    How much RAM is on the video adapter?

    _____

    Are any DirectX features enabled? If so, which ones?

    _____

    Research the words *RAM*, *video adapter*, and *DirectX* on the Internet to help with this answer and give a brief description of the features.

    _____

    _____

    _____

5.　Ensure that the *Sound* tab is selected.

What is the device type used?

_____

What is WDM? If you do not know, research it on the Internet.

_____

Which driver file is used?

_____

What does the WHQL logo mean? If you do not know, research this term on the Internet.

_____

6.　Click the *Input* tab.

List any direct input devices displayed.

_____

7.　Expand any USB devices in the Input Related Devices section.

List any USB devices that are considered to be input devices.

_____

8.　Close the DirectX Diagnostics window.

Lab 8.4 Installing a Sound Card and Speakers in Windows 7, 8, or 10

Objective:　　To install and configure a sound card

Parts:　　A computer with Windows 7, 8, or 10 loaded and an available expansion slot

Sound card with drivers or Internet access

Optional audio disc

Procedure:　　Complete the following procedure and answer the accompanying questions.

1.　Before powering on the computer, determine the current audio capabilities.

How many sound ports are integrated into the motherboard?

_____

Draw each port and state its purpose. If you do not know, use the Internet to research the computer model.

_____

_____

_____

2.　Connect power to the speakers and attach the speakers to the computer, if necessary.

3.　Power on the computer and log in to Windows. Access the *Hardware and Sound* section of the Control Panel. Select the *Sound* link.

On the Playback tab, how many playback devices are listed?

_____

4.　Right-click the icon that represents the enabled speaker(s) and select *Properties*.

Which name is currently assigned to the output device?

_____

5.　Click in the *General Tab* textbox and change the name to something more meaningful.

List the name assigned.

_____

LAB 8

Which output jacks are available for this output device?

_____

What controller is controlling the speakers?

_____

6.   Click the speaker controller *Properties* button.

Which driver version is installed?

_____

7.   Close the Properties window. Back in the Speakers Properties window, select the *Levels* tab.

Which settings can you control on this tab?

_____

The tabs that are available vary depending on the speakers installed. Which tabs are available for the speakers on your computer?

_____

8.   Select the *Advanced* tab. Test the quality of the sound output by clicking the *Test* button. Troubleshoot the system if the speakers do not emit a sound.

How many bits are used in converting analog sounds into digital audio?

_____

9.   Select the *Default Format* drop-down menu. Note that this is the window where you allow applications to control or change the speaker settings.

List two other available formats, if possible.

_____

10. Click *Cancel* twice to close the Speaker Properties windows. Power off the computer.

11. Power on the computer and enter the BIOS/UEFI Setup program.

Which key or process did you use to enter Setup?

_____

12. Locate and disable the integrated sound ports. Save the settings and exit BIOS/UEFI Setup.

13. Log in to Windows.

14. Using any method you would like, ensure that the speakers do not emit sound.

Which method did you use?

_____

15. Shut down the computer and remove the power cord.

16. Access the computer expansion slots and, if necessary, remove any slot covers or retention bars.

17. Install the sound adapter into an empty expansion slot and ensure it fits snugly into the slot. Reinstall any retention bar as necessary.

18. Attach the power cord and power on the computer. The computer should detect that a new device has been installed. You may be prompted for a device driver and to restart the computer in order to use the new adapter. If you don't have a device driver, go to a computer that has Internet access and download the appropriate driver for the sound card you installed. Note that you may have to power down the computer and look at the sound card (and possibly remove it) in order to get the appropriate model required to download the correct driver.

19. Attach the speakers to the appropriate ports on the newly installed sound card.

20. Using any method, including previously demonstrated methods or by playing an audio disc, test the new sound card.

21. Access *Device Manager* and expand the *Sound, Video and Game Controllers* section.

22. Right-click the newly installed sound card and select *Properties*.

    Which I/O address does the adapter use?

    _____

    What is the device status?

    _____

Instructor initials: _____

23. Power down the computer and remove the power cord.

24. Unplug the speakers from the sound card. Remove the sound card and attach any slot covers.

25. Power on the computer and access BIOS/UEFI Setup.

26. Enable the integrated sound ports and save the settings.

27. Attach the speakers to the motherboard speaker port.

28. Attach the power cord. Boot the computer and log in to Windows again. Test the speakers.

29. Return all parts to the proper location.

Lab 8.5 Installing a USB Scanner

Objective: To be able to install a USB scanner and driver on a Windows-based computer

Parts: USB scanner, USB cable, scanner driver, scanner software/utilities, computer with Windows loaded

Procedure: The procedures outlined below are guidelines. Refer to the scanner's installation instructions for exact procedures.

Installing the Scanner Driver

1. Insert the scanner driver media into the drive. Sometimes you must also select which type of interface connection is going to be used. If this is the case, select *USB*. The software installer sometimes includes additional software programs that can be used to control the scanner and to manipulate scanned images. Many drivers require the computer to be restarted when the installation process is complete.

Connecting the Scanner

2. A scanner may ship with a carriage safety lock. If this is the case, remove the safety lock.

3. With the computer powered on, connect one end of the USB cable to the scanner's USB port and attach the other end to a USB computer port or a USB hub port.

4. If necessary, attach the power cable to the scanner. Attach the other power cable end to an electrical outlet.

5. Power on the scanner.

6. Optionally, if the scanner has a calibrate routine, execute it.

Using the Scanner

7. If the scanner software program(s) did not install during driver installation, install the scanner software program(s) now.

8. Insert a document to be scanned.

9. Access the scanner software program by clicking the *Start* button and scan the document.

Instructor initials: _____

Lab 8.6 Changing the Drive Letter of an Optical Drive by Using Disk Management and the `diskpart` Utility

Objective: To reassign the optical drive letter

Parts: Windows computer with administrator rights

Procedure: Complete the following procedure and answer the accompanying questions.

1.   Using Windows/File Explorer, determine the current optical drive letter.

     What drive letter is being used by the optical drive?

     _____

2.   In Windows 7, from the Start button menu in the Search Program and Files textbox, type **Disk Management** and press (↵Enter). In Windows 8/10, use the *Administrative Tools* Control Panel to access and open the *Computer Management* tool. Expand the *Storage* section and select *Disk Management*.

3.   Locate the optical drive in the bottom half of the Disk Management window.

4.   Right-click or tap and briefly hold the drive icon in the left side of the panel where the drive letter is located and select *Change Drive Letter and Paths*.

5.   Select *Change* and use the *Assign the Following Drive Letter:* drop-down menu to select a different drive letter.

     What drive letter did you choose?

     _____

6.   Click *OK* and click *Yes* to the notification that some programs might not work properly.

7.   At a command prompt, type **diskpart** and press (↵Enter). Type **list volume** and press (↵Enter). Look down the Type column for an optical drive and locate the drive to be changed. Ensure that the drive letter in the Ltr column is the same drive letter written down in step 5.

     Write the volume number that is listed in the same row as the optical drive.

     _____

8.   At a command prompt, type select volume x (where x is the number you wrote in step 7). A message appears, stating that the volume is selected. If the message does not appear, recheck your steps, starting from the beginning of the lab.

9.   Type **assign letter=x** (where x is the newly assigned drive letter). A message appears, stating that the drive letter assignment was successful. If this message does not appear, redo the exercise.

10. Use *Windows Explorer* (Windows 7)/*File Explorer* (Windows 8 or 10) to verify the reassignment, refreshing the screen if necessary. Show the instructor or lab assistant your reassigned drive letter.

Instructor initials: _____

11. In the `diskpart` utility or the Disk Management window, return the drive to the original drive letter. Refer to the answer to the question in step 1 if you do not remember the original drive letter. Use Windows Explorer/File Explorer to show the instructor or lab assistant that the drive letter has been reassigned.

Instructor initials: _____

9 Printers Labs

Lab 9.1 Installing a Generic/Text-Only Print Driver on a Windows 7, 8, or 10 Computer

Objective: To install a generic print driver on a Windows computer and examine printer properties

Parts: Computer with Windows 7, 8, or 10 installed

Procedure: Complete the following procedure and answer the accompanying questions.

Notes: A printer is not required to be attached to the computer for this lab to be executed.

In order to install a printer, you must have the specific permission to install a printer and install a device driver.

1. Power on the computer and log on using the user ID and password provided by the instructor or lab assistant.

   Is a printer attached to the PC? If so, does it attach wirelessly or using the USB port?

   _____

2. In Windows 7: Click the *Start* button > *Control Panel* > *Hardware and Sound* > *Devices and Printers* > *Add a Printer* link > *Add a Local Printer* > ensure that the *Use an Existing Port* radio button is selected and the *LPT1: (Printer Port)* option is selected (even if a printer attaches to the PC already; you will not be printing from this print driver) > *Next* > in the *Manufacturer* column, select *Generic* > in the *Printers* column, select *Generic/Text Only* > *Next* > in the *Printer name* textbox, type Class Printer > *Next* > ensure that the *Do Not Share This Printer* radio button is enabled > *Next* > ensure that the *Set as the Default Printer* checkbox is unchecked > *Finish*.

   In Windows 8: Search for **printers** and select *Devices and Printers* from the resulting list > *Add a Printer* link > when the system starts searching for printers, select the *Stop* button > *The Printer That I Want Isn't Listed* link > enable (select) the radio button for *Add a Local Printer or Network Printer with Manual Settings* > *Next* > ensure that the *Use an Existing Port* radio button is selected and the *LPT1: (Printer Port)* option is selected (even if a printer attaches to the PC already; you will not be printing from this print driver) > *Next* > in the *Manufacturer* column, select *Generic* > in the *Printers* column, select *Generic/Text Only* > *Next* > in the *Printer name* textbox, type **Class Printer** > *Next* > ensure that the *Set as the Default Printer* checkbox is unchecked > *Finish*.

   In Windows 10: Search for **printers** and select *Printers and Scanners* from the resulting list > *Add a Printer or Scanner* link > when the system starts searching for printers, *The Printer That I Want Isn't Listed* link > enable (select) the radio button for *Add a Local Printer or Network Printer with Manual Settings* > *Next* > ensure that the *Use an Existing Port* radio button is selected and the *LPT1: (Printer Port)* option is selected (even if a printer attaches to the PC already; you will not be printing from this print driver) > *Next* > in the *Manufacturer* column, select *Generic* > in the *Printers* column, select *Generic/Text Only* > *Next* > in the *Printer Name* textbox, type **Class Printer** > *Next* > ensure the *Set as the Default Printer* checkbox is unchecked > *Finish*.

3. From the *Devices and Printers* section of the Control Panel > right-click the *Class Printer icon >* *Properties.*

    Which tabs are available with the generic print driver?

    _____

4. Click *OK* > right-click the *Class Printer* icon > *Printer properties.*

    Which tabs are available through this option?

    _____

    _____

    Use Lab Table 9.1 to list what is important about each tab or why a technician might use the tab.

LAB TABLE 9.1   Generic printer *Properties* window tabs

Tab	Notes
General	
Sharing	
Ports	
Advanced	
Color Management	
Security	
Device Settings	
Printer Commands	
Font Selection	

On the Ports tab, what do you think printer pooling is?

_____

Which button on the General tab do you think would be useful to a technician when troubleshooting a printing problem?

_____

5. Close the window. Right-click on *Class Printer* and select *Printing Preferences*. In the *Orientation* section, select the *Landscape* option.

    How does this change printing?

    _____

6. Select the *Paper/Quality* tab. Click the *Paper Source* drop-down menu.

    Which options are available, even with a generic print driver?

    _____

7. Select the *Advanced* button.

    List three paper size options.

    _____

    _____

8. Click *Cancel*; click *Cancel* again. Then access the *Printer Properties* window.

9. Click the *Ports* tab. Notice that LPT1 is checked. If you made a mistake during installation and selected the wrong port, you can change it here. Notice that File: and XPS are options.

10. Access the *Advanced* tab. Select the *Printing Defaults* button. Through this option, you can select the default quality and orientation the printer uses to print. Users must change the settings if they want something other than this. Click *Cancel*. Click the *Separator Page* button.

What is the purpose of a separator page?

_____

_____

11. Click *Cancel*. Click *OK*.

12. To rename the Class Printer driver, right-click on *Class Printer* in the Control Panel > *Printer Properties*. On the *General* tab, change the name of the printer in the first textbox to *IT Printer* > *OK*.

13. To delete the IT Printer, right-click on *IT Printer* > *Remove Device* > *Yes*.

Lab 9.2 Installing a Local Printer on a Windows 7, 8, or 10 Computer

Objective:　　To install a local printer on a Windows 7, 8, or 10 computer

Parts:　　A computer with Windows 7, 8, or 10 installed and a printer physically attached to an LPT, COM, or USB port

An appropriate printer driver for the operating system (with Internet connectivity or a printer driver provided)

Procedure:　　Complete the following procedure and answer the accompanying questions.

Notes:　　Refer to the printer installation guide when installing a new printer. A printer may have its own CD and installation wizard that installs the driver and software.

In order to install a printer, you must log on as an administrator (or use a user ID that belongs to the Administrators group).

1. Power on the computer and log on using the user ID and password provided by the instructor or lab assistant.

2. Use the Internet to research and download the printer driver appropriate for the printer and operating system version installed. Otherwise, use the driver provided by the instructor or lab assistant.

Which version of the printer driver did you download or do you have?

_____

3. Attach the printer cable to the correct computer port. Attach the power cord to the printer, if necessary, and insert the other end into a wall outlet. Power on the printer.

4. Windows normally detects a plug-and-play printer and may complete all the installation steps automatically.

Does Windows automatically detect and install the printer?

_____

5. If Windows cannot find the driver, browse for a printer driver when you are prompted to do so.

6. When the driver is installed, print a test page to ensure communication between the computer and the printer.

Did the printer print correctly? If not, delete the printer and complete the installation again.

_____

Lab 9.3 Exploring a Windows 7, 8, or 10 Printer

Objective: To explore printer options available through Windows 7, 8, or 10

Parts: A computer with Windows 7, 8, or 10 installed and an installed printer

                    Optionally, access to the Internet for researching the latest printer driver

Procedure: Complete the following procedure and answer the accompanying questions.

Note: This process depends on the printer manufacturer. You may need to modify the initial steps to find the details for the specific printer.

1. Power on the computer and log in to Windows.

2. Access the *Devices and Printers* section of the Control Panel. Right-click on the installed printer and select *Printing Preferences*.

    What is the default print quality mode for this printer?

    _____

    Is this the most cost-efficient mode available? If not, what is?

    _____

3. Using various Control Panel options, answer the following questions.

    a. List one instance in which a technician might use the *Pause Printing* option. If you do not know for sure, research the answer on the Internet.

        _____

        _____

    b. List the steps necessary to share this printer with other computers.

        _____

        _____

        _____

        _____

        _____

    c. Which printer option would you use to see how many documents have been sent to the printer?

        _____

    d. List information that might be important for business documentation purposes.

        _____

        _____

        _____

    e. What information is provided for troubleshooting printing problems?

        _____

    f. To what port does the printer attach?

        _____

    g. Which print spooler option is used?

        _____

    h. Which security options are currently used?

        _____

    i. If the printer is shared, does the printer have the option to render print jobs on client computers?

        _____

4. Close any open windows.

10 Mobile Devices Labs

Lab 10.1 Backing Up an iOS Device to a PC or Mac by Using iTunes

Objective: To be able to use the iTunes application to back up the operating system and settings on an iOS device

Parts: An iOS-based device

A PC or Mac computer

A USB cable to connect the iOS device to the PC or Mac

An Apple ID and password

Procedure: Complete the following procedure and answer the accompanying questions.

1. Power on the PC or Mac and the iOS device. Log in as required.

2. Ensure that the PC or Mac has iTunes installed. If the application is not installed, download and install it. Open iTunes.

3. Attach the USB cable from the iOS device to the computer.

4. On the Mac or PC, the iOS device should display, or you can choose it from the top, left where the music notes icon is located. Note that you may have to click *Continue > Get Started* if this device has never been connected before.

   What iOS version does iTunes show is on the iOS device?

   _____

   What is the iOS serial number shown in iTunes?

   _____

5. In the *Backups* section, select the *This Computer* radio button.

   Looking at the screen, does this Mac or PC have the ability to encrypt the backup file where the backup is to be stored? [Yes | No]

   How do you know?

   _____

6. Click the *Back Up Now* button.

   What information displays under the *Latest Backup* section?

   _____

What option on the screen would you use if you needed to reinstall the iOS operating system?

_____

Lab 10.2 Determining Memory Resources in an iOS-Based Device

Objective: To be able to use the Apple iOS operating system to determine the amount of memory

Parts: An Apple iPhone or iPad

Procedure: Complete the following procedure and answer the accompanying questions.

1.   Ensure that the Apple device is powered on.

2.   Access the Home screen (by pressing the Home screen button or swiping up from the bottom). Tap the *Settings* option. Note that you may have to swipe your finger to access the *Settings* option if multiple pages of icons are present.

3.   Tap the *General* option. Tap the *About* option. Locate the *Capacity* option, which shows the total amount of memory installed.

How much memory is available on the device?

_____

4.   Locate the *Available* option, which shows the amount of memory that is not being used.

How much memory is free?

_____

5.   Return to the *Home* screen.

Lab 10.3 Determining Memory Resources in an Android-Based Device

Objective: To be able to use the Android operating system to determine the amount of memory

Parts: An Android-based device

Procedure: Complete the following procedure and answer the accompanying questions.

Note: The Android operating system is an open source operating system. Options vary from device to device, but most configuration options are similar.

1.   Ensure that the Android device is powered on.

2.   Access the *Home* screen by tapping the *Home* icon. Tap the *Settings* option. Note that you may have to swipe your finger to access the Settings option if multiple pages of icons are present.

3.   Tap the *Storage* option. Locate the total amount of storage.

How much memory is available on the device?

_____

4.   Locate how much memory is available (not being used).

How much memory is free?

_____

How much memory is being used by applications?

_____

Does this device have external storage? If so, how can you tell?

_____

5.   Return to the *Home* screen.

Lab 10.4 Managing Files on a Mobile Device

Objective: To be able to copy files or send files using an Android or Apple iOS-based device

Parts: Android device or Apple iOS device

Procedure: Complete the following procedure and answer the accompanying questions.

Android

1.   If working on an Apple device, please go to step 16. Power on the Android device.

2.   Access the Camera app by touching the *Camera* icon on the *Home* screen.

3.   Normally in the Camera app, there is an icon of a camera or a circle that you touch to take the picture. Take a picture. You may hear a sound effect of a camera shutter.

4.   Return to the *Home* screen by touching the *Home* icon. If the *Home* icon is not showing, touch the screen where it normally appears (bottom left, center icon).

5.   Locate and tap the *File Manager* app.

6.   Unless the settings have been changed, most photos are stored by default on internal storage. Tap the *Internal Storage* option. The internal storage folders are listed to the right.

7.   Locate and tap the *DCIM* folder.

8.   Locate and open the *Camera* folder.

9.   To open a picture, touch the filename. Frequently there are options such as rotating or cropping the photo found by touching just outside the photograph.

   What photo options are available?

   _____

10.   Return to the file listing by using the *Return* button (the button on the screen that is a return arrow that looks like this: ↰). If the *Return* button is not shown, you can touch the bottom left of the screen, and the *Return* arrow should appear.

11.   Enable the checkbox by the name of the photograph by touching the checkbox.

12.   Options either appear or you can touch an icon normally located in the upper-right or upper-left corner to allow options to appear. Locate the options that include the copy function.

13.   Go to another folder located on your internal storage. Select the *Paste* option.

Instructor initials: _____

14.   Delete the original and copied photographs.

Instructor initials: _____

15.   Power off the device.

Apple

16.   If working on an Android device, please go to step 1. Power on the Apple device.

17.   Access the Camera app by tapping the *Camera* icon on the *Home* screen.

18.   Tap the icon of the camera to take the picture. Take a picture. You may hear a sound effect of a camera shutter.

19.   Notice that a small image of the photograph is available in the lower-left corner. Tap the graphic of the photo. Note that you can also access the photograph by using the *Photos* home screen icon.

20.   Options are available in the top-right corner. If these options have disappeared, just tap the photo.

   Describe three options available at the top of a photograph.

   _____

   _____

21. Select the option that has a box with an arrow in it. Select *Email Photo*.

22. In the *To:* textbox, type a valid email address such as your own by tapping inside the blank space to the right of To:. See the instructor if you don't know of an email address to use.

    What email address did you use?

    _____

23. In the *Subject* textbox, type *Class Photo*. Notice that the photo is already attached to the email.

24. Tap the *Send* button in the top-right corner of the email.

25. Take another photograph.

26. Either using the *Camera* app or the *Photos* app, locate the original photograph.

27. Tap the photo to bring up the options in the right corner if they are not showing. Select the *Slideshow* icon.

28. Select a type of transition by tapping the *Transitions* option.

    What transition did you choose?

    _____

29. Select *Start Slideshow*. Stop the slideshow by tapping on the screen.

Instructor initials: _____

30. Delete the two photographs.

Instructor initials: _____

31. Power off the device.

Lab 10.5 Connecting a Mobile Device to a WiFi Network

Objective: To be able to connect an Android or Apple iOS-based device to an IEEE 802.11 WiFi network

Parts: Android device or Apple iOS device

Procedure: Complete the following procedure and answer the accompanying questions.

Note: Android is an open source operating system. The operating system may be modified by the vendor. Android simulators are available for free and can be used for the Android portion of this lab.

Android

1. If working on an Apple device, please go to step 7. Power on the Android device.

2. Access the *Home* screen by pressing the *Home* button. Locate the *Settings* option by swiping if necessary.

3. Tap the *Settings* option > optionally *Wireless and Network* > *Wi-Fi/Wi-Fi Settings*.

4. Tap the WiFi network you want to join. Enter the security credentials if needed > *Connect*. Note that if the WiFi network is not shown because the wireless access point is not broadcasting the SSID (see Chapter 14, "Introduction to Operating Systems," for more information), you can tap the *Add Wi-Fi Network* option at the bottom of the page and enter the relevant SSID and security credentials.

5. Verify that the wireless symbol shows at the top of the mobile device.

6. To disconnect from the network, tap the connected network > *Forget*.

Apple

7. If working on an Android device, please go to step 1. Power on the Apple device.

8. Access the *Home* screen by pressing the *Home* button or swiping up from the bottom. Locate the *Settings* option by swiping if necessary.

9.   Tap the *Settings* option > *Wi-Fi.* Ensure that WiFi is enabled by tapping the button to the far right of the option to the enabled (right) side.

10. Tap the WiFi network you want to join. Enter the security credentials if needed > *Join.* Note that if the WiFi network is not shown because the wireless access point is not broadcasting the SSID (see Chapter 13, "Networking" for more information), you can tap the *Other* option at the bottom of the page and enter the relevant SSID and security credentials.

11. Verify the wireless symbol shows at the top of the mobile device.

12. To disconnect from the network, tap the connected network > *Forget This Network.*

11 Computer Design and Troubleshooting Review Labs

Lab 11.1 Logical Troubleshooting

Objective: To use logic to solve a computer problem

Parts: Computer

Procedure: Complete the following procedure and answer the accompanying questions.

1. In teams of two, one person leaves the room, while the other person inserts a problem in the machine and powers it down.

2. The person who left the room powers on the computer with the problem and performs troubleshooting. Use the flowchart shown in Lab Figure 11.1 and answer the questions that follow. When the problem is solved, swap roles.

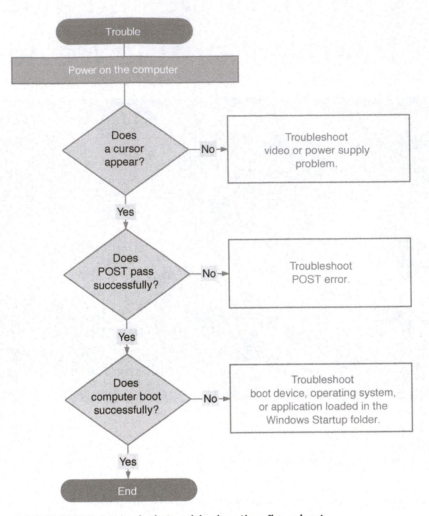

LAB FIGURE 11.1   Lab troubleshooting flowchart

Do you hear any audio clues? If yes, list the symptoms.

_____

Do any POST errors appear? If so, list them.

_____

Are there any startup errors? If so, list them.

_____

Are there any application-specific problems? If so, list them.

_____

List any possible techniques to test. Test them one at a time. Document the solution.

_____

Lab 11.2 Designing a Computer Subsystem

Objective: To design an upgrade for a particular subsystem

Parts: Computer

Procedure: Complete the following procedure and answer the accompanying questions.

1.   Look at a particular computer within the classroom or that you have seen in your own home or a friend's home. Think of the computer in terms of one of the following subsystems. Note that the instructor may assign a particular subsystem.

> Motherboard and case

> Power supply and case

> Storage

> Audio

> Display

Can the subsystem be upgraded? Why or why not? [Yes | No]

_____

Is the system a proprietary one? In other words are you limited in your upgrade options because the system is sold by a particular manufacturer? [Yes | No] Describe the limitations, if any.

_____

_____

2.   Before you design an upgrade for that particular subsystem, remove the parts for the subsystem in order to see the particulars about the parts. Document your findings.

_____

_____

_____

3.   Design an upgrade for the subsystem. Write a proposal for a prospective customer on what the parts would cost and what you would charge them to upgrade the chosen or assigned subsystem.

_____

_____

_____

_____

_____

_____

_____

_____

_____

_____

4.   In three or more complete sentences, describe the challenges associated with designing for a particular subsystem rather than designing an entire computer system that serves a specific purpose.

_____

12 Internet Connectivity, Virtualization, and Cloud Technologies Labs

Lab 12.1 Exploring Serial Devices in Windows 7

Objective: To explore serial devices and their properties using Windows 7

Parts: A computer with Windows 7 installed

Either a serial port with an external modem attached or an internal modem

Procedure: Complete the following procedure and answer the accompanying questions.

1. Power on the computer and log on using the user ID and password provided by the instructor or lab assistant.

2. Click the *Start* button and access *Control Panel*.

3. Click the *System and Security* Control Panel.

4. Click the *Device Manager* link. Note that you may have to scroll down to see this option.

5. Expand the *Ports* option.

6. If *Communications Port (Com1)* is available, right-click it and select *Properties*.

   What tabs are available?

   _____

   What is the status of the serial port?

   _____

7. Click the *Port Settings* tab.

   What is the maximum number of bits per second?

   _____

8. Click the *Advanced* button.

   What UART is being used?

   _____

What COM port is assigned?

_____

9. Click *Cancel*.

10. Click the *Driver* tab and click the *Driver Details* button.

    List any drivers, including the complete path associated with the serial port.

    _____

11. Click the *OK* button.

    What is the purpose of the *Roll Back Driver* button?

    _____

12. Click the *Resources* tab.

    What IRQ and I/O addresses are assigned?

    _____

Instructor initials: _____

13. Click the *OK* button.

Modems

Note: Skip this section if an internal modem is not installed. If unsure, perform the tasks to see if the steps work.

14. Expand the *Modems* Device Manager category. Right-click a specific modem and select *Properties*. Click the *Modem* tab.

    What COM port does the modem use?

    _____

    What is the maximum port speed?

    _____

    Is the setting for the maximum bits per second on a serial port the speed at which the external modem transmits over the phone line? Explain your answer.

    _____

    Why would you want the speaker volume enabled when first installing a modem?

    _____

15. Click the *Diagnostics* tab and click the *Query Modem* button.

    What was the first AT command that was sent to the modem?

    _____

16. Click the *View Log* button. Scroll to the bottom of the log.

    What communications standard or standards does the modem use?

    _____

17. Close the *Notepad Log* window. Click the *Resources* tab.

    What IRQ and I/O addresses does the modem use?

    _____

Instructor initials: _____

18. Close the *Modem Properties* window. Close the *Device Manager* window.

19. Close the *Control Panel* window.

Lab 12.2 Installing a Windows 7 Internal or External Modem

Objective: To be able to install an internal or external modem

Parts: Internal or external modem

Procedure: Complete the following procedure and answer the accompanying questions.

1.   Power on the computer and ensure that it boots properly.

2.   Shut down the computer properly and remove the power cord from the back of the computer. Complete steps 3 and 4 that are appropriate for the type of modem you have. Then move to step 5.

Internal Modem Installation

3.   Install the internal modem into an available slot.

4.   Reinstall the computer cover, reinstall the computer power cord, and power on the computer. The *Found New Hardware* wizard appears if this is the first time the computer has had this adapter installed.

External Modem Installation

3.   Attach the external modem to the USB port. Attach power to the external modem, if necessary.

4.   Reinstall the computer power cord and power on the computer. The *Found New Hardware* wizard appears.

Both Modem Installation Types

5.   Install the correct modem driver, using either the one provided with the modem, the one downloaded, or the one provided as part of the operating system.

6.   Access *Device Manager* > expand *Modems* > right-click the internal modem that was just installed > *Properties*.

     Under the General tab, what is the device status? It should be that the modem is working properly. If it is not, perform appropriate troubleshooting until it does display that message.

     _____

7.   Click the *Diagnostics* tab. Click the *Query Modem* button.

     List at least two AT commands and the response that is shown in the information window.

     _____

8.   Click the *View Log* button.

     What do you think a technician could do with the information shown?

     _____

9.   Close the *Notepad Log* window.

10. Click the *Resources* tab.

     What memory range does the adapter use?

     _____

     Which IRQ is the adapter using?

     _____

11. Click the *Advanced* tab.

     When do you think you would use the Extra Initialization Commands textbox?

     _____

12. Click the *Advanced Port Settings* button.

Which COM port is used with this adapter?

_____

Are FIFO buffers used by default?

_____

13. Click the *Cancel* button on the next two screens to exit the *Properties* window.

14. If an external modem was installed, power off the modem and disconnect it from the PC. If an internal modem was installed, power down the PC, remove the adapter, and install the slot cover.

15. Power on or reboot the computer and ensure that it boots properly.

Lab 12.3 Introduction to Internet Explorer (IE) Configuration

Objective: To become familiar with basic Internet Explorer configuration options

Parts: Windows computer

Procedure: Complete the following procedure and answer the accompanying questions.

1. Power on the computer and ensure that it boots properly.

2. Open Internet Explorer. From the *Tools* (gear) icon, select *About Internet Explorer* to determine the IE version.

Which version of IE is being used?

_____

3. Re-access the *Tools* link.

4. Select *Internet Options*.

What URL is listed as the home page?

_____

Is the *Delete Browsing History on Exit* option enabled or disabled?
[enabled | disabled]

List one corporate scenario for which you think the business security policy would require the *Delete Browsing History on Exit* option be enabled.

_____

_____

_____

_____

_____

_____

5. Click the *Settings* button in the *Browsing History* section.

How often does the IE browser check to see if there is a newer version of a web page?

_____

What drive partition currently holds temporary Internet files?

_____

If the drive partition that currently holds temporary Internet files is an SSD, would it be better to change this to a different folder? Why or why not?

_____

_____

_____

_____

6. Access the *History* tab from within the *Website Data Settings* window.

   What is the number of days the web browsing history is kept?

   _____

7. Access the *Caches and Databases* tab from within the *Website Data Settings* window.

   How much drive space can be used before the user is notified that a website cache or database exceeds that amount?

   _____

8. Use the *Cancel* button to close the *Website Data Settings* window. Click the *Tabs* button in the *Tabs* section.

   [T | F] To enable tabbed browsing when it has been disabled, you must close all Internet Explorer windows and then reopen Internet Explorer to activate the change.

   Based on the configured options, what currently happens when a new tab is opened?

   _____

   _____

   Based on the information in the *Tabbed Browsing Settings* window, what do you think would be the most secure pop-up setting for a corporate environment, and why do you think this?

   _____

   _____

   From the choices provided, what is your favorite way of handling program links provided in a website?

   _____

   _____

9. Click *Cancel*. Click the *Colors* button.

   Is the *Use Windows Colors* option enabled or disabled? [enabled | disabled]

   _____

10. Disable the *Use Windows Colors* option. Select the *Use Hover Color* option.

    Based on what you see as the default settings, which option might you change for a person with red-green colorblindness?

    _____

    _____

    What color is the default hover color?

    _____

11. Click *Cancel*. Click the *Languages* button.

    What two prefix and suffix options are available?

    _____

    _____

12. Click *Cancel*. Click the *Fonts* button.

    What is the current font setting for web pages?

    _____

13. Click *Cancel*. Click the *Accessibility* button.

   List one example of when you might use the formatting options presented in a home computer environment.

   _____

   _____

14. Click *Cancel* twice and close *Internet Explorer*.

Lab 12.4 Verifying Computer Support for Microsoft Hyper-V Virtualization

Objective: To determine if a Windows computer can use the Microsoft Hyper-V virtualization tool

Parts: Windows computer

               Internet access if BIOS/UEFI research is needed

Procedure: Complete the following procedure and answer the accompanying questions.

1. Power on the computer and ensure that it boots properly.

2. Access the BIOS/UEFI. Locate and enable the virtualization extensions. These are commonly found in either the Chipset, Processor, or Security menu option. Look for Intel Virtualization Technology, Intel VT, AMD Virtualization, AMD-V, or Virtualization extensions. Research the computer on the Internet for BIOS/UEFI options.

   Which option did you enable?

   _____

3. Also enable hardware-enforced data execution prevention (DEP). On an Intel-based system this is the execute disable (XD) bit. On an AMD-based system, this is called the no execute (NX) bit.

   Where did you find the DEP option to enable within the BIOS/UEFI?

   _____

4. Save and exit the BIOS/UEFI.

5. Once Windows starts, launch the *System Information* Windows tool.

6. Look for the Hyper-V requirements, as detailed in Lab Table 12.1 and as shown in Lab Figure 12.1. Note that there should be a Yes next to each requirement, or Hyper-V cannot be used on the computer.

   Do all four options show as Yes? Only if they all show as Yes can Hyper-V be used on the computer.

   _____

LAB TABLE 12.1   Hyper-V Requirements Explanation

Requirement	Description
Processor	64-bit
Processor nested paging	Also known as second-level address translation (SLAT) extensions. Intel provides this through the extended page table (EPT) in Core i9, i7, i5, and i3 processors. AMD calls this nested page tables (NPT) or rapid virtualization indexing (RVI).
Processor support for virtualization (VM Monitor Mode extension)	Intel lists this as Virtualization Technology (VT); VT-*x*, such as VT-c or VT-d. AMD lists it as AMD-V.
RAM	4 GB or higher
BIOS/UEFI support	Enable virtualization and hardware-enforced data execution prevention.

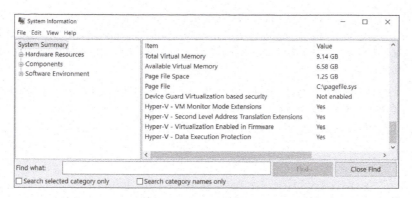

LAB FIGURE 12.1   Windows System Information Hyper-V requirements

Lab 12.5 Installing Another Operating System Within Microsoft Hyper-V

Objective: To create a virtual machine using Microsoft Hyper-V

Parts: Windows 8 or 10 computer

Any other operating system ISO file

Internet access if an ISO file needs to be downloaded

Note: Additional steps may be needed for installation of the operating system.

Procedure: Complete the following procedure and answer the accompanying questions.

1. Power on the computer and ensure that it boots properly.

2. Download or otherwise obtain an ISO operating system image.

3. Ensure that the computer has BIOS/UEFI virtualization options enabled. See Lab 12.4 or the Tech Tip in the "Virtualization Basics" section of Chapter 12.

4. Access the *Turn Windows Features On or Off* Control Panel. Ensure that the following two Hyper-V options are enabled: (1) *Hyper-V Management Tools* and (2) *Hyper-V Platform > OK*. Reboot the computer by selecting *Restart Now*.

5. Access the *Hyper-V Manager* app. Use the *Action* menu option to select *New > Virtual Machine*. Note that if this option is not available, you may need to select the item immediately under the Hyper-V Manager in the left window. Click *Next*.

6. Name the virtual machine.

What name did you select?

_____

7. Select the default location to store the virtual machine > *Next* > leave the default of *Generation 1* > *Next* > select the proper amount of RAM for the operating system you are going to install.

How much RAM did you select?

_____

Are you sure this is at least the minimum required for the operating system that will be installed? If not, research on the Internet the minimum required before proceeding. [Yes | No]

8. Click *Next* only after you are sure you have at least the minimum amount of RAM required for the operating system to be installed.

9. For the networking portion, select *Not Connected > Next*. For the virtual hard disk, in the *Size* option, ensure that you select the minimum hard drive space required for the operating system.

How much hard drive space did you select?

_____

Are you sure this is at least the minimum required for the operating system that will be installed? If not, research on the Internet the minimum required before proceeding. [Yes | No]

10. Leave all the other defaults and click *Next* in the virtual hard disk window. In the *Installation Options section, select the Install an Operating System from a Bootable CD/DVD-ROM option* > *select the Image File (.iso)* radio button > select the path where the ISO file is located by using the *Browse* button > *Next* > *Finish*.

11. From within the Hyper-V Manager window under *Virtual Machines* > right-click the newly created device > *Connect* > *Start* (Power) button.

12. Install the operating system. Steps will vary based on the operating system chosen.

Instructor initials: _____

Lab 12.6 Introduction to Amazon AWS Cloud

Objective: To become familiar with cloud technologies using AWS

Parts: Windows computer

Notes: A credit card is required but is not charged unless you exceed the AWS Free Tier limits.

                  Vendors frequently change their online products, so although the examples shown in this lab were relevant at the time of press, they may not be relevant when you work through this lab.

                  The AWS Educate website, at awseducate.com, is available for use with reduced functionality.

Procedure: Complete the following procedure and answer the accompanying questions.

1. Power on the computer and ensure that it boots properly. Open a web browser and use the following URL to access Amazon Web Services (AWS): https://aws.amazon.com.

2. Create an account, if necessary, and log in. Note that if you do not have a credit card and are so directed by your instructor, skip to the note in step 9.

3. From the *Products* menu, select *Amazon EC2*. The AWS Free Tier includes 750 hours of Linux and Windows usage. Select the *Try Amazon EC2 for Free* button if this is your first time using it.

4. Select the *Launch a Virtual Machine* option from within the *Build a Solution* section.

   Which version of Amazon Linux AMI is shown?

   _____

   Which root device type is the Microsoft Windows Server 2016 Base with Containers?

   _____

   Which virtualization type is used with the Deep Learning AMI (Microsoft Windows Server 2016)? Note that if the server version is not available, the answer should be the answer for another version.

   _____

   Does the Windows Server 2008 SP2 base allow you to choose whether you use a 32-bit or a 64-bit version?

   _____

   How many machine images are available?

   _____

5. Enable the *Free Tier Only* checkbox.

   How many machine images are available within the free tier?

   _____

6. Click the *Cancel* and *Exit* link at the top right. Click on the letters *aws* in the top-left corner to return to the home page.

7. Select the *Backup* and *Recovery* option from within the *Learn to Build* section.

8. Locate the *Explore with Tutorials and Labs* section and click the *Introduction to Amazon Simple Storage Service (S3)* self-paced lab. Note that you will just be watching the Introductory 3-minute video and not doing the full 45-minute lab. In the *Overview* section, select the link *Here Is a 3-Minute Introductory Video*.

9. Note: If you did not create an account within AWS, then use the Internet to access www.youtube.com. Search for the *Introduction to Amazon Simple Storage Service (S3) - Cloud Storage on AWS* video. This is the same video you would watch if you had an account.

   According to the video, what are two drawbacks of building your own storage repository? (Choose two.)

   [time-consuming | technically difficult | space invasive | expensive | unsecure]

   According to the video, what must you also have if you have your own storage repository?

   a. PATA hard drives

   b. Lots and lots of space

   c. Different manufacturers (and often incompatible) products

   d. Racks and racks of hardware and software

   According to the video, guessing how much capacity you need in your own storage repository is

   _____.

   [pretty easy | usually easy | sometimes tedious | difficult]

   According to the video, is S3 secure? [if you pay for it | yes | no]

   If you used Amazon S3 Cloud Storage, what are the two steps required to store data? (Choose two.)

   a. Select a type of drive.

   b. Choose the region.

   c. Create a bucket.

   d. Select a drive.

   e. Select the capacity needed.

   How does S3 ensure that your data is not lost?

   _____

   Which Amazon plan would be used for data that is kept for archival purposes?

   [S3 Prime | S3 Standard | Amazon Glacier | S3 Standard Infrequent Access]

Lab 12.7 Installing VMware Workstation

Objective: To install VMware Workstation 15 Pro in preparation for future VMware Workstation labs

Parts: Windows computer with administrator rights to install software

Internet access to download a 30-day trial of VMware Workstation Pro

Procedure: Complete the following procedure and answer the accompanying questions.

1. If VMware Workstation Pro is not already downloaded on the computer, go to http://www.vmware.com and download the software.

   Is VMware Workstation already installed on the computer?

   _____

   Is the same version of VMware Workstation downloaded for 32-bit Windows as 64-bit Windows? If you do not know, research this on the Internet.

   _____

2. Start the VMware installer. Accept the end-user agreement. When the Customer Setup window appears, keep the default location selection unless directed otherwise.

3. Leave the *Check for Product Updates on startup* option enabled and click *Next*.

4.   Either enable or disable the *Join the VMware Customer Experience Program* checkbox.

Which option did you choose?

_____

5.   Leave the shortcut checkboxes enabled and click *Next*. Click *Install*

6.   Either enter a license key provided by the instructor or lab assistant or select the *Finish* button. Note that no key is needed for the 30-day trial.

7.   When the installation is complete, the VMware Workstation icon appears on the desktop. Note that you may be prompted to restart the computer before using the software.

Instructor initials: _____

Lab 12.8 Installing Windows and Ubuntu as a VMware Workstation Virtual Machine

Objective: To install a version of Windows 7 and Ubuntu as a VMware Workstation virtual machine

Parts: Windows computer with administrator rights that has VMware Workstation installed

Procedure: Complete the following procedure and answer the accompanying questions.

Notes: This lab does not require .iso discs, but uses the integrated guest operating systems simply to expose the student to the environment.

1.   Double-click the *VMware Workstation* icon on the desktop or access the software from the *Start* button menu. VMware Workstation opens. If this is the first time starting VMware Workstation, you will be prompted to enter a license key or you can select the *I want to try VMware Workstation 15 for 30 days* radio button. Make your selection and click *Continue > Yes > Finish*. Lab Figure 12.2 shows the VMware Workstation area.

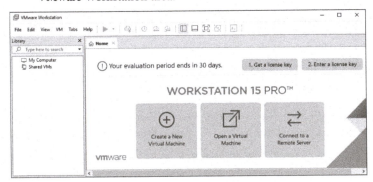

LAB FIGURE 12.2   VMware Workstation

2.   On the *Home* tab, select the *Create a New Virtual Machine* option.

3.   Select the *Typical (Recommended)* radio button and click *Next*.

4.   Select the *I will install the operating system later* radio button and click *Next*.

5.   Select the *Microsoft Windows* radio button. Set the version to *Windows 7* and click *Next*. Answer the questions based on what you see on the screen.

Were a username and password selected as part of this installation process?
[Yes | No] If so, document the username and password.

_____

6.   Enter a name for the machine (or leave the default) and select a hard drive location to store the virtual machine file. Click *Next* after you have answered the questions.

What name did you use for the virtual machine?

_____

Document the path to the folder that contains the virtual machine file.

_____

7. Keep the default disk size and accept the default of the *Split virtual disk into multiple files* radio button. Click *Next*.

8. Look over the virtual machine settings to answer the questions.

   What is the default amount of RAM?

   _____

   What type of network adapter is installed?

   _____

   What other devices are automatically installed?

   _____

9. Click *Finish*. Notice that the virtual machine is within its own tab. Right-click the tab that contains your new virtual machine.

   Document at least four menu options that are available when you right-click the virtual machine tab.

   _____

10. Locate the VM in the Library panel on the left. The virtual machine name is under *My Computer* and has a name that you assigned. Right-click the virtual machine you just created.

    Are the options the same as the ones you saw when you right-clicked the virtual machine tab?

    [Yes | No]

11. Ensure the VM is still selected in the left panel. In the right panel, select the *Edit virtual machine settings* link. Ensure *Memory* is selected in the Device column.

    Based on what is shown, what is the maximum recommended memory?

    _____

    What is the recommended memory amount?

    _____

    What is the Guest OS recommended minimum?

    _____

12. Select *Processors* in the left window.

    What is the default number of processors for the VM?

    _____

    What is the default number of cores per processors for the VM?

    _____

    What is the maximum number of processors that can be selected for the VM?

    _____

    How many processor cores are available on each processor?

    _____

13. Select the *Hard Disk* option.

    Which drive interface is used by default? [PATA | SAS | SATA | SCSI]

    Which disk utilities are available for this drive? (Choose all that apply.)

    [Mark as active | Convert to GPT | Map | Defragment | Compact | Compress |

    Expand | Disconnect | Partition]

14. Click the *Advanced* button. Look in the mode section. If the *Independent* option was selected, you are allowed to select either the persistent or nonpersistent mode. Persistent mode is when any changes you make take effect immediately. Nonpersistent mode means that you can make changes to the VM, but when you power the VM off, the changes are not kept. Click *Cancel*.

15. Select *Network Adapter* from the device list on the left. An important part of virtualization is how you configure the NIC.

   What are the five types of network connections? (Choose five answers.)

   [Bridged | Custom | Disconnected | Host-only | LAN segment | NAT | PAT]

   Which network connection type is the default?

   [Bridged | Custom | Disconnected | Host-only | LAN segment | NAT | PAT]

   Looking at the other devices, is a printer detected by default? [Yes | No]

16. Click *Cancel* to return to the main VM Workstation window.

17. Using the process you just learned, return to the *Home* tab and create a new VM using the guest OS of *Ubuntu*.

   What is the default amount of memory allocated to this VM?

   _____

   Is the hard drive interface the same that was used for the Windows 7 VM?
   [Yes | No]

   Which network connection is the default for the Ubuntu VM?

   [Bridged | Custom | Disconnected | Host-only | LAN segment | NAT | PAT]

Instructor initials: _____

18. Ensure that one of your VMs is selected in the left window. Select the *VM* menu option. Notice the *Snapshot* option. A snapshot is used to create an image or backup of the VM in its current state. This is good when making changes or trying something new so that you could revert back to the VM at a particular point in time if something happens or you do not like the results of a particular change.

19. Right-click on the *Windows 7* VM. Select *Remove* > click the *Remove* button.

20. Right-click on the *Ubuntu* VM. Select *Remove* > click the *Remove* button.

21. Close the *VMWare Workstation* window.

Lab 12.9 Installing VirtualBox

Objective: To download and install VirtualBox on a Windows 10 computer

Parts: Windows computer with administrator rights

                 Access to the Internet or a disc/drive with the VirtualBox installer file

Procedure: Complete the following procedure and answer the accompanying questions.

1. VirtualBox is software that allows you to create virtual machines. Inside a virtual machine, you can run multiple guest operating systems. If you need to download the VirtualBox installer, access the *www.virtualbox.org* > *Downloads* page. Download the binary version for Windows hosts.

2. From the location where you downloaded the VirtualBox installer or disc that has the file, launch the executable file by double-clicking it.

3. Click *Next*. Most people accept the default features and location where VirtualBox is to be installed, but your instructor may have specific requirements. If the instructor has not provided any specifics, select *Next* > select the options to be installed or accept the default > *Next*. Note that the installation process disables the network connection temporarily. Select *Yes* > *Install*. Click *Yes* to install. Make sure you select *Install* from any security window that pops up, depending on which options are to be installed.

4. Click *New* to create a new virtual machine (VM).

   List three types of VMs supported by VirtualBox.

   _____

If you selected the macOS X operating system, what versions are available?

_____

5.   In the *Name* textbox, type a name for the VM, select the Linux operating system from the *Type* drop-down menu, and select *Ubuntu (32-bit)* from the *Version* drop-down menu > *Next*.

     What is the maximum memory that can be used for the VM?

_____

6.   For *Memory Size*, leave the default and click *Next*. Leave the default of *Create a Virtual Hard Disk Now* > *Create*. Leave the default hard disk file type set to *VDI* > *Next*. Leave the default storage type as *Dynamically Allocated* > *Next. For File Location and Size*, leave the default > *Create*. Lab Figure 12.3 shows the Oracle VM VirtualBox Manager window with the new VM installed.

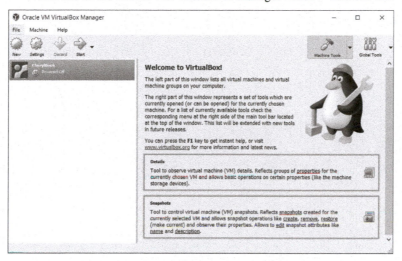

LAB FIGURE 12.3   Oracle VM VirtualBox Manager

     Is the VM powered on or off by default? [On | Off]

Instructor initials: _____

7.   With the name of the VM highlighted in the left window, select the *Settings* icon. Use the menu options on the left to answer the following questions.

     How many CPUs are allocated to the VM by default? [1 | 2 | 4 | 8 | 16]

_____

     [None | 4 MB | 8 MB | 16MB | 64 MB | 128 MB]

     Is video capture available? [Yes | No]

     On which type of hard drive is the VM built by default?
     [IDE | PATA | SATA | USB]

     Is the network adapter enabled by default? [Yes | No]

     Which USB controllers are supported? Select all that apply.
     [1.1 | 2.0 | 2.2 | 3.0 | 3.1]

8.   Click *OK*. With the VM name still highlighted in the left window, select the *Start* menu icon. The VM powers on. Notice that the VM requires a startup disk or an operating system. Either browse to an ISO or click *Cancel* to close the VM.

13 Networking Labs

Lab 13.1 Creating a Straight-Through CAT 5, 5e, or 6 Network Patch Cable

Objective: To create a functional CAT 5, 5e, or 6 UTP network cable

Parts: UTP cable

RJ-45 connectors

Stripper/crimper tool

UTP cable tester

Note: Standard Ethernet networks are cabled with either UTP cable or RG-58 coaxial cable. In this exercise, you create a standard cable for use with Ethernet networks connected through a central hub or switch.

Procedure: Complete the following procedure and answer the accompanying questions.

1. Category 5 and higher UTP cable consists of four twisted pairs of wires, color coded for easy identification. The color-coded wires are colored as follows:

   Pair 1: White/orange and orange

   Pair 2: White/blue and blue

   Pair 3: White/green and green

   Pair 4: White/brown and brown

2. Using the stripper/crimper tool, strip approximately 1/2 inch (1 centimeter) of the protective outer sheath to expose the four twisted pairs of wires. Most strippers have a strip gauge to ensure stripping the proper length. See Lab Figure 13.1.

   Note: To make it easier to sort the wire pairs, the sheathing can be stripped farther than 1/2 inch (1 centimeter), and the wires can be sorted properly and then trimmed to the proper length.

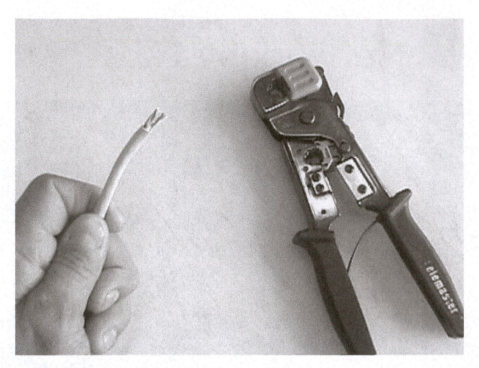

LAB FIGURE 13.1   Strip the cable sheathing

3.   Untwist the exposed wire pairs. Be careful that you do not remove more twist than necessary. Sort the wires according to the following:

Wire 1: White/orange

Wire 2: Orange

Wire 3: White/green

Wire 4: Blue

Wire 5: White/blue

Wire 6: Green

Wire 7: White/brown

Wire 8: Brown

Ethernet cable utilizes wires 1, 2, 3, and 6. Using the preceding wiring scheme means that the cable will use the white/orange-orange and white/green-green wire pairs.

Will both ends of the cable need to follow the same wiring schematic?

[Yes | No]

4.   Insert the sorted and trimmed cable into an RJ-45 connector. The RJ-45 connector key (tang) should face downward with the open end toward you while you insert the wires. Verify that all eight wires fully insert into the RJ-45 connector and that they are inserted in the proper order. See Lab Figure 13.2.

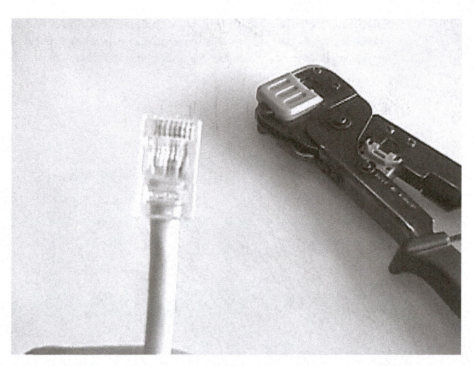

LAB FIGURE 13.2   Push wires firmly into the RJ-45 connector in the correct color order

5.   Insert the cable-connector assembly into the stripper/crimper tool and crimp the connector firmly. See Lab Figure 13.3.

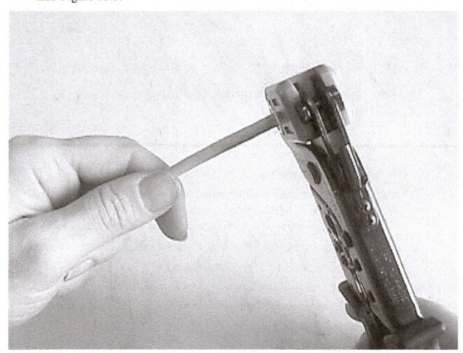

LAB FIGURE 13.3   Crimp the RJ-45 connector firmly

6.   Remove the cable/connector assembly from the stripper/crimper tool and verify that the wires fully insert into the connector and that they are in the proper order.

7.   Repeat steps 2 through 6 for the other end of the CAT 5 or higher UTP cable.

Can the cable be used at this point? [Yes | No]

8.   Before using the cable, it should be tested with a cable tester to verify that you have end-to-end continuity on individual wires and proper continuity between wire pairs. Insert the RJ-45 connector into the proper cable tester receptacle and verify that the cable is functional. See Lab Figure 13.4.

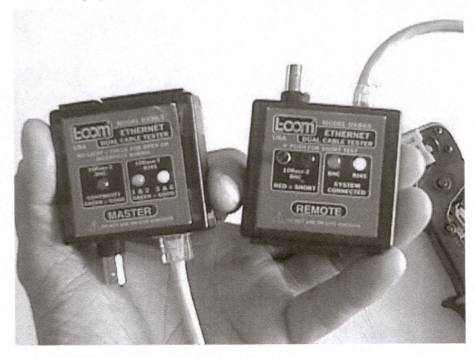

LAB FIGURE 13.4   Network cable tester

Instructor initials: _____

Lab 13.2 Creating a CAT 5, 5e, or 6 Crossover Network Cable

Objective: To create a functional UTP crossover cable

Parts: UTP cable

RJ-45 connectors

Stripper/crimper tool

UTP cable tester

Note: In normal situations, straight-through UTP cable is used to connect to a central hub or switch. In this exercise, you create a crossover cable for use when directly connecting two network devices (computers *without* using a central hub or switch).

Procedure: Complete the following procedure and answer the accompanying questions.

1.   Category 5, 5e, 6, and 7 UTP cable consists of four twisted pairs of wires that are color coded for easy identification. The color-coded wires are as follows:

Pair 1: White/orange and orange

Pair 2: White/blue and blue

Pair 3: White/green and green

Pair 4: White/brown and brown

2.   Using the stripper/crimper tool, strip approximately 1/2 inch (1 centimeter) of the protective outer sheath to expose the four twisted pairs of wires. Most tools have a strip gauge to ensure stripping the proper length.

Note: To make it easier to sort the wire pairs, the sheathing can be stripped farther than 1/2 inch (1 centimeter). The wires can then be sorted properly and then trimmed to the proper length.

3. Untwist the exposed wire pairs. Be careful that you do not remove more twist than necessary. Sort the wires as follows:

    Wire 1: White/orange

    Wire 2: Orange

    Wire 3: White/green

    Wire 4: Blue

    Wire 5: White/blue

    Wire 6: Green

    Wire 7: White/brown

    Wire 8: Brown

    Ethernet networks utilize wires 1, 2, 3, and 6. Using the above wiring scheme means the cable will use the white/orange-orange and white/green-green wire pairs.

    When making a crossover cable, will both ends of the cable need to follow the same wiring schematic? [Yes | No]

4. Insert the sorted and trimmed cable into an RJ-45 connector. The RJ-45 connector key (tang) should face downward with the open end toward you while you insert the wires. Verify that all eight wires fully insert into the RJ-45 connector and that they are inserted in the proper order.

5. Insert the cable-connector assembly into the stripper/crimper tool and crimp the connector firmly.

6. Remove the cable/connector assembly from the stripper/crimper tool and verify that the wires are fully inserted into the connector and that they are in the proper order.

7. To create the crossover cable, the wire pairs must be put in a different order. To accomplish this, repeat steps 2 through 6 on the *opposite* end of the cable, but when sorting the wire pairs, use the following color codes.

    Wire 1: White/green   Wire 5: White/blue

    Wire 2: Green   Wire 6: Orange

    Wire 3: White/orange   Wire 7: White/brown

    Wire 4: Blue Wire 8: Brown

8. Verify both ends of the cables, ensuring that the tang is downward and the colored wires are in the correct order. You can also check the ends of the connectors to see if you see the tip of the copper wire pushed against the end. See Lab Figure 13.5.

    Can the crossover cable be used at this point? [Yes | No]

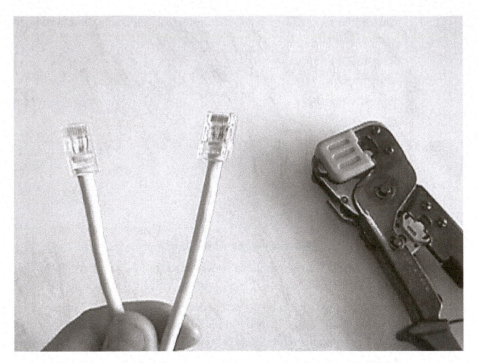

LAB FIGURE 13.5   Verify the color codes on both connectors

9.   Before using the crossover cable, it should be tested with a cable tester to verify that you have end-to-end continuity on individual wires and proper continuity between wire pairs. Insert the RJ-45 connector into the proper cable tester receptacle and verify that the cable is functional.

Note: Your cable tester must have the capability to test crossover cables.

Instructor initials: _____

Lab 13.3 Exploring NIC Properties with Windows 7, 8, or 10

Objective: To examine and modify NIC properties, including manually setting IP address information
Parts: One computer with Windows 7, 8, or 10 installed
Procedure: Complete the following procedure and answer the accompanying questions.

1.   Power on the computer and log on to Windows, if necessary.

2.   Access the *Network and Sharing Center* section of the Control Panel.

3.   Select the *Change Adapter Settings* link.

4.   Double-click or tap the wired or wireless connection that is currently used to connect the computer to the network.

5.   Select the *Details* button. Use Lab Table 13.1 to document key pieces of information assigned to this NIC. For any property that is not shown, simply write *not applicable* for that setting.

LAB TABLE 13.1   NIC lab documentation

Property	Setting
Physical (MAC) address	
DHCP Enabled	[Yes | No]
IPv4 Address	
IPv4 Subnet Mask	
Leased Obtained	

Property	Setting
Lease Expires	
IPv4 Default Gateway	
IPv4 DHCP Server	
IPv4 DNS Server	
IPv6 Address	
IPv6 Default Gateway	

6. Close the *Network Connection Details* window. In the *Local Area Connection Status* window, notice that you can disable the NIC. You can also do this by right-clicking or tapping and briefly holding on the NIC icon. Select the *Disable* button.

   What indication do you have that the NIC is actually disabled?

   _____

7. Right-click or tap and briefly hold on the NIC icon and select *Enable*. Double-click the NIC icon again.

   How many bytes have been sent?

   _____

   How many bytes have been received?

   _____

8. Select the *Properties* button. The *Local Area Connection Properties* window opens. Select the *Configure* button. The properties for the specific NIC card appear. The tabs at the top of the window are manufacturer specific, but most manufacturers tend to have the same basic tabs.

   Which company manufactured the NIC?

   _____

   Which data bus does the card use? [PCI | PCIe | _____]

   What key information would be important to the tech in the *Device Status* window?

   _____

   Using the various tabs, determine the following information:

   Which driver version is installed?

   _____

   Are any power management options enabled? If so, which ones?

   _____

   _____

   Which tab can be used to disable the device?

   _____

9. Access the *Advanced* tab. Locate and select the option that allows you to manually set the NIC speed (and optionally the duplex).

   What default value is shown?

   _____

10. Select the down arrow in the Value menu.

    List the available options.

    _____

    _____

If you were to manually configure this NIC for speed and/or duplex, which option would be best?

_____

In your opinion, why do you think that a 1.0 Gbps option shows only full duplex?

_____

_____

11. Leave the speed at the original setting and return to looking at the specific properties.

Look through the advanced property options and list which ones relate to Wake on LAN. Note that you may have to access the option and look at the values to answer this completely.

_____

_____

12. Select *Cancel > Close*.

Lab 13.4 Networking with Windows 7, 8, or 10

Objective: To put two Windows 7, 8, or 10 computers into a network workgroup

Parts: Two computers with Windows 7, 8, or 10 installed

One crossover cable *or* two straight-through cables and a hub or switch

Procedure: Complete the following procedure and answer the accompanying questions.

1. Power on the first computer and log on to Windows, if necessary. Do one of the following: (1) connect a crossover between the two computer's NICs or (2) connect a straight-through cable from each computer to the hub or switch and power on the switch. Note that the computer may already be on a wired network.

2. In Windows 7, right-click the *Start* button and select *Open Windows Explorer*. Right-click *Computer* in the left pane and select *Properties*. Locate the *Computer Name, Domain, and Workgroup Settings* section.

In Windows 8/10, open *File Explorer*. Right-click or tap and briefly hold *This PC* in the left pane and select *Properties*. Locate the *Computer Name, Domain, and Workgroup Settings* section.

Document the current settings:

Original Computer 1 name: _____

_____

Original Full computer 1 name: _____

_____

Original Computer 1 description, if entered:_____

_____

Is Computer 1 on a workgroup or domain? [Workgroup I Domain]

Original workgroup/domain name for Computer 1: _____

_____

3. On the first computer, select the *Change Settings* link to the right of the computer name section. Click *Continue*, if necessary.

4. On the first computer, select the *Computer Name* tab. Click the *Change* button. Select the *Workgroup* radio button. Name the workgroup something unique.

Changed workgroup/domain name: _____

5. On the first computer, click the *OK* button, and a Computer Name/Domain Changes window appears. Click *OK* and/or *Close* until prompted to *Restart Now*.

6. Power on the second computer and log on to Windows, if necessary.

7. In Windows 7, right-click the *Start* button and select *Open Windows Explorer*. Right-click *Computer* in the left pane and select *Properties*. Locate the *Computer Name, Domain, and Workgroup settings* section.

    In Windows 8/10, open *File Explorer*. Right-click or tap and briefly hold *This PC* in the left pane and select *Properties*. Locate the *Computer Name, Domain, and Workgroup Settings* section.

    Document the current settings:

    Original Computer 2 name: _____

    _____

    Original Full computer 2 name: _____

    _____

    Original Computer 2 description if entered: _____

    _____

    Is Computer 2 on a workgroup or domain? [Workgroup | Domain]

    Original workgroup/domain name for Computer 2: _____

    _____

8. On the second computer, select the *Change Settings* link to the right of the computer name section. Click *Continue*, if necessary.

9. Select the *Computer Name* tab. Click the *Change* button. Select the *Workgroup* radio button.

    Name the Workgroup the same workgroup name as used on Computer 1.

    Changed workgroup/domain name: _____

    _____

10. Click the *OK* button, and a Computer Name/Domain Changes window appears. Click *OK* and/or *Close* until prompted to *Restart Now*.

11. When both computers have rebooted, the IP addresses need to be configured manually.

    On Windows 7 (both computers), click the *Start* button > *All Programs* > *Accessories* > *Command Prompt*. In the new window, type `ipconfig /all`.

    On Windows 8/10 (both computers), locate and access the *Command Prompt* app. In the new window, type `ipconfig /all`.

    On Computer 1, what is the IPv4 address on the Ethernet adapter?

    _____

    On Computer 1, what is the IPv6 link-local address on the Ethernet adapter?

    _____

    On Computer 1, what is the IPv4 subnet mask?

    _____

    On Computer 1, what is the default gateway?

    _____

    On Computer 1, what is the MAC address?

    _____

    On Computer 2, what is the IPv4 address on the Ethernet adapter?

    _____

    On Computer 2, what is the IPv6 link-local address on the Ethernet adapter?

    _____

    On Computer 2, what is the IPv4 subnet mask?

    _____

On Computer 2, what is the default gateway?

_____

On Computer 2, what is the MAC address?

_____

Who is the network adapter manufacturer for Computer 2?

_____

How many hexadecimal characters are shown in the Computer 1 IPv6 address?

_____

How many bits does this represent?

_____

12. Complete this step on both computers. Close the Command Prompt window. Access the *Network and Sharing Center* Control Panel > access the *Change Advanced Sharing Settings* link in the left pane.

    Document the current Sharing and Discovery settings for both computers. Note that all options may not be available in Windows Home versions, but the lab still works. You may also have to expand some sections to find them in the particular type of network currently being used.

	Computer 1	Computer 2
Network discovery	_____	_____
File sharing	_____	_____
Printer sharing	_____	_____
Password protected sharing	_____	_____
Media sharing/streaming	_____	_____
Public folder sharing	_____	_____

13. On both computers, select *Cancel*. From the *Network and Sharing Center* section of the Control Panel, select the *Change Adapter Settings* link from the left panel. Right-click or tap and briefly hold *Local Area Connection* or *Ethernet* Adapter > *Properties*. In the center window, locate and select *Internet Protocol Version 4 (TCP/IPv4)* > *Properties* button.

    Document the settings for Computer 1 and Computer 2:

    Is Computer 1 configured with an IP address, mask and default gateway OR is Computer 1 configured to obtain an IP address automatically?

    _____

    Is Computer 1 configured with a preferred and alternate DNS server(s) IP addresses OR does Computer 1 obtain DNS server address information automatically?

    _____

    Is Computer 2 configured with an IP address, mask and default gateway OR is Computer 2 configured to obtain an IP address automatically?

    _____

    Is Computer 2 configured with a preferred and alternate DNS server(s) IP addresses OR does Computer 2 obtain DNS server address information automatically?

    _____

14. On Computer 1, select the *Use the Following IP Address* radio button and type in the following information:

    IP address: `192.168.1.1`

    Subnet mask: `255.255.255.0`

    Default gateway: `192.168.1.254`

    Click the *OK* button. Click the *OK* button at the bottom of the *Local Area Connection Properties* screen.

15. On Computer 2, select the *Use the Following IP Address* radio button and type in the following information:

    IP address: `192.168.1.2`

    Subnet mask: `255.255.255.0`

    Default gateway: `192.168.1.254`

    Click the *OK* button. Click the *OK* button at the bottom of the *Local Area Connection Properties* screen.

16. On both computers, using previously described procedures, open a command prompt and verify that the IPv4 address has been applied. Note that you may have to scroll up to see the IPv4 address.

    From a Computer 1 command prompt, type `ping 192.168.1.2`.

    What was the response? Note that the default Windows Firewall behavior is to deny pings. When File and Print Sharing is enabled, the firewall automatically enables ICMP messages that include pings.

Sharing and Accessing a Shared Folder

Note: This section can take a little patience depending on the type of network the computer uses.

17. On both computers, access the *Network and Sharing Center* Control Panel > *Change Advanced Sharing Settings* link. Configure the following settings:
    > Network discovery: *Turn on Network Discovery*
    > File and print sharing: *Turn on File and Print Sharing*

    Click the *Save Changes* button.

18. On Computer 1, using *Windows Explorer* (Windows 7) or *File Explorer* (Windows 8/10), create a text file called *Surprise.txt* in a Documents folder you create called ABC; place this message in the text file:

    `Technology makes it possible for people to gain control over`
    `everything, except over technology. -John Tudor`

19. On Computer 1, right-click or tap to select the *ABC* folder > *Share* menu option.

    The options you have here depend on the type of network the computer is on. Note that not all options will be available, depending on the type of network configured. Select the option that best suits your network environment. If necessary, ask the instructor or student assistant what type of network is used.
    > If connected to a HomeGroup, you can select *Homegroup (View)* or *Homegroup (View and Edit)*. If you want to configure a HomeGroup to use this option, see the steps in Chapter 13.
    > On a domain or workgroup, you can select specific users listed that are available to add or select using the *Add* option to add other users.
    > On Windows 8 and 10, you can also select the *Email* icon and email a link to the share.
    > OneDrive can be used instead of sharing the folder. Drag the folder into OneDrive and share from there.

An older method of sharing folders is to right-click the folder (or tap and briefly hold) > *Properties* > *Sharing* tab > *Share* button > access the down arrow and choose *Everyone* > *Add* button > *Share* button.

20. On Computer 2, there are several ways to view the share, depending on the type of network the computer is on. Note that not all options will be available, depending on the type of network configured. Select the option that best suits your network environment. If necessary, ask the instructor or student assistant what type of network is used.
    > If on a HomeGroup, use *Windows Explorer/File Explorer* to expand the *Homegroup* option from the left pane. Expand the particular computer to view the shared files.
    > If using OneDrive, access it through *Windows Explorer/File Explorer* or a web browser.
    > If using the older method of folder sharing, use *Windows Explorer/File Explorer* to select the *Network* option from the left pane. In the right pane, double-click the *Computer 1 Name*.

    Note: If Computer 1 does not appear in the right pane (it can take quite a few minutes to do so), do what many IT personnel do and access the computer by using its UNC. From a command prompt or Search textbox, type the following: \\`computer_name`\`share_name` (where `computer_name` is the name of Computer 1 and `share_name` is ABC, the name of the share). An example would be \\`Cheryl-PC`\`ABC`.

    Note: If no passwords are assigned to the existing user account, a password will have to be applied to the account on both machines.

21. Access the *ABC* folder. Open the *Surprise.txt* document. Try modifying the text inside and saving it on Computer 1.

    Were you successful? [Yes | No]

Instructor initials: _____

22. Close the *Surprise.txt* document on both computers.

Instructor initials: _____

23. Place both computers back in the original workgroup/domain. Refer to step 7 for the original settings.

24. Configure both computers to the original Sharing and Discovery settings. Refer to step 12 for the original settings.

25. Place both computers to the original IPv4 IP address, mask, default gateway, and DNS settings. Refer to step 13 for the original settings.

26. Remove the cable and put the computers back to the original cabling configuration. Ensure that the computer works and has the same access as it had before you began this lab.

Instructor initials: _____

Lab 13.5 Connecting to a Windows 7 Shared or Networked Printer

Objective: To properly share a printer and use a shared or networked printer using Windows 7
Parts: Two networked computers with a printer attached to one and Windows 7 installed
Procedure: Complete the following procedure and answer the accompanying questions.

Sharing a Printer on the Network

1. Power on the computer that has the printer attached. If necessary, log on to Windows, using the appropriate user ID and password.

2. Click the *Start* button and select *Control Panel*.

3. In Windows 7, access the *Network and Sharing Center* Control Panel. Ensure that *Printer Sharing* is enabled through the *Change Advanced Sharing Settings* link.

4. Access the *Devices and Printers* Control Panel. Right-click the printer to be shared and select the *Properties* option.

5.   Click the *Sharing* tab. (If the *Sharing* tab is not available, return to the *Devices and Printers* Control Panel, right-click the printer icon > select *Printer Properties*.) Select the *Share This Printer* radio button/checkbox. (If the option is grayed out, select the *Network and Sharing Center* link. Make changes as necessary. Then continue with the rest of this step.) Ensure that the *Render Print Jobs on Client Computers* checkbox is enabled.

6.   In the *Share Name* textbox, type in a unique printer name, limited to eight characters, if possible. It is important that this name be unique.

What name was assigned to the printer? _____

_____

7.   Click the *OK* button.

Printing to a Shared or Networked Printer

8.   On the computer that does not have the printer attached, open the *Devices and Printers* Control Panel.

9.   Click the *Add a Printer* menu option. The Add Printer Wizard opens. Click the *Next* button.

10. Click the *Add a Network, Wireless, or Bluetooth Printer* option.

11. The printer link should be listed in the window. Click *Next* if the printer is there and then click the *Install Driver* button. If the printer is missing, click *The Printer That I Want Isn't Listed*. Three methods can be used to find a shared or networked printer:

> Click the *Browse for a Printer Radio* button and click *Next*. Double-click the computer icon that has the printer attached. Select the printer and click the *Select* button and click *Next*.

> Select the *Shared Printer by Name* radio button. Either type the name of the printer using the format `\\computer_name\printer_share_name` (the computer name that has the printer attached and the printer name set in step 6) or browse the network for the printer name, click the *Next* button, select the printer, and click *Next*.

> Select the *Add a Printer Using a TCP/IP Address or Hostname* radio button and click *Next*. Type the hostname or IP address. Click *Next*.

12. Select one of these options and locate the shared printer. Print a test page to the shared printer.

Does the test page print properly? If not, perform appropriate printer troubleshooting. [Yes | No]

Lab 13.6 Connecting to a Windows 8 Shared or Networked Printer

Objective: To properly share a printer and use a shared or networked printer using Windows 8

Parts: Two networked computers with a printer attached to one and Windows 8 installed

Procedure: Complete the following procedure and answer the accompanying questions.

Sharing a Printer on the Network

1.   Power on the computer that has the printer attached. If necessary, log on to Windows, using the appropriate user ID and password/PIN.

2.   Access the *Network and Sharing Center* Control Panel. Ensure that *Printer Sharing* is enabled through the *Change Advanced Sharing Settings* link.

3.   Using *Devices and Printers* Control Panel, locate the *Printers* section. Locate the printer to be shared. Right-click or tap and briefly hold the printer icon > *Properties*.

4. Click the *Sharing* tab. (If the Sharing tab is not available, return to the *Devices and Printers* Control Panel, right-click or tap and briefly hold the printer icon > select *Printer Properties*.)

5. Select the *Share This Printer* radio button/checkbox. (If the option is grayed out, go back to the *Network and Sharing Center* Control Panel and ensure that sharing options are enabled. Make changes as necessary. Then continue with the rest of this step.) Ensure that the *Render Print Jobs on Client Computers* checkbox is enabled.

6. In the *Share* Name textbox, type in a unique printer name, limited to eight characters, if possible. It is very important that this name be unique.

    What name was assigned to the printer? _____

7. Click the *OK* button.

Printing to a Shared or Networked Printer in Windows 8

8. On the Windows 8 computer that does not have the printer attached, select *Settings > PC and Devices > Devices*.

9. Select the *Add a Device* option.

10. The printer should be listed in the window. If the printer is missing, click *The Printer That I Want Isn't Listed*. Four methods can be used to find a shared or networked printer:
    > Method 1: Select the *My Printer Is a Little Older. Help Me Find It* link > *Next*.
    > Method 2: Select the Shared Printer by Name radio button. Either type the name of the printer using the format `\\computer_name\printer_share_name` or browse the network for the printer name, click the *Next* button, select the printer, and click *Next*. Note that this is sometimes the quickest method for a shared printer as it directly accesses the printer across the network. To locate the computer name, use the *System* Control Panel. The printer share name was issued and documented in step 6.
    > Method 3: Select the *Add a Printer Using a TCP/IP Address or Hostname* radio button and click *Next*. Type the hostname or IP address. Click *Next*.
    > Method 4: Select the *Add a Bluetooth, Wireless or Network Discoverable Printer* radio button.

11. Select one of these options and locate the shared printer. Print a test page to the shared printer.

    Does the test page print properly? If not, perform appropriate printer troubleshooting. [Yes | No]

Lab 13.7 Connecting to a Windows 10 Shared or Networked Printer

Objective: To properly share a printer and use a shared or networked printer using Windows 10

Parts: Two networked computers with a printer attached to one and Windows 10 installed

Procedure: Complete the following procedure and answer the accompanying questions.

Sharing a Printer on the Network

1. Power on the computer that has the printer attached. If necessary, log on to Windows, using the appropriate user ID and password/PIN.

2. Access the *Network and Sharing Center* Control Panel. Ensure that *Printer Sharing* is enabled through the *Change Advanced Sharing Settings* link.

3. Using *Devices and Printers* Control Panel, locate the *Printers* section. Locate the printer to be shared. Right-click or tap and briefly hold the printer icon > *Properties*.

4. Click the *Sharing* tab. (If the Sharing tab is not available, return to the *Devices and Printers* Control Panel, right-click, or tap and briefly hold the printer icon > select *Printer Properties*.)

5. Select the *Share This Printer* radio button/checkbox. (If the option is grayed out, go back to the *Network and Sharing Center* Control Panel and ensure sharing options are enabled. Make changes as necessary. Then continue with the rest of this step.) Ensure that the *Render Print Jobs on Client Computers* checkbox is enabled.

6. In the *Share* Name textbox, type in a unique printer name, limited to eight characters, if possible. It is important that this name be unique.

   What name was assigned to the printer? _____

7. Click the *OK* button.

Printing to a Shared or Networked Printer Windows 10

8. On the Windows 10 computer that does not have the printer attached, use *Settings > Devices > Printers & Scanners.*

9. Select the *Add a Printer* option.

10. The printer should be listed in the window. Click *Next* if the printer is there and then click the *Install Driver* button.

    If the printer is missing, click *The Printer That I Want Isn't Listed.* Four methods can be used to find a shared or networked printer:
    > Method 1: Select the *My Printer Is a Little Older. Help Me Find It* link > *Next.*
    > Method 2: Select the *Shared Printer by Name* radio button. Either type the name of the printer using the format \\computer_name\printer_share_name or browse the network for the printer name, click the *Next* button, select the printer, and click *Next.* Note that this is sometimes the quickest method for a shared as it directly accesses the printer across the network. To locate the computer name, use the *System* Control Panel. The printer share name was issued and documented in step 6.
    > Method 3: Select the *Add a Printer Using a TCP/IP Address or Hostname* radio button and click *Next.* Type the hostname or IP address. Click *Next.*
    > Method 4: Select the *Add a Bluetooth, Wireless or Network Discoverable Printer* radio button.

11. Select one of these options and locate the shared printer. Print a test page to the shared printer.

    Does the test page print properly? If not, perform appropriate printer troubleshooting. [Yes | No]

Lab 13.8 Installing a Wireless NIC

Objective: To install a wireless NIC into a computer and have it attach to an access point

Parts: A computer with access to the Internet and permission to download files

                A wireless NIC

                An access point that has already been configured by the instructor or lab assistant

Note: To verify that a wireless NIC works after it is installed, it must have another wireless device such as another computer with a wireless NIC installed or an access point. This lab assumes that an access point is available and allows attachment of wireless devices. The students will need any security information such as WEP key or WPA2 password before they begin. Each student will download the installation instructions and driver for the wireless NIC. Frequently, these files may be in zipped or PDF format. The computer they use may need to have Adobe's Acrobat Reader and/or a decompression software package loaded.

Procedure: Complete the following procedure and answer the accompanying questions.

1. Determine which type of wireless NIC is being installed.

   What type of wireless NIC is being installed?
   [USB | PCI | integrated | PCIe]

Who is the manufacturer of the wireless NIC?

_____

What operating system is used on the computer in which the wireless NIC will be installed?

_____

2.   Using the Internet, determine the latest version of wireless NIC driver for the operating system being used and download the driver.

What is the latest driver version?

_____

3.   Using the Internet, download the installation instructions for the wireless NIC being used.

What is the name of the installation document?

_____

4.   Open the document that details how to install the wireless NIC.

5.   Follow the directions and install the wireless NIC.

Does the wireless NIC automatically detect a wireless network?

_____

List any specifications given to you by the instructor/lab assistant.

_____

Lab 13.9 Configuring a Wireless Network

Objective: To configure a wireless AP (access point) or router and attach a wireless client

Parts: One wireless access point or router

A computer with an integrated wireless NIC or a wireless NIC installed as well as an Ethernet NIC

One straight-through cable

Procedure: Complete the following procedure and answer the accompanying questions.

1.   Obtain the documentation for the wireless AP or router from the instructor or the Internet.

2.   Reset the wireless AP or router as directed by the wireless device manufacturer.

Document the current Ethernet NIC IPv4 settings. [DHCP | Static IP address]

If a static IP address is assigned, document the IP address, subnet mask, default gateway, and DNS configuration settings.

_____

3.   Attach a straight-through cable from the computer Ethernet NIC to the wireless AP or router.

4.   Power on the computer and log on, if necessary.

5.   Configure the computer NIC with a static IP address or DHCP, as directed by the wireless device manufacturer.

6.   Document the current settings first. Then open a web browser and configure the wireless AP or router with the following parameters:

> Change the default SSID.
> Leave SSID broadcasting enabled for this lab.
> Do not configure wireless security at this time.
> Change the default password used to access the wireless AP/router.

Document the current settings:

SSID: _____

Password for wireless device access: _____

7. Save the wireless AP or router configuration.

8. Disconnect the Ethernet cable.

9. Enable the wireless NIC and configure it for the appropriate SSID.

10. Configure the wireless NIC for a static IP address or DHCP as directed by the wireless AP or router manufacturer.

11. Open a web browser and access the wireless AP or router. If access cannot be obtained, troubleshoot as necessary, or reset the wireless AP or router to default configurations and restart the lab.

    What frequency (channel) is used by the wireless AP or router and the wireless NIC for connectivity?

    _____

12. Show the instructor the connectivity.

Instructor initials: _____

13. Reset the wireless AP or router to the default configuration settings.

14. Reset the computer(s) to the original configuration settings.

Lab 13.10 Using an FTP Server and Client

Objective: To transfer files from one network device to another, using an FTP server and client software

Parts: An application or freeware application that provides the FTP server service

               An application or freeware application that provides the FTP client service

Procedure: Complete the following procedure and answer the accompanying questions.

FTP Server

1. Download, install, and open an FTP server freeware application such as FileZilla. This lab has directions specifically for Home FTP Server, but the steps for other applications are similar.

2. Start the FTP server. You may need to start the FTP server or the FTP server service. In the Home FTP Server application, click the *FTP Server* tab > *Start Server*.

3. Some FTP server applications allow anonymous users or anyone who connects to the server to download files. Also, some applications allow you to specify what the anonymous user can do such as download, upload, and delete files and directories. To enable anonymous logins within Home FTP Server, click the *FTP Server* tab > enable *Allow Anonymous Users (Allow All Active)* checkbox. This same tab can be used to enable specific permissions for creation and deletion of files and directories.

   Write down where the default anonymous directory is located.

   _____

4. FTP server applications frequently allow web connectivity. To enable the web interface within Home FTP Server, select the *Web Interface* tab > enable the *Web Interface Enabled* checkbox.

   What is the default port number used for the FTP server?

   _____

   What is the IP address of the FTP server?

   _____

5. Copy some files into the default anonymous directory on the FTP server.

FTP Client

6. Download, install, and open an FTP client freeware application. This lab has directions specifically for the SmartFTP client, but the steps for other applications are similar.

7. Usually, a client requires the following configuration:
   > Address of the FTP server
   > User login ID and password *or* anonymous login selected

   In the SmartFTP client, type in the FTP server IP address in the *Address* textbox > click the *Anonymous* button (option) > click the green arrow to connect. The FTP client displays the files that were copied into the anonymous directory.

Instructor initials: _____

Tightening Security

8. Create a user on the FTP server. In Home FTP Server, click the *New Member* button > *General* tab > type a name in the *User Name* textbox > type **class999** in the *Password* textbox.

   Make a note of the home directory and permissions for this user.

   _____

9. Click *Apply*. Test the user account from the FTP client application by creating a new entry with the appropriate user ID and password. In SmartFTP, click the *File* menu option > select *Disconnect* to disconnect the previous login session. Click the *File* menu option > *New Remote Browser* > in the *Host* textbox, type the FTP server IP address > in the *User Name* textbox, type the *exact* username that was typed in the FTP server application > in the *Password* textbox, type **class999** > in the *Name* textbox, type **FTP with login** > *OK*. The client connects to the FTP server.

Instructor initials: _____

10. Within the client application, close the FTP session. For the SmartFTP client, use the *Close* button in the upper-right corner of the *FTP with Login* tab. Close all tabs and sessions.

11. Delete FTP client entries. From within SmartFTP client, click the *Favorites* menu option > *Edit Favorites Quick Connect* option in the left pane > click once on the FTP server IP address in the right pane > *Edit* menu option > *Delete* > *Yes*. Delete the FTP with login option using the same technique.

Instructor initials: _____

14 Introduction to Operating Systems Labs

Lab 14.1 Windows 7 Basic Usage

Objective: To work effectively with the Windows 7 desktop, including working with the Start button; managing the display through the Control Panel; changing Start button properties; obtaining help; performing file, folder, and computer searches; and accessing programs

Parts: Computer with Windows 7 and the Windows Notepad application installed

Procedure: Complete the following procedure and answer the accompanying questions.

1. Power on the computer and log on to Windows if necessary.

Working with the Start Menu

2. Click the *Start* button. The top right of the Start menu on some systems shows who is currently logged on to the computer. Users are created so that the system can be individualized when multiple people use the same computer. If the computers are re-imaged every time the computer boots, no programs are pinned to the left Start menu.

   What do you think is the difference between the applications listed on the left and those listed on the right side of the Start button menu?

   _____

3. You can make changes to the Start button menu by right-clicking the *Start* button > *Properties* > *Start Menu* tab > *Customize* button. The resulting window has different alphabetized sections that can be enabled by clicking within checkboxes to enable or disable options. Some sections have several radio button options, in which case you can select only of the options.

   What is the current setting for the Control Panel option?
   [Display as a Link | Display as a Menu | Don't Display This Item]

   What is the current setting for Games?
   [Display as a Link | Display as a Menu | Don't Display This Item]

   How many recent programs are currently set to display?

   _____

4.   Click *Cancel*. Select the *Taskbar* tab.

List three options that can be customized through this tab.

_____

5.   Select the *How Do I Customize the Taskbar* link. Using the information available, answer the following questions.

How can you tell if the taskbar is locked or unlocked without moving it?

_____

_____

6.   Close the Windows Help and Support and Taskbar and Start Menu Properties windows.

7.   Re-access the *Start* menu.

What are the top four options in the right column of the *Start* menu?

_____

_____

8.   The *Documents* option represents a folder that is the default storage location for saved files. *Pictures*, *Music*, *Computer*, and *Control Panel* also represent folders. A folder can contain another folder, and this folder is commonly called a subfolder. A file is a document created by an application. Files are stored and organized in folders. Click the *Computer* option. The *Computer* option contains access to drives installed or connected to the computer. Flash drives, hard drives, optical drives, and so on are given drive letters such as E: or C:.

What drive letters are available through the *Computer* option?

_____

Working with Control Panel

9.   Close the *Computer* window and re-access the Start button menu. Select the *Control Panel* Start button option. The Windows Control Panel icons or links are used to configure the computer. There are two views for the Control Panel: *Classic* and *Category*. The default view is Category. Select *Category* in the *View By* drop-down menu.

List two Control Panel categories shown on the screen.

_____

_____

10.   Select *Large Icons* or *Small Icons* from the *View By* drop-down menu. The classic view/large or small icons is the older method for accessing any particular Control Panel. Return to the *Category* Control Panel view.

Use Lab Table 14.1 as a reference. Note that some systems have special Control Panel utilities due to the hardware installed or type of computer, such as a laptop or tablet. Notice that some of the options are listed in multiple categories.

Use Lab Table 14.2 (several pages away) to explore Windows Control Panels and document what Control Panel category and subcategory you would use to perform particular tasks.

LAB TABLE 14.1   Common Windows 7 Control Panel categories*

Control Panel category	Subcategory	Function
System and Security	Backup and Restore	Save or restore files and folders to or from a different location.
	System	View basic computer properties, such as RAM, processor type, and computer name.
	Windows Update	Customize how updates are received and installed.
	Power Options	Configure power saving modes.
	Administrative Tools	Free up hard disk space, manage hard drive partitions, schedule tasks, and view event logs.
	Action Center	View personal information, view a history of computer problems, view performance information, configure backup, troubleshoot problems, and restore the computer to a previous point.
	Windows Firewall	Enable and customize firewall security features.
	Windows Update	Customize how updates are received and installed.
	Windows Defender*	Scan the computer for unwanted software.
	BitLocker Drive Encryption	Change or use encryption options.
Network and Internet	Network and Sharing Center	Check the status and modify network-related settings as well as share files, folders, and devices on the network.
	Internet Options	Customize Internet Explorer.
	People Near Me*	Configure the computer for software such as Windows Meeting Place.
	Sync Center*	Synchronize mobile devices or network shares.
	HomeGroup	View and change sharing and password options.
Hardware and Sound	Devices and Printers	Add/remove/configure/remove a device, scanner, camera, printer, and mouse as well as access Device Manager.
	AutoPlay	Change how media are automatically handled when a disc, flash drive, or type of file is added or inserted.
	Sound	Manage audio devices and change sound schemes.
	Power Options	Configure power saving modes.
	Keyboard*	Customize keyboard settings.
	Phone and Modem Options*	Install a modem and control modem and phone dialing properties.

LAB 14

Control Panel category	Subcategory	Function
	Game Controllers*	Add/remove/configure/remove devices, scanners, cameras, printers, and mice as well as access Device Manager.
	Pen and Input Devices	Configure pen options for a tablet PC.
	Color Management*	View/change advanced color settings on disc plays, scanners, and printers.
	Tablet PC Settings	Configure tablet and screen settings on a tablet PC.
	Display	Adjust resolution, configure an external display, or make text larger/smaller.
	Bluetooth Devices	Install, configure, and adjust Bluetooth wireless devices.
Programs	Programs and Features	Uninstall and change programs as well as enable/disable Windows features such as games, Telnet server, Telnet client, TFTP client, and print services.
	Windows Defender*	Scan the computer for unwanted software.
	Default Programs	Remove a startup program, associate a file extension with a particular application, or select the program used with a particular type of file.
	Desktop Gadgets	Add/remove/restore desktop interactive objects.
Mobile PC	Windows Mobility Center	Adjust laptop screen brightness, audio volume, wireless enabling and strength status, presentation settings, and external display control.
	Power Options	Used on laptops to configure power saving modes.
	Personalization	Used on laptops to assign visuals and sounds such as the Windows theme used.
	Tablet PC Settings	Used on laptops and has the same function as in the Programs category.
	Pen and Input Devices/Touch	Used on mobile devices to calibrate the screen, set tablet buttons, and control screen rotation.
	Sync Center	Used to configure synchronization options, view sync settings, conflicts, and results, and manage offline files.
User Accounts and Family Safety	User Accounts	Add, remove, or modify accounts on the computer.
	Parental Controls	Used to create a user that has security control settings available for children.
	Windows CardSpace	Manage relationships and information such as a user ID and password for websites and online services. The personal card information is kept encrypted on the local hard drive.

Control Panel category	Subcategory	Function
	Credential Manager	Store usernames/passwords in a vault for easy logon to sites and/or computers.
Appearance and Personalization	Personalization	Used to assign visuals and sounds such as the Windows theme.
	Taskbar and Start menu	Customize the Start menu and taskbar by adding or removing icons.
	Fonts	Customize available fonts.
	Folder Options	Configure how folders are viewed and acted upon, including what files are seen.
Clock, Language, and Region	Date and Time	Configure time, date, time zone, and clocks for different time zones.
	Region and Language Options	Configure the format for date, time, currency, and so on that are region-specific options. Also used to customize keyboard settings.
Additional Options		Holds special Control Panel utilities that are system specific, such as an NVIDIA video display or Java Control Panel.

* Note that particular options can be found by typing in the subcategory in the *Search Control Panel* textbox.

Fill in Lab Table 14.2 with the correct Control Panel category and subcategory for each task.

LAB TABLE 14.2   Determine the correct Windows 7 Control Panel categories and subcategories

Control Panel category	Control Panel subcategory	Task
		Configure mouse buttons for a left-handed person.
		Mute the computer speaker sound.
		Configure the date to be in the format April 15, 202X.
		Define how quickly a character repeats when a specific key is held down.
		Define what page (home page) appears every time Internet Explorer starts.
		Configure an IP address on a wired or wireless network adapter.
		Set a printer as the default printer.
		Verify if Windows recognizes a particular piece of hardware.

Working with the Display

11. Ensure that you are in the *Category* view. Select the *Hardware and Sound* Control Panel category. Select *Display*. Note that you may be required to search throughout this area to answer the questions.

    What is the current resolution?

    _____

    How many bits are used for color?

    _____

12. Continue working with the *Display* link. Locate and select the *Advanced Settings* button or link. *Note:* You may have to click *Change Display* or use another Control Panel, depending on the manufacturer.

    What adapter is used?

    _____

    How much video memory does the adapter have?

    _____

    How much total video memory is available?

    _____

13. Click the *Monitor* tab.

    What refresh rate is used?

    _____

14. Click *Cancel* on this window and on the next window. Select the *Personalization* link in the bottom left; select the *Screen Saver* link in the bottom right. Use the *Screen Saver* down arrow to see a list of preinstalled screen savers and click one of the options. Click the *Preview* button. The screen saver appears. Move the mouse to regain control.

Dealing with Power Settings

15. Click the *Change Power Settings* link. The Power Options Properties window appears. Lab Table 14.3 shows the various power options available in Windows 7.

    What power option would be applied to a laptop being used by a teacher during a four-hour class?

    _____

LAB TABLE 14.3   Windows 7 default power schemes*

Power scheme	Purpose
Balanced	Default mode; processor adapts to activity being performed; performance provided when the computer is in use; power savings when the computer is inactive. Display powers down after 15 minutes; hard drive powers down after 20 minutes and goes to sleep after 20 minutes.
Power Saver	Provides maximum battery life for laptops. Display and hard drive power down after 20 minutes, and the system goes to sleep after 1 hour.
High Performance	Maximum system performance and responsiveness. Display and hard drive power down after 20 minutes, but the system never sleeps.
Customized	A scheme created by the user that has different settings than the three default schemes.

* Note that a computer manufacturer may provide additional power schemes.

16. Close all Control Panel windows.

Obtaining Help

17.   Click *Help and Support* from the Start button menu. The Help and Support window contains links to online and locally stored help documents.

18.   The standard three links are How to Get Started with Your Computer, Learn About Windows Basics, and Browse Help Topics.

      The Search Help textbox is used by typing a word or series of words on a specific topic. Note that the Help and Support window may vary depending on the computer manufacturer.

      What is the first link listed in the help window?

      _____

19.   Type **monitor quality** in the *Search* textbox and press ⏎Enter.

      List three settings used to improve display quality.

      _____

      _____

      _____

20.   To see a list of troubleshooting topics, type **troubleshooting** in the *Search Help* textbox. A list of troubleshooting topics immediately appears. Select the *Offline Help* menu arrow in the bottom-right corner.

      What menu options appear?

      _____

21.   Select *Settings* from the *Options* menu. Notice that you can customize the type of help you receive by enabling or disabling the online help checkbox.

22.   Close any open window.

Searching for Files, Folders, and Computers

23.   Click the *Start* Button and find the *Search Programs and Files* textbox, located directly above the Start button. This option is used to hunt for files, other computers on the network, people listed in your address book, and information located on the Internet.

24.   In the *Search Programs and Files* textbox, type **system configuration** but do not press ⏎Enter. Notice that the program appears in the panel. Always keep in mind that applications are simply a type of file that brings up the specific software. Also, any files that contain the words "System Configuration" appear in the list of files when you do this search. Select the System Configuration program from the list.

      List five tabs found in the System Configuration window.

      _____

      Close the window.

25.   Again bring up the search list for **system configuration** but don't press ⏎Enter.

TECH TIP

Changing UAC (User Access Control) settings

Windows 7 has a UAC dialog box that frequently appears, asking for permission to do something. To change UAC settings, use the *User Accounts* Control Panel > select an account > *Change User Account Control Settings*. The UAC settings can also be disabled through the *System Configuration* utility (`msconfig` command) > *Tools* tab > *Change UAC Settings* option > *Launch* button > select the appropriate level.

26. Click the *See More Result*s link and scroll to the bottom of the list; locate and select the *Internet* icon. List one URL that the system found.

_____

27. Locate the name of the computer by using a Control Panel section previously explored. Exchange computer names with a classmate, if possible. If not, locate another computer on the same network and document that computer name, found through a Windows Control Panel.

    Your computer name: _____

    Other computer name: _____

28. Return to the computer *Search Programs and Files* textbox, type in the other computer name, and press ⏎Enter. In the resulting window in the *Folders* panel on the left, select the *Network* option. (*Note:* You may have to change the default settings of the computer: *Start* > *Control Panel* > *Network and Internet* > *Network and Sharing Center* > *Change Advanced Sharing Settings* > expand *Home or Work* as necessary to enable to following: *Turn On Network Discovery*.) Use Windows Explorer to locate a remote network device.

    Does the remote computer name appear? [Yes | No]

Instructor initials: _____

29. Close the window.

Starting Applications

30. Software applications are accessed through the Start button. Click the Start button. The left column contains the most recently used applications. If a program is not listed there and the application is installed, you can access it through the All Programs option. Point to *All Programs*; locate and click the Accessories option. Locate and click *Notepad*. The Notepad application opens.

31. Type **Whatever you are, be a good one.-Abraham Lincoln**. Click the *File* menu option > *Save* > then type quote in the File Name textbox. Notice the path for where the document is saved, located at the top of the window. The folder and subfolders are separated by arrows. The path is shown at the top of the *Save as* window. An example of the path is Libraries>Documents.

    Write the path for where the document will be saved.

_____

_____

32. Click the *Save* button. Click the *Close* button (the button with the X) in the top-right corner. Re-access the *Start* button menu.

    Does the Notepad application now appear in the left column of the Start menu?

    [Yes | No]

33. In the *Search Programs and Files* textbox, type **notepad** but do not press the ⏎Enter key. The Notepad application is listed under the Programs section. In the *Search Programs and Files* textbox, delete the word *notepad* and type **quote**, but do not press ⏎Enter. Your file (and any others that have the word quote in the filename or document) will appear under the Files section of the list. Notice the icon beside the filename. Click the *Quote* document. The document opens. Close the document and the application.

Recycle Bin

34. Right-click the *Start* button and select the *Open Windows Explorer* option. Using the information you wrote down for step 31, click the first folder you wrote down. It should be located under the Desktop or Documents section in the left panel. Double-click the second (and any subsequent) folder you wrote down. Locate the file called `quote`. Do not open the file; just browse until the filename appears in the major window.

35. Right-click the `quote` filename. Notice that there is a Delete option. Do not click this option. Click away from the filename on an empty part of the window and then click once on the `quote` filename to select it. The name is highlighted when it is selected. Press the ⎙Del key. A dialog message does not appear if you saved the file to a flash drive. It does appear for files saved to the hard drive.

The Recycle Bin holds deleted files and folders. When a file or folder is deleted, it is not immediately discarded; instead, it goes into the Recycle Bin folder. When a file or folder is in the Recycle Bin, it can be removed. This is similar to a piece of trash being retrieved from an office trash can. A technician must remember that the files and folders in the Recycle Bin take up hard drive space and that users frequently forget to empty these deleted files and folders.

> **TECH TIP**
>
> **Files deleted from the Recycle Bin cannot be retrieved**
>
> When the Recycle Bin has been emptied, the deleted files cannot be recovered without the use of special software.

36. From the window where you located the now-deleted `quote` document, locate the *Recycle Bin* icon. In Windows 7, the Recycle Bin icon is commonly located on the desktop. Select *Desktop* from the Favorites section. Double-click the Recycle Bin icon.

Does the `quote` text document appear in the Recycle Bin window? [Yes | No]

If not, redo the steps in this section to create and delete the file.

Instructor initials: _____

37. Select the *Empty the Recycle Bin* option from the top menu. A confirmation window appears, asking if you are sure you want to permanently delete the file. Click *Yes*. The name disappears from the Recycle Bin window (as do the names of any other files that were located in the Recycle Bin). Close the window.

Pinning an Application to the Start Menu

38. Click *Start* > *All Programs* > *Accessories* and locate the *Notepad* application. Right-click the *Notepad* application and select the *Pin to Start Menu* option.

39. Click the *Start* button. Notice that the Notepad application appears at the top of the Start menu. After the application is pinned, it always appears in that top list.

Instructor initials: _____

40. Right-click the *Notepad* Start button option and select *Unpin from Start Menu*. The application is removed immediately but still resides in All Programs.

Other Windows 7 Differences

41. One of the things that is different in Windows 7 from previous Windows versions is the gadgets. Gadgets are mini applications that stay on the desktop. By default, they load to the right, but you can customize where they go. Right-click the desktop and select *Gadgets*.

List three gadgets you would find useful to have on the desktop.

Windows 7 Shutdown Options

42. When you're finished working on the computer for the day, the computer needs to be turned off or shut down properly. All applications and windows should be closed, and then special steps need to be taken to shut down the machine. Click *Start* and locate the *Search Programs and Files* textbox you have been using. Immediately to the right of that textbox is a Shutdown button.

    The shutdown options that commonly appear are listed in Lab Table 14.4, along with the purpose of each one.

LAB TABLE 14.4   Windows 7 shutdown options

Option	Purpose
Switch user	Allows another user to switch to his or her own environment (desktop, files, and so on).
Log Off	Keeps the computer powered on but logs off the current user.
Lock	Locks the computer, such as when someone goes to lunch. All settings and current applications are left untouched.
Restart	Used when new software or hardware has been installed or when the computer locks.
Sleep	Reduces power consumption but keeps the applications and settings that are currently on the screen.
Shut down	Powers off the computer.

43. Select the *Shutdown* option unless you have another lab to do.

Lab 14.2 Modifying the Windows 7 Start Button

Objective: To modify the Start button menu

Parts: Computer with Windows 7 installed

Procedure: Complete the following procedure and answer the accompanying questions.

Start Menu Icon Size

1. After Windows boots, right-click the *Start* button > *Properties* > *Start Menu* tab > *Customize* button. The radio buttons and checkboxes configure the look of the Start menu. The icon size is controlled by a checkbox at the end of the list.

    What Start menu icon size radio button is currently selected? [Normal | Large]

2. Set the setting to the opposite (that is, if the box is already checked, uncheck it, and if the box is unchecked, then check it). Click *OK* > *Apply* > *OK*.

3. Click the *Start* button to test the icon size change.

4. Return the icon size to the original setting.

Customizing the Number of Start Menu Programs Shown

5. Right-click the *Start* button > *Properties* > *Start Menu* tab > *Customize* button. Locate the *Number of Recent Programs to Display* selectable number option at the bottom of the window. The number of programs shown on the left side (bottom portion) of the *Start* button menu can be modified using the up and down arrows that control the number.

   How many programs are currently set to appear on the *Start* button?

   _____

6. Click the *Cancel* button and, when returned to the previous menu, click *Cancel* again. Click the *Start* button and verify that the number of programs shown is correct. Windows automatically adds the most often used programs to the list, but the maximum is set through the window from which you just returned.

7. Right-click the *Start* button > *Properties* > *Start Menu* tab > *Customize* button.

   What is the maximum number of recent programs that you can have on the *Start* button?

   _____

8. Increase the number of programs shown on the *Start* button menu. When finished, click *OK* > *Apply* > *OK*.

9. Click the *Start* button. The number of programs shown on the bottom left of the *Start* menu should be the number specified. If it is not, access an application not listed on the menu, close the application, and click the *Start* button again.

10. Return the number of Start button menu programs to the original setting.

Customizing the Start Menu Programs

11. By default, the Start menu has links to Documents, Pictures, Music, Help and Support, and so on in the right column. Click the *Start* button.

    What are three items found in the Start button menu right column?

    _____

    _____

12. Right-click the *Start* button > *Properties* > *Start Menu* tab > *Customize* button. Locate the *Computer* section. Some of the options located in this window have three possible selections, similar to the Computer section: (1) Display as a Link, (2) Display as a Menu, and (3) Don't Display This Item.

    Display as a Link means that when the menu option is selected, it opens in a new window. With *Display as a Menu*, the option has an arrow to the side allowing you to access all options that windows would normally contain.

    What is the current setting for Control Panel?

    _____

13. Click the *Cancel* button and, when returned to the previous menu, click *Cancel* again. Click the *Start* button and observe the current *Control Panel* option on the menu.

    Does the Control Panel option appear as configured? [Yes | No]

14. Right-click the *Start* button > *Properties* > *Customize* button. Locate the *Control Panel* section. Change the *Control Panel* menu option to one of the other menu settings. Click *OK* > *Apply* > *OK*.

15. Click the *Start* button and select the *Control Panel* menu option.

    How is the Control Panel option different now?

    _____

    _____

16. Return the Control Panel item to its original setting.

Adding a Program to the Start Menu

17. Click the *Start* button > type **charmap** in the *Search Programs and Files* textbox. charmap is the file used to execute the Character Map program. It is commonly found in the C:\Windows\System32 folder.

    Note: If the charmap file is not installed, you can use any program file for this part of the exercise.

18. Locate charmap in the resulting *Programs* list. Right-click the charmap file and select the *Pin to Start Menu* option. Click the *Start* button.

    Where on the Start button menu is the Character Map application added?

    _____

    Instructor initials: _____

19. To remove a customized application, click the *Start* button, right-click the unwanted item (charmap in this case), and select *Unpin from Start Menu*.

Lab 14.3 Windows 8/8.1 Basic Usage: Introduction to the Start Screen

Objective: To work effectively with the Windows 8/8.1 Start screen, including working with charms, apps, and tiles

Parts: Computer with Windows 8/8.1 and administrator privileges

Procedure: Complete the following procedure and answer the accompanying questions.

1. Power on the computer and log on to Windows 8/8.1. Note that you may have to swipe up or press a key to access the logon screen.

Working with the Start Screen

2. Access the *Start* screen. This is the screen with all the tiles. If it is not shown, press the ▦ key. The top right of the Start screen shows who is currently logged on to the computer. Users are created so that the system can be individualized when multiple people use the same computer.

3. The four corners of the Windows 8/8.1 computer are hot corners. You can move the pointer to the tip of the corner of the screen (maybe even a little off the screen) to quickly access other tools and screens.

   For example, move the pointer to the top-left corner. A small icon of a recently used app appears (if one has been used). Move the pointer to the bottom-left corner. The Start button icon appears. Selecting the *Start* button toggles between the Start screen and the traditional desktop. Now move the pointer to the top right. Moving the pointer to the top right and bottom right does the same thing: brings up the charms. Note that the pointer needs to hover to the far right.

   What are the five charms?

   _____

4. Re-access the *Search* charm. Click the down arrow beside *Everywhere*.

   What are the choices for where you might select to search?

   _____

   _____

5. Access *Charms* and select the *Start* charm. The *Start* charm brings up the Start screen, but if you are already on the Start screen, it returns you to the last app you were using.

   What happened when you clicked the Start charm?

   _____

   _____

6. Re-access *Charms* and select *Devices*. The *Play* option enables you to stream music, a PowerPoint slide show, or a video. The *Print* option enables you to print if the app being used supports it. The last option is *Project*, which enables you to send whatever is on the display to a projector, TV, or a second display.

7. Re-access *Charms* and select *Settings*. The Settings option contains what most users want to do (but not always what most technicians want to configure or are accustomed to). Note that the Settings option can also be launched from the *System Settings* tile.

   List three Settings options at the bottom of the panel that can be configured from this charm.

   _____

   _____

Manipulating the Start Screen

8. Now explore how to modify tiles. Move your pointer to one of the hot corners to return to the Start screen. See if you can figure out which one will get you there. Tiles that appear in the Start screen can be modified by selecting and dragging them to another location.

   What tile is currently located in the far-left position?

   _____

9. If multiple ties are shown, select and drag the tile located in the far-left position to the last position in the first block of tiles. Then return the tile to the current position.

10. To add an app to the Start screen, access the *Search* charm. Type **command** in the *Search* textbox. The Command Prompt option appears in the resulting list. Right-click or tap and briefly hold on the *Command Prompt* option in the search list.

    List the options available from the context menu.

    _____

11. Note that sometimes you need the *Run as Administrator* option in order to use a tool. Select the *Pin to Start* option.

12. Move the pointer over and click or tap within the Start screen. If necessary, use the scrollbar to go to the far right, where you see the Command Prompt tile.

    Does the Command Prompt tile appear on the Start screen? If not, redo steps 10, 11, and 12. [Yes | No]

13. Tap or select the *Command Prompt* tile. The Command Prompt window opens. Close the command prompt window by using the *Close* button (the X in the top-right corner).

14. Re-access the *Start* screen using whatever method you prefer. Tap and briefly hold or right-click the *Command Prompt* tile to access the context menu.

    List any menu options that were not available from the context menu previously accessed before you pinned the app to the Start screen.

    _____

    _____

15. Hover the pointer over the *Resize* option.

    What choices do you have?

    _____

16. Select a different tile size. Re-access the *Command Prompt* tile context menu. Select *Open File Location*. Windows *File Explorer* opens, showing the folder that contains this file (and other files within the same folder). Notice that the Command Prompt option is a shortcut. You can tell because the icon on the left has a bent arrow on it. Also, in the *Type* column, you can see the word *Shortcut*.

17. To see where the original file is located, right-click or tap and hold the *Command Prompt* icon > select *Properties*. Ensure that the *Shortcut* tab is selected. The *Target* textbox shows where the file is actually located. `%windir%` is used to describe the folder where Windows was installed. Commonly, it is `C:\Windows`, but because this might be on another drive letter or installed to a different folder, Microsoft simply describes it as `%windir%`. The full path for the command prompt is commonly `C:\Windows\Systems32\cmd.exe`.

18. Click *Cancel* to return to File Explorer. Close *File Explorer*. Return to the *Start* screen (the one with the tiles).

19. Re-access the *Command Prompt* context menu. Select *Unpin from Start*.

20. To see all the tiles at once, select the minus sign located at the far right of the scrollbar, at the bottom of the display. Note that you may have to click or tap at the bottom of the screen to see the scrollbar and to select the minus sign to the far right. All the tiles on the Start screen are shown. Select any tile, and the normal tile sizes are shown, with that particular tile viewable in the window.

21. Select the minus sign icon again. This time click any empty space on the screen; the last view you were on is shown in normal size.

Power Options

22. The *Power Options* icon is on the top right of the Start screen. It is a circle with a vertical line that extends through the top part of the circle. You often see the symbol on power buttons. Click this icon once.

What options are available?

_____

_____

What other icon is available to the right of the power options icon? If you do not know what this is, hover the pointer over it to receive context-sensitive help.

_____

The shutdown options that commonly appear are listed in Lab Table 14.5, along with the purpose of each one.

LAB TABLE 14.5   Windows 8/8.1 power button shutdown options

Option	Purpose
Lock	Locks the computer, such as when someone goes to lunch. All settings and current applications are left untouched.
Restart	Used when new software or hardware has been installed or when the computer locks.
Sleep	Reduces power consumption but keeps the applications and settings that are currently on the screen.
Hibernate	Reduces power consumption even more so than the sleep mode. Takes longer to resume operations than sleep mode but not as long as with a cold boot.
Shut down	Powers off the computer.

Apps

23. Select the symbol that is a circle with a down arrow inside it (⊕) located at the bottom of the Start screen. Note that you may have to move the pointer for it to appear. All of the installed apps are shown.

24. Apps can be shown in different orders. The option at the top tells you how the apps are sorted.

     What is the current sort option? [Apps by Name | Apps by Date Installed | Apps by Most Used | Apps by Category]

     _____

25. Use the down arrow by Apps to select *Apps by Name*. The app icons are then shown in alphabetical order. Scroll to the right, and you may see some apps provided by the device manufacturer. Scroll further to the right, and you may see groupings for the Microsoft Office suite or a particular security software manufacturer. Continue scrolling to the right until you reach the grouping called Windows Accessories.

     What three accessories do you think technicians might use the most?

     _____

     _____

26. The Windows Ease of Access apps are listed next. These are tools to configure the device for those with visual, auditory, or mobility issues. At the far right are the Windows System apps, including the Command Prompt. Return to the *Windows Accessories* section. Access the context menu for *Notepad* by right-clicking it or tap and briefly hold. Notice that you can pin an app from the App menu to the Start menu or taskbar. Move the pointer away from the context menu without selecting any option and click or tap in an empty space.

27. Open both the *Notepad* app and the *Snipping Tool* app.

28. Access and launch any program from the *Start Screen* tiles.

29. Return to the *Start* screen. Use the left hot-corner button to locate, access, and close the running apps. Locate the app or utility that you launched from a *Start* screen tile. Right-click that thumbnail > select *Close*.

30. Locate the thumbnail for *Desktop*. Windows Accessories run in desktop mode. Click the thumbnail, and you can see Notepad and the Snipping Tool app. Close both apps.

Lab 14.4 Windows 8/8.1 Basic Usage: Introduction to PC Settings

Objective: To be familiar with the Windows 8/8.1 PC Settings

Parts: Computer with Windows 8/8.1 installed

                Optional flash drive

Procedure: Complete the following procedure and answer the accompanying questions.

1. Power on the computer and log on to Windows 8/8.1. Note that you may have to swipe up or press a key to access the logon screen.

2. Use *Charms* to access the *Settings* charm. Select the *Change PC Settings* link.

Working with the PC and Devices Setting

3. Select the *PC and Devices* category from the *PC Settings* list.

    Looking over the list, which option are you curious about?

    _____

4.   Ensure that the *Lock Screen* option is selected in the left menu. This particular setting enables you to control how the display reacts and possibly the camera as well (if one is installed). The lock screen function is a screen that appears when you have not interacted with the device after a specified amount of time. The lock screen commonly shows information such as time, date, battery status, and network status. Notice that to enable an option, you select one side of a particular option.

What is the current option to play a slide show on the lock screen? [On | Off] Note that if you have trouble telling, the black side of the option points toward one side or the other. The selection chosen is shown as a particular word on the left (either On or Off). Change the option by clicking or tapping the side away from the black bar.

5.   Choose the opposite selection for *Play a Slide Show on the Lock Screen* by clicking or tapping the opposite side of the gray box so that the black bar goes to the opposite side. If the answer to Question 4 was *On*, you should turn the option *Off*. If the answer to Question 4 was *Off*, you should turn the option *On*.

What visual clue did you have that the option changed?

_____

_____

6.   Return the setting to the original *On* or *Off* position.

7.   Select the *Display* setting from the left panel. This setting is commonly used to reset the screen resolution if the user has set it to something less than optimal. You can also use it to connect to a wireless display such as a TV.

What is the current resolution?

_____

8.   Select the *Devices* setting from the left panel. This setting is used to quickly see what devices are attached to the computer. Scroll to the bottom of the option. The last option allows you to configure the saving of videos, music, and photos to a removable drive instead of the local hard drive that may be an SSD.

9.   If possible, attach a flash drive. Notice how the flash drive appears under *Other Devices*.

10. Locate the *Default Save Locations* section > select the *Set Up* button. Notice the types of files you can unselect (because all of them are selected by default). Note that if you have more than one external storage device attached, the system selects the lowest drive letter by default. This would commonly be an external medium that stays attached to the computer.

What drive letter is assigned to your flash drive where media are now automatically stored?

_____

11. Click *OK*. Notice that the *Default Save Locations* button changes to read *Stop Saving Here*. Select the *Stop Saving Here* button. A message appears that music, pictures, and videos will now be saved to this PC. Click *OK*.

12. Hover the pointer over the flash drive listed in the *Other Devices* section and select the drive. Note that a flash drive might be seen as a mass storage device. Notice that you can eject the device from here by selecting the *Remove Device* link. Select *Remove Device*. When asked if you are sure you want to remove the device, select *Yes*. You might have to do this a second time to get this message to appear.

13. Select the *Mouse and Touchpad* option from the left panel.

Which mouse button is the primary one? [Left | Right]

14. Select the *Typing* option from the left panel. The two features here are used to spell check, highlight, and automatically fix any spelling errors you make. This might be annoying to you, especially if you have an unusual name or if you send things to someone with an unusual name.

15. Select the *Corners and Edges* option from the left panel. This is where you can enable or disable the hot-corner options.

16. Select the *Power and Sleep* option from the left panel. The options that appear here depend on the type of device that has Windows 8/8.1 loaded.

After how much time will the screen dim if there is no activity?

_____

17. Select the *AutoPlay* option from the left panel. Note that if a big orange arrow is in the way, click on the arrow tip to remove the message and arrow. AutoPlay is sometimes disabled in the corporate environment so that people who have executable files on their removable media can't automatically launch those files. When AutoPlay is disabled (turned off), the user is prompted about what to do when digital media are inserted into the computer.

18. Select the *Disk Space* option from the left panel.

How much free space is on this device?

_____

How much free space is taken up by files in the Recycle Bin?

_____

19. Finally, select the *PC Info* option from the left panel. This information is important to a technician because the type of computer, name of the computer, amount of RAM, processor, and system type can be used to research problems the machine might be having.

20. Click the left arrow to return to the PC settings screen.

Accounts

21. Rather than going through each option, you can answer questions in each section to make sure you are looking at important options. Explore the Accounts options to answer the questions.

What three sign-in options can you use with Windows 8/8.1?

_____

How many digits does a PIN need to be in Windows 8/8.1?

_____

How would you add an additional account to this machine? Give exact steps.

_____

_____

22. Click the left arrow at the top of the menu panel to return to the PC settings screen.

OneDrive

23. Select *OneDrive* from the PC settings screen. Explore the different *OneDrive* options to answer the questions.

What is OneDrive?

_____

_____

What is a metered connection?

_____

What would be the drawback to allowing upload and download files over metered connections?

_____

Would you personally configure the OneDrive uploads and downloads to be on even when the device might be roaming? Explain your choice.

_____

24. Click the left arrow at the top of the menu panel to return to the PC settings screen.

Search and Apps

25. Select *Search and Apps* from the PC settings screen. Explore the different options to answer the questions.

    List one example of why someone would want to clear the search history.

    _____

    _____

    _____

    What is the default search engine?

    _____

    Can the default search engine be changed? If so, describe how.

    _____

    What app opens `.arw` files by default?

    _____

    How much memory does the *Calculator* app take?

    _____

    What are quiet hours, and how does that relate to a PC's settings?

    _____

26. Click the left arrow at the top of the menu panel to return to the PC settings screen.

Privacy

27. Select *Privacy* from the PC settings screen. Explore the different options to answer the questions.

    Does Windows 8/8.1 allow you to disable and enable the capability to let apps access the name, picture, and account information found on the computer?

    _____

    What apps, if any, can use the computer's location?

    _____

    Does the device have a webcam? If so, are any devices allowed to use it? Where did you find this information?

    _____

    _____

    What apps are allowed to use the computer's microphone?

    _____

28. Click the left arrow at the top of the menu panel to return to the PC settings screen.

Network

29. Select *Network* on the PC settings screen. Explore the different options to answer the questions.

    What types of networks are supported?

    _____

    If you worked in a corporate environment in which a proxy server was used and you were required to configure an executive's laptop, what configuration settings would you need to obtain from the network support staff to manually configure the settings?

    _____

Which option would you use to join a corporate domain?

[HomeGroup I Domain I Workplace I Connections]

Which option would you use to attach the device to the wireless network?

[Connections I Airplane mode I Proxy I Homegroup I Workplace]

30. Click the left arrow at the top of the menu panel to return to the PC settings screen.

Time and Language

31. Select *Time and Language* from the PC settings screen. Explore the different options to answer the questions.

    Can you manually configure the time, or is it automatic with Windows 8/8.1?
    [Manual I Automatic]

    Does Windows 8/8.1 support multiple languages to be installed at the same time? [Yes I No]

32. Click the left arrow at the top of the menu panel to return to the PC settings screen.

Ease of Access

33. Select *Ease of Access* from the PC settings screen. Explore the different options to answer the questions.

    Can the Narrator be turned on and the *Start Narrator Automatically* option be turned off at the same time? [Yes I No]

    What is the purpose of the magnifier?

    _____

    Does the magnifier have to be on to invert colors? [Yes I No]

    In what other way could you adjust color settings for a person who is color blind?

    _____

    Why do you think someone would want to have the on-screen keyboard enabled?

    _____

    _____

    What is the purpose of the last pointer color option?

    _____

    _____

34. Click the left arrow at the top of the menu panel to return to the PC settings screen.

Update and Recovery

    Note: Be very careful in this section to follow the directions exactly. You can lose all data if you're not careful.

35. Select *Update and Recovery* from the PC settings screen. Explore the different options to answer the questions.

    Use the *View Your Update History* link to determine when the last update installed on this computer. Document what you found.

    _____

    Does Windows 8/8.1 allow you to choose how updates get installed?
    [Yes I No]

LAB 14

How does Microsoft handle Windows 8/8.1 updates when the computer is connected to the Internet on a metered connection?

_____

What is the purpose of the *File History* option?

_____

What three recovery options are available?

_____

_____

Which recovery option would enable you to access advanced options, especially if an SSD is installed in the computer and you cannot press the F8 key quickly enough to access the options?
[Refresh Your PC | Remove Everything | Advanced Startup]

36. Select the *Restart Now* button.

What options are available to you?

_____

_____

_____

37. From the screen shown, select *Troubleshoot*.

What options are available to you?

_____

38. Select *Advanced Options*.

What options are available to you?

_____

_____

39. Select *Startup Repair*. Note that this provides the same function as pressing the F8 key during the boot process.

What options are available to you?

_____

40. Select an account and enter the appropriate password > select *Continue*.

41. The system attempts to repair the PC. Select *Advanced Options*. You are returned to the same screen as in step 37. Select the *Continue* option.

Lab 14.5 Windows 8/8.1 Basic Usage: Working with the Traditional Desktop and Control Panel Utilities

Objective: To work effectively with the Windows 8/8.1 traditional desktop, including accessing Control Panel utilities; managing the display through the Control Panel; performing file, folder, and computer searches; and accessing programs

Parts: Two computers with Windows 8/8.1 with administrator rights

Note: This lab could actually be done with one computer; in that case, only step 38 cannot be completed.

Procedure: Complete the following procedure and answer the accompanying questions.

1. Power on the computer and log on to Windows, if necessary.

Working with the Start Menu

2. Windows 8.1 enables you to work with the Start screen where tiles are located, with the more traditional desktop, or both. Move the pointer to the lower-left corner and select the Windows icon that appears. The traditional desktop appears.

3. Notice that the traditional desktop has a Start button (in Windows 8.1 but not Windows 8) that is a little different. The Windows 8.1 desktop also has a taskbar and notification area, and the hot-corners options used to access the Start screen, charms, and switching between applications still work.

4. Right-click or select and briefly hold on an empty space within the taskbar (the bar that runs across the bottom of the display).

    List the options available in the context menu.

    _____

    _____

    How can you tell if the taskbar is locked or unlocked without moving it?

    _____

    _____

    What toolbars can be added to the taskbar?

    _____

    _____

5. Select the *Customize* link in the notification area. Note that you may have to select an up arrow to see the link. After you answer the question, select *Cancel*.

    List three system icons that can be customized within the notification area.

    _____

    _____

Working with Control Panel

6. To access Control Panel in Windows 8.1, access and select the *Settings* charm > select *Change PC Settings* > select *Control Panel* or right-click the *Start* button and select *Control Panel*.

TECH TIP

Different ways to access Control Panel utilities in Windows 8.1

> Use the *Settings* charm > select *PC Settings* > select *Control Panel*.

> Type control in *Search* textbox > select *Control Panel*.

> After searching for *Control Panel*, right-click or tap and briefly hold the icon > select *Pin to Start* so you have a Control Panel tile on the Start screen or select *Pin to Taskbar* so it will be available on the traditional desktop taskbar.

> Keypress ⊞+Ⓧ > select *Control Panel*.

> With the Control Panel window open, locate the words *Control Panel* in the address bar > select and drag the words *Control Panel* to the desktop so that a shortcut icon will be created.

> From the *Start* screen, locate the *Control Panel* app tile.

> From *File Explorer*, select *This PC* in the window to the left > select *Computer* from the menu ribbon (previously called just "the menu") > select the *Open Control Panel* icon.

7. *Control Panel* allows access to Control Panel icons or links used to configure the computer. There are two basic ways to view Control Panels: the classic view (small and large icons for each Control Panel) and category view (where eight major categories are shown with a few links under each category but more links are available after you select the link). The default view is by category. To ensure that you are in the default view, locate and select the *View By* down arrow on the top right. Ensure that *Category* is selected.

List two Control Panel categories shown on the screen.

_____

_____

_____

8. Select *Large Icons* or *Small Icons* in the *View By* drop-down menu. This view is the older method for accessing any particular Control Panel utility. Return to the *Category* Control Panel view.

9. Use Lab Table 14.6 as a reference. Note that some systems have special Control Panel utilities because of the type of computer being used. Also, some of the options are found in multiple categories. Use Lab Table 14.7 to explore the Windows Control Panel and document which Control Panel category and subcategory you would use to perform particular tasks.

LAB TABLE 14.6   Common Windows 8/8.1 Control Panel categories*

Control Panel category	Subcategory	Function
System and Security	Action Center	View messages about security and maintenance issues and change security or maintenance-related settings.
	Windows Firewall	Enable and customize security features.
	System	View basic computer properties, such as RAM, processor type, and computer name.
	Windows Update	Customize how updates are received and installed.
	Power Options	Configure power-saving modes.
	File History	Periodically back up files in the Documents, Music, Pictures, Videos, and Desktop folders.
	BitLocker Drive Encryption	Change or use encryption options.
	Storage Spaces	Create a single storage space from multiple drives (and drive types).
	Work Folders	Save files that are accessible from multiple devices that may or may not be connected to the Internet at the time.
	Administrative Tools	Perform such tasks as freeing up hard disk space, managing hard drive partitions, scheduling tasks, and viewing event logs.
Network and Internet	Network and Sharing Center	Check the status and modify network-related settings as well as share files, folders, and devices on the network.
	Internet Options	Customize Internet Explorer.
	HomeGroup	View and change sharing and password options.

Control Panel category	Subcategory	Function
Hardware and Sound	Devices and Printers	Add/remove devices, scanners, cameras, printers, and mice as well as access Device Manager.
	AutoPlay	Change how media are automatically handled when a disc or type of file is added or inserted.
	Sound	Manage audio devices and change sound schemes.
	Power Options	Configure power saving modes.
	Display	Adjust resolution, configure an external display, or make text larger/smaller.
	Windows Mobility Center	On mobile devices, set the most commonly used settings, such as volume, battery status, wireless network status, and display status.
	Pen and Touch	Configure pen or touch options for a tablet.
	Tablet PC Settings	Calibrate the screen, adjust for left- or right-handed controls, and set the order in which the screen rotates.
	Location Settings	Control how apps use the device's location.
Programs	Programs and Features	Uninstall and change programs as well as enable/disable Windows features such as games, Telnet server, Telnet client, TFTP client, and print services.
	Default Programs	Remove a startup program, associate a file extension with a particular application, or select the program used with a particular type of file.
User Accounts and Family Safety	User Accounts	Add, remove, or modify accounts allowed access to the computer.
	Family Safety	Obtain reports of other users' computer activities, select what can be seen online, and configure time restrictions.
	Credential Manager	Store usernames/passwords in a vault for easy logon to sites or computers.
Appearance and Personalization	Personalization	Configure the desktop, background, colors, themes, and screen saver.
	Display	Adjust resolution, configure an external display, or make text larger/smaller.
	Taskbar and Navigation	Customize the Start screen and taskbar.
	Ease of Access Center	Configure visual, auditory, and mobility options.
	Folder Options	Configure how folders are viewed and acted upon, including what files are seen.
	Fonts	Customize available fonts.

LAB 14

Control Panel category	Subcategory	Function
Clock, Language, and Region	Date and Time	Configure time, date, time zone, and clocks for different time zones.
	Language	Add a language.
	Region	Configure the formatting of date, time, currency, and other options that are region specific.

* Note that you can find particular options by typing in the subcategory in the *Search Control Panel* textbox.

Fill in Lab Table 14.7 with the correct Control Panel category and subcategory.

LAB TABLE 14.7   Determine the correct Control Panel categories and subcategories

Control Panel category	Control Panel subcategory	Task
		Configure the mouse buttons for a left-handed person.
		Mute the computer speaker sound.
		Configure the date to be in the format April 15, 202X.
		Define how quickly a character repeats when a specific key is held down.
		Define what page (home page) appears every time Internet Explorer starts.
		Configure an IP address on a wired or wireless network adapter.
		Set a printer as the default printer.
		Verify if Windows recognizes a particular piece of hardware.

Working with the Display

10. Select the *Hardware and Sound* Control Panel category > select *Display*. Note that you may be required to search throughout this area and select various options to answer the questions.

    What is the current resolution?

    _____

    How many bits are used for color?

    _____

11. Continue working with the *Display* link. Locate and select the *Advanced Settings* link. *Note:* You may have to select the *Change Display Settings* link or use another Control Panel, depending on the manufacturer.

    What adapter is used?

    _____

How much video memory does the adapter have?

_____

How much total video memory (dedicated video memory) is available?

_____

12. Select the *Monitor* tab.

What refresh rate is used?

_____

13. Click *Cancel* on this window and on the next window to return to the *Control Panel* main screen. Select the *Appearance and Personalization* link > select the *Personalization* link > select the *Screen Saver/Change Screen Saver* link in the bottom right.

What screen saver, if any, is currently set?

_____

14. Use the *Screen Saver* down arrow to see a list of preinstalled screen savers and click one of the options. Click the *Preview* button. The screen saver appears. Move the pointer to regain control. Return the screen saver to the original setting (see the answer to Question 13).

Dealing with Power Settings

15. Select the *Change Power Settings* link. The Power Options window appears. Lab Table 14.8 shows the various power options available in Windows 8/8.1.

What power option would a teacher use when using a laptop to teach a four-hour class?

_____

LAB TABLE 14.8   Windows 8/8.1 default power schemes*

Power scheme	Purpose
Balanced	Default mode; processor adapts to activity being performed; performance provided when the computer is in use; power savings when the computer is inactive. Display powers down after 15 minutes; hard drive powers down after 20 minutes and goes to sleep after 20 minutes.
Power saver	Provides maximum battery life for mobile devices. Display and hard drive power down after 20 minutes, and the system goes to sleep after 1 hour.
High performance	Maximum system performance and responsiveness. Display and hard drive power down after 20 minutes, but the system never sleeps.
Customized	A scheme created by the user that has different settings than the three default schemes.

* Note that a computer manufacturer may provide additional power schemes.

16. Close all Control Panel windows.

Obtaining Help

17. Use the *Search* charm and type **help**. Two main sources of Windows 8/8.1 help are *Help+Tips* and *Help and Support*. Access the *Help+Tips* link. Notice how this help is a user-type Help feature.

18. Re-access the *Search* charm and access the *Help and Support* link. The standard categories for Help are Get Started, Internet and Networking, and Security, Privacy, & Accounts. You can use the textbox in the top center to search for specific help topics, or you can access the *Browse Help* link.

19. Select the *Browse Help* link.

What is the first link listed in the Help window?

_____

LAB 14

20. Type **monitor quality** in the *Search* textbox and press ⏎Enter or click the magnifying glass icon to the right of the textbox.

   List two settings used to improve display quality.

   _____

   _____

21. To see a list of troubleshooting topics, type **troubleshooting** in the Search textbox. A list of troubleshooting topics immediately displays.

22. Close the *Windows Help and Support* window.

Searching for Files, Folders, Applications, and Computers

23. Folders and files, including executable files, can be located using Windows File Explorer. Open Windows *File Explorer* > locate and select *This PC* in the *Search This PC* textbox located directly across from the path address box. Type **msconfig** and pause a moment before doing anything else.

24. Notice at the top of the ribbon menu that a Search menu option has appeared. Within this option, you can specify whether to include subfolders, the type of file, and advanced options including searching system files. You can also save the results of a particular search.

   List three kinds of items that could be used in a search.

   _____

   _____

25. By now your search should be complete. The msconfig command is an important one for technicians because it launches the System Configuration utility. In the resulting list, locate and launch (by double-clicking or double-tapping) the msconfig utility (normally the second or third option in the list).

   List the five tabs in the System Configuration window.

   _____

26. Click *Cancel* to close the System Configuration window. Close *File Explorer*.

27. Another way to locate files is through the Search charm. Type **msconfig** in the *Search* textbox and select msconfig.exe from the resulting list.

28. Click *Cancel* to close the System Configuration window.

29. Using any search method you want, find the *WordPad* application and launch it. Type the following message:

   Your profession is not what brings home your weekly paycheck. Your profession is what you're put here on earth to do with such passion and such intensity that it becomes spiritual in calling.-van Gogh

30. Select the *Save* icon in the top-left corner (the icon looks like a floppy disk, 🖫).

31. Ensure that the address bar shows that the file is saving into *Documents*. If it is not, scroll in the left window to locate and select *Documents*. In the *File Name* textbox, type **Lab4test** and click *Save*.

32. Close WordPad by using the *Close* button in the top-right corner.

33. Using the *Search* charm, type **lab** in the textbox.

   Did your Lab4test file appear in the resulting search list? If not, redo steps 29 through 33. [Yes | No]

34. Close the *Search* charm by selecting or clicking somewhere on the desktop.

35. Use the *System* Control Panel to document your computer name.

   Computer name: _____

36. To locate other computers on a network from a Windows 8/8.1 computer, on your own computer access *File Explorer* > select *Network* from the left. If computers and devices are configured to be seen on the network, then the computers appear in the screen to the right.

37. To configure your computer to be seen through File Explorer, access the *Network and Internet* Control Panel > *Network and Sharing Center* > *Change Advanced Sharing Settings* > expand the section that shows your current profile by selecting or tapping on the down chevron > enable the following: *Turn on Network Discovery* and *Turn on File and Printer Sharing* > *Save Changes*. Do the same process on the second computer or ask a classmate to do it.

    Second computer name: _____

38. Use *File Explorer* to locate a remote network device or computer. Do the same on the second Windows 8/8.1 computer.

    Does the remote device appear? [Yes | No]

    Does your device appear in File Explorer on the remote device?
    [Yes | No]

    Instructor initials: _____

Changing UAC (User Account Control) settings

Windows has a UAC dialog box that appears, asking for permission to do something. To change UAC settings, use the *User Accounts and Family Safety* Control Panel > select an account > *Change User Account Control Settings* > move the UAC control bar to have more notifications, fewer notifications, or no notifications > *OK*.

The UAC settings can also be disabled through the *System Configuration* (**msconfig** command) > *Tools* tab > *Change UAC Settings* > *Launch* button > select the appropriate level > *OK*.

LAB 14

39. Close all windows.

Recycle Bin

40. Open *File Explorer* > locate the Lab4test document created earlier in the lab. Ensure that the file is showing in the right window.

41. Right-click and briefly hold on the Lab4test filename. Notice that there is a Delete option. Do not click this option. This is just one way you could delete the file, but here you are going to use a different way. With the Lab4test filename still highlighted (but no context menu showing), press the Del key. The file is sent to the Recycle Bin, which is just a folder on the hard drive. You do not get message asking if you are sure, as you would in Windows 7 and older operating systems.

    The Recycle Bin holds deleted files and folders. When a file or folder is deleted, it is not immediately discarded; instead, it goes into the Recycle Bin folder. When a deleted file or folder is in the Recycle Bin, it can be removed. This is similar to a piece of trash being retrieved from an office trash can. A technician must remember that the files and folders in the Recycle Bin take up hard drive space and that users frequently forget to empty these deleted files and folders.

Files deleted from the Recycle Bin cannot be retrieved

After the Recycle Bin has been emptied, the deleted files cannot be recovered without the use of special software.

42. Locate the *Recycle Bin* icon on the desktop. If the Recycle Bin is not on the desktop, search for the Recycle Bin folder. Double-click or double-tap the *Recycle Bin* icon.

    Does the `Lab4test` WordPad document appear in the Recycle Bin window?
    [Yes | No] If no, redo the steps in this section to create and delete the file.

43. Select *Empty Recycle Bin* from the *Manage* menu ribbon option. A confirmation window appears, asking if you are sure you want to permanently delete the file. Select *Yes*. The name disappears from the Recycle Bin window (as do those of any other files that were located in the Recycle Bin). Close the *Recycle Bin* window.

Lab 14.6 Windows 10 Basic Usage: Introduction to the Start Screen

Objective: To work effectively with the Windows 10 Start screen

Parts: Computer with Windows 10 and administrator privileges

Procedure: Complete the following procedure and answer the accompanying questions.

1. Power on the computer and log on to Windows 10. Note that you may have to swipe up or press a key to access the logon screen.

Working with the Start Screen

2. The Start screen that displays is customizable so that it can look similar to the traditional desktop, the Windows 8/8.1 Start screen with all tiles, or a combination of the two.

    Which type of Start screen do you see?

    a. The traditional Windows Start screen with a Start button in the lower-left corner and a taskbar across the bottom

    b. A screen similar to the default Windows 8 screen, where the entire Start screen shows tiles representing apps

    c. A combination of the two, where some tiles show, but the taskbar still shows across the bottom or appears when the pointer is moved to the bottom of the screen

3. To see what options are available on the Start screen, start by opening *Settings*. How you do this depends on how your Start screen is already configured (and you will put it back that way later in this lab). Open *Settings* using one of the following methods. Note that all methods may not be available due to the type of device or configuration settings:
    > Hold down the ⊞ key and then press the ⓘ key.
    > Select the *Start* button, located in the bottom-left corner. You may have to move the pointer to the bottom of the screen for it to appear. Select *Settings* from the menu.
    > Select the *Start* button located in the bottom-left corner. You may have to move the pointer to the bottom of the screen for it to appear. Select the icon that looks like a bulleted list (located below the power icon). Scroll to the S section and select *Settings*.
    > Select the icon that has three horizontal lines located in the top-left corner > select *Settings* from the resulting menu.

4. Select *Personalization* > select *Start*.

    Document your current settings so that you can reinstate them later in the lab. Document any not settings not given in the list.:
    > Show More Tiles [On | Off]
    > Occasionally Show Suggestions in Start [On | Off]
    > Show Most Used Apps [On | Off]
    > Show Recently Added Apps [On | Off]
    > Use Start Full Screen [On | Off]
    > Show Recently Opened Items in Jump Lists on Start or the Taskbar [On | Off]

5. Set all options to the *Off* position. Select the *Choose Which Folders Appear on Start* link at the bottom of the pane.

    Document your current settings so that you can reinstate them later in the lab:
    > File Explorer [On | Off]
    > Settings [On | Off]
    > Documents [On | Off]
    > Downloads [On | Off]
    > Music [On | Off]
    > Pictures [On | Off]
    > Videos [On | Off]
    > HomeGroup [On | Off]
    > Network [On | Off]
    > Personal Folder [On | Off]

6. Set all the folders to *Off*. Close the *Settings* window to return to the Start screen. Which Start screen do you now see?

    a. The traditional Windows Start screen with a Start button in the lower-left corner and a taskbar across the bottom

    b. A screen similar to the default Windows 8 screen, where the entire Start screen shows tiles representing apps

    c. A combination of the two, where some tiles show, but the taskbar still shows across the bottom or appears when the pointer is moved to the bottom of the screen

7. Select the *Start* button from the Start screen.

    What menu options appear directly above the Start button?

    _____

8. Select the *All Apps* option > scroll to the *S* section > select *Settings* > *Personalization* > select the *Start* option. Notice that the preview window shows an example of the Windows Start screen and its layout.

9. Turn the *Show More Tiles on Start* option *On*.

    How did the preview window change (if at all)?

    _____

    If you enable the *Show suggestions occasionally in Start* option, how does the preview window change, if at all?

    _____

10. Lab Table 14.9 shows the purpose of each of these options. Lab Figure 14.1 shows where these options would be located on the Start menu. Explore these options to see their effects.

LAB TABLE 14.9   Windows 10 Start screen settings

Setting	Purpose
Show more tiles on Start	Shows one more column of tiles. Note that you can drag the edge of a tile to make any size you want.
Show suggestions occasionally in Start	Displays ads for suggested apps.
Show most used apps	Dynamically populates with the most commonly used apps.
Show recently added apps	Lists the apps recently installed.

Setting	Purpose
Use Start full screen	Start screen is more like the Windows 8 tiles view full screen. Use the menu icon in the left-top corner to access apps.
Show recently opened items in jump lists on Start or the taskbar	Displays as an arrow from the Start menu or on the Start screen. Jump lists are recently used documents, websites, and so on related to a particular app. On the taskbar, right-click an app icon to see the associated jump list.

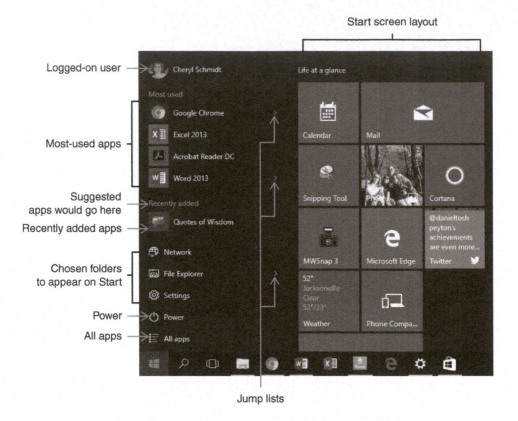

LAB FIGURE 14.1   Windows 10 Start menu areas

11. Within the *Start* settings, ensure that the *Use Start full screen* option is *Off*. Access the *Chose which folders appear on Start* link at the bottom of the right pane.

12. Select several of the settings and re-access the Start screen.

    List which options you think would be most beneficial for people in a work environment.

    _____

    _____

13. Within the *Personalization > Start* settings, ensure that the *Use Start Full Screen* option is *On*.

14. Re-access the Start menu by selecting the *Start* icon from the desktop.

Manipulating the Start Screen

15. To learn how to modify tiles, examine the tiles shown in the Start screen.

    Which tile is currently located in the far-left position?

    _____

16. Select and drag the tile located in the far-left position to the last position in the first block of tiles. Then return the tile to the current position.

17. To add a tile that represents an app to the Start screen, access the *All Apps* Start menu icon that looks like a bulleted list. Select the *Windows Accessories* menu item and locate but do not select the *Notepad* application. Right-click or tap and briefly hold on the *Notepad* option. A context menu appears. Move the pointer to the *More* option.

    Which additional options are available?

    _____

18. Select the *Pin to Start* option. A Notepad tile appears. Right-click on the *Notepad* tile.

    List the options available in the context menu.

    _____

19. Tap or select the *Notepad* tile. The Notepad application window opens. Close the window using the *Close* button in the upper-right corner.

20. Re-access the *Start* menu using whatever method you prefer. Locate the *Notepad* tile. Tap and briefly hold or right-click the *Notepad* tile to access the context menu.

21. Hover the pointer over the *Resize* option.

    What choices do you have?

    _____

22. Select a different tile size than the one currently used. Re-access the *Notepad* tile context menu again. Using the *More* option, select *Open File Location*. Windows *File Explorer* opens, showing the folder that contains this file (and other files in the same folder). Notice that the Notepad option is a shortcut. You can tell because the icon on the left has a bent arrow on it. Also, in the *Type* column, you can see the word *Shortcut*.

23. To see where the original file is located, right-click or tap and hold on the *Notepad* icon from within *File Explorer* > select *Properties*. Ensure that the *Shortcut* tab is selected. The Target textbox shows where the file is actually located. `%windir%` is used to describe the folder where Windows was installed. Commonly it is `C:\Windows`, but because this might be on another drive letter or installed to a different folder, Microsoft simply describes it as `%windir%`. The full path for the Notepad application is commonly `C:\Windows\Systems32\notepad.exe`.

24. Click *Cancel* to return to File Explorer. Close *File Explorer*. Return to the *Start* screen (the one with the tiles).

25. Re-access the *Notepad* context menu. Select *Unpin from Start*.

Conducting Searches

26. Searches in Windows 10 are done through the taskbar, using the *Search the Web and Windows* textbox. Note that if you have the Cortana feature turned on, you can speak or type questions or conduct searches through that interface. To ensure that everyone is on the same page, let's document some original configuration stuff and, if necessary, change.

    From the *Start* menu, start typing (note that you do not have to click anywhere) **cor** and select *Cortana & Search Settings* from the resulting list.

    Document the device's current settings related to searching. Note that you may have to explore the links to answer. Document any settings not given.
    > SafeSearch [Strict | Moderate | Off]
    > Windows Cloud Search [On | Off]
    > View activity history [On | Off]
    > My device history [On | Off]
    > My search history [On | Off]

27. Ensure that the *My search history* is turned *On*.

28. Select the *Search* icon from the taskbar or select inside the *Search the Web and Windows* textbox. Type `comm` in the textbox. A list separated by Best Match, Apps, Store, Web, and Settings appears. Select the *Command Prompt* option. The Command Prompt window appears. Close the Command Prompt window by using the *Close* button in the top-right corner.

29. Re-access the search function and type `word`. From the resulting list, right-click or tap and briefly hold on the *WordPad* app. Notice from the search result that you still have access to the context menu that allows you to pin a particular app to the Start menu or taskbar. You also have the option to run an app as an administrator. This is sometimes required with Windows utilities used by technicians, although it is not needed with WordPad. Click away from the Search list.

30. In the textbox at the bottom of the list, remove `word` and type `trinkets` instead. Notice that because there is nothing in the Windows 10 environment related to trinkets, web links are provided if this computer is connected to the Internet. Select somewhere away from the search list.

Power Options

31. The Power Button icon is in the Start menu. It is a circle with a vertical line that extends through the top part of the circle. You often see the symbol on power buttons. Click this icon once. Lab Table 14.10 explains the various power options that might be seen.

LAB TABLE 14.10   Windows 10 power button shutdown options

Option	Purpose
Sign out	Allows the current user to log off from the account being used.
Restart	Used when new software or hardware has been installed or when the computer locks.
Sleep	Reduces power consumption but keeps the applications and settings that are currently on the screen.
Hibernate	Reduces power consumption even more so than the sleep mode. Takes longer to resume operations than sleep mode, but not as long as with a cold boot.
Shut down	Powers off the computer.

What options are available?

_____

_____

Controlling the Desktop

32. The desktop is the main screen area that you see when you log in to Windows 10. What is shown on the desktop and default options are customizable like the Start menu.

33. Right-click or tap and briefly hold on an empty space on the desktop. Point to the *View* option.

What options are available in the context menu?

_____

_____

What options are currently enabled?

_____

34. Select the *Show Desktop Icons* option to disable it (if necessary, remove the check mark beside the option).

    What changed?

    _____

35. Re-access the *View* context menu and ensure that the *Show Desktop Icons* option is set to the original configuration.

Task View

36. On the taskbar is the Task View option. Task View allows you to view thumbnails of open apps and easily switch between them. Let's explore how this works.

37. Open the *Notepad, Snipping Tool*, and *Command Prompt* apps.

38. Locate and select the *Task View* option on the taskbar. It is located to the right of the search function. It is a rectangle with handles on the side. If you hold your cursor over the icon, the handles extend outward.

    What happened when you selected the *Task View* option?

    _____

39. Locate and select the *Notepad* app. Note that you may have to select a down arrow below the thumbnails to see more thumbnails if you have more apps open than can fit on the screen. Leave these apps open.

40. Task View can also be used to create more than one desktop. That way you have one or more apps open within one desktop and different apps open within another desktop. Then you can use Task View to easily swap between them. Re-access *Task View* from the taskbar.

41. Select the *New Desktop* option from the bottom of the *Task View* desktop. If you don't see the words *New Desktop* in the bottom-right corner, click on the *Task View* icon from the taskbar again. Then click on *New Desktop*.

42. Access the new desktop by clicking that numbered desktop on the far right (usually *Desktop 2*).

43. On this desktop, open the *WordPad* app.

44. Now select the *Task View* taskbar option again. The multiple desktops show. Move the pointer to the first desktop (*Desktop 1*), and all open apps appear in the window above. Move the pointer to the desktop you just created, and the WordPad app thumbnail appears.

    One thing to note about the virtual desktops is that they are not totally separated from one another. For example, if you enable the *Use Start Full Screen* option, it will be enabled across all desktops.

45. Ensure that the pointer is pointing toward the last desktop that was just created (usually Desktop 2). Click the X in the upper-right corner to delete that virtual desktop. If you have clicked within that virtual desktop and see the opened WordPad app, you are in the wrong place. Click the *Task View* icon on the taskbar and then hover the pointer over the miniature icon representing the last desktop created. Then click the X in the upper-right corner to delete that particular virtual desktop.

46. In the original desktop, ensure that any apps you have open are closed (for example, *Notepad, Snipping Tool*, and *Command Prompt*).

Getting the Machine Back in Order

47. Refer to steps 4, 5, and 26 and return all Start settings to their original configuration.

48. Have a classmate verify that the settings are configured properly.

    Are the computer settings back to the original configuration, as listed in steps 4, 5, and 26? [Yes | No]

    Classmate's printed name: _____

    Classmate's signature: _____

Lab 14.7 Windows 10 Basic Usage: Introduction to Settings

Objective: To be familiar with the Windows 10 Settings

Parts: Computer with Windows 10 installed

             Flash drive

Procedure: Complete the following procedure and answer the accompanying questions.

1. Power on the computer and log on to Windows 10. Note that you may have to swipe up or press a key to access the logon screen.

2. Use the *Start* menu to access *Settings*. Without using Control Panel utilities, you have more configurable options in Windows 10 Settings than you have in Windows 8/8.1.

Working with Windows 10 System Settings

3. Select the *System* option from the *Settings* screen.

    Looking over the list, which option(s) are you curious about?

    _____

4. Select the *Display* setting. This setting is commonly used to set the size of text and the orientation of the display, and it shows the number of displays detected.

    What is the current orientation? [Landscape | Portrait | Landscape (flipped) | Portrait (flipped)]

5. Change the orientation to something else, such as *Landscape (Flipped)*. Select *Apply*. Select the *Revert* option if you can after you answer the questions that follow. If you cannot select this option, do not worry because if you don't accept the change, the display will automatically change back to the original setting.

    What happened?

    _____

    _____

6. Select the *Advanced Display Settings* link at the bottom of the *Display* settings option. This option allows you to reset the screen resolution if the user has set it to something less than optimal. Normally, you will see the *(Recommended)* beside the resolution that is best for the screen being used. You might also have the *Color Calibration* link to ensure the colors on the display appear best.

    What is the current resolution?

    _____

7. Return to the *System* settings window by selecting the *left arrow* in the top-left corner of the window.

8. Select the *Multitasking* option. The multitasking option has items related to snapping and resizing windows as well as virtual desktop settings that relate to Task View (covered in Lab 14.6).

    What is the current setting for showing windows that are open?
    [Only the Desktop I Am Using | All Desktops]

9. Return to the *System* settings window by selecting the *left arrow* in the top-left corner.

10. Select the *Power & Sleep* option. This is where you can select a power plan for the system.

    At what point will the screen turn off after a period of inactivity?

    _____

    At what point will the PC go to sleep after a period of inactivity?

    _____

    Could you configure a Windows 10 computer so that it never goes to sleep?
    [Yes | No]

11. Select the *Additional Power Settings* link. Notice that you are taken to the *Power Options* Control Panel utility.

12. Return to the *System* settings by closing the *Power Options* Control Panel window. In the *System Power & Sleep* settings window select the *left arrow* in the top-left corner to return to the main Settings window.

13. Attach a flash drive to the PC.

14. Select the *Storage* system setting. In the Storage section, select the flash drive that has just been attached. Windows categorizes the type of documents found on the drive (system files, apps and games, documents, pictures, music, videos, maps, temporary files, and others) and shows you how much of each type are on the chosen file media.

     Return to the *Storage* settings screen and scroll down to the *Save Locations* section or use the *Change where new content is saved* link.

     Use Lab Table 14.11 to document current save locations.

LAB TABLE 14.11   Windows 10 save locations

Option	Current setting
New apps will save to	
New documents will save to	
New music will save to	
New pictures will save to	
New videos will save to	

Describe a situation in which you think someone might want to change one or more of these settings.

_____

_____

_____

15. Return to the *System* settings. On the left menu, select and access the *About* setting. This screen is full of information that is important to an IT person.

     List five items that you think might be useful to a technical person that are not usually useful to the end user.

_____

_____

Can you rename the computer from this window? [Yes | No]

From the *Related* settings area, select the *System Info* link. If you access the *Device Manager* link, does the Device Manager tool open in another window or display within the settings window? [another window | same window]

What information is displayed when the *System Information* link is chosen that was not available from the *About* system setting?

_____

_____

16. Close any Control Panel, Device Manager, or System Info window that is open. Return to the main *Settings* window.

Devices

17. Select the *Devices* setting. This setting is used to quickly see and configure attached devices. Rather than go through each option, answer some questions in each section to make sure you are looking at important options. Explore the different *Devices* options to answer the questions.

    Does the *Printer & Scanners* option have any settings related to devices other than printers and scanners? [Yes | No] If yes, explain what is there.

    _____

    Can you configure Bluetooth devices through the *Connected Devices* link?
    [Yes | No]

    Does the attached flash drive appear as a connected device? [Yes | No]

    List two connected devices.

    _____

    Describe which steps can be taken so the PC can be found by other Bluetooth devices. Note that not all devices have Bluetooth installed. Write "not applicable" as an answer if this is the case.

    _____

    _____

    Which button is the primary mouse button? [Left | Center | Right]

    If the mouse has a scroll wheel, how many lines scroll each time the mouse wheel is rolled?

    _____

    Can the computer scroll inactive windows when the user hovers the mouse pointer over them?
    [Yes | No]

    Can the Windows operating system be configured to automatically correct misspelled words?
    [Yes | No]

    Can the Windows operating system be configured to recommend alternative words? [Yes | No]

    Can you disable AutoPlay through the *AutoPlay Devices* settings? [Yes | No]

    What is the default web browser for the machine? How did you find this through Settings?

    _____

    _____

18. Return to the *System* settings window by selecting the *left arrow* in the top-left corner of the window.

Network & Internet

19. Select *Network & Internet* from the *Settings* window. Explore the different options to answer the questions.

    What types of networks are supported?

    _____

    Does Windows 10 allow you to turn on airplane mode? [Yes | No]

    If you work in a corporate environment in which a proxy server is used and you are required to configure an executive's laptop, what configuration settings do you need to obtain from the network support staff to manually configure the settings?

    _____

    Which option would you use to see the MAC address of the Ethernet network card?

    _____

Which option would you use to attach the device to the wireless network?

[Wi-Fi | Airplane Mode | Proxy | Ethernet | Dial-up]

20. Return to the *Settings* screen.

Personalization

21. Select *Personalization* from the *Settings* window.

22. Select the *Lock Screen* option. This particular setting allows you to control how the display reacts and possibly the camera as well (if one is installed). The lock screen function is a screen that appears when you have not interacted with the device after a specified amount of time. The lock screen commonly shows information such as time, date, battery status, and network status. Notice that to enable an option, you select one side of a particular option.

What is the current option to play a slide show on the lock screen? [On | Off] Note that if you are having trouble telling, a dot points toward one side or the other. The selection chosen is shown as a particular word on the left (either on or off). Change the option by clicking or tapping on the side away from the dot.

23. Choose the opposite selection for the *Show Windows Background Picture on the Sign-in Screen* by clicking or tapping the opposite side of the colored oval so that the dot goes to the opposite side. If the answer to Question 22 was *On*, you should turn the option *Off*. If the answer to Question 22 was *Off*, you should turn the option to *On*.

What visual clue did you have that the option changed?

_____

_____

_____

24. Return the setting to the original *On* or *Off* position.

25. Access the *Screen Saver Settings* link at the bottom of the window. Screen timeout and screen saver settings are important options in the business environment for security reasons. Return to *Settings*.

Accounts

26. Rather than go through each option, answer some questions in each section to make sure you are looking at important options. Explore the different *Accounts* options to answer the questions.

What three sign-in options can be used with Windows 10?

_____

How many digits does a PIN need to be in Windows 10?

_____

How would you add an additional account to this machine? Give exact steps.

_____

_____

What does *Sync Your Settings* mean?

_____

27. Return to the *Settings* screen.

Time & Language

28. Select *Time & Language* from the *Settings* screen. Explore the different options to answer the questions.

   Can the time be manually configured?

   [Yes | No]

   If the date setting was set to the *dddd, MMMM d, yyyy* option, how would today's date appear?

   _____

   Does Windows 10 support multiple languages being installed at the same time? [Yes | No]

   Is any option available that might help with speech recognition for a person from the deep South? If so, what?

   _____

   What is the default voice for text-to-speech apps?

   _____

29. Return to the *Settings* screen.

Ease of Access

30. Select *Ease of Access* from the *Settings* screen. Explore the different options to answer the questions.

   Can the Narrator be turned on and the *Start Narrator Automatically* option be turned off at the same time? [Yes | No]

   What is the purpose of the magnifier?

   _____

   Does the magnifier have to be on to invert colors? [Yes | No]

   In what other way could you adjust color settings for a person who is color blind?

   _____

   Why do you think someone would want to have the on-screen keyboard enabled?

   _____

   _____

   What is the purpose of the last pointer color option?

   _____

   _____

   What option would be used to increase the thickness of the cursor?

   _____

   Does Windows 10 support closed captioning? [Yes | Not that I can tell]

31. Select the *left arrow* to return to the *Settings* screen.

Privacy

32. Select *Privacy* from the *Settings* screen. Explore the different options to answer the questions.

   Does Windows 10 allow you to disable and enable the capability to let apps access the name, picture, and account information found on the computer?

   [Yes | No]

   What apps, if any, can use the computer's location?

   _____

   Does the computer have a webcam? [Yes | No]

If so, are any devices allowed to use it? Where did you find this information?

_____

Which apps are allowed to use the computer's microphone?

_____

Which apps are allowed to access your call history?

_____

33. Return to the PC settings screen.

Update & Security

Note: Be very careful in this section to follow the directions exactly. You can lose all data if you're not careful.

34. Select *Update & Security* from the *Settings* screen. Explore the different options to answer the questions.

When was the last update installed on this computer? How did you find this information? Document your process.

_____

_____

Does Windows 10 allow you to choose how updates get installed? [Yes | No]

What steps would you take to uninstall an update?

_____

_____

What is the purpose of the *File History* option?

_____

What recovery options are available?

_____

Which recovery option would allow you to access advanced options, especially if an SSD is installed in the computer and you cannot press the [F8] key quickly enough to access the options?
[Reset This PC | Remove Everything | Advanced Startup]

35. From the *Recovery Update & Security* option, select the *Restart Now* button.

What options are available to you?

_____

_____

36. From the screen shown, select *Troubleshoot*.

What options are available to you?

_____

37. Select Advanced Options.

What options are available to you?

_____

_____

38. Select *Startup Repair*. Note that this provides the same function as pressing the [F8] key during the boot process.

39. Select an account and enter the appropriate password > select *Continue*.

40. The system attempts to repair the PC. Select *Advanced Options*. You are returned to the same screen as in step 36. Select the *Continue* option.

Lab 14.8 Windows 10 Basic Usage: Working with Control Panel Utilities

Objective: To work effectively with the Windows 10 traditional desktop, including accessing Control Panel utilities; managing the display through the Control Panel; performing file, folder, and computer searches; and accessing programs

Parts: Two computers with Windows 10 with administrator rights

Note: This lab can be done with one computer; in this case, only step 27 cannot be completed.

Procedure: Complete the following procedure and answer the accompanying questions.

1.   Power on the computer and log on to Windows, if necessary.

Working with Control Panel Utilities

2.   Control Panel utilities are used to configure the operating system and hardware. There are various ways to open Control Panels:

> Right-click or tap and briefly hold the *Start* button > *Control Panel*.

> Type **control** in the *Search* textbox > select *Control Panel*. After searching for Control Panel, right-click or tap and briefly hold the icon > select *Pin to Start* so that you have a Control Panel tile on the Start screen or select *Pin to Taskbar* so it displays on the taskbar.

> Use ■+ⓧ > select *Control Panel*. With the Control Panel window open, locate the word *Control Panel* in the address bar > select and drag the words *Control Panel* to the desktop so that a shortcut icon is created.

> From the *Start* menu, select the *All Apps* icon > locate and expand the *Windows System* folder > locate and select *Control Panel*.

3.   There are two basic ways to view Control Panels: the classic view (small and large icons for each Control Panel) and category view (where eight major categories are shown with a few links under each category, but more links are available after you select the link). The default view is Category. To ensure that you are in the default view, locate and select the *View By* down arrow on the top right. Ensure that *Category* is selected.

4.   List two Control Panel categories shown on the screen.

_____

_____

_____

5.   Select *Large Icons* or *Small Icons* in the *View By* drop-down menu. This view is the older method for accessing any particular Control Panel utility. Return to the *Category* Control Panel view.

Use Lab Table 14.12 as a reference. Note that some systems have special Control Panel utilities due to the hardware installed or type of computer, such as a laptop or tablet. Notice in Lab Table 14.12 that some of the options are available in multiple categories. Use Lab Table 14.13 to fill in and document which Control Panel categories and subcategories you would use to perform particular tasks.

LAB TABLE 14.12   Common Windows 10 Control Panel categories*

Control Panel category	Subcategory	Function
System and Security	Security and Maintenance	View messages about security and maintenance issues and change security or maintenance-related settings. Similar to the Action Center Control Panel in previous Windows editions.
	Windows Firewall	Enable and customize security features.

Control Panel category	Subcategory	Function
	System	View basic computer properties, such as RAM, processor type, and computer name.
	Power Options	Configure power-saving modes.
	File History	Periodically back up files in the Documents, Music, Pictures, Videos, and Desktop folders.
	Backup and Restore (Windows 7)	Save or restore files and folders to/from a different location.
	BitLocker Drive Encryption	Change or use encryption options.
	Storage Spaces	Create a single storage space from multiple drives (and drive types).
	Work Folders	Save files that are accessible from multiple devices that may or may not be connected to the Internet at the time.
	Administrative Tools	Do tasks such as free up hard disk space, manage hard drive partitions, schedule tasks, and view event logs
Network and Internet	Network and Sharing Center	Check the status and modify network-related settings as well as share files, folders, and devices on the network.
	HomeGroup (through version 1803)	View and change sharing and password options.
	Internet Options	Customize Internet Explorer.
Hardware and Sound	Devices and Printers	Add/remove devices, scanners, cameras, printers, and mice and as access Device Manager.
	AutoPlay	Change how media are automatically handled when a disc or type of file is added or inserted.
	Sound	Manage audio devices and change sound schemes.
	Power Options	Configure power saving modes.
	Display	Adjust resolution, configure an external display, or make text larger/smaller.
Programs	Programs and Features	Uninstall and change programs as well as enable/disable Windows features such as games, Telnet server, Telnet client, TFTP client, and print services.
	Default Programs	Remove a startup program, associate a file extension with a particular application, or select the program used with a particular type of file.

LAB 14

Control Panel category	Subcategory	Function
User Accounts	User Accounts	Add, remove, or modify accounts allowed access to the computer.
	Credential Manager	Store usernames/passwords in a vault for easy logon to sites or computers.
Appearance and Personalization	Personalization	Configure the desktop, background, colors, themes, and screen saver.
	Display	Adjust resolution, configure an external display, or make text larger/smaller.
	Taskbar and Navigation	Customize the Start screen and taskbar.
	Ease of Access Center	Configure visual, auditory, and mobility options.
	File Explorer Options	Configure how folders are viewed and acted upon, including which files are seen.
	Fonts	Customize available fonts.
Clock, Language, and Region	Date and Time	Configure time, date, time zone, and clocks for different time zones.
	Language	Add a language.
	Region	Configure the formatting of date, time, currency, and so on that are region specific.

* Note that particular options can be found by typing in the subcategory in the *Search Control Panel* textbox.

Fill in Lab Table 14.13 with the correct Control Panel categories and subcategories.

LAB TABLE 14.13   Determine the correct Control Panel categories and subcategories

Control Panel category	Control Panel subcategory	Task
		Configure the mouse buttons for a left-handed person.
		Mute the computer speaker sound.
		Configure the date to be in the format April 15, 202X.
		Define how quickly a character repeats when a specific key is held down.
		Define what page (home page) appears every time Edge starts.
		Verify if Windows recognizes a particular piece of hardware.
		Configure an IP address on a wired or wireless network adapter.
		Set a printer as the default printer.

Power Settings

6. From the *Hardware and Sound* Control Panel category, select the *Change power-savings settings* link within the *Power Options* section. The Power Options window appears. Lab Table 14.14 shows the various power options available in Windows 10.

    What power option would a teacher use when using a laptop to teach a 4-hour class?

LAB TABLE 14.14   Windows 10 default power schemes*

Power scheme	Purpose
Balanced	Default mode; processor adapts to activity being performed; performance provided when the computer is in use; power savings when the computer is inactive. Display powers down after 15 minutes; hard drive powers down after 20 minutes and goes to sleep after 20 minutes.
Power saver	Provides maximum battery life for mobile devices. Display and hard drive power down after 20 minutes, and the system goes to sleep after 1 hour.
High performance	Maximum system performance and responsiveness. Display and hard drive power down after 20 minutes, but the system never sleeps.
Customized	A scheme created by the user that has different settings than the three default schemes.

* Note that a computer manufacturer may provide additional power schemes.

7. Close all Control Panel windows.

Obtaining Help

8. Use the *Search* textbox (this could be *I'm Cortana* and you need to go through the dialogs until you select that you are sure you do not want Cortana help, then the *Search the Web and Windows* textbox appears) and type **windows help**. Access one of the search results.

9. Windows 10 relies on search results from the Internet more than any prior operating system. Close all windows you might have opened.

Searching for Files, Folders, Applications, and Computers

10. Folders and files, including executable files, can be located using Windows File Explorer. Open Windows *File Explorer* using any method described in a previous lab. You can also right-click or tap and briefly hold the *Start* button and select *File Explorer*.

11. Locate and select *This PC* in the left window.

12. In the *Search This PC* textbox (located directly across from the path address box), type **msconfig** and pause a moment before doing anything else. Notice at the top of the ribbon menu that a Search option has appeared.

13. Select the *Search* ribbon menu option. Within this option, you can specify whether to include subfolders, the type of file, and advanced options including searching system files. You can also save the results of a particular search.

    Click on the *Kind* option from the *Search* menu option. List three types of items that could be used in a search.

---

14. By now your search should be complete. You can click off of the list to see the search results. The `msconfig` command is an important one for technicians because it launches the System Configuration utility. In the resulting list, locate and launch (by double-clicking) the `msconfig` utility (normally the second through sixth options in the list). It has an icon of a computer with a check in it.

List the five tabs in the System Configuration window.

_____

15. Select *Cancel* to close the System Configuration window. Close the search results window, too.

16. Another way to locate files is through the Search textbox on the taskbar. Type **msconfig** in the Search textbox and select *System Configuration* from the resulting list.

17. Select *Cancel* to close the System Configuration window.

18. Using any search method you want, find the *WordPad* application and launch it. Type the following message:

    Your profession is not what brings home your weekly paycheck. Your profession is what you're put here on earth to do with such passion and such intensity that it becomes spiritual in calling.-van Gogh

19. Select the *Save* icon in the top-left corner (the icon looks like an old floppy disk, 🖫).

20. Ensure that the address bar shows that the file is saving into *Documents*. If it is not, scroll down in the left window to locate and select *Documents*. In the *File Name* textbox, type **Lab4test** and click *Save*.

21. Close WordPad by using the *Close* button in the top right.

22. Using the *Search* textbox, type **lab** in the textbox.

    Did your `Lab4test` file appear in the resulting search list? If not, redo steps 18 through 22. [Yes | No]

23. Close the *Search* results list by selecting or clicking somewhere on the desktop.

24. Access and use the *System* Control Panel to document your computer name.

    Instructor initials: _____

    Computer name: _____

25. To locate other computers on a network from a Windows 10 computer, on your own computer access *File Explorer* > select *Network* from the left panel. If computers and devices are configured to be seen on the network, then the computers appear in the screen to the right. If your computer is not listed there or a classmate's Windows 10 computer is not listed, proceed to the next step to configure for that.

    Computer name shown through the Network option: _____

26. To configure your computer to be seen through File Explorer, access the *Network and Internet* Control Panel category > *Network and Sharing Center* > *Change Advanced Sharing Settings* > expand the section that shows your current profile (it should be expanded already) by selecting or tapping on the down chevron > enable the following: *Turn on Network Discovery* > *Save Changes*.

27. Do the same process on the second computer or ask a classmate to do it on a computer. Use File Explorer on both computers to locate the remote computer.

    Does the remote device appear? [Yes | No]

    Computer names shown through the Network option: _____

TECH TIP

Changing UAC (User Account Control) settings

Windows has a UAC dialog box that asks for permission to do something. To change UAC settings, use the *User Accounts* Control Panel > select an account > *Change User Account Control settings* > move the UAC control bar to have more notifications, fewer notifications, or no notifications > *OK*.

The UAC settings can also be disabled through the *System Configuration* utility (`msconfig` command) > *Tools* tab > *Change UAC Settings* > *Launch* button > select the appropriate level > *OK*.

28. Close all windows.

Recycle Bin

29. Open *File Explorer* > locate the `Lab4test` document created earlier in the lab. Ensure that the file is showing in the right window of File Explorer.

30. Right-click or tap and briefly hold on the `Lab4test` filename. Notice that there is a *Delete* option. (If you do not have this option, you did not actually right-click the `Lab4test` filename or you are not in *This PC > Documents*.) With the `Lab4test` filename still highlighted (but no context menu showing), press the ⌨Del key. The file is sent to the Recycle Bin, and you do not get message asking if you are sure, as you would in previous Windows versions. Remember that the Recycle Bin is just a folder on the hard drive.

    The Recycle Bin holds deleted files and folders. When a file or folder is deleted, it is not immediately discarded; instead, it goes into the Recycle Bin folder. When a deleted file or folder is in the Recycle Bin, it can be removed. This is similar to a piece of trash being retrieved from an office trash can. A technician must remember that the files and folders in the Recycle Bin take up hard drive space and that users frequently forget to empty these deleted files and folders.

TECH TIP

Files deleted from Recycle Bin cannot be retrieved

Once the Recycle Bin has been emptied, the deleted files cannot be recovered without the use of special software.

31. Locate the *Recycle Bin* icon on the desktop. If the Recycle Bin is not on the desktop, search for the Recycle Bin folder. Double-click or double-tap the *Recycle Bin* icon.

    Does the `Lab4test` WordPad document appear in the Recycle Bin window?

    [Yes | No] If not, redo the steps in this section to create and delete the file.

32. Select the *Empty Recycle Bin* from the *Manage* menu ribbon option. A confirmation window appears, asking if you are sure you want to permanently delete the file. Select *Yes*. The name disappears from the Recycle Bin window (as do those of any other files that were located in the Recycle Bin). Close the *Recycle Bin* window.

Lab 14.9 Windows 7 Taskbar Options

Objective: To interact with and customize the Windows taskbar

Parts: Computer with Windows 7 installed

Procedure: Complete the following procedure and answer the accompanying questions.

1.   Turn on the computer and verify that the operating system loads. Log on, if necessary.

Taskbar Options

2.   Locate the taskbar at the bottom of the screen. If it is not showing, move the mouse to the bottom of the screen, and the taskbar pops up.

3.   To modify or view the taskbar settings, right-click a blank area of the taskbar. A menu appears. (Note that you can also modify the taskbar through the *Taskbar and Navigation* Control Panel utility.)

4.   Select the *Properties* option. The *Taskbar and Start Menu Properties* window appears.

5.   Ensure that you are on the *Taskbar* tab. The options available on this screen relate to how things are shown on the taskbar. The checked items are active. To remove a check mark, click in that checkbox. To put a check mark in a box, click once in an empty box. Lab Table 14.15 shows the functions of the options.

Document each enabled option.

Lock the taskbar [enabled | disabled]

Auto-hide the taskbar [enabled | disabled]

Use small icons [enabled | disabled]

Taskbar location on screen [Bottom | Left | Right | Top]

Taskbar buttons: [Always combine, hide labels | Combine when taskbar is full | Never combine]

LAB TABLE 14.15   Windows taskbar options and functions

Option	Function
Lock the taskbar	Prevents the taskbar from being moved
Auto-hide the taskbar	Hides the taskbar until the pointer is moved to the taskbar area; use the *Keep the Taskbar on Top of Other Windows* option with this option to ensure that the taskbar is visible when selected
Use small icons	Makes the icons on the taskbar smaller than the default view
Taskbar location on screen	Sets whether the taskbar appears at the bottom (default) or to the left, right, or top
Taskbar buttons	Optionally combines similar labels
Notification area	Customizes the icons and types of notifications that can appear here
Preview desktop with Aero Peek	Enables the desktop to be shown when the pointer is moved to the Show Desktop button at the far end of the taskbar

6.   Ensure that the *Auto-Hide the Taskbar* option is enabled and all other taskbar options are disabled. Select *Apply* and then *OK*. The taskbar disappears from view. If it does not, redo this step.

7.   Point to the screen where the taskbar is normally located. The taskbar appears. Open the *Notepad* app using any method you know. Maximize the screen by clicking the *Maximize* button (the center button at the top-right side of the window).

What happened to the taskbar?

_____

8.   Move the pointer to the screen area where the taskbar is normally located.

Did the taskbar appear? [Yes | No]

9.   Close the *Notepad* window. Bring the taskbar options back up and reset them to their original configuration. Refer to the answer to Question 5 for enabled options. Close the *Taskbar and Start Menu Properties* window.

Instructor initials: _____

10.   A sign (<, <<, or ▲) marks the beginning of the notification area of the taskbar found on the far right of the taskbar. Three common options within the notification area are *Clock, Volume*, and *Network*. The *Clock* option displays the time in the notification area. The *Volume* option is used to change the sound output level. The *Network* option is used to show Internet access status.

11.   On the taskbar, click the notification area sign (▲) to view hidden icons.

Did the computer have any inactive icons that displayed? [Yes | No]

12.   Right-click or tap and briefly hold an empty taskbar space and select *Properties*. At the bottom of the Taskbar tab is the Notification Area section. The Customize button is used to change the settings. Click *Customize*. Locate an icon that has the *Show Icon and Notifications* option enabled and select the down arrow by this option.

Which two other options did you see?

_____

Which option do you personally prefer for the Action Center icon? Explain your reasoning.

_____

13.   Select the *Turn System Icons On or Off* link. This is where the most common icons are located. On a desktop computer, the power system icon defaults to *off*, but on a laptop or a tablet, the default setting is on. Select *Cancel* two times to return to the taskbar properties window. Close the *Taskbar and Start Menu Properties* window.

Quick Launch Taskbar

14.   There are several ways to add an item to the taskbar. The easiest way is demonstrated here. Use the *Start* button menu > *Search Programs and Files* textbox and type **wordpad** in the textbox but do not press ⏎Enter.

15.   In the *Search Results* window, drag the `wordpad` filename to the taskbar area. The *Pin to Taskbar* message displays, and then you can release the mouse button.

16.   Any application pinned to the taskbar can be opened by simply clicking once on the icon. Click the *WordPad* icon in the taskbar.

Instructor initials: _____

17.   The WordPad application appears. Close the WordPad window.

18.   To remove the WordPad icon from the taskbar, right-click the taskbar *WordPad* option. Select the *Unpin This Program from Taskbar* option.

19.   Use the *All Programs* > *Accessories* Start menu option to access the *WordPad* application.

Is the WordPad application still available? [Yes | No]

If so, show the window to the instructor or lab assistant. If WordPad does not start, you did not select the proper option earlier. If this is the case, the WordPad application must be removed from the Recycle Bin and placed in its proper folder. The default folder is `Program Files\Windows NT\ Accessories`.

Instructor initials: _____

20. Close the WordPad application and power off the computer properly if you do not have any more labs to do.

Lab 14.10 Windows 8/8.1 Taskbar Options

Objective: To interact with and customize the Windows taskbar

Parts: Computer with Windows 8/8.1 installed

Procedure: Complete the following procedure and answer the accompanying questions.

1. Turn on the computer and verify that the operating system loads. Log on, if necessary. If the Windows Start screen is showing tiles, press the ▦ key so the traditional desktop appears.

Taskbar Options

2. Locate the taskbar on the bottom of the screen. If it is not showing, move the mouse to the bottom of the screen, and the taskbar pops up.

3. To modify or view the taskbar settings, right-click a blank area of the taskbar. A menu appears. Select the *Properties* option. The *Taskbar and Navigation Properties* window appears. (Note that you can also modify the taskbar through the *Taskbar and Navigation* Control Panel utility.)

4. Ensure that you are on the *Taskbar* tab. The options available on this screen relate to how things are shown on the taskbar. The checked items are active. To remove a check mark, click in the checkbox that already contains a check. To put a check mark in a box, click once in an empty box. Lab Table 14.16 shows the functions of the options.

   Document the current settings:
   > Lock the Taskbar [Enabled | Disabled]
   > Auto-Hide the Taskbar [Enabled | Disabled]
   > Use Small Taskbar Buttons [Enabled | Disabled]
   > Taskbar Location on Screen [Bottom | Right | Left | Top]
   > Show Windows Store Apps on the Taskbar [Enabled | Disabled]
   > Use Peek to Preview the Desktop When You Move Your Mouse to the Show Desktop Button at the End of the Taskbar [Enabled | Disabled]

LAB TABLE 14.16   Windows 8/8.1 taskbar options and functions

Option	Function
Lock the taskbar	Prevents the taskbar from being moved
Auto-hide the taskbar	Hides the taskbar until the pointer is moved to the taskbar area; use the *Keep the Taskbar on Top of Other Windows* option with this option to ensure that the taskbar is visible when selected
Taskbar location on screen	Sets whether the taskbar appears at the bottom (default), or to the left, right, or top
Taskbar buttons	Optionally combines similar labels
Use small taskbar buttons	Makes icons on the taskbar smaller
Show Windows Store apps on the taskbar	Displays downloaded apps
Use Peek to preview the desktop when you move your mouse to the Show desktop button at the end of the taskbar	Hides all open windows when the pointer is moved to the last spot past the date and time at the end of the taskbar

5. Select the notification area *Customize* button.

    Document the current settings:
    > Notification area *Customize* button options:
        > Action Center [Show Icon and Notifications | Hide Icon and Notifications | Only Show
          Notifications]
        > Network [Show Icon and Notifications | Hide Icon and Notifications | Only Show Notifications]
        > Volume [Show Icon and Notifications | Hide Icon and Notifications | Only Show Notifications]
        > Windows Explorer [Show Icon and Notifications | Hide Icon and Notifications | Only Show
          Notifications]
        > Any others?

6. Select the *Turn System Icons On or Off* link.

    Document the current settings:
    > Clock [On | Off]
    > Volume [On | Off]
    > Network [On | Off]
    > Power [On | Off]
    > Action Center [On | Off]
    > Input Indicator [On | Off]
    > Any others?

7. Return to the *Taskbar and Start Menu Properties* window by selecting *Cancel* two times.

8. Ensure that the *Auto-Hide the Taskbar* option is enabled and all other taskbar options on the *Taskbar* tab
    are disabled. Select *Apply* and then *OK*. The taskbar disappears from view. If it does not, redo this step.

9. Point to the screen where the taskbar is normally located. The taskbar appears. Open the *Notepad*
    app, using any method previously described or one of your own methods. Maximize the screen by
    clicking the maximize button, which is the center button at the top-right side of the window.

    What happened to the taskbar?

    _____

10. Move the pointer to the screen area where the taskbar is normally located.

    Did the taskbar appear? [Yes | No]

11. Close the *Notepad* window.

12. Move the pointer so that the taskbar appears. Notice how a sign (▲) marks the beginning of the
    notification area of the taskbar (to the far right on the taskbar). Three common options are *Clock,
    Volume,* and *Network*. The *Clock* option displays the time in the notification area. The Volume option
    is used to change the sound output level. The *Network* option is used to show Internet access status.

    Make the taskbar reappear. On the taskbar, select the notification area sign (▲) to show and view
    hidden icons.

    Did the computer have any inactive icons that displayed? [Yes | No]

    _____

13. Right-click or tap and briefly hold an empty taskbar space and select *Properties*. Locate and click or
    tap the *Customize* button in the notification area to change the settings. Locate an icon that has the
    Show Icon and Notifications option enabled and disable it. Verify that the changes were applied.

    Which option do you prefer for the Action Center icon? Explain your reasoning.

    _____

14. Select the *Turn System Icons On or Off* link. This is where the most common icons are located. The
    default on a desktop computer is *Off*, but on a laptop or a tablet, the default setting is *On*. Select
    Cancel two times to return to the taskbar properties window.

LAB 14

15. Select the *Navigation* tab. This tab is not in previous versions of Windows because it customizes how corners, charms, the desktop, Start screen, and apps are handled. For traditional Windows users, it is important that a technician be familiar with this configuration tab.

   Which options are currently enabled?

   Corner navigation:
   > When I Point to the Upper-Right Corner, Show the Charms [Enabled | Disabled]
   > When I Click the Upper-Left Corner, Switch Between My Recent Apps [Enabled | Disabled]
   > Replace Command Prompt with Windows PowerShell in the Menu When I Right-click the Lower-Left Corner or Press ⊞ Key+Ⓧ [Enabled | Disabled]

   Start screen:
   > When I Sign In or Close All Apps on a Screen, Go to the Desktop Instead of Start [Enabled | Disabled]
   > Show My Desktop Background on Start [Enabled | Disabled]
   > Show the Apps View Automatically When I Go to Start [Enabled | Disabled]
   > Search Everywhere Instead of Just My Apps When I Search from the Apps View [Enabled | Disabled]
   > List Desktop Apps First in the Apps View When It's Sorted By Category [Enabled | Disabled]

16. Select the *Jump Lists* tab. Jump lists allow you to right-click or tap and briefly hold on a taskbar icon and display other items related to that particular icon. For example, if you pinned a browser icon to the taskbar, the jump list for that browser icon would be included in most often visited websites. For a word processing application, the jump list would contain recently opened files.

   What is the default number of items to display in a jump list?

   _____

17. Select the *Toolbars* tab. Some of the common Windows toolbars are described in Lab Table 14.17.

LAB TABLE 14.17   Windows 8 taskbar toolbars

Toolbar	Description
Address	Holds commonly used folders, files, and websites
Links	Contains favorite website URLs
Desktop	Displays desktop items in a list format

18. Click *Cancel* to close the *Taskbar and Navigation Properties* window.

19. Right-click or tap and briefly hold on an empty space on the taskbar. Notice that toolbars can also be set from the context menu.

20. Bring the taskbar options back up and reset them to their original configuration. Refer to the answers in steps 4, 5, 6, and 15 for enabled options.

Instructor initials: _____

Lab 14.11 Windows 10 Taskbar Options

Objective: To interact with and customize the Windows taskbar

Parts: Computer with Windows 10 installed

Procedure: Complete the following procedure and answer the accompanying questions.

1. Turn on the computer and verify that the operating system loads. Log on, if necessary.

Taskbar Options

2. Locate the taskbar on the bottom of the screen. If it is not showing, move the mouse to the bottom of the screen, and the taskbar pops up.

3. To modify or view the taskbar settings, right-click a blank area of the taskbar. A menu appears. Select the *Properties* option. The *Taskbar and Start Menu Properties* window appears. (Note that you can also modify the taskbar through the *Taskbar and Navigation* Control Panel utility.)

4. Ensure that you are on the *Taskbar* tab. The options available on this screen relate to how things are shown on the taskbar. The checked items are active. To remove a check mark (that is, to not use an option), click or tap in the checkbox that already contains a check. To put a check mark in a box (enable an option), click or tap once in an empty box. Lab Table 14.18 shows the functions of the options.

   Document the current settings:
   > Lock the Taskbar [Enabled | Disabled]
   > Auto-Hide the Taskbar [Enabled | Disabled]
   > Use Small Taskbar Buttons [Enabled | Disabled]
   > Taskbar Location on Screen [Bottom | Right | Left | Top]
   > Use Peek to Preview the Desktop When You Move Your Mouse to the Show Desktop Button at the End of the Taskbar [Enabled | Disabled]

LAB TABLE 14.18   Windows 10 taskbar options and functions

Option	Function
Lock the taskbar	Prevents the taskbar from being moved
Auto-hide the taskbar	Hides the taskbar until the pointer is moved to the taskbar area; use the *Keep the Taskbar on Top of Other Windows* option with this option to ensure that the taskbar is visible when selected
Taskbar location on screen	Sets whether the taskbar appears at the bottom (default) or to the left, right, or top
Taskbar buttons	Optionally combines similar labels
Use small taskbar buttons	Makes icons on the taskbar smaller
Use Peek to Preview the desktop when you move your mouse to the Show desktop button at the end of the taskbar	Hides all open windows when the pointer is moved to the last spot past the date and time at the end of the taskbar

5. Select the notification area *Customize* button. You are redirected to the *Settings > System > Notifications & Actions* window.

   Document the current settings:
   > Show Me Tips About Windows [On | Off]
   > Show App Notifications [On | Off]
   > Show Notifications on the Lock Screen [On | Off]
   > Show Alarms, Reminders, and Incoming VoIP Calls on the Lock Screen [On | Off]
   > Hide Notifications While Presenting [On | Off]

6. If possible, select the *Select Which Icons Appear on the Taskbar* link.

   Document the current settings:
   > Always Show All Icons in the Notification Area [On | Off]
   > Network [On | Off]
   > Volume [On | Off]
   > Windows Explorer [On | Off]
   > Microsoft OneDrive [On | Off]
   > Any others?

7. Select the *back (left) arrow* beside the word *Settings* to return to the *Notifications & Actions* window.

8. If possible, select the *Turn System Icons On or Off* link.

   Document the current settings:
   > Clock [On | Off]
   > Volume [On | Off]
   > Network [On | Off]
   > Power [On | Off]
   > Input Indicator [On | Off]
   > Location [On | Off]
   > Action Center [On | Off]
   > Any others?

9. Return to the *Taskbar and Start Menu Properties* window. It might be easier to close all windows and right-click or tap and briefly hold on an empty taskbar space > select *Properties*.

10. On the *Taskbar* tab, ensure that the *Auto-Hide the Taskbar* option is enabled and all other taskbar options on the *Taskbar* tab are disabled. Select *Apply* and then *OK*. The taskbar disappears from view. If it does not, redo this step.

11. Point to the screen where the taskbar is normally located. The taskbar appears. Open the *Notepad* app using any method previously described or one of your own methods. Maximize the screen by clicking the *Maximize* button, which is the center button at the top-right side of the window.

    What happened to the taskbar?

    _____

12. Move the pointer to the screen area where the taskbar is normally located.

    Did the taskbar appear? [Yes | No]

13. Close the *Notepad* window.

14. Move the pointer to the taskbar area so that the taskbar appears. Notice that a caret sign (^) marks the beginning of the notification area of the taskbar. Three common options are Clock, Volume, and Network. The Clock option displays the time in the notification area. The Volume option is used to change the sound output level. The Network option is used to show Internet access status.

15. Make the taskbar reappear. On the taskbar, select the notification area sign (^) to show and view hidden icons.

    Did the computer have any inactive icons that displayed? [Yes | No]

    _____

16. Right-click or tap and briefly hold an empty taskbar space and select *Properties*. Locate the *Notification Area* > select *Customize* > select *Turn System Icons On or Off*.

17. Locate an icon that is currently enabled (turned on). Turn off that option.

    Which option do you prefer for the Action Center icon? Explain your reasoning.

    _____

18. Verify that the setting modification is validated by making the taskbar reappear and verifying in the notification area.

19. Close the *Settings* window and re-access the *Taskbar and Start Menu Properties* window.

20. Select the *Navigation* tab. This is was not in previous versions of Windows because it customizes corner navigation. In Windows 10 it gives you the option to use Windows PowerShell instead of the command prompt. Windows PowerShell allows commands and scripts to be executed, so it may be more useful than the command prompt environment.

    Document your current option.

    _____

21. Select the *Toolbars* tab. Some of the common Windows toolbars are described in Lab Table 14.19.

LAB TABLE 14.19   Windows 10 taskbar toolbars

Toolbar	Description
Address	Holds commonly used folders, files, and websites
Links	Contains favorite website URLs
Desktop	Displays desktop items in a list format

22. Click *Cancel* to close the *Taskbar and Start Menu* properties window.

23. Right-click or tap and briefly hold on an empty space on the taskbar. Notice that toolbars can also be set from the context menu.

24. Bring the taskbar options back up and reset them to their original configuration. Refer to the answer to questions in Steps 4, 5, 6, 8, and 20 for option settings.

Instructor initials: _____

Lab 14.12 Windows 7 File and Folder Management

Objective: To create folders, move files, and copy files to new locations

Parts: Computer with Windows 7 installed

        Flash drive

Procedure: Complete the following procedure and answer the accompanying questions.

Note: There are multiple ways to do some of the steps in this exercise. Some steps have an alternative method for doing the same procedure. For these steps, you may use either method.

1. Attach a flash drive. Ensure that it is recognizable through *Windows Explorer* and is assigned a drive letter.

   What drive letter is assigned to the flash drive?

   _____

2. Access the *Notepad* Windows accessory or app. Type the following in Notepad:

   Develop a passion for learning. If you do, you will never cease to grow.-Anthony J. D'Angelo

3. Click the *File* menu option > *Save*.

4. Select the flash drive letter in the left window panel. Note that you may have to scroll down to view it in the left window panel (see Lab Figure 14.2) and expand the *Computer* area by clicking on the arrow beside the Computer icon. Notice that the flash drive letter appears in the address bar when the flash drive is selected in the left panel. Whenever you are at the start of any drive, this is known as the root directory of that drive.

5. In the *File Name* textbox, click once, and the entire filename `*.txt` is highlighted. Simply start typing **Quote1** as the filename. Notice that the default *Save as Type* option is *Text Documents (*.txt)*. You do not have to add a file extension when you type the filename if your file is of that type. `Quote1` will be the name of the file, and it will have the extension `.txt` because of the *Save As* type of document. The full filename will be `Quote1.txt`. Click the *Save* button. If you accidentally click somewhere else and *.txt is not highlighted, simply erase all that and type **Quote1**.

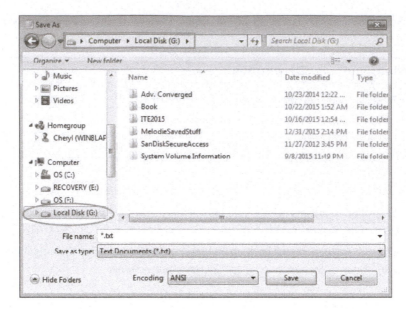

LAB FIGURE 14.2   Windows 7 Saving a Notepad file to a flash drive

6.   In Notepad, click *File > New*. Type the following:

The man who graduates today and stops learning tomorrow is uneducated the day after.-Newton D. Baker

7.   In the *File Name* textbox, save the file as Quote2, using the skills you just learned or know already.

8.   Click *File > New*. Type the following:

Don't just learn the tricks of the trade. Learn the trade.-James Bennis

9.   In the *File Name* textbox, save the file as Quote3.

10.   Click *File > New*. Type the following:

Nine-tenths of education is encouragement.-Anatole France

11.   In the *File Name* textbox, save the file as Quote4.

12.   Click *File > New*. Type the following:

Technology is dominated by two types of people:-- those who understand what they do not manage, and those who manage what they do not understand.-Source Unknown

13.   In the *File Name* textbox, save the file as Quote5.

14.   Close the *Notepad* application by clicking the *Close* button (the X) in the upper-right corner.

15.   Right-click the *Start* button and select *Open Windows Explorer*. In the left window, use the vertical scrollbar to locate and select the flash drive you are using. Remember that you might have to expand the *Computer* section to see the flash drive.

16.   In the right window panel, locate the five files you just created, called Quote1, Quote2, Quote3, Quote4, and Quote5. If the files are not there, redo the lab from the beginning.

Instructor initials: _____

Create a Folder

Note: Items preceded by the label *Alternative* denote alternative ways to perform the same steps. You may use either method, and you might consider using one method in one step and then trying it a different way on another step.

17. Ensure that the flash drive is selected in the left Windows Explorer panel. Right-click on an empty space in the right panel. Point to the *New* option and click the *Folder* option. A folder appears in the right window with the words *New Folder* highlighted. Type **LearningQuotes** and press ⏎Enter.

    Alternative: Click the *New Folder* option from the top line. A folder appears in the right window panel, with the words *New Folder* highlighted. Type **LearningQuotes** and press ⏎Enter.

On Your Own

18. Create another new folder in the root directory of the flash drive called GeneralQuotes, using the steps outlined in step 17.

Instructor initials: _____

Copy a File

19. In the right *Windows Explorer* window panel, right-click the file named Quote1. A context menu appears. Select the *Copy* option. The file is placed in a Windows utility called the Clipboard, which works in the background.

    Alternative: In the right *Windows Explorer* window panel, click once to select the file named Quote1. Click the *Organize* ribbon menu and select the *Copy* option from the drop-down menu.

20. In the right window panel, double-click the *LearningQuotes* folder. The path appears across the top of the window. The right window panel is empty because the folder does not have any files or subfolders in it yet.

21. In the right window panel, right-click and a context menu appears. Click *Paste*, and the Quote1 file appears in the right window.

    Alternative: Click the *Organize* down arrow. Select *Paste*. The Quote1 file appears in the right window.

22. In the left *Windows Explorer* window panel, click the drive option for the flash drive you are using. The path across the top of the window changes.

On Your Own

23. Copy the files named Quote2 and Quote3 from the root directory of the flash drive into the *LearningQuotes* folder, using the methods outlined in previous steps.

Copy Multiple Files

24. In the left *Windows Explorer* window, click the drive option for the media you are using.

    Alternative: In the address bar, select the left arrow to return to the root directory of the flash drive or click on the flash drive.

25. Locate the files called Quote4 and Quote5 in the right window panel.

26. In the right *Windows Explorer* window panel, click once on the Quote4 filename. The name is highlighted.

27. Hold down ⬆Shift and select the Quote5 filename. Both the Quote4 and Quote5 filenames are highlighted. *Note:* The ⬆Shift key is used to select files that are consecutive in a list (one right after the other). If you want to select files that are not consecutive, hold down the Ctrl key while selecting the files.

28. Right-click the files named Quote4 and Quote5. A context menu appears. Click the *Copy* option.

    Alternative: Click the *Organize* down arrow and select *Copy*.

29. Double-click the *GeneralQuotes* folder.

LAB 14

The path across the top changes to **X:\GeneralQuotes** (where *X:* is the drive for the media you are using), and the right window is empty because the folder does not have any files or subfolders in it yet.

30. In the right window panel, right-click an empty space, and a context menu appears. Select *Paste*. The `Quote4` and `Quote5` files appear in the right window.

Alternative: Click the *Organize* down arrow and select *Paste*. The `Quote4` and `Quote5` files appear in the right window panel.

How many folders are located in the root directory of the flash drive?

_____

How many files are in the root directory of the flash drive?

_____

How many files are in the LearningQuotes folder?

_____

How many files are in the GeneralQuotes folder?

_____

Instructor initials: _____

Copying a File from One Folder to Another

31. In the left window panel, click the drive option for the media you are using.

32. Open the *LearningQuotes* folder. The files `Quote1`, `Quote2`, and `Quote3` appear in the right window.

33. In the right window panel, right-click the `Quote3` file. From the context menu that appears, select *Copy*.

34. Open the *GeneralQuotes* folder located under the drive for the media option you are using. The `Quote4` and `Quote5` files appear in the right window panel, and the Address textbox shows `GeneralQuotes`.

35. In the right window panel, right-click an empty space, and a context menu appears. Select *Paste*, and the `Quote3`, `Quote4`, and `Quote5` files appear.

36. Using the same procedures previously described, copy the `Quote1` and `Quote2` files from the *LearningQuotes* folder into the *GeneralQuotes* folder. At the end of this step you should have three files (`Quote1`, `Quote2`, and `Quote3`) in the *LearningQuotes* folder and five files (`Quote1`, `Quote2`, `Quote3`, `Quote4`, and `Quote5`) in the *GeneralQuotes* folder.

TECH TIP

The purpose of Cut and Paste

The Cut and Paste options are used to move a file from one folder to another. When a file is cut, it no longer exists in the original folder.

Moving a File

37. Create a folder called *MyStuff* in the root directory of the drive you are using. Refer to the steps earlier in the lab if you need assistance.

38. Open the folder called *GeneralQuotes*. In the right window panel, all five files appear.

39. In the right window, click once on the `Quote1` file to highlight it. Hold down the Ctrl key and click the `Quote2` file. Both the `Quote1` and `Quote2` filenames are highlighted.

40. Right-click either the `Quote1` or `Quote2` filename (with both filenames still highlighted). A context menu appears. Select the Cut option.

    Alternative: Click the *Organize* down arrow and select *Cut*. The Cut option moves a file from one folder to another.

41. Open the *MyStuff* folder. The right window is empty because no files have been copied or moved into the *MyStuff* folder yet. In the right window panel, right-click and select Paste. The `Quote1` and `Quote2` files appear in the right window.

    Alternative: Click the *Organize* down arrow and select *Paste*. The `Quote1` and `Quote2` files appear in the right window.

42. Using the procedures just learned, move the `Quote1` file from the *LearningQuotes* folder into the *GeneralQuotes* folder.

    How many files are in the *LearningQuotes* folder?

    _____

    How many files are in the *GeneralQuotes* folder?

    _____

    How many files are in the *MyStuff* folder?

    _____

    Instructor initials: _____

Deleting Files and Folders

43. Open the *MyStuff* folder. The `Quote1` and `Quote2` files appear in the right window.

44. In the right window panel, select the `Quote1` and the `Quote2` files. Both the `Quote1` and `Quote2` filenames are highlighted.

45. Press the [Del] key on the keyboard. A message appears on the screen that asks *Are You Sure You Want to Delete These 2 Items*? Click *Yes*.

    Alternative: Click on the *Organize* down arrow and select *Delete*. A confirmation message appears. Select *Yes*.

TECH TIP

Deleted files on external media are not put in the Recycle Bin

When deleting files from an optical disc, a thumb drive, or other external media, the files are not placed in the Recycle Bin. They are deleted. When deleting files from a hard drive, the files get placed in the Recycle Bin.

46. From the flash drive root directory, select the *MyStuff* folder. The *MyStuff* folder is highlighted. Press the [Del] key on the keyboard. A message appears on the screen asking if you are sure you want to delete the *MyStuff* folder. Click the *Yes* button.

    Alternative: Click the *Organize* down arrow and select *Delete*. A confirmation message appears. Select *Yes*

    Instructor initials: _____

> **TECH TIP**
>
> **Skipping the Recycle Bin for deleted hard drive files**
>
> If you want to permanently delete a file from a hard drive without first putting the file into the Recycle Bin, hold down the ⬆Shift key while pressing the Del key.

47. Using the previously demonstrated procedures, delete the *LearningQuotes* folder, the *GeneralQuotes* folders, all files contained within each folder, as well as the original Quote1, Quote2, Quote3, Quote4, and Quote5 files.

48. Close the *Windows Explorer* window.

> **TECH TIP**
>
> **Retrieving a deleted file**
>
> To restore a file that has been accidentally placed in the Recycle Bin, open the Recycle Bin, right-click the file, and click the *Restore* option or click *Restore This Item*.

Challenge

49. Using Notepad, create three text files and save them to the flash drive in a folder called *MyFiles*.

50. On the hard drive or on external media, create a folder called *ComputerText*.

51. Copy the two of the three text files from the *MyFiles* folder into the folder called *ComputerText*.

52. Move the third text file from the *MyFiles* folder into the folder called *ComputerText*.

Instructor initials: _____

How many files are in the *MyFiles* folder?

_____

How many files are in the *ComputerText* folder?

_____

53. Permanently delete the folder called *ComputerText* and all files within it.

54. Permanently delete the folder called *MyFiles* and all files within it.

Lab 14.13 Windows 8/8.1/10 File and Folder Management

Objective:	To create folders, move files, and copy files to new locations
Parts:	Computer with Windows 8, 8.1, or 10 installed
	Flash drive
Procedure:	Complete the following procedure and answer the accompanying questions.
Note:	There are multiple ways to do some of the steps in this exercise. Some steps have an alternative method for doing the same procedure. For these steps, you may use either method.

1. Attach a flash drive. Ensure that it is recognizable through File Explorer and is assigned a drive letter.

What drive letter is assigned to the flash drive?

_____

2.   Access the *Notepad* Windows accessory or app using whatever method you like, including using the *Search* charm/function. Type the following in Notepad:

Develop a passion for learning. If you do, you will never cease to grow.-Anthony J. D'Angelo

3.   Select the *File* menu > *Save*.

4.   Select the flash drive letter in the left window panel. Note that you may have to scroll down to view it in the left window panel (see Lab Figure 14.3). Notice that the flash drive letter appears in the address bar. Whenever you are at the start of any drive, this is known as the root directory of that drive.

5.   In the *File Name* textbox, click once, and the entire filename with ***.txt** highlights. Simply start typing **Quote1** as the filename. Notice that the default *Save as Type* option is *Text Documents (*.txt)*. You do not have to add a file extension when you type a filename for a document of that file type. Quote1 will be the name of the file, and it will have the extension .txt because of the *Save as* type of document. The full filename will be Quote1.txt. Click or tap the *Save* button. If you accidentally selected somewhere else and **.txt* is not highlighted, simply erase all that and type **Quote1.**

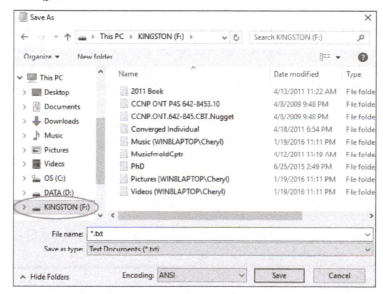

LAB FIGURE 14.3   Windows 10 Notepad flash drive selection

6.   In Notepad, select *File > New*. Type the following:

The man who graduates today and stops learning tomorrow is uneducated the day after.-Newton D. Baker

7.   In the *File Name* textbox, save the file as Quote2, using the skills you just learned or know already.

8.   Select *File > New*. Type the following:

Don't just learn the tricks of the trade. Learn the trade.-James Bennis

9.   In the *File Name* textbox, save the file as Quote3.

10. Select *File > New*. Type the following:

Nine-tenths of education is encouragement.-Anatole France

11. In the *File Name* textbox, save the file as Quote4.

12. Select *File > New*. Type the following:

    ```
    Technology is dominated by two types of people--Those who
    understand what they do not manage, and those who manage what they
    do not understand.-Source Unknown
    ```

13. In the *File Name* textbox, save the file as Quote5.

14. Close the *Notepad* application by selecting the *Close* button (the X) in the upper-right corner.

15. Open *File Explorer*. In the left window, use the vertical scrollbar to locate and select the drive media you are using. Remember that you might have to expand the *This PC* area in order to be able to see the drive.

16. In the right window, locate the five files you just created (Quote1, Quote2, Quote3, Quote4, and Quote5). If the files are not there, redo the lab from the beginning.

Instructor initials: _____

Create a Folder

Note: The label *Alternative* denotes an alternative way to perform the same steps. For these steps, you may use either method, and you might consider using one method in one step and then trying it a different way on another step.

17. Ensure that the flash drive is selected in the left *File Explorer* panel. Right-click or tap and briefly hold an empty space. Point to the *New* option and select the *Folder* option. A folder appears in the right window with the words *New Folder* highlighted. Type **LearningQuotes** and press ⏎Enter. The *LearningQuotes* folder now appears in the right window panel.

    Alternative: Select the *New Folder* option from the top corner by hovering the pointer over the top-left corner icons to locate the option that looks like a folder. Another alternative is to select the *Home* ribbon menu option and select *New Folder*. A folder appears in the right window with the words *New Folder* highlighted. Type **LearningQuotes** and press ⏎Enter.

On Your Own

18. Create another new folder in the root directory of the flash drive called *GeneralQuotes* using the procedure outlined in step 17.

Instructor initials: _____

Copy a File

19. In the right *File Explorer* window panel, right-click or tap and briefly hold the file named Quote1. A context menu appears. Select the *Copy* option. The file is placed in a Windows utility called the Clipboard, which works in the background.

    Alternative: In the right *File Explorer* window panel, select the file named Quote1 > select the *Home* menu option > select *Copy*. The file is copied to the Windows utility called the Clipboard, which works in the background.

20. In the right window panel, double-click or double-tap the *LearningQuotes* folder to open it. Notice that the address bar changes to X: (where X: is the name and drive letter of the flash drive) > LearningQuotes. The right window panel is empty because the folder does not have any files or subfolders in it yet.

21. In the right window, right-click or tap and briefly hold and a context menu appears. Select *Paste*, and the Quote1 file appears in the right window panel.

    Alternative: In the *File Explorer* window, select the *Home* menu option > select *Paste*. The Quote1 file appears in the right window panel.

22. In the left *File Explorer* window, click the option for the flash drive you are using. Note that the path changes in the address bar of File Explorer.

On Your Own

23. Copy the files named `Quote2` and `Quote3` from the root directory of the flash drive into the *LearningQuotes* folder, using the methods outlined in previous steps.

Copy Multiple Files

24. In the left *File Explorer* window panel, select the drive option for the media you are using.

    Alternative: In the address bar, select the left arrow to return to the root directory of the flash drive.

25. Locate the files called `Quote4` and `Quote5` in the right *File Explorer* window panel.

26. In the right *File Explorer* window panel, click once on the `Quote4` filename. The name is highlighted.

27. Hold down ⚹Shift and select the `Quote5` filename. Both the `Quote4` and `Quote5` filenames are highlighted.

    Note: The ⚹Shift key is used to select files that are consecutive in a list (one right after the other). If you wanted to select files that are not consecutive, hold down the Ctrl key while selecting the files.

28. Right-click or tap and briefly hold the files named `Quote4` and `Quote5`. A context menu appears. Select the *Copy* option.

    Alternative: Select the *Home* menu option > select *Copy*.

29. Double-click or double-tap the *GeneralQuotes* folder.

    The path across the top changes to $X:$ > `GeneralQuotes` (where X is the name and drive letter of the flash drive). The right window panel is empty because the folder does not have any files or subfolders in it yet.

30. In the right *File Explorer* window panel, right-click or tap and briefly hold an empty space, and a context menu appears. Select *Paste*. The `Quote4` and `Quote5` files appear in the right window panel.

    Alternative: Select the *Home* menu option > select *Paste*. The `Quote4` and `Quote5` files appear in the right window panel.

    How many folders are located in the flash drive root directory?

    _____

    How many files are in the root directory?

    _____

    How many files are in the *LearningQuotes* folder?

    _____

    How many files are in the *GeneralQuotes* folder?

    _____

Instructor initials: _____

Copying a File from One Folder to Another

31. In the left window panel, select the flash drive you are using. The flash drive root directory files and folders appear in the right window panel.

    Alternative: Select the name of the flash drive in the address bar. The flash drive root directory files and folders appear in the right window panel.

LAB 14

32. Open the *LearningQuotes* folder. The files Quote1, Quote2, and Quote3 appear in the right window panel.

33. In the right *File Explorer* window panel, right-click or tap and briefly hold the Quote3 file. From the context menu that appears, select *Copy*.

34. Open the *GeneralQuotes* folder located under the flash drive option you are using. The Quote4 and Quote5 files appear in the right *File Explorer* window panel, and the address bar shows GeneralQuotes.

35. In the right *File Explorer* window panel, right-click or tap and briefly hold an empty space and a context menu appears. Select *Paste*, and the Quote3, Quote4, and Quote5 files appear.

On Your Own

36. Using the same procedures previously described, copy the Quote1 and Quote2 files from the *LearningQuotes* folder into the *GeneralQuotes* folder. At the end of this step you should have three files (Quote1, Quote2, and Quote3) in the *LearningQuotes* folder and five files (Quote1, Quote2, Quote3, Quote4, and Quote5) in the *GeneralQuotes* folder.

37. Create a folder on the flash drive and name it *MyStuff*. Refer to the steps earlier in the exercise if you need assistance.

TECH TIP

The purpose of Cut and Paste

The Cut and Paste options move a file from one folder to another. When a file is cut, it no longer exists in the original folder.

Moving a File

38. Open the folder called *GeneralQuotes*. In the right window panel, all five files appear.

39. In the right *File Explorer* window, select the Quote1 file to highlight it. Hold down the Ctrl key and select the Quote3 file. Both the Quote1 and Quote3 filenames are highlighted. *Note*: The Ctrl key is used to select nonconsecutive files, whereas the ⬆Shift key is used to select files that are listed consecutively.

40. Right-click or tap and briefly hold either the Quote1 or Quote3 filename (both filenames are still highlighted). A context menu appears. Select the *Cut* option. The Cut option is used to move a file from one folder to another.

    Alternative: Select the *Home* menu option > select *Cut*.

41. Open the *MyStuff* folder. The right *File Explorer* window panel is empty because no files have been copied or moved into the *MyStuff* folder yet. In the right *File Explorer* window panel, right-click or tap and briefly hold > from the context menu select *Paste*. The Quote1 and Quote3 files appear in the right *File Explorer* window panel.

    Alternative: Select the *Home* menu option > select *Paste*. The Quote1 and Quote3 files appear in the right *File Explorer* window panel.

On Your Own

42. Using the procedures just learned, move the Quote1 file from the *LearningQuotes* folder into the *GeneralQuotes* folder.

    How many files are in the *GeneralQuotes* folder? _____

How many files are in the *LearningQuotes* folder?

_____

How many files are in the *MyStuff* folder?

_____

Instructor initials: _____

TECH TIP

Deleted files on external media are not put in the Recycle Bin

When deleting files from an optical disc, a flash drive, or other external media, the files are not placed in the Recycle Bin; they are deleted. When deleting files from a hard drive, the files are placed in the Recycle Bin.

Deleting Files and Folders

43. Open the *MyStuff* folder. The Quote1 and Quote3 files appear in the right window panel.

44. In the right *File Explorer* window panel, select the Quote1 and the Quote3 files. Both the Quote1 and Quote3 filenames are highlighted.

45. Press the Del key on the keyboard. A message appears on the screen asking *Are You Sure You Want to Delete These Two Items*? if you are on a flash drive. Select *Yes*.

   Alternative: Select the *Customize Quick Access Toolbar* down arrow and select *Delete*. Note that the Delete icon may have been added to the top icons, and in this case, the Customize Quick Access Toolbar option does not have to be used. If deleting from a flash drive, a confirmation message appears. Select *Yes*.

   Alternative 2: Select the *Home* menu option > select *Delete*.

46. From the flash drive root directory, select the *MyStuff* folder. The *MyStuff* folder is highlighted. Press the Del key on the keyboard. If working from a flash drive, a message appears on the screen asking *Are You Sure You Want to Permanently Delete This Folder*? Select the *Yes* button.

TECH TIP

Skipping the Recycle Bin for deleted hard drive files

If you want to permanently delete a file from a hard drive so that the file will not first be placed in the Recycle Bin, hold down the ⬆Shift key while pressing the Del key.

Instructor initials: _____

On Your Own

47. Using the previously demonstrated procedures, delete the *LearningQuotes* folder, the *GeneralQuotes* folders, all files contained within each folder, and the original Quote1, Quote2, Quote3, Quote4, and Quote5 files.

48. Close the *File Explorer* window.

LAB 14

TECH TIP

Retrieving a deleted file

To restore a file that has been accidentally placed in the Recycle Bin, open the Recycle Bin, right-click the file, and click the *Restore* option or click *Restore This Item*.

Challenge

49. Using Notepad, create three text files and save them to the external media in a folder called *MyFiles*.

50. On the flash drive, create a folder called *ComputerText*.

51. Copy two of the three text files from the *MyFiles* folder into the folder called *ComputerText*.

52. Move the third text file from the *MyFiles* folder into the folder called *ComputerText*.

Instructor initials: _____

How many files are in the *MyFiles* folder?

_____

How many files are in the *ComputerText* folder?

_____

53. Permanently delete the folder called *ComputerText* and all files within it.

54. Delete the folder called *MyFiles* and all files within it.

Lab 14.14 Windows 7 File Extension

Objective: To associate a file extension with a file type

Parts: Computer with Windows 7 installed

                Flash drive

Procedure: Complete the following procedure and answer the accompanying questions.

1. Access and launch the *Notepad* application. Type the following:

   I hear and I forget. I see and I remember. I do and I understand.-Confucius

2. Select the *File* menu > *Save*.

3. Attach a flash drive. Select the appropriate drive option for the media you are using. In the *File Name* textbox, type **Junk**. Click the *Save* button.

4. Close the *Notepad* application.

5. Right-click the *Start* button and select *Open Windows Explorer*.

6. Select the *Organize* menu option and select *Folder and Search Options*.

   Click the *View* tab. If the *Hide (File) Extensions for Known File Types* checkbox contains a check mark, click inside the checkbox to remove the check mark. If the checkbox is empty, ignore this step. Click *OK*.

7. In the left *Windows Explorer* window panel, use the vertical scrollbar to locate and select the disk media you used to save the file. Locate the Junk.txt file in the right window panel and double-click the icon.

   What happened?

   _____

8. Close the *Notepad* application.

9.   In the *Windows Explorer* window panel, right-click the file called Junk.txt. Click the *Rename* option. Ensure the entire filename, Junk.txt, is highlighted. Type **junk.abc** and press ⏎Enter. A rename warning box appears, stating *If You Change a Filename Extension, the File May Become Unusable.* It also asks *Are You Sure You Want to Change It?* Click *Yes*. Junk.txt is renamed junk.abc.

     What does the junk.abc file icon look like now?

     _____

10. Double-click the junk.abc file icon.

     What happened when you double-clicked on the junk.abc file icon?

     _____

     _____

11. Click the *Select the Program from a List of Installed Programs* radio button and click *OK*. Locate and click the *Notepad* icon. Click *OK*.

     What happened when you clicked the *OK* button?

     _____

     _____

12. In the Notepad application, select the *File* menu > *New*.

13. Type the following:

     The only real mistake is the one from which we learn nothing.-John Powell

14. Select the *File* menu > *Save As*. Ensure the disk media option that you are using is the destination. In the *File Name* textbox, type **Junk2** and click *Save*.

15. Close the *Notepad* application.

16. Using Windows Explorer, rename the Junk2.txt file to Junk2.abc. A rename warning box appears stating *If You Change a Filename Extension, the File May Become Unusable.* It also asks *Are You Sure You Want to Change It?* Click *Yes*. Notice the file icon after the change.

     How is the icon different from before?

     _____

     _____

17. Double-click the Junk2.abc icon.

     What happened when you double-clicked the Junk2.abc icon?

     _____

     Instructor initials: _____

18. Close *Notepad*. Delete both files.

Lab 14.15 Windows 8/8.1/10 File Extension

Objective: To associate a file extension with a file type

Parts: Computer with Windows 8, 8.1, or 10 installed

                Flash drive

Procedure: Complete the following procedure and answer the accompanying questions.

1.   Access and launch the *Notepad* application. Type the following:

     I hear and I forget. I see and I remember. I do and I understand.-Confucius

2.   Select the *File* menu > *Save*.

3.   Attach a flash drive. Select the appropriate drive option for the media you are using. In the *File Name* textbox, type `Junk`. Click the *Save* button.

4.   Close the *Notepad* application.

5.   Right-click the *Start* button and select *File Explorer*.

6.   Select the *View* ribbon menu option, click on the *Options* down arrow and select *Change Folder and Search Options*.

Click the *View* tab. If the *Hide (File) Extensions for Known File Types* checkbox contains a check mark, click inside the checkbox to remove the check mark. If the checkbox is empty, ignore this step. Click *OK*.

7.   In the left *File Explorer* window panel, use the vertical scrollbar to locate and select the disk media you used to save the file. Locate the `Junk.txt` file in the right window panel and double-click the icon.

What happened?

_____

8.   Close the *Notepad* appli*cation.*

9.   *In the right* File Explorer window panel, right-click the file called `Junk.txt`. Click the *Rename* option. Ensure the entire filename, `Junk.txt`, is highlighted. Type `junk.abc` and press ⏎Enter. A rename warning box appears stating that, *If You Change a Filename Extension, the File May Become Unusable.* It also asks *Are You Sure You Want to Change It?* Click *Yes.* `Junk.txt` is renamed `junk.abc`.

What does the `junk.abc` file icon look like now?

_____

10.   Double-click the `junk.abc` file icon.

What happened when you double-clicked on the `junk.abc` file icon?

_____

11.   Click the *More Options* link. Locate and click the *Notepad* icon. Click *OK* (Windows 10 only).

What happened when you selected Notepad?

_____

_____

12.   In the Notepad application, select the *File* menu > *New*.

13.   Type the following:

The only real mistake is the one from which we learn nothing.-John Powell

14.   Select the *File* menu option and click *Save As*. Ensure that the disk media option that you are using is the destination. In the *File Name* textbox, type `Junk2` and click *Save*.

15.   Close the *Notepad* application.

16.   Using File Explorer, rename the `Junk2.txt` file to `Junk2.abc`. A rename warning box appears, stating *If You Change a Filename Extension, the File May Become Unusable.* It also asks *Are You Sure You Want to Change It?* Click *Yes*. Notice the file icon after the change.

How is the icon different from before?

_____

17.   Double-click the `Junk2.abc` icon.

What happened when you double-clicked the `Junk2.abc` icon?

_____

Instructor initials: _____

18. Select *Notepad* from the dialog box.

19. Close *Notepad*. Delete both files.

Lab 14.16 Windows 7/8//10 Attributes, Compression, and Encryption

Objective: To identify and set file and folder attributes, compression, and encryption

Parts: Computer with Windows 7, 8, 8.1, 10 installed

     Ability to save a file to an NTFS partition

Note: The compression and encryption portions of this exercise require an NTFS partition.

Procedure: Complete the following procedure and answer the accompanying questions.

Managing File Attributes

1. Access and open the *Notepad* application. Type the following:

   Aim for success, not perfection.-Dr. David M. Burns

2. Select the *File* menu > *Save*. In the *Windows Explorer/File Explorer* left pane, select a location such as *Documents* or *Desktop*. In the *File Name* textbox, replace the highlighted `*.txt` by typing **Attribute File** and select *Save*.

   Document which folder holds the file.

   _____

3. Close the *Notepad* application.

4. Open *Window Explorer* (Windows 7)/*File Explorer* (Windows 8, 8.1, or 10).

5. In the left pane, select the option where you stored the file. The `Attribute File` file should be listed in the right pane. If not, redo the previous steps to create the file.

6. Select (but do not open) the `Attribute File` file in the right pane.

7. In Windows 7, select the *Organize* menu option and select *Properties*. The same results can be obtained by right-clicking or tapping and briefly holding on the filename and selecting *Properties*.

   In Windows 8/8.1/10, select the *Home* menu option > select *Properties*. The same results can be obtained by right-clicking or tapping and briefly holding on the filename and selecting *Properties*.

   The file attributes are listed at the bottom. Additional attributes can be viewed for a file stored on an NTFS partition by clicking the *Advanced* button. Note that the *Advanced* button is not available on a flash drive that uses a file system other than NTFS.

   What file attributes are listed for the `Attribute File` file?

   _____

   _____

   _____

   What file attribute is enabled by default?

   _____

   _____

   _____

8. When the Archive attribute (File Is Ready for Archiving) is enabled, the file is selected for backup by default. Backup applications use this attribute when backing up data. On the main *Attribute File Properties* window (*General* tab), select (enable) the *Read-Only Attribute* checkbox and click *OK*.

LAB 14

9. Open the *Attribute File* filename. The application opens with the typed text shown. Add the following to the quote:

    ```
    Never give up your right to be wrong, because then you will lose
    the ability to learn new things and move forward with your life.-
    David M. Burns
    ```

10. Select the *File* menu option and select *Save*. With the same name listed (do not change it), click the *Save* button.

    What happens when the *Save* option is chosen?

    _____

    _____

11. Select *Yes > OK > Cancel* to return to the changed document, open in Notepad.

12. Click the *Close* button in the Notepad window. When asked if you want to save the changes, select *Don't Save*. The read-only attribute prevents the file from being changed.

13. In the *Windows Explorer/File Explorer* window, right-click or tap and briefly hold the *Attribute File* filename > select *Properties*. Select the *Hidden* file attribute checkbox > select *OK*.

    What happens to the *Attribute File* filename in Windows Explorer/File Explorer?

    _____

    _____

14. In Windows 7 in the *Windows Explorer* window, select the *Organize > Folder and Search Options > View* tab *> Hidden Files and Folders > Show Hidden Files, Folders, and Drives* radio button. This option is used to see files or folders that have the hidden attribute set or enabled. To make this change applicable to all folders, click the *Apply to Folders* button. A Folder Views dialog box appears, stating that the change will occur the next time the folder is opened. Click *Yes* > click *OK*.

    In Windows 8/8.1/10 in the *File Explorer* window, select the *View* menu option > select *Options* > select *Change Folder and Search Option*s *> View* tab.

    Which one of the following options is enabled? [Don't Show Hidden Files, Folders, or Drives | Show Hidden Files, Folders, and Drives]

    _____

15. Select (enable) the *Show Hidden Files, Folders, and Drives* radio button or ensure that it is enabled. This option is used to see files or folders that have the hidden attribute set or enabled.

    Note: If you want to make this change applicable to all folders, you can select the *Apply to Folders* button, but you do not do this in this lab.

    Does the `Attribute File` file appear in the Windows Explorer/File Explorer right pane? [Yes | No]

    If the file does not reappear, press the F5 key to refresh the window, click the *Refresh Documents* icon, which is a curved arrow at the end of the address bar, or select the *Refresh* option from the *View* menu.

    How does the file icon differ from before? Note that you may need to create another text file just to see the difference.

    _____

16. In Windows 7 *Windows Explorer*, click the *Change Your View* icon, which contains a down arrow on the right side of the menu bar > select *Small Icons*.

    In Windows 8/8.1/10 *File Explorer*, select the *View* menu option > select *Small Icons*.

    How do the icons now appear in the Windows Explorer/File Explorer right pane?

    _____

17. In Windows 7, click the *Change Your View* menu option > select *List*.

In Windows 8/8.1/10, select the *View* menu option > select *List*.

How does the *Attribute File* now appear in the right pane?

_____

18. In Windows 7, select the *Change Your View* menu option > *Details*.

In Windows 8/10, select the *View* menu option > *Details*.

Why do you think that a technician would prefer the Details option over any other view?

_____

_____

Instructor initials: _____

19. Delete the `Attribute File` file.

Did either the hidden or read-only attribute stop the `Attribute File` file from being deleted?
[Yes | No]

20. Put the folder option back to the original setting (see step 14).

Using Compression

Note: The disk volume must have an NTFS file system on it in order for you to complete this section. To check the file system, in Windows Explorer/File Explorer open *Computer* (Windows 7)/*This PC* (Windows 8/8.1/10). Right-click or tap and briefly hold the hard drive volume that contains Windows and select *Properties*. In the Properties window near the top, the file system is listed.

21. Create a WordPad file called `CompressionFile` and save it in the *Documents* folder on the hard drive. If necessary, refer to a previous exercise for steps. The text to be placed in the file follows:

The most successful career must show a waste of strength that might have removed mountains, and the most unsuccessful is not that of the man who is taken unprepared, but of him who has prepared and is never taken. On a tragedy of that kind, our national morality is duly silent.-Edward M. Forster

22. Copy this text repeatedly in the document until you have four pages of text. You could also copy a picture from the Internet, use the Windows *Snipping Tool* accessory to make screen captures and windows captures that are pasted into the document, and use different kinds of fonts and texts to make the document of decent size so this step will work. (*Note*: If you do not make the file size large enough, compression will not occur.)

23. Close the *WordPad* application window. Using Windows Explorer/File Explorer, locate the `CompressionFile` file. (*Note*: You might need to change the view or get the properties of the file to answer the question that follows.)

What is the file size of the `CompressionFile` file?

_____

24. Right-click or tap and briefly hold on the *CompressionFile* and select *Properties*. Select the *Advanced* button. In the Advanced Attributes dialog box, locate the *Compress or Encrypt Attributes* section.

25. Select (enable) the *Compress Contents to Save Disk Space* checkbox. This option is used to compress a file or folder. Select the *OK* button > select *OK* again. Keep in mind that to save disk space efficiently, the file needs to be at least 4 kB of disk space.

26. Using *Windows Explorer/File Explorer*, locate the file called `CompressionFile` and open the file's *Properties* window again.

LAB 14

27. On the *General* tab, notice the *Size* and *Size on Disk* numbers. If the numbers are the same, you don't have enough information in the file to compress it. Copy more information into it, make sure you use graphics to increase the size, or recopy and paste the information you have to increase the size of the file so it can be compressed. After compression occurs, you can verify through the *General* tab. Leave this window open to show the instructor the reduction.

Instructor initials: _____

Document the file size.

_____

What visual clue do you have in Windows Explorer/File Explorer that a file is compressed?

_____

28. Click *OK* to close the *CompressionFile Properties* window.

Enabling Encryption

Note: The disk volume must have an NTFS file system on it for you to complete this section.

29. Create a file called `EncryptionFile` by using Notepad or WordPad and save it to *Documents*. If necessary, refer to a previous exercise for steps. Enter the following text in the file:

    I do not fear computers. I fear the lack of them.-Isaac Asimov

30. Close the *Notepad/WordPad* application window. Using *Windows Explorer/File Explorer*, locate the file named `EncryptionFile`.

    What is the current size of `EncryptionFile`?

_____

31. Right-click or tap and briefly hold on the filename (`EncryptionFile`) > *select Properties* > *Advanced* button. In the Advanced Attributes dialog box, locate the *Compress or Encrypt Attributes* section. Select (enable) the *Encrypt Contents to Secure Data* checkbox, the option used to encrypt a file or folder. (*Note*: The checkbox may not be available on some Windows Home versions. See the Tech Tip.) Click *OK* twice. A dialog box appears, asking if you want to encrypt the file and the parent file or encrypt only the file. Select the *Encrypt the File Only* radio button > *OK*.

TECH TIP

Limited encryption support on Home versions

Windows Home versions do not fully support encrypting files. In these versions, the `cipher` command can be used at the command prompt to decrypt files, to modify an encrypted file, and to copy an encrypted file to the computer.

32. The first time that you select to encrypt a file, a prompt appears, telling you that you should back up the recovery key. This is *extremely* important. If the encryption key used to encrypt your file ever has an issue, you will not be able to get into your file again. For now, ignore the message, and later you will see how to access it and back it up.

    What is the size of the `Encryption File` file after encryption?

_____

Instructor initials: _____

Backing Up the File Encryption Certificate and Key

33. Open *Control Panel*. In the *Search Control Panel* textbox, type **encrypt** and select the *Manage File Encryption Certificates* link > *Next* > ensure that the *Use This Certificate* radio button is selected > *Next* > in the *Back Up the Certificate and Key* window, ensure that the *Back Up the Certificate and Key Now* radio button is selected (enabled) > use the *Browse* button to specify a backup location that is on some type of removable media and type in a filename so you will know it is your encryption certificate > select *Save*. In the *Password* and *Confirm Password* textboxes, issue a password that you won't forget > *Next* > Do not select any files within the *Update Your Previously Encrypted Files* window > *Next* > *Close*.

Instructor initials: _____

> **TECH TIP**
>
> **Recovering EFS-protected files**
>
> If your encryption key ever becomes corrupted or you move a drive that has encrypted files to another computer, it is possible to recover it if you have that encryption certificate and key backed up. Use the following steps:
>
> **Step 1.** Enter the `certmgr.msc` command from the search textbox or from a command prompt.
>
> **Step 2.** In the left window, select *Personal*.
>
> **Step 3.** From the *Action* menu, select *All Tasks* > *Import* > *Next* > *Browse* > in the drop-down menu to the right of the *File Name* textbox, select *Personal Information Exchange (*.pfx; *.p12)* and browse to where the encryption certificate and key are located in the external media. Select the *File* > *Open* button > *Next* > in the *Password* textbox, type the password (that you were never supposed to forget!) > select the checkbox *Mark This key As Exportable. This Will Allow You to Back Up or Transport Your Keys at a Later Time* > leave the *Include All Extended Properties* textbox enabled > *Next* > on the certificate store window click *Next* > *Finish*. A message appears that it was successful.

34. Permanently delete the `CompressionFile` file.

35. Permanently delete the `EncryptionFile` file.

Lab 14.17 Using `regedit` in Windows 7/8/8.1/10

Objective:	To become familiar with the `regedit` registry-editing utility
Parts:	Computer with Windows 7, 8, 8.1, or 10 installed and administrator rights
	Flash drive
Procedure:	Complete the following procedure and answer the accompanying questions.
Notes:	`regedit` is a utility used for editing the Windows registry. With `regedit`, you can view existing registry settings, modify registry settings values, or create new registry entries to change or enhance the way Windows operates. In this lab, you will use `regedit` to view the system BIOS and component information on your computer.
Caution:	Editing the registry can cause your computer to run erratically or not run at all! When performing any registry editing, follow all directions carefully, including spelling, syntax use, and so on. Failure to do so may cause your computer to fail!

Viewing Registry Information

1.   In Windows 7, in the Search Programs and Files textbox, type **regedit** > in the *Programs* section, click the *Regedit > Yes* button, if necessary. The regedit utility opens.

In Windows 8/8.1/10, search for *regedit* using the *Search* charm or any other search method > open the Windows Registry Editor.

2.   In the left Registry Editor window, expand Hkey_Local_Machine, Hardware, and Description by selecting the arrow located to the left of each name. Select the *System* option located under *Description*. In the right window, the system BIOS and component information displays.

What is the system BIOS version?

_____

Who is the manufacturer of the system BIOS?

_____

What values are listed in the *Component Information* option?

_____

Exporting and Importing a Registry Section

3.   regedit can be used to back up and restore part or all of the registry. To illustrate this point, a portion of the registry will be exported to disk and then imported into the registry. Ensure that Hkey_Local_Machine\Hardware\Description\System is still selected in the left Registry Editor window. (Ensure that the word *System* is selected under *Description*.)

4.   Select the *File* menu option and choose *Export*. The Export Registry File window opens.

5.   Attach a flash drive. Select the down arrow in the *Save In* textbox and select the appropriate drive option for the flash drive you are using. In the *File Name* textbox, type **Registry System Section** and select *Save*. The specific registry key is saved to disk.

6.   To restore the registry (or a portion of it, as in this exercise), select the *File* menu option and select *Import*. The screen should list the file located on the external disk media, but if it does not, select the appropriate drive letter option for the disk media you are using.

7.   Select the *Registry System Section* filename and click the *Open* button. A message appears when the section is successfully inserted into the registry. Show this message to the instructor or lab assistant.

Instructor initials: _____

8.   Close the regedit utility.

Lab 14.18 Windows 7 Backup Tool

Objective: To be able to use the Backup tool provided with Windows 7

Parts: Windows 7 computer and administrator rights

Flash drive with 1 GB of free space (2 GB drive is recommended)

Procedure: Complete the following procedure and answer the accompanying questions.

Notes: This lab does not back up the hard drive but simply illustrates the concept of using the Backup tool.

1.   Power on the computer and log on using a user ID and password that has administrator rights.

2.   Use the *Windows Help and Support* tool to answer the following questions. Use the key terms **backup tool** to get started.

Is Shadow Copies of Shared Folders a feature found in Windows 7? [Yes | No]

What is the purpose of the Shadow Copies of Shared Folders feature?

_____

_____

What command is used to create and manage system image backups for Windows 7 computers?

_____

What are four Windows-based backup tools?

_____

_____

List one recommended location for storing a backup.

_____

_____

_____

If a flash drive is to be used, what is the minimum amount of free space that must be available on that drive?

_____

3.   Copy at least one file to the Recycle bin.

4.   Insert a flash drive. Ensure that the drive is visible in Windows Explorer.

5.   Using Windows Explorer, create a folder called Backup on the flash drive.

6.   Locate the *System and Security* Control Panel and select the *Backup and Restore* link.

7.   If a backup has not been performed before, you need to select the *Set up Backup* link. If a backup has been performed before, select the *Change Settings* link.

   Note: You may need to use the *Refresh* button to be able to see the flash drive. If the flash drive does not appear, ensure that it is viewable through Windows and has more than 1 GB of free space available. Select the appropriate drive letter. Click Next.

   Select the *Let Me Choose* radio button. Click *Next*. If the system is not set up to do the backup on demand, you may have to click the *Change Schedule* link to modify it so the backup can be done. Then select the *$Recycle Bin* checkbox. Note that you may have to expand the *Computer* option as well as the C: drive in order to locate this checkbox. Click *Next*. Select the Save *Settings and Run Backup* button.

8.   While the backup is occurring, select the *View Details* button.

   Why do you think a technician would use this option?

   _____

   _____

   Were you surprised at the time it took to perform the backup?

   _____

Instructor initials: _____

9.   When the backup is complete, click the *Close* button, delete the backup from the flash drive, eject the flash drive and give it to the instructor, if necessary, and close all windows.

LAB 14

Lab 14.19 Windows 8/8.1 File History Utility

Objective: To explore backing up data using the Windows File History utility

Parts: Computer with Windows 8/8.1 installed

                  Flash drive

Procedure: Complete the following procedure and answer the accompanying questions.

1.   Power on the computer and log in to Windows.

2.   Attach the flash drive to the computer.

     Which drive letter is assigned to the flash drive?

     _____

3.   Search by typing in the words **file history** in the *Search* textbox. Select *File History Settings* from the resulting search list.

4.   Ensure that the *File History* option is turned *On*.

5.   If the flash drive is not shown as the drive to back up personal files, use the *Select a Drive* or *Select a Different Drive* link to select the drive.

6.   Notice that you cannot select what is backed up. In Windows 8.1, sentences at the top of the screen describe what information is automatically backed up. Also notice that this backup occurs automatically (meaning you need to leave that drive attached). Select the *Back Up Now* button.

     How much space is the backup going to take?

     _____

7.   Open *File Explorer* and access the flash drive.

     What is the name of the file that contains the backed up data?

     `FileHistory`

8.   Return to the *File History Settings* window and set the option to *Off*.

9.   Return to *File Explorer* and access the flash drive. Right-click or tap and briefly hold on the *FileHistory* folder > select *Delete* > *Yes*.

     Do you think most people will use this option? Why or why not?

     _____

Lab 14.20 Windows 10 File History Utility

Objective: To explore backing up data using the Windows File History utility

Parts: Computer with Windows 10 installed

                  Flash drive

Procedure: Complete the following procedure and answer the accompanying questions.

1.   Power on the computer and log in to Windows.

2.   Attach the flash drive to the computer.

     Which drive letter is assigned to the flash drive?

     _____

3.   Search by typing in the words **file history** in the *Search* textbox. Select *File History Settings* from the resulting search list.

4.   Select the + *Add a Drive* option. Note that if this option has been used before, you can simply turn on the *Automatically Backup My Files* option and select the *More Options* link to select what files/folders are backed up, how often to back up the files, and how long to keep the backups.

5. After all settings have been configured, click the *Back Up Now* button.

   How much space is the backup going to take?

   _____

6. Open *File Explorer* and access the flash drive.

   What is the name of the file that contains the backed-up data?

   `FileHistory`

7. Return to the *File History Settings* window and set the option to *Off*.

8. Return to *File Explorer* and access the flash drive. Right-click or tap and briefly hold on the *FileHistory* folder > select *Delete* > *Yes*.

   Do you think most people will use this option? Why or why not?

   _____

Lab 14.21 Creating a Windows 7 System Repair Disc

Objective: To create a system repair disc in the Windows 7 environment

Parts: Computer with Windows 7 installed

                Blank DVD or 8 GB+ flash drive

Procedure: Complete the following procedure and answer the accompanying questions.

1. Boot the computer and access the system BIOS. Ensure that the system is set to boot first from the drive you are using.

2. Save the settings and exit BIOS. Boot into Windows.

3. Click the *Start* button > *Control Panel* > *System and Security* link > *Backup and Restore* > *Create a System Repair Disc* link.

4. Ensure that the appropriate media is ready (blank DVD or 8 GB flash drive). Select the appropriate media > *Next*.

5. Click the *Create Disc* button.

   How often do you think a home user should create a system repair disc?

   _____

   _____

   When the system repair disc is complete, what is the recommended label for the repair disc?

   _____

   What is the difference between a system repair disc and a system image disc?

   _____

   _____

6. After the disc/drive has been created, click the *Close* button followed by *OK*.

Using the System Repair Disc/Drive

7. After labeling the system repair disc, re-insert it into the drive or ensure that the System Repair drive is attached.

8. Power down the computer.

9. Power on the computer using the power button. A prompt may appear that tells you to press any key to start the computer from a CD or DVD. Press any key to boot from the system repair disc.

10. Select the appropriate language and keyboard settings. Click Next.

11. From this screen, you can either use Windows recovery tools or restore the system from a previously created system image. For this exercise, select the radio button that begins *Use Recovery Tools*, ensure that the correct operating system is highlighted, and click *Next*.

List three options from the resulting menu.

_____

_____

Instructor initials: _____

Lab 14.22 Creating a Windows 7 System Image Disc

Objective: To create a system image disc in the Windows 7 environment

Parts: Computer with Windows 7 that has an optical drive installed

                 Blank DVD

Procedure: Complete the following procedure and answer the accompanying questions.

1. Boot the computer and access the system BIOS. Ensure that the system is set to boot from the optical drive first.

2. Save the settings and exit BIOS. Boot into Windows 7.

3. Click the *Start* button > *Control Panel* > *System and Security* link > *Backup and Restore* > *Create a System Image* link.

What three options are available?

_____

4. Determine from the instructor or lab assistant the appropriate storage medium and select the appropriate radio button. Click *Next*.

5. Select at least the operating system to back up.

What is the amount of space required to do the system image?

_____

6. Click *Next*. Optionally insert media as directed and click *Start Backup*.

While the image is being created, what option(s) do you have on the screen?

_____

Instructor initials: _____

(Optional) Using the System Image Disc

7. To use the system image disc:
   > You can use the Recovery Control Panel.
   > You can restore, starting from a Windows 7 installation disc or system repair disk, using the following steps once you boot from the disc: A prompt may appear that tells you to press any key to start the computer from a CD or DVD. Press any key to boot from the system repair disc or Windows 7 installation disc. Select the appropriate language and keyboard settings. Click Next. If you booted from a system recovery disc, select the radio button for a system repair disc and click Next. If you booted from the Windows installation disc, select *Repair Your Computer*.
   > Finally, you can do the following if you don't have a Windows 7 installation disc or a system repair disc. Reboot the computer, and as the computer is booting press (F8) to access the Windows Advanced Boot Options screen. Select *Repair Your Computer*, select the appropriate keyboard, and click *Next*. Select a username, type a password, and click *OK*. Select *Image Recovery* and follow the instructions.

8. For this lab, use the Recovery Control Panel because the computer is working. Click the *Start* button and type **recovery** in the *Search Programs and Files* textbox.

9.   Select *Recovery* from the resulting list.

Document the path through Control Panel utilities to reach this option.

_____

10.   Select the *Advanced Recovery Methods* link. Select the *Use a System Image You Created Earlier to Recover Your Computer* option. Follow the instructions on the screen to recovery your computer.

Instructor initials: _____

Lab 14.23 Creating a Windows 8/8.1/10 System Recovery Drive

Objective: To create a system recovery drive in the Windows 8/8.1/10 environment

Parts: Computer with Windows 8, 8.1, or 10 installed

Flash drive or external drive (whose entire contents will be erased)

Procedure: Complete the following procedure and answer the accompanying questions.

1.   Boot the computer and log in to Windows.

2.   Optionally, attach external media if that is what is being used. Otherwise, a second drive should be available. Note that the amount of space needed on the external media or second hard drive depends on the size of drive (and possibly the size of the recovery partition) of the computer being backed up.

How much space is used on the drive being backed up?

_____

3.   Use the *Search* function to search on the words `recovery drive`. Select the *Create a Recovery Drive* in the resulting search list > *Yes*.

4.   Optionally, ensure the *Copy the Recovery Partition from the PC to the Recovery Drive* option is selected > *Next*.

5.   Select the appropriate media in the *Available Drive(s)* list > *Next* > *Create*.

While the image is being created, what option(s) do you have on the screen?

_____

How long did the backup take to finish?

_____

Instructor initials: _____

6.   Select *Finish*.

(Optional) Using the System Recovery Drive in Windows 8.1

7.   To use the system recovery drive, access the BIOS/UEFI BIOS and ensure that the computer is configured to boot from the USB drive.

8.   Attach the USB drive to the computer.

9.   Boot the computer from the USB drive. The *Windows Boot Manager* window appears with the following choices:

1. Insert your Windows installation disc and restart your computer.

2. Choose your language settings and then click *Next*.

3. Click *Repair Your Computer*.

Instructor initials: _____

10.   You do not have to go any further because the computer is not broken. Return the system to the original configuration.

15 Introduction to Scripting Labs

Lab 15.1 Using Basic Commands from a Command Prompt

Objective: To execute basic commands at a command prompt

Parts: A Windows-based computer with command prompt access

                The ability to save a file to the hard drive *or* access to a flash drive

Procedure: Complete the following procedure and answer the accompanying questions.

Note: For each step requiring a typed command, the ⏎Enter key must be pressed to execute the command. This instruction will *not* be given with each step.

1. Power on the computer and log on, if necessary.

2. Create a file in Notepad called `LadyVOLS.txt` and save the file to the flash drive. Here is some text for your file:

   This is a fine mess you've gotten me into, Ollie.

   Go get that Earth creature and bring back the Uranium Pew36 Space Modulator.

   Can you sing "Rocky Top"?

   What drive letter does the flash drive use?

   _____

3. Close Notepad. This file will be used later in the lab.

4. Exit to a command prompt using the directions that follow, based on the particular operating system you are using:
   > Windows 7: Use the *Search programs and files* textbox and type **cmd** > press ⏎Enter.
   > Windows 8, use the Search charm and type **command** > select the *Command Prompt* option from the resulting list.
   > Windows 10, search for **command** > select the *Command Prompt* option from the resulting list.

   Does a prompt display? [Yes | No]

   If not and you followed every step correctly, contact your instructor.

   What prompt displays on the screen? This is the folder (directory) from which you are starting.

   _____

5. At the command prompt, type the following:

    cd

    The prompt changes to C:\>. If a message appears, stating this is an invalid command or an invalid directory, you made a typing error. If you suspect an error, verify that the backslash is after cd and that there are no extra spaces. The backslash starts from the left side and goes down to the right (\). Other commands use a forward slash (/).

    cd is the command to change the directory, which tells the operating system to go to a different directory in the tree structure. The \ after the **cd** command tells the operating system to go to the root directory. An alternative way of typing this command is **cd **, with a space between the **cd** command and the backslash. There are usually different ways to use every command from a prompt. The **cd** or **cd ** command allows you to return to the root directory at any time.

6. At the command prompt, type the following:

    dir

    A list of files and directories appears. In this list, next to each filename, you see an extension to the right of the filename, the file size, and the file creation date. File extensions give clues about which application created the file. Each directory has a <DIR> entry to the right of the name.

    List two files, including their extensions, and one directory shown on the screen. Using your own knowledge or the Internet, try to determine the application that created each file and write that application (if found) beside the filename. Document your findings in Lab Table 15.1.

LAB TABLE 15.1   Files and directory

Information displayed	Name	Application
File		
File		
Directory		N/A

7. When the number of files shown exceeds what can display on the screen, the files quickly scroll off the screen until all files finish displaying. The **DIR** command has a switch that controls this scrolling. A command switch begins with a forward slash and enhances or changes the way a command performs. At the command prompt, type **dir /p**.

    After looking at the data on the screen, press ⏎Enter again. Continue pressing ⏎Enter until the prompt reappears. The /p switch when used with the dir command tells the operating system to display the files one page at a time.

8. At the prompt, type the following:

    dir /w

    What is the function of the /w switch?

    _____

9. At the prompt, type **dir /p**. The information shows one page at a time. If there were more than one page of files and directories, you would press any key to see another page of information.

10. Multiple switches can be used with a command. At the prompt, type the following command:

    dir /w/l

    Using the **dir** command with the **/w** and **/l** switches causes files to display in a wide format and displays the information in lowercase.

11. Different versions of Windows have documentation with online help. To find out the operating system version loaded on the computer, type **ver**.

What company is the operating system manufacturer, and what version is used on the computer?

_____

12. At the prompt, type **dir /? | more**. To create the vertical bar used in the command, hold down the ⟨⬆Shift⟩ key and, while keeping it held down, press the key directly above the ⟨⏎Enter⟩ key, which is the same key as the backslash. A short explanation of the command appears, followed by the command syntax (that is, the instructions or rules for how the command is to be typed). A technician needs to understand command syntax to determine what commands to type when unfamiliar with a command. The | symbol is called the pipe symbol. The | more command tells the operating system to display the output one page at a time. Perform the following activity and then press any key to continue until you return to a prompt.

    Based on the output, list two switches that can be used with the dir command.

    _____

    _____

    _____

    _____

    Write one switch that can be used with the dir command along with a short explanation of its purpose.

    _____

13. Type **cd\XXXXX**, where the **XXXXX** is replaced by the name of the directory you wrote as the answer to the question in step 6. For example, if you wrote the directory name *Windows*, you would type **cd\Windows** at the prompt. Note that if you get an *Access Is Denied* message, simply use the Windows directory. The prompt changes to the name of the directory (folder), such as **C:\Windows>**.

14. Type the following command:

    dir a*.*

    The **a*.*** is not a switch. This command is directing the operating system to list all files or subdirectories that start with the letter A. The ***.*** part means all files. The directory you chose may not have any files or subdirectories that start with the letter A. If this occurs, the operating system displays the message File not found. The * is known as a wildcard. A wildcard substitutes for one or more characters. The first asterisk (*) is the wildcard for any name of a file. The second asterisk is the wildcard for any extension.

    Does the operating system list any files or subdirectories that start with the letter A? If so, write one of them in the following space. If not, did the operating system let you know this? If so, write the message displayed.

    _____

    _____

15. Type the following command:

    cd..

    The .. tells the operating system to move back (or up, if you think about the structure in Windows Explorer/File Explorer) one directory in the directory structure. Because you are one level down (because of typing the **cd\XXXXX** command), this command returns you to the root directory.

    If you want to display a list of all files or directories in the root directory that start with the letter C, what command would you type? Try the command you think is right on the computer to see if it works.

    _____

    Do any files or directories start with the letter C? If so, write at least one of them down.

    _____

On Your Own

16a. Change to the directory that contains Windows. The directory name is normally *Windows*. If you cannot determine what directory contains Windows, use the **dir** command again. Try repeating the lab until it is easier to do this step.

Write the command you used to do this.

_____

List two Windows files that begin with the letter D.

_____

_____

16b. Return to the root directory.

Write the command you used.

_____

17. At the prompt, access the flash drive. To do this, type the drive letter assigned to the flash drive (see the answer to the question in step 2), followed by a colon, and then press the ⏎Enter key. If a flash drive was assigned the letter G, type **G:** and press ⏎Enter. Whenever directions are given where the drive letter is not known, such as in this lab, *X*: (italicized *X* and then a colon) is used. You always need to substitute your drive letter for *X*:. Type the following command, based on your own drive letter:

X:

Notice that the prompt changes to the drive letter of the flash drive. If it does not, you might have forgotten to press ⏎Enter or may not have replaced the *X* with your own drive letter, documented in step 2.

18. From the root directory, the **type** command allows you to view the text file you just created. Enter the following command:

type ladyvols.txt

What is the result of using the **type** command?

_____

Can you edit and change the file by using this command? [Yes | No]

Have a classmate verify your file displays and sign his or her name beside your answer.

Classmate's printed name: _____

Classmate's signature: _____

19. The **del** command is used to delete files. From the root directory, delete the file you just created by using the following command:

del ladyvols.txt

Why do you think you did not have to type **del x:\ladyvols.txt** (the full path) in this last step?

_____

_____

Lab 15.2 Using the `copy`, `md`, `del`, and `rd` Commands

Objective: To correctly use the `copy`, `md`, `del`, and `rd` commands

Parts: Windows computer with command prompt access

Flash drive

Procedure: Complete the following procedure and answer the accompanying questions.

Notes: For each step requiring a typed command, the ⏎Enter key must be pressed to execute the command. This instruction will *not* be given with each step.

The directions given in the previous command prompt lab are not repeated. If you have trouble with this lab, it is recommended that you return to and do Lab 15.1 until you are proficient with the concepts, and then do this lab again.

It is critical that you follow directions. For example, if the lab directs you to make a directory called SubFolder1 and use the command md subfolder1, a common mistake is for students to type the following: md subfolder 1. Notice the difference? A space was added after subfolder, and that means that the name of the directory is subfolder, not subfolder1. When the student has to create subfolder2 and the command md subfolder 2 is typed by accident, a message appears that the directory already exists. Why? The md subfolder 2 command was giving the computer the direction to create a directory called subfolder because the space and the 2 in the typed command were ignored.

1. Power on the computer and log on, if necessary.

2. Using Notepad, create four text files, putting any professional data that you want into the files. Name the files with your first initial and last name plus a number, a dash, and another number (flast1-1). For example, since my name is Cheryl Schmidt, my files could be named cschmidt1-1, cschmidt1-2, cschmidt2-1, and cschmidt2-2. Save the files to the root directory of your flash drive.

   What drive letter does the flash drive use?

   _____

   What application did you use to verify what drive letter the flash drive uses?

   _____

   Have a classmate verify that your four files are in the flash drive root directory. Then close Windows Explorer/File Explorer and Notepad.

   Classmate's printed name: _____

3. Access a command prompt. Multiple methods can be used. Use a previous lab or the textbook for instructions.

   At the command prompt, type the command to go to the drive you will be using and press ⏎Enter. For example, if you are using a flash drive that uses the drive letter G, you would type G: and press ⏎Enter. The command is as follows: X: (where X is the drive letter where you are allowed to create files). The prompt changes to the appropriate drive letter, such as G:\>.

4. At the command prompt, type the following command: **cd**

   What is the purpose of the cd command?

   _____

   What is the purpose of the cd\ command?

   _____

5. Create a directory (folder) called *Class* by entering the following command:

   md class

6. Use the **dir** command to verify the directory creation. If it is not created, redo step 5.

7. When the directory is created, move into the *Class* directory by using the cd command:

   cd class

   If you use the dir command at this point, what two entries are automatically created in a directory?

   _____

8.   Within the *Class* directory, create a subdirectory (subfolder) called *SubFolder1* by entering the following command:

md subfolder1

9.   Move from the *Class* folder into the subfolder just created:

cd subfolder1

In this step, would the cd *X:*\Class\SubFolder1 (where *X:* represents the flash drive you are using) command have worked as well? Why or why not?

_____

_____

_____

10.   From the *SubFolder1* directory, move back one directory:

cd..

What does the prompt look like at this point?

_____

11.   Make another subdirectory called *SubFolder2* that is located under the *Class* directory.

Have another student verify that both subdirectories have been created by using the dir command. Have that classmate sign his or her name on your answer sheet if the *Class* directory has two subdirectories that have the correct names.

Classmate's printed name: _____

Classmate's signature: _____

12.   Return to the root directory of the flash drive. Redo Lab 15.1 if you cannot remember how to do this step.

On Your Own

13a.   From the prompt, create two directories on the root directory of the flash drive. Name the directories *Sara* and *Josh*. Use the dir command to verify that the *Sara* and *Josh* directories exist in the root directory of the flash drive.

Have another student verify that two directories are created in the root directory. Ensure that the two names are correct and are readable.

Classmate's printed name: _____

13b.   Return to the root directory of the *X:* drive (the flash drive root directory).

Draw a picture of the directory structure that you have created on the flash drive.

_____

_____

_____

_____

_____

You are sitting at the root directory of the flash drive. What do you think would be the results of entering the following command:

COPY C:\WINDOWS\SYSTEM32\ATTRIB.EXE

_____

_____

_____

14. *Note*: This step assumes that Windows has been loaded in a directory (folder) called *Windows*. If it is loaded in a different directory, substitute the name of that directory for *Windows* in the commands. You also have to substitute `X:\Class` with a drive letter different from `X:` for the flash drive letter you are using.

    From the root directory, type the following command. Notice that the `copy` command is first. Then the source (the complete path of where the file is located: `C:\windows\system32\attrib.exe`). Last is the destination—where the file is to be placed (in the *Class* directory found on the flash drive).

    `copy C:\windows\system32\attrib.exe X:\class`

    If you did this step correctly, a message appears, saying that one file copied. If you did not get such a message, try the command again. Remember that `X:` is your flash drive letter, and you are supposed to type that drive letter rather than the `X`.

    To what location do you think the file was copied?

    _____

15. From the root directory, verify that the file has been copied by typing the following command:

    `dir \class`

    What is the size of the `attrib.exe` file?

    _____

    _____

16. To copy the `attrib.exe` command from the *Class* folder into *SubFolder2* (from the root directory), use the following command:

    `copy \class\attrib.exe \class\subfolder2`

    Notice the command comes first, and because everything is on the flash drive and the prompt is showing the flash drive, the flash drive letter can be omitted from both the source and the destination. The drive letter for the flash drive could precede the backslash (\) before the source and the destination part of the command, and it would work just as well (that is, `copy X:\class\attrib.exe X:\class\subfolder2`).

17. Verify that the file copied correctly by using the following command:

    `dir \class\subfolder2`

    Notice that with the `dir` command, you are instructing the computer to show a directory listing starting from the root drive (because the next part starts with the backslash [\]) and then instructing the computer to go into the *Class* directory, and then go into the *subfolder2* directory. You are giving the computer the exact path to take to get to the correct directory to show the listing.

    The `attrib.exe` file should be listed. If it is not, redo step 16.

    Are any other files or folders in the class directory? [Yes | No]

18. Copy the *flast1-1.txt* text file into the *Subfolder1* directory (which is located under the *Class* directory) by using the following command:

    `copy \flast1-1.txt \class\subfolder1`

    Remember that *flast1-1.txt* is your first initial and last name followed by `1-1.txt`. You created this file at the beginning of the lab.

    A message should appear that one file copied. If it does not, redo step 18.

19. Verify that the file copied by using the following command:

    `dir \class\subfolder1`

    Write the exact command to copy the *flast1-1* text file from *Subfolder1* into the *Subfolder2* directory. Remember that both *Subfolder1* and *Subfolder2* are subdirectories located under the *Class* directory. The *Class* directory is directly off of the root directory.

    _____

    _____

20. Execute the command documented in step 19. If the message that one file copied does not appear, redo the command or rewrite the command in step 19. Once the file is copied, verify the copy by using the `dir` command.

    What is the full command used to verify the copy in step 20?

    _____

21. From the flash drive root directory, use the `tree` command to verify your structure:

    `tree /f | more`

    There should be four text files in the root directory with your first initital and last name and 1-1, 1-2, 2-1, and 2-2 as part of the filename. There should be directories called *Class*, *Sara*, and *Josh*. Under the *Class* directory, there should be one file and two subfolders. The file is `attrib.exe`. The directories are *Subfolder1* and *Subfolder2*. Under the *Subfolder2* directory are the file *flast1-1*. `txt` and `attrib.exe`. Under the *Subfolder2* directory is the file *flast1-1*.`txt`. If any of these are not correct, use *Windows Explorer/File Explorer* to delete any files, directories, and subdirectories you have created and restart the lab.

On Your Own

22a. From the flash drive root directory prompt, copy the *flast1-2*.`txt` file from the flash drive root directory into the *Sara* directory. Use the space that follows to write your command before attempting to type it.

    Document the command to copy the *flast1-2*.`txt` file from the root directory of the flash drive into the *Sara* directory.

    _____

22b. From the flash drive root directory prompt, copy the *flast2-1*.`txt` file into the *Josh* directory. Use the space that follows to write your command before attempting to type it.

    Document the command to copy the *flast2-1*.`txt` file from the root directory of the flash drive into the *Josh* directory.

    _____

22c. From the flash drive root directory prompt, copy the *flast2-2*.`txt` file into the *Class* directory. Use the space that follows to write your command before attempting to type it.

    Document the command to copy the *flast2-2*.`txt` file from the root directory of the flash drive into the *Class* directory.

    _____

    Have another student verify that a file is copied into each of the three subdirectories. Ensure that the names are correct and are readable. Windows Explorer/File Explorer can be used to verify but not to correct. A better option would be to use the `dir` and `cd` commands.

    Classmate's printed name: _____

    Classmate's signature: _____

22d. Return to the root directory of the `X:` drive (the flash drive root directory). Close all other windows except the command prompt window.

23. A subdirectory can be created within a subdirectory from the root directory. To create a subdirectory called *Fun* within the *SubFolder2* subdirectory (which is under the *Class* directory), use the following command from the root directory. Notice that you must insert the backslashes when you have multiple directories to go through to create the subdirectory.

    ```
    md \class\subfolder2\fun
    ```

24. Verify the subdirectory creation by using the following command:

    ```
    dir \class\subfolder2
    ```

    A directory called *Fun* should be listed in the output.

    How much space do the files located within *SubFolder2* occupy?

    _____

25. Use the tree command to verify the *Class* folder structure:

    ```
    tree \class
    ```

    There should be two subdirectories (*Subfolder1* and *Subfolder2*) and one subdirectory (*Fun*) under *Subfolder2*.

26. To copy all the files from *SubFolder2* into the newly created *Fun* subdirectory, use the following command:

    ```
    copy \class\subfolder2 \class\subfolder2\fun
    ```

    A message should appear that two files copied. If you do not receive this message, do not go any further. Try redoing the command. Make sure there is a space between the copy command and the first backslash. Make sure there is a space between the first time you type subfolder2 and the next backslash (between the source and the destination parts).

27. Use the dir command as follows to verify the copy:

    ```
    dir \class\subfolder2\fun
    ```

28. Wildcards can be used with the copy command. To copy all the files that start with the letter A from the *Fun* subdirectory into the *Subfolder1* subdirectory, use the following command:

    ```
    copy \class\subfolder2\fun\a*.* \class\subfolder1
    ```

    A message should appear, stating that one file copied. If you do not receive this message, do not go any further. Try redoing the command. Make sure there is a space between the copy command and the first backslash (\). Make sure there is a space between the last asterisk (*) and the next backslash (between the source and the destination parts).

    How many files were copied?

    _____

Instructor initials: _____

29. The del command is used to delete files. Wildcards can also be used with this command. Delete all the files located in the *Fun* subdirectory using the following command (where the *.* is the wildcard representing all files with any extension):

    ```
    del \class\subfolder2\fun\*.*
    ```

    When prompted if you are sure, type **Y** and press ⏎Enter. Verify that the files are deleted with the dir command:

    ```
    dir \class\subfolder2\fun
    ```

30. The rd command removes directories and subdirectories. Note that you cannot remove a directory or subdirectory with the rd command unless that directory or subdirectory is empty. Remove the *Fun* subdirectory:

    ```
    rd \class\subfolder2\fun
    ```

31. Type the following command to remove the *SubFolder2* subdirectory:

    `rd \class\subfolder2`

    What is the operating system response, and what do you think has to be done as a result?

    _____

    _____

32. Delete the files in the *Subfolder2* subdirectory:

    `del \class\subfolder2\*.*`

    When prompted if you are sure, type **Y** and press (←Enter). Verify that the files are deleted with the `dir` command:

    `dir \class\subfolder2`

33a. Remove the *Subfolder2* subdirectory:

    `rd \class\subfolder2`

    Verify the results:

    `dir \class`

On Your Own

33b. From the command prompt, use the `del`, `rd`, and `dir` commands to delete all files that you have created in the root directory and verify the deletions.

    Write each command you are going to use *before* attempting this part. An important part of learning the commands and the prompt is to think about what and how you are going to type something before executing the command.

    _____

    _____

    _____

    _____

    _____

    Write each command used to delete the files in the *Class*, *Subfolder1*, *Sara*, and *Josh* directories and subdirectories.

    _____

    _____

    _____

    _____

    Write each command used to delete the *Class*, *Subfolder1*, *Sara*, and *Josh* directories and subdirectories.

    _____

    _____

    _____

    _____

    Have another student verify your work. Have that student sign and print his or her name to verify that all of the files created during this lab have been deleted.

    Classmate's printed name: _____

    Classmate's signature: _____

Lab 15.3 Using the `attrib` Command and Moving Around in the Directory Structure

Objective: To use the `attrib` command and to work correctly from a prompt when dealing with directories and subdirectories

Parts: A computer with a Windows operating system loaded

Access to modify files on the hard drive or on a flash drive

Procedure: Complete the following procedure and answer the accompanying questions.

Note: For each step requiring a typed command, the ⏎Enter key must be pressed to execute the command. This instruction will *not* be given with each step.

1.   Power on the computer and log on, if necessary.

2.   Using Notepad, create three files, named `Special1.txt`, `Special2.txt`, and `Tickle.txt`, and save them in the root directory of the flash drive.

   What drive letter is assigned to the flash drive?

   _____

3.   Access a command prompt. Ensure that the prompt represents the root directory of the flash drive. Do not use Windows Explorer or File Explorer to verify anything for the rest of the lab. If you cannot use the command prompt for all of this, you should practice the previous labs some more.

   What does your command prompt look like? Note that it should be the drive letter of the flash drive, a colon, a backslash, and a greater than sign. If it is not, review the previous labs before going to step 4.

   _____

4.   From the root directory of the flash drive, type the following command to create a directory called *Junk*:

   md junk

5.   Under the *Junk* directory, make subdirectories called *Sub1*, *Sub2*, and *Sub3* by using the following commands:

   cd junk
   md sub1
   md sub2
   md sub3

6.   Return to the root directory. Verify that you are in the correct directory by looking at the command prompt.

   What command makes the root directory the current directory?

   _____

   Write the command prompt as it appears on your screen.

   _____

7.   Make a new directory called *Trash* from the root directory and within the *Trash* directory, make subdirectories called *Sub1*, *Sub2*, and *Sub3* by using the following commands:

   md trash

   cd trash

   md sub1

   md sub2

   md sub3

8.   Return to the root directory of the flash drive.

On Your Own

9. Make a new directory called *Garbage* from the root directory. Within the *Garbage* directory, make subdirectories called *Sub1*, *Sub2*, and *Sub3*. Verify that the directory and subdirectories were created.

    Write the commands to create a directory called *Garbage* and the three subdirectories.

    _____

    _____

    _____

    _____

    _____

    _____

    _____

10. Place the `Special1.txt`, `Special2.txt`, and `Tickle.txt` files in the `Garbage\Sub1` subdirectory.

11. From the root directory, copy all files that begin with the letter *S* from the `Garbage\Sub1` subdirectory and place them in the `Trash\Sub3` subdirectory.

    Write the commands to copy these files from the `Garbage\Sub1` subdirectory to the `Trash\Sub3` subdirectory.

    _____

    _____

    How many files were copied?

    _____

12. Copy any file that begins with *T* from the `Garbage\Sub1` subdirectory and place it in the *Sub2* subdirectory of the *Junk* directory.

    Write the commands to copy files that begin with T from one subdirectory to another subdirectory.

    _____

    How many files were copied?

    _____

    Draw a diagram of the directory structure that you have created in this exercise, including all directories, subdirectories, and files.

    _____

    _____

    _____

    _____

    _____

    _____

    _____

    _____

    _____

    _____

    _____

    _____

    _____

    _____

Setting/Removing Attributes

13. To make all files in the *Sub3* subdirectory of the *Trash* directory read-only, use the `attrib` command with the `+r` switch. From the root directory, type the following command:

    `attrib +r \trash\sub3\*.*`

14. To verify that the read-only attribute is set, type the following command:

    `attrib \trash\sub3\*.*`

    The *Sub3* subdirectory should list two files. Both should have an R beside them, indicating that the read-only attribute is set. If the two files do *not* have the read-only attribute set, perform steps 13 and 14 again.

15. The best way to prove that the files are read-only is to try to delete them. Type the following command:

    `del \trash\sub3\*.*`

16. When asked if you are sure, type **Y** and press ⏎Enter. A message should appear on the screen, stating Access is denied. Then the command prompt appears. If the access denied message does not appear, the files were deleted, which means the read-only attribute was not set. If this is the case, redo this exercise, starting with step 11.

17. Hide the `Junk\Sub2` subdirectory by using the following command:

    `attrib +h \junk\sub2`

    No message appears on the screen. The command prompt appears again.

18. To verify that the directory is hidden, type the following command:

    `dir \junk`

    The *Sub2* subdirectory should not appear in the list.

19. Use the `attrib` command to verify that the directory is hidden by typing the following command:

    `attrib \junk\sub2`

    The directory listing should appears with an H beside the name.

20. Some operating system files are automatically marked as system files when the operating system is installed. Type the following command to see what files are already marked as system files:

    `attrib c:\*.*`

    List any files that have the system attribute.

    _____

    _____

    _____

On Your Own

21. Hide the `Special1.txt` file located in the *Sub1* subdirectory of the *Garbage* directory.

    Write the command you used for this step.

    _____

22. Verify that the `Special1.txt` file is hidden by using the **dir** and **attrib** commands.

    Write the commands you used for this step.

    _____

    _____

Have another student verify your work. Have that student sign and print his or her name and write the commands he or she used to verify that you were in the correct directory.

Classmate's printed name: _____

Classmate's signature: _____

_____

_____

_____

Instructor initials: _____

23. Remove the hidden attribute from the `Special1.txt` file in the *Sub1* subdirectory of the *Garbage* directory. If necessary, use the **attrib /?** command to find the switch to remove an attribute.

    Write the command used in this step.

    _____

24. Have a classmate verify that the `Special1.txt` file is no longer hidden.

    Have that student sign and print his or her name and write the commands he or she used to verify that the `Special1.txt` file is no longer hidden.

    Classmate's printed name: _____

    Classmate's signature: _____

    _____

    _____

    _____

25. Ensure that you are at the root directory.

26. Moving around within subdirectories can be challenging when you are first learning commands. Move to the *Sub3* subdirectory of the *Trash* directory.

    What command did you use to perform this step?

    _____

27. To move to the *Sub1* subdirectory from within the *Sub3* subdirectory, type the following:

    cd..

    Then type the following to move into the correct subdirectory:

    cd sub1

    What does the command prompt look like now?

    _____

28. A shortcut to move up one directory is to type **cd..** from within the *Sub1* subdirectory. The prompt immediately changes to one level up (the *Trash* directory). Type the following:

    cd..

    The command prompt changes to *X:*\`\Trash>`.

29. Using the **cd..** command again takes you one level back in the directory structure, to the root directory. Type the following:

    cd..

    The command prompt changes appropriately.

On Your Own

30. From the root directory change to the *Sub2* subdirectory of the *Garbage* directory.

    Write the command used in this step.

    _____

How can you verify that the current directory is `Garbage\Sub2`?

_____

31. From the *Garbage\Sub2* subdirectory, change the current directory to the *Sub3* subdirectory of the *Trash* directory.

Write the command you used in this step.

_____

Have a classmate verify your work. Have that student sign and print his or her name and describe how he or she verified that you were in the correct directory.

Classmate's printed name: _____

Classmate's signature: _____

_____

32. Using the **cd..** command, move from `Trash\Sub3` to *Trash*.

33. Using the **cd..** command, move from *Trash* to the root directory.

34. Using the `attrib`, `del`, and `rd` commands, delete the *Trash* and *Garbage* directories, including all subdirectories underneath them. Write all commands needed for this before you attempt this step at the command prompt.

Write all commands used in this step.

_____

_____

_____

_____

_____

_____

_____

_____

_____

_____

_____

35. Using the `attrib`, `del`, and `rd` commands, delete the *Junk* directory and all its subdirectories. Write all commands needed for this before you attempt this step at the command prompt.

Write all commands used in this step.

_____

_____

_____

_____

_____

_____

Instructor initials: _____

Lab 15.4 Windows 7/10 Backup Software and the Archive Bit

Objective: To explore backup options and how they affect the archive attribute, using Windows 7 or 10

Parts: A computer with Windows 7 or 10 installed

               Flash drive

Procedure: Complete the following procedure and answer the accompanying questions.

Note: This lab requires both command prompt and Windows skills.

1.   Power on the computer and log in to Windows.

2.   Attach the flash drive.

      What drive letter is assigned to the flash drive?

      _____

3.   Ensure that there are at least three files in the *Documents* folder on the hard drive. You may have to create three files. This will be the folder that contains the data to be backed up.

      What are the names of your three files?

      _____

4.   In Windows 7, from the *Start* menu, access *All Programs > Accessories >* right-click *Command Prompt > Run as Administrator > Yes.* In Windows 10, search for command prompt, in the resulting list right-click or tap and briefly hold on the words *Command Prompt >* select *Run as Administrator > Yes.*

5.   Use the `cd` command to move into the directory (folder) chosen in step 2. Hint: You must change into the directory *Users* and the folder with the username used to log in to the computer before you can locate the *Documents* folder. For example, my username is CASchmidt, so my prompt will be `C:\Users\CASchmidt\Documents>`.

      Document the command(s) used to accomplish this step.

      _____

      _____

      _____

      _____

      _____

      _____

      _____

      _____

6.   Use the `DIR` command to verify that at least three files are in the folder.

      Have another student verify that three files are there.

      Classmate's signature: _____

7.   Use the `attrib` command to determine the attributes set by default on a file saved on a Windows computer. The attributes are listed to the far left, then there is a space, and then there is the full path to the filename. Leave the command prompt window open.

      Document the attributes found for the three files, keeping in mind that A is the archive attribute, R is the read-only attribute, and H is the hidden attribute.

      _____

      _____

      _____

      _____

8. Search for, locate, and select the Windows 7 *Backup and Restore* or Windows 10 *Backup and Restore (Windows 7)* section of the Control Panel.

9. If a backup has been done before, select the *Change Settings* link; otherwise, select the *Set Up Backup* link.

10. Select the appropriate backup destination (the flash drive letter, as specified in the answer to the question in step 2) > *Next*.

11. Select the *Let Me Choose* button > *Next*.

12. Expand folders as necessary by clicking on the arrows and locate and select the folder chosen in step 2 > *Next*.

13. Click the *Save Settings and Run Backup* button.

14. When the backup finishes, return to the command prompt window and reissue the **attrib** command.

    Did the archive attribute change for the three files? [Yes | No]

    Describe the backup file on the flash drive. In other words, how does the Windows Backup software save the file?

    _____

    _____

15. Using *Windows Explorer/File Explorer*, copy one of the files from the *Documents* folder to the desktop.

16. In the command prompt window, type **cd** to return to the root directory.

17. Use the **cd** command to access the *Desktop* directory. A sample command would be **cd \users\ Cheryl\desktop** if the person who signed onto the computer used the Cheryl account.

    Document the exact command you used to access the *Desktop* directory.

    _____

18. Use the **attrib** command to determine whether the archive bit changes when a file is copied.

    Document your findings.

    _____

Instructor initials: _____

Cleanup

19. Permanently delete the file copied to the desktop and the three files created in the *Documents* folder.

20. Close all windows.

Lab 15.5 Setting Windows Environment Variables

Objective: To access environment variables in Windows

Parts: Windows computer and administrator rights

Procedure: Complete the following steps and answer the accompanying questions.

1. Power on the computer and log on using a user ID and password that has administrator rights.

2. Open the *System* Control Panel utility > *Advanced System Settings* link. Explore within the *System Properties* window to answer the following questions.

    Which options did you select to find the Environment Variables window?

    _____

    _____

Which system variable name is used for the PowerShell environment variable?

_____

What is the value of this variable?

_____

_____

Is the PowerShell environment variable a system variable or a user variable?
[system variable | user variable]

Can you edit this environment variable? [Yes | No] Why or why not?

_____

_____

_____

What variable is used for temporary files?

_____

What is the value associated with this variable?

_____

_____

Instructor initials: _____

Describe another way to access environment variables in Windows.

_____

Which option would you use, and why?

_____

3.   Use the Internet to research how to find Python environment variables. Document three findings and the URL where you found them.

_____

_____

_____

_____

On Your Own

4.   Change the environment variable for one user's program so that it includes a new directory named `TestDir`. Document how you did this.

_____

_____

5.   Do your own research to find out where user environment variables are stored in the registry. Document your findings and be sure to list the specific registry key.

_____

6.   Do your own research to find out where system environment variables are stored in the registry. Document your findings and be sure to list the specific registry key.

_____

_____

7. For the following environment variables, locate the values on your computer and record them in the spaces provided here:

    %*COMPUTERNAME*% _____

    %*APPDATA*% _____

    %*HOMEPATH*% _____

    %*LOCALAPPDATA*% _____

    %*PATHEXT*% _____

Instructor initials: _____

Lab 15.6 Creating a Batch File

Objective: To create and run a script using command line and batch files

Parts: Windows computer with Microsoft Office or OpenOffice or access to five user-created files and administrator rights

     Flash drive

Procedure: Complete the following steps and answer the accompanying questions.

1. Power on the computer and log on.

2. In Windows Explorer/File Explorer, locate and select the flash drive. Create a folder (directory) on the flash drive named *batchTest*.

3. Next, put five files inside the *batchTest* folder. You can use any files already on the computer, or you can create five simple files yourself. The files can be from any application and can contain anything you want; the content is not important. It is recommended that you use at least three different applications to make the results more interesting, such as an Excel file, a Word file, a text file, and so on. OpenOffice is also acceptable. Suggested filenames and content are given in Lab Table 15.2.

LAB TABLE 15.2   Suggested batch file content*

Sample filename	Sample content
`drones.docx, drones.odt`	A drone is an unmanned aircraft, like a flying robot.
`addition.xlsx, addition.ods`	2 + 2 = 4 (normally)
`scripting.pptx, scripting.odp`	My First Scripting Presentation
`firstScript.txt`	The echo command displays messages on the console.
`smile.png, smile.jpg, smil.bmp`	Draw a smiley face.

* These are only suggestions. You can create any five files you want.

4. Open Notepad and create a batch file as shown below:

```
echo
REM create a list of files in the batchTest folder
dir "X:\batchTest" > X:\file_list.txt
echo "Check out the list of files now!"
```

This should create a new file with a list of all the files that are in the *batchTest* directory. Make sure you replace the X: with the drive letter assigned to the flash drive. For example, if your flash drive is F:, then everywhere you see X: above, use F: instead.

Note that batch file commands are not case sensitive. You could substitute ECHO for echo, and DIR for dir. The comment command (REM) is normally written in uppercase simply to set it off from the comment text.

Save the file on the flash drive with the filename batch1*xxx*.bat, replacing *xxx* with your initials. When you save the file, be sure to use the drop-down menu under *Save as Type* and select the

All Files option. Otherwise, Notepad will add the `.txt` extension to your file, and the script will not run. Close the file.

5.   Search for **command prompt** to open the command prompt. Then enter the following command to run your file:

X: (where *X*: is the drive letter of your flash drive) ⏎Enter

cd batchTest ⏎Enter

start batch1xxx.bat (where *xxx* is your initials) ⏎Enter

What is displayed on the console?

_____

_____

_____

_____

_____

_____

_____

In Windows Explorer/File Explorer, locate the file named `file_list.txt` and open it. What are its contents?

_____

Instructor initials: _____

6.   Modify your batch file as follows: Locate the `batch1xxx.bat` file, right-click it, and choose *Edit* to open it in Notepad. Add or modify the commands to do the following:
     > Edit the file so it creates a new directory (folder) in the root directory of the flash drive called *myFiles*. Recall that the command to make a new directory is `md` or `mkdir`.
     > Edit the file so it saves the `file_list.txt` file to the new *myFiles* folder.

     What changes did you make? List them.

_____

_____

_____

_____

7.   Add comments to your batch file to explain what each line does.

8.   Execute the batch file and then verify that the `file_list.txt` file is located in a folder called *myFiles*.

     Where is `file_list.txt` located now? Verify that it is in the location where you want it to be.

_____

Instructor initials: _____

9.   Create a second batch file, named `batch2xxx.bat`, to add two numbers, stored in variables named `number1` and `number2`. Store the sum in a third variable, named `sum`, and then store a message to display the results in another variable, named `message1`. Output only the results. The code is as follows:

```
@echo off
REM doing math
SET /A number1=5
SET /A number2=3
SET /A sum=%number1% + %number2%
SET message1=The result of adding %number1% and %number2% is %sum%
echo %message1%
```

10. Execute the batch file from a command prompt to verify your code.

    What message displays on the screen?

    _____

Instructor initials: _____

11. Modify your batch file as follows:
    > Add a third variable, named `product`, to store the results of multiplying the two numbers.
    > Add a variable named `message2` to store a message that gives the result of the multiplication and output this message.

    Your final display should look like this:

    ```
    The result of adding 5 and 3 is 8.

    The result of multiplying 5 by 3 is 15.
    ```

Instructor initials: _____

12. Create a third batch file, named `batch3xxx.bat`, to count by twos from 2 through 20, using a loop and an `if` clause. The output should be a vertical list of the following numbers:

    2 4 6 8 10 12 14 16 18 20

    Note that batch files do not actually have a true `while` loop. However, there are several ways to mimic the `while` loop syntax available in Python, JavaScript, and shell scripting. A true `while` loop begins with a test condition that compares a variable or an expression to another value. This is followed by a block of statements that are executed over and over until the test condition is no longer true. In the block of statements, the variable or expression to be tested is changed (normally incremented or decremented). All of this can be simulated in a batch file by using the `goto` command and an `if` clause.

    A loop in a batch file begins with a colon (`:`) and a label. The label can be almost anything you choose. It is followed by an `if` clause that tests a condition. If the condition is `true`, the statements in the `if` clause will execute. You must remember to change the test item somewhere in the `if` clause, or the loop will run forever. After these statements have executed, the `goto` command is used with the label name to tell the computer to start again, back at the first line. In general terms, the syntax is as follows:

    ```
    :label
    if test condition is true
        do stuff
        increment or decrement the test variable
        goto :label
    ```

    However, if you use the word `while` as your label, your batch file loop looks a lot like a `while` loop. Here's the code.

    ```
    @echo off
    REM Using a loop and an if clause to count by two's from 2 through
    20
    SET /A number=1
    SET /A count=2
    SET /A limit=22
    :while
    if %count% LEQ %limit%  (
        SET /A result=%number%*%count%
        echo %result%
        SET /A count=count+2
        goto :while
    )
    ```

13. Execute the third batch file and ensure it works properly. Troubleshoot as necessary.

Instructor initials: _____

14. Create a fourth batch file, named `batch4xxx.bat`, and save it inside your *batchTest* folder. Use the `forfiles` command to have this batch file output to the console a list of all the files in the *batchTest* folder with the date and time last modified. Here's the code:

```
echo

REM use a forfiles loop to create a list of files in the batchTest
folder

forfiles /C "cmd /c echo @file @fdate @ftime"
```

What is displayed?

_____

_____

_____

_____

_____

_____

_____

_____

_____

_____

_____

Instructor initials: _____

On Your Own

15. Create a batch file to output the following. Change the name of Bobby to your own name:

Hello, Bobby. Your operating system is Windows 10.

Do this by creating a variable named `name` that holds the value `Bobby`. Use a second variable, named `systemOS`, to hold the value `Windows 10`. Write your code below.

_____

_____

_____

_____

_____

16. Modify your batch file from step 15 to detect the computer's operating system version. Search the Internet to find out how to do this. Document your results.

_____

_____

_____

_____

_____

_____

_____

_____

_____

_____

Instructor initials: _____

17. Create a batch file script to output only files created after a specific date. The command to do that is:

```
forfiles ... [/D [+] {MM/DD/YYYY}]
```

This command selects files with a last modified date greater than or equal to (+) the specified date using the *MM/DD/YYYY* format. Document your results.

_____

_____

_____

Instructor initials: _____

Lab 15.7 Windows 7/10 Backup Software

Objective: To explore backup options using Windows 7 or 10

Parts: A computer with Windows 7 or 10 installed

                   Flash drive

Procedure: Complete the following procedure and answer the accompanying questions.

Note: This lab requires both Windows skills and use of the command prompt.

1.   Power on the computer and log in to Windows.

2.   Attach the flash drive.

     What drive letter is assigned to the flash drive?

_____

3.   Ensure that there are at least one subdirectory that contains three files under the *Documents* folder on the hard drive. You may have to create these three files. This will be the folder that contains the data to be backed up.

     What are the names of your three files and the subfolder name?

_____

4.   In Windows 7, from the *Start* menu, access *All Programs > Accessories >* right-click *Command Prompt > Run as Administrator > Yes.*
     In Windows 10, search for **command prompt** > in the resulting list right-click or tap and briefly hold on the words *Command Prompt >* select *Run as Administrator > Yes.*

5.   Use the cd command to move into the directory (folder) recorded in step 2. Hint: You must change into the directory *Users* and the folder with the username used to log in to the computer before you can locate the *Documents* folder. For example, my username is CASchmidt, so my prompt will be C:\Users\CASchmidt\Documents>.

     Document the command(s) used to accomplish this step.

_____

_____

_____

_____

_____

_____

6.   Use the dir command to verify that at least three files are in the folder.

     Have another student verify that the three files are there.

     Classmate's signature: _____

7.   Search, locate, and select the Windows 7 *Backup and Restore* or Windows 10 *Backup and Restore (Windows 7)* Control Panel.

LAB 15

8. If a backup has been done before, select the *Change Settings* link; otherwise, select the *Set Up Backup* link.

9. Select the appropriate backup destination (the flash drive letter, as specified in the answer to the question in step 2) > *Next*.

10. Select the *Let Me Choose* button > *Next*.

11. Expand folders, as necessary, by clicking on the arrows and locate and select the folder chosen in step 3 > *Next*.

12. Click the *Save Settings and Run Backup* button.

Instructor initials: _____

Cleanup

13. Permanently delete the subfolder and the three files created in the *Documents* folder.

14. Close all windows.

Lab 15.8 Introduction to PowerShell

Objective: To create and run PowerShell scripts using cmdlets and scripting code

Parts: Windows computer with Microsoft Office or OpenOffice or access to five user-created files and administrator rights

Procedure: Complete the following steps and answer the accompanying questions.

1. Power on the computer and log on.

2. In Windows Explorer/File Explorer, in the C: drive, create a folder (directory) in *Documents* named *PowerShellTest*.

3. Next, put five files inside the *PowerShellTest* folder. You can use any files from the user of the computer or you can create five simple files yourself. The files can be from any application and can contain anything you want; the content is not important. It is recommended that you use at least three different applications to make the results more interesting, such as an Excel file, a Word file, a text file, and so on. OpenOffice is also acceptable. Suggested filenames and content are given in Lab Table 15.3.

LAB TABLE 15.3   Suggested filenames and content for PowerShell*

Filename	Content
drones.docx, drones.odt	A drone is an unstaffed aircraft, like a flying robot.
addition.xlsx, addition.ods	2 + 2 = 4 (normally)
scripting.pptx, scripting.odp	My First Scripting Presentation
firstScript.txt	The echo command displays messages on the console.
smile.png, smile.jpg, smil.bmp	Draw a smiley face.

* These are only suggestions. You can create any five files you want.

4. Use *Cortana* or the *Windows Search* box to open the *PowerShell ISE*. (ISE stands for Integrated Scripting Environment.) Your screen should look like the one in Lab Figure 15.1.

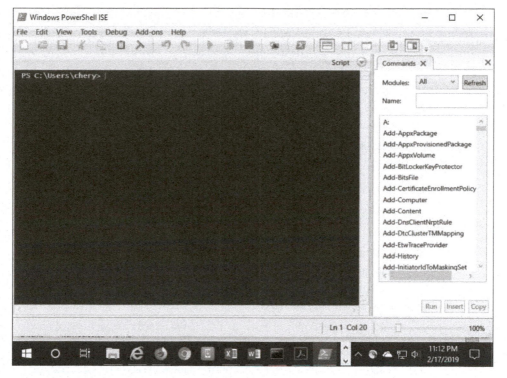

LAB FIGURE 15.1   The PowerShell ISE

5. Look on the right side of the screen. Use the *Modules* drop-down menu to select *CimCmdlets*. Use the Internet to research what CIM stands for and record your answer and the URL where you found that information:

     _____

     _____

     _____

6. Using *Windows Explorer/File Explorer*, go inside the *PowerShellTest* folder. Click in a blank space of the address bar to see the full path (for example, `C:\Users\student\Documents\PowerShellTest`). While the path is highlighted, use Ctrl+C to copy that path.

7. In the PowerShell ISE environment, use the `Get-Childitem` cmdlet to view the files in the *PowerShellTest* folder. In the left-side area, type the following command after the prompt:

     `Get-ChildItem C:\users\`*`username`*`\Documents\PowerShellTest`

     Note: You can type `Get-Childitem`, add a space, and then use the Ctrl+V keys to paste the path into the command line.

     What happens?

     _____

     _____

     _____

Instructor initials: _____

8. To create a PowerShell script, open Notepad or any other simple text editor and enter the following:

     `Write-Host "Hello! This is my first PowerShell script."`

     Save the file inside your *PowerShellTest* folder with the filename `powershell1`*`xxx`*`.ps1`, where *xxx* is your initials. When you save the file, be sure to use the drop-down menu under *Save as Type* and select the *All Files* option. Otherwise, Notepad will add the `.txt` extension to your file, and the script will not run.

9. Return to the PowerShell window and run the script with the following command, remembering to replace username with the username you used to log into the computer:

& "C:\Users*username*\Documents\PowerShellTest\powershell1*xxx*.ps1"

If you get an error, it may be because PowerShell has enforced an execution policy. Be sure you have opened PowerShell as an administrator. (Close PowerShell, rerun the search, right-click on the search results for Windows PowerShell ISE and select *Run As an Administrator.*) Then run the following command:

Set-ExecutionPolicy RemoteSigned

Select *Yes* in the message that displays. Then try running your script again.

You should see the following:

Hello! This is my first PowerShell script.

Instructor initials: _____

10. Edit the powershell1*xxx*.ps1 file and add the line from step 7 to see a list of all the files in that directory. Run the script again. What is the result now? You should see the line of text, a line that displays the path to your *PowerShellTest* directory, and a list of all the files in that directory. If you do not see this, start the lab over.

What properties are shown for the files in the directory (that is, what are the column headings shown)?

_____

11. Create a second PowerShell script file, named powershell2*xxx*.ps1, to count by twos from 2 through 20, using the ForEach-Object command. The output should include a line of text and a vertical list of these numbers, as shown in Lab Figure 15.2:

2 4 6 8 10 12 14 16 18 20

LAB FIGURE 15.2   Results of a PowerShell script file

The command to process the numbers is as follows:

```
1,2,3,4,5,6,7,8,9,10 | ForEach-Object -Process {$_*2}
```

Here's the code:

Write-Host "Counting by twos"

```
1,2,3,4,5,6,7,8,9,10 | ForEach-Object -Process {$_*2}
```

12. To execute the code, use your ⬆ and change the name of the file from powershell1*xxx*.ps1 to powershell2*xxx*.ps1 (where *xxx* is your initials). If you can't get this to work, type the full command to execute the script.

Did the script work? [Yes | No] If no, redo the code and execute it again.

Instructor initials: _____

13. Create a third PowerShell script file named powershell3*xxx*.ps1. Use the Get-Date cmdlet to get the current date and time.

Now use this command to find all files that are more than a year old in your *PowerShellTest* directory. Be sure you have at least one file that was created over a year ago so you can check that your script works. Use the code that follows, replacing username with the name you used when you logged into Windows. Note that there is no space between (Get-Date) and .AddDays.

```
$time = (Get-Date).AddDays(-365)
$path = "C:\Users\username\Documents\PowerShellTest"
Get-ChildItem $path |
Where-Object {$_.LastWriteTime -lt $time}
```

Instructor initials: _____

On Your Own

14. Add comments to your PowerShell scripts. In PowerShell, a single-line comment begins with the # symbol and ends at the end of that line. A multi-line comment begins with <# and ends with #>.

    List an example of one of your comments.

    _____

15. Create a new script, powershell4xxx.ps1, to multiply each number in a list (2, 4, 6, 8) by 100 and divide each number in the list by 4 so the output is as shown in Lab Figure 15.3.

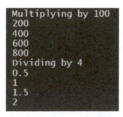

LAB FIGURE 15.3   Output of a PowerShell script

    List your code.

    _____

    _____

    _____

    _____

Instructor initials: _____

16. Create a new script, powershell5xxx.ps1, to find all files that are older than 60 days in your *PowerShellTest* directory.

    List your code.

    _____

    _____

    _____

Instructor initials: _____

17. Create a new script, powershell5xxx.ps1, to get all the files in your *PowerShellTest* directory that have a specific extension. To do this, you use the Select-String command.

    List your code.

    _____

    _____

    _____

    _____

    _____

Instructor initials: _____

Lab 15.9 Introduction to Python Scripting

Objective: To create and run Python scripts using IDLE

Parts: Windows computer with access to the Internet and rights to download and install free software

Procedure: Complete the following steps and answer the accompanying questions

1. Power on the computer and log on. Open a browser.

2. In the browser, go to https://www.python.org/. Click on *Downloads* and then *Python 3.7.0*. Save the file `python-3.7.0.exe` to a place on the computer where you can find it. At the time of this writing, Python 3.7.0 was the latest version. If that has changed, you can download a later version. However, to do this lab, you must have a version of Python 3 installed (*not* Python 2!).

This executable file installs Python on your computer. This will allow you to create programs in the Python language, using the integrated development environment (IDE) named IDLE. (Note that IDE is a generic term for a program used by a language to write programs, and IDLE is the name of the IDE used here to write Python programs.)

3. Click on the executable file and follow the prompts. Accept all the default options. If your installation is successful, you should see a verification similar to that shown in Lab Figure 15.4.

LAB FIGURE 15.4   Successful installation of Python

4. From Windows *Start*, expand the *Python* folder, if necessary, and click on *IDLE* (see Lab Figure 15.5).

LAB FIGURE 15.5   The *Python* folder expanded

5. You should see the Python 3.7 Shell window. Make it active by clicking anywhere in its blank area. The cursor should be blinking to the right of the three chevrons: >>>. Press ⏎Enter two times, and you should see two more rows of chevrons. This means that Python is working and waiting for you to do something.

6. In the Python Shell window, type the following:

```
print("I got it to work!")
```

Press ⏎Enter, and you should see a screen like the one shown in Lab Figure 15.6.

```
Python 3.7.0 Shell                                    —  □  ×
File  Edit  Shell  Debug  Options  Window  Help
Python 3.7.0 (v3.7.0:1bf9cc5093, Jun 27 2018, 04:06:47) [MSC v.1914 32 bit (Inte
l)] on win32
Type "copyright", "credits" or "license()" for more information.
>>>
>>>
>>> print("I got it to work!")
I got it to work!
>>> |
```

LAB FIGURE 15.6   Working in the Python IDLE shell

7. To prepare for your work, create a folder called *PythonTest*. Make sure you know where this folder is located.

8. The Python Shell window is where you see a script run. To create a script, you need to work in the Python editor. From the menu within the Python Shell window, select *File > New File* to open the Python editor.

   Type the following into the editor:

```
# display a greeting and generate a password
# get input from the user
first_name = input("First name: ")
last_name = input("Last name: ")
id_number = input("Enter your school ID number: ")
# create strings
name = first_name + " " + last_name
temp_password = first_name + "*" + id_number
# display the results
print("Welcome " + name + "!")
print("Your temporary password is: " + temp_password)
```

Be sure to type this code exactly as shown. In Python, indents, spaces, and line spacing are very important:

> In this program, any line that begins with a hash symbol (#) is a comment and will be ignored by the computer when the program runs.

> The following are the variable names in this script: `first_name`, `last_name`, `id_number`, `name`, and `temp_password`. The value on the right side of the equals sign is the value stored in the variable on the left side.

> In the line `first_name = input("First name: ")`, the variable is `first_name`. The word `input` is a Python function that tells the computer to put a prompt on the screen. The text of the prompt is whatever is enclosed in quotes inside the parentheses. In this case, the text `First name:` will be displayed. When the user enters his or her name, that value is stored in the variable `first_name`.

> The `name` variable joins the values of two variables and adds a space between those values because of the space within quotes (`" "`).

> The `print()` command tells the computer to display something on the screen. It can be text, the value of a variable, or a combination of text and variables.

9. Save your program with the filename python1*xxx*.py (where *xxx* is your initials) inside your *PythonTest* folder by going to the *File* tab and selecting *Save As*.

10. Now you can run your program. Go to the *Run* tab at the top of the Python Editor screen, as shown in Lab Figure 15.7, and click on *Run Module*. The program should open in the Python shell and prompt you for your first name.

```
File  Edit  Format  Run  Options  Window  Help

# display a greeting and generate a password
# get input from the user
first_name = input("First name: ")
last name = input("Last name: ")
```

LAB FIGURE 15.7   The *Run* tab in the Python IDLE editor

If you get an error, go back to the editor and compare your code with the code given above. Fix any errors you find, save the changes, and try again.

11. Until you enter something, nothing will happen. Enter **Jackie** for the first name and enter **Cho** for the last name. Enter **123456** for the school ID number. You should see the results in the Python shell, as shown in Lab Figure 15.8.

```
First name: Jackie
Last name: Cho
Enter your school ID number: 123456
Welcome Jackie Cho!
Your temporary password is: Jackie*123456
>>> |
```

LAB FIGURE 15.8   Results of the first Python script

Did the script work? [Yes | No] If no, troubleshoot and edit your code as necessary until it does.

Instructor initials: _____

12. Create a new Python program. You can simply write over your first program and save the program inside the *PythonTest* folder with a new filename. Name this new file python2*xxx*.py (where *xxx* is your initials). This new program will use a decision structure to decide whether a user is eligible for a 20%, 10%, or 0% discount on a purchase. In this program, the user will enter the cost of a purchase. If the purchase value is over $100.00 the discount is 20%. If the purchase value is $50.00 to $99.99, the discount is 10%. Anything under $50.00 is not eligible for a discount. The code for this program is as follows:

```
# prompt user for cost of purchase
cost = float(input("How much is your purchase? $ "))
# check for discount amount
if cost >= 100:
    discount = cost * .20
    percent = "20%"
    cost = cost - discount
elif cost >= 50:
    discount = cost * .10
    percent = "10%"
    cost = cost - discount
else:
    discount = 0
    percent = "0%"
# display the results
print("You have received a " , percent, " discount")
print("Your final cost is $ ", cost)
```

13. Run the program at least three times to check that all the discount options (0%, 10%, or 20%) work. You can enter any numbers you want, but here are some suggestions for input:

105

87

50

34

If you enter **87** at the prompt, you should see the results shown in Lab Figure 15.9.

```
How much is your purchase? $ 87
You have received a  10%  discount
Your final cost is $  78.3
>>>
```

LAB FIGURE 15.9   Results of the second Python script

You might notice that there are some things that could be improved in this program:

> Try entering a negative number. The program will still run, but it makes no sense to have a negative value as an input. You can fix this later as an On Your Own exercise.

> The output shows a dollar amount but has only one decimal place where you would expect two. There are ways to deal with this issue, but they require more advanced coding, so for now, this is fine.

> Each time you want to enter a new value, you must run the program again. By using a loop, you can allow the user to enter as many values as desired. You will add this functionality in the next step.

14. Save your `python2xxx.py` file with a new filename: **python3xxx.py**. For this script, you will add a `while` loop so a user can repeat the process of entering values as often as desired.

Add the following lines to the top of the program:

```
# loop to re-enter a new value
choice = "y"
    while choice == "y":
```

Next, indent each line of your previous code one time by pressing [Tab⇄] at the start of each line.

Add the following line at the end, also indented once:

```
choice = input("Enter another value? (y/n) ")
```

An abbreviated version of the code looks like this:

```
# loop to re-enter a new value
choice = "y"
while choice == "y":
    # prompt user for cost of purchase
    cost = float(input("How much is your purchase? $ "))
    # check for discount amount
    if cost >= 100:
        discount = cost * .20
        percent = "20%"
        cost = cost - discount
    ...(remainder of code)
    print("Your final cost is $ ", cost)
    choice = input("Enter another value? (y/n) ")
```

Note that your entire program from the previous file must be between the new lines. The first new line of code is a comment. The next line declares a variable named `choice` and sets its value to `y`. The `while` loop tests to see if `choice` has the value `y`. If it does, the loop is entered, and the program proceeds. After running once, you are prompted to enter `y` or `n`. Then control returns to the `while` test. If you entered **y**, the condition is `true`, and the program runs again. If the condition is anything but `y`, the condition is `false`, and the loop block of statements are skipped. In this case, the program ends.

15. Now save and run your program. If you enter **63** at the first prompt, **y** at the second prompt, **245** at the third prompt, and **n** at the last prompt, you should see the results shown in Lab Figure 15.10 in the Python Shell window.

```
How much is your purchase? $ 63
You have received a  10%  discount
Your final cost is $  56.7
Enter another value? (y/n) y
How much is your purchase? $ 245
You have received a  20%  discount
Your final cost is $  196.0
Enter another value? (y/n) n
>>>
```

LAB FIGURE 15.10   Results of the improved Python script

16. You may have noticed that the user can enter anything when prompted for a decision to run the program again or not. If the user enters a lowercase **y**, the program loops around again. But any other entry from the keyboard will stop the program. However, the prompt specifies entering either y or n. This is done mainly for the user's sake because it seems to make more sense to allow the user to say, in effect, yes or no in answer to the question. However, you can change this by changing this line:

```
choice = input("Enter another value? (y/n) ")
```

to the following:

```
choice = input("Enter another value? Type y to
continue or any other key to end. ")
```

Note: Because of space constraints in this text, the code shown above appears on two lines. But you must type the whole thing on a single line.

Add this change to your program and run it again. Be sure it works correctly before continuing.

Instructor initials: _____

17. You may also have noticed that a user can type an uppercase **Y** to continue, but the program will end. This is because computers are case sensitive. If you want to give the user the option to use uppercase or lowercase entries, you can use a logical operator.

Change this line:

```
while choice == "y":
```

to the following:

```
while choice == "y" or choice == "Y":
```

Make this change and test your program with both upper- and lowercase entries.

Instructor initials: _____

On Your Own

Note: Most programming problems can be solved in a variety of ways. Your solution may not be exactly like your classmates' but, as long as the problem is solved, one method is not "better" than another. As you become more proficient with writing scripts, you may find more efficient ways to write code.

18. Revise the code of your `python3`*xxx*`.py` file to check if the purchase price for a 0% discount is both less than 50.00 and greater than or equal to 0. Execute the program to test it.

Add an `elif` clause to check if the cost entered is greater than 0 and revise the `else` clause so it will display a message that any other amount is invalid. Write the code.

_____

_____

_____

_____

_____

_____

_____

_____

_____

_____

_____

_____

_____

_____

_____

_____

_____

_____

_____

_____

_____

Instructor initials: _____

19. Add tax to the final cost in the `python3xxx.py` program. Assume that the tax rate is 6.25%. The final output should include the discounted cost plus 6.25% tax. Run the program to verify your code. *Hint:* The code `cost = cost + (.0625*cost)` can help here.

Did the code run properly? [Yes | No]

Instructor initials: _____

20. Create a new Python program, `python4xxx.py`, to assign a letter grade to a student when a numerical grade is input. The grades should be as follows:

     90–100: A

     80–89.99: B

     70–79.99: C

     60–69.99: D

     Under 60: F

     Did the code run properly? [Yes | No]

     Write the code you used for this program.

     _____

     _____

     _____

     _____

21. Add a loop to your `python4xxx.py` program that will allow the user to enter information for as many students as desired. Test the program.

     Did the code run properly? [Yes | No]

     Write the code you used to modify the program.

     _____

     _____

     _____

LAB 15

22. Add to your `python4`*xxx*`.py` program a greeting that explains to the user what the program does. Consider the placement of this greeting within the program (before or inside the loop).

Did the code run properly? [Yes | No]

Write the code you used to modify the program.

_____

_____

Instructor initials: _____

23. Create a new Python program, `python5`*xxx*`.py`, that accepts input from the user and generates an email address, as follows:

First name: Sam

Last name: Throckmorton

Welcome Sam!

Your new email address is Sam.Throckmorton@mycollege.edu

The email address should consist of the user's first name, a dot, the user's last name, joined with the text `@mycollege.edu`.

Did the code run properly? [Yes | No]

Write the code you used to create the program.

_____

_____

_____

_____

_____

_____

_____

_____

_____

_____

Instructor initials: _____

Lab 15.10 Introduction to JavaScript

Objective: To create and run JavaScript programs in a web browser

Parts: Windows computer with access to the Internet and rights to download and install free software

Procedure: Complete the following steps and answer the accompanying questions.

Notes: JavaScript runs in a browser. A JavaScript program is called from a web page, which is written in HTML. Normally web pages are stored on a server and opened on the Internet. However, for this lab, you will create a simple HTML file, add some JavaScript, and open your file in the browser from your computer. An HTML file is a text file. There are many HTML editors available, and many of them are free. But here you will simply use Notepad.

1. Power on the computer and log on.

2. Using *Windows Explorer* or *File Explorer*, create a folder to save your work. Name the folder *JavaScriptTest*.

3. Open Notepad or any other text editor. In this step you will be creating a simple web page. All items in web pages are defined by tags, which are keywords that help organize, format, and classify content. Most tags are in pairs—an opening tag (start tag) and a closing tag (end tag). Everything between the

start and end tags will have the formatting associated with that tag. While this can be changed by a web designer, here you can accept the default formatting. All web pages start with an <html> start tag and end, at the very bottom of the page, with a </html> end tag. Notice that an end tag begins with a slash (/). All web pages have two important parts: a head section and a body section. The head section includes information needed by the browser that is not seen by the user. The body section is where the content within the browser is displayed. Type the following into Notepad to create the web page. Note that it is very important that you type all punctuation correctly. Also note that in the third line from the bottom <h1> and </h1> has the number 1 (one) after the h, not a lower case L.

```
<html lang="en">
<head>
    <meta charset="utf-8" />
    <title>First JavaScript Program</title>
</head>
<body>
    <h1>My First JavaScript Program</h1>

</body>
</html>
```

> The <html> tag in the first line contains an attribute of lang="en". Attributes provide additional formatting and descriptive information associated with the tag. Not all tags contain attributes. The lang="en" attribute in this example sets the default language of the page to English, which is important for programs such as screen readers and search engines that may read the page.

> The third line, <meta charset="utf-8" />, specifies the character set. In this case, utf-8 is capable of encoding all the characters in Unicode. ASCII is a subset of Unicode. Note that the meta tag is a type of tag called an *empty tag* because it has no end tag. Instead, there is a slash before the closing angle bracket (>).

> The next line uses the <title></title> tag pair to define a page title. The page title is the text that shows up in your browser on the very top whenever you go to any web page. This web page will have **First JavaScript Program** as its title.

> The head section must be closed with the </head> end tag before the body section begins with the <body> start tag. Anything between <body> and </body> will be visible when the page is opened in a browser.

> This web page has one line only. The text **My First JavaScript Program** will be displayed. Since it is enclosed in <h1></h1> tags, by default the text will be large and black. Other tag pairs can be used for different formats.

4. Read this entire step before taking action. Now save your file inside the *JavaScriptTest* folder with the filename javascript1*xxx*.html, where *xxx* is your initials. Be sure to use the drop-down menu in the Notepad *Save As* window to change *Save as Type* to *All Files* and be sure to save your file with the .html extension by including the file extension (.html) as part of the filename. If you let Notepad use the default extension (.txt), your page will not be a web page.

5. Now open your web page in a browser by right-clicking on the javascript1*xxx*.html file in *Windows Explorer/File Explorer* and use the *Open With* option to select a web browser such as Microsoft Edge or Internet Explorer. If you have done everything correctly, you should see a page like the one in Lab Figure 15.11 in your browser.

LAB FIGURE 15.11   HTML code in the Firefox browser

Notice the page title in the upper-left corner. Notice the path to the file in the browser's address bar. In this case, the path is `file:///C:/JavascriptTest/javascript1end.html`, but your path will be slightly different, depending on where you saved your file (and your own initials, of course). If your web page appeared properly, you are now ready to add some JavaScript. If it did not appear properly, correct the code using Notepad and rerun it until it does.

Did the proper web page appear? [Yes | No]

Instructor initials: _____

6. In this first JavaScript program, you will return to Notepad and create a button that the user will click to start the JavaScript program. The button and the area where the result of the JavaScript code will appear are enclosed in `<p></p>` tags. The button is nested inside the `<p></p>` tags and enclosed in `<button></button>` tags. Enter the following code under the first line of the body (`<h1>My First JavaScript Program<h1>`):

    ```
    <p><button type="button" onclick="welcome()">Click me
         </button> <span id="greet"> </span></p>
    ```

    Note: While character spacing and line spacing are not essential in JavaScript or HTML, it is important to follow standard spacing and indentation conventions to make reading and debugging code easier: separate operators like + and = with a space, and indent all JavaScript statements inside of functions as demonstrated in the next step.

    This code will put a button on the web page with the text `Click Me`. A space for the result is identified by `id="greet"`, and the result will be placed in the area between the `<span></span>` tags. When the page loads, there is nothing in this space, so ` ` is simply a placeholder. It stands for "non-breaking space."

7. Add the JavaScript code. In the head section, under the `<title></title>` line which is, (`<title>First JavaScript Program</title>`) line, add the following code:

    ```
    <script type = "text/javascript">
    function welcome(){
                        var name = prompt("What's your name? ", " ");
                var greeting = ("Hello there, " + name + "!");
                document.getElementById('greet').innerHTML =
                        greeting;
    }
    </script>
    ```

    > JavaScript scripts (or programs) are enclosed in `<script></script>` tags. In this small script, the code is enclosed in a function named `welcome()`. When the button on the HTML page is clicked, control transfers to the `welcome()` function. All the code to be executed when the `welcome()` function is called is contained between an opening curly brace (`{`) and a closing curly brace (`}`).

    > The first line of the function declares a variable named `name`. A variable is a named memory location that stores data. In a script, variables are declared in order to tell the JavaScript interpreter to create the memory location that will store the value. A prompt will appear on the screen with the text `What's Your Name?`, and execution of the code will pause until the user types in a name. That value is stored in the variable `name`.

    > The next line declares a second variable, named `greeting`. The value of `greeting` consists of text (`"Hello there, "`) joined with the value of `name` and then joined with an exclamation point. Note, by the way, that the text to be displayed includes a space after the comma. A space is considered a character. Without the space, the output would be something like this:

    `Hello there,Cheryl!`

    when what you want is this in order to make the output more readable:

    `Hello there, Cheryl!`

> The last line of the function outputs the value of greeting into the space on the web page identified by id="greet". This line has several parts:

```
document.getElementById('greet').innerHTML = greeting;
```

The word document refers to an object which represents the current web page. getElementById() is a JavaScript function that tells the computer to look for an element with a tag on the page with the id attribute that matches what is inside the parentheses. In this case, it is the <span> tag with id="greet" attribute. Assigning the variable greeting, which is on the right side of this statement, to the innerHTML property of the element on the left side of the statement using the equal (=) sign is a way for JavaScript to tell the computer to replace whatever currently is in the <span> element with the value of the variable.

8.   Save your new file with the filename javascript2*xxx*.html inside your *JavaScript Test* folder. Now open the file in a browser as you did before.

9.   If you see the *Click Me* button, click it. If you do not see the *Click Me* button, redo the code. Do not proceed until you see the *Click Me* button.

Does the *Click Me* button work properly? [Yes | No]

Instructor initials: _____

10. Enter your name and see if it works. If your name is Cheryl, you should see the prompt and, after entering **Cheryl**, the screen should display the correct greeting. Compare your results to Lab Figure 15.12 (which shows the page opened in Firefox).

LAB FIGURE 15.12   Enhanced JavaScript program with a button and a prompt

11. Now create a JavaScript program that allows the user to enter two numbers and either add or multiply them. You can start with your first program and make the following changes to the HTML body:
> Change the page title to **Second JavaScript Program**.
> In the <button> section, change the text on the button from Click me to **Do the math!**
> Change the id attribute of the span element from greet to **'calc'**.
> The new JavaScript function you create in the next step is named do_math(), so you need to change this in the HTML body (onclick= section) as well.

12. Between the <script></script> tags in the head section, replace the welcome() function with the following do_math() function:

```
function do_math()
{
        var num1 = parseFloat(prompt("Enter the first
            number: "));
    var num2 = parseFloat(prompt("Enter the second
            number: "));
    var result = prompt("Enter A to add the numbers
            or M to multiply them: ");
    if (result == 'A')
        var answer = num1 + num2;
    else if (result == 'M')
        var answer = num1 * num2;
    else
        var answer = "Invalid entry";
    document.getElementById('calc').innerHTML=
```

```
        "The result is " + answer;
    }
```

JavaScript does not have strict rules regarding spacing or indentation. In fact, a whole program could be typed on a single line, although this would never be a good idea since the resulting code would be difficult to read. The spacing and indentation you see in the code shown here follows standard coding conventions for readability and also to help developers with debugging. You should make every effort to follow these conventions in your own code.

13. Save this new file inside your *JavaScript Test* folder with the filename **javascript3xxx.html**. There are a few new things worth discussing in this program. It uses a decision structure (if/else) to determine whether to add the numbers or multiply them. It also validates the user input by displaying an error message of "Invalid entry" if the user has not selected either A to add or M to multiply.

    > You will notice that the prompt() statements are enclosed in a new JavaScript function—the parseFloat() function. When a user types in anything in response to a prompt, it is automatically stored as a string (a sequence of text that is not interpreted as numbers). But, in order to do mathematical calculations, the numbers must be stored as numbers. The parseFloat() function will change the text the user has entered into a floating-point number (a number with a decimal point).

14. Run your new program in a browser. Click on the *Do the Math!* button. If the button is not there, redo the code until it appears. Do not proceed until the button appears.

    Does the Do the Math! button work properly? [Yes | No]

Instructor initials: _____

15. Enter **3** and **5** for the two numbers and **A** to add (make sure it is a capital *A*). Lab Figure 15.13 shows the results you should see, given the inputs listed. If you do not see this output, redo your code until you do.

LAB FIGURE 15.13   JavaScript math program using addition

16. Click on the *Do the Math!* button again. Enter **4.6** and **6.9** for the two numbers and **M** to multiply (ensuring it is a capital M). Lab Figure 15.14 shows what you should see now.

LAB FIGURE 15.14   JavaScript math program using multiplication

17. Click on the *Do the Math!* button again. Enter **35** and **63** for the two numbers and **m** to multiply. Note that the lowercase m is intentional so you can see the result, as shown in Lab Figure 15.15.

LAB FIGURE 15.15   JavaScript math program, with an error due to case

18. Click on the *Do the Math!* button again. Enter **two** and **six** for the two numbers and **A** to add.

LAB FIGURE 15.16   JavaScript math program, with invalid entries

In Lab Figure 15.16, the result is shown as NaN. This stands for "not a number," and it is what happens when the JavaScript `parseFloat()` function attempts to convert text that has no numerical value to a number. The way a developer would deal with this to avoid the NaN error is to validate the input by checking if the value stored in `num1` or `num2` was an actual number and, if necessary, prompt the user for a valid entry.

19. To deal with the situation that arose in Lab Figure 15.15, where a lowercase letter is entered instead of the required uppercase letter, you can add a logical operator (the | | is an OR operator checking whether either situation is true) to ensure that both lowercase and uppercase entries are valid. Change the `if/else` statements in your program as shown in this step in bold, save it again with a new filename, `javascript4xxx.html`, then run the program several times to make sure all of the entries (**A**, **a**, **M**, and **m**) are now valid. The replaced lines should be as follows:

```
if (result == 'A' || result == 'a')
```

and:

```
else if (result == 'M' || result == 'm')
```

There are a few things to be careful about when you make these changes. You can enclose the text within the conditions with either double or single quotes (" " or ' '), but whichever you choose, it should be consistent. The entire condition must be enclosed in parentheses, and the two sides of the **OR** symbol (| |) must be complete conditions. Consider these examples:

```
if (result == "A" || result == 'a') is not correct.
if (result == 'A') || (result == "a") is not correct.
if (result == 'A' || 'a')  will not work.
```

20. Test the code by running it within a web browser. See if you can press the lowercase a to add two numbers. Also see if the lowercase m works properly. Troubleshoot your code until it works before proceeding.

Does the *Do the Math!* button work with lowercase letters now? [Yes | No]

Instructor initials: _____

21. Now you will add a loop to this program to allow the user to run the program as often as desired without having to use the Back button or refresh the screen. To do this, you add a variable, `rerun`, and set its initial value to y. Then you open a `while` loop and enclose the entire block of statements in the loop within curly braces ({ }). You will also call the alert function to display an alert box to the user containing the result, followed by a prompt asking the user if the program should run again.

The new code looks like this:

```
function do_math()
{
    var rerun = 'y';
    while (rerun == 'y' || rerun == 'Y')
    {
    var num1= parseInt(prompt("Enter the first number: "));
    var num2 = parseInt(prompt("Enter the second number: "));
```

```
                    var result = prompt("Enter A to add the numbers or M to
       multiply them: ");
                    if (result == 'A' || result == 'a')
                        var answer = num1 + num2;
                    else if (result == 'M' || result == 'm')
                        var answer = num1 * num2;
                    else
                        var answer = "Invalid entry";
                    alert("The result is " + answer);
                    rerun = prompt("Enter y to continue or press any key to
       end: ");
                }
            }
```

Note the two closing curly braces at the end. One closes the `while` loop, and one closes the `do_math()` function; the indentation should help make it clear to you. The `parseInt()` function changes any value the user has typed into an integer, if possible. Refer to the section where the `parseFloat` was used as a comparison. Save this program as `javascript5xxx.html` and run it in a browser. After you enter two numbers and get the result, you should see a screen like the one in Lab Figure 15.17.

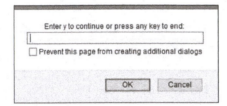

LAB FIGURE 15.17   JavaScript math program with a fix for uppercase and lowercase entries

Test your loop by entering **y** and making sure the program runs again.

Does the prompt appear, allowing you to rerun the program? [Yes | No]

Instructor initials: _____

On Your Own

Note: With all scripting languages, there are multiple ways to solve most programming problems. As you become more proficient with writing code, you may find new or more efficient ways to solve problems.

22. Run the `javascript3xxx.html` or `javascript4xxx.html` program but enter the values **3.3** and **3.3** and select the option to multiply. What is the result? Did you get what you expected? Why or why not? Use the Internet to research how floating-point numbers are stored. See if you can explain why the results of doing math with floating-point numbers is not truly accurate.

_____
_____
_____
_____

23. Change the code of your `javascript3xxx.html` or `javascript4xxx.html` file to offer the user the option to subtract the two numbers. Provide the code that you changed to make this work.

    _____

    _____

    _____

    _____

    _____

    _____

Instructor initials: _____

24. Change the input prompts in the `javascript3xxx.html` file to use integers instead of floating-point numbers. Save this file as `javascript6xxx.html`. Use the `parseInt()` function instead of the `parseFloat()` function. Make sure the program works when integers are input by the user. Provide the code that you changed to make this work.

    _____

    _____

    _____

Instructor initials: _____

25. Try entering the following in your `javascript6xxx.html` program: **4.5**, **2**, **M**. What is the result? Is it what you would expect? Can you explain what happened? Do some research on the Internet to find out what happens when a floating-point number is entered in JavaScript if an integer is expected.

    _____

    _____

26. Consider the `do_math()` function. What special circumstances might arise if you attempt to include the option to divide two numbers?

    _____

    _____

    _____

    _____

LAB 15

16 Advanced Windows Labs

Lab 16.1 Windows 7 Installation

Objective:	To install Windows 7 on a hard drive that does not have an existing operating system
Parts:	A computer with the minimum hardware requirements for Windows 7
	Windows 7 DVD or virtual image of the installation disc
Note:	The screens may appear a little differently with different service packs and Windows 7 versions.
Procedure:	Complete the following procedure and answer the accompanying questions.

1. Configure the BIOS to boot from the CD/DVD drive.

2. Insert the Windows 7 installation DVD into an optical drive and turn on the computer. The Windows 7 Setup program starts automatically if the BIOS is configured correctly.

3. Select the appropriate regional options and click *Next*.

4. Select *Install Now* to start the Windows 7 installation.

5. Read the EULA (end user licensing agreement). Select the *I Accept the License Terms* option and click *Next*.

6. Two options appear for Windows 7: to upgrade or to perform a custom installation. To install Windows 7 as a clean install, click the *Custom (Advanced)* option.

7. When prompted for where to install Windows 7, select the *Drive Options (Advanced)* option.

8. Delete a partition, create a partition, and format a partition, as needed. When finished selecting the partition, click *Next*. If a RAID or SCSI driver is needed, install it at this point.

9. The computer restarts, and Windows 7 loads and completes the installation. A username and a computer name are required. The computer name must be unique. Contact the instructor or lab assistant for a unique name, if necessary.

10. Contact the instructor for a password for the user account.

    Print the exact password to be used, with appropriate uppercase and lowercase letters.

    _____

11. Enter the password, enter a hint, and then click *Next*.

12. Enter the product key provided. Check with the instructor or lab assistant if you do not have one. Note that you can leave this blank to experiment with the different versions of Windows 7. They all come on the same DVD. You must eventually install a version for which you have a license. Do not experiment with different Windows 7 versions if upgrading from a prior version of Windows as this is not allowed after the old version is upgraded.

13. In the *Help Protect Your Computer and Improve Windows Automatically* dialog box, select the *Use Recommended Settings* option.

14. In the *Review Your Time and Date Settings* dialog box, select the appropriate time zone and date options. Click *Finish*.

Instructor initials: _____

15. Contact your instructor or lab assistant for the appropriate computer location. If the instructor or assistant is not available, select the *Work* option.

16. Click *Start*, and the Windows logon appears.

Instructor initials: _____

Lab 16.2 Windows 8/8.1 Installation

Objective: To install Windows 8 or 8.1 on a hard drive that does not have an existing operating system

Parts: A computer with the minimum hardware requirements for Windows 8/8.1

Windows 8/8.1 DVD, virtual image of the installation disc, or image on an eSATA or USB drive

Note: The screens may appear a little differently with different service packs and Windows 8/8.1 versions.

Procedure: Complete the following procedure and answer the accompanying questions.

1. Configure the BIOS to boot from the optical drive, USB drive, or eSATA drive.

2. Insert or attach the Windows 8/8.1 installation media and turn on/restart the computer. The Windows Setup program starts automatically if the BIOS is configured correctly.

3. Select the appropriate regional options, such as language, time/currency, and keyboard/input method and click *Next*.

4. Select *Install Now* to start the Windows installation.

5. Read and accept the EULA (end user licensing agreement).

6. Two installation options appear for Windows: to upgrade or to perform a custom installation. To install Windows as a clean install, click the *Custom (Advanced)* option.

7. When prompted for where to install Windows, select the *Drive Options (Advanced)* option.

8. Delete a partition, create a partition, and format a partition, as needed. When finished selecting the partition, click *Next*. If a RAID or SCSI driver is needed, install it at this point.

9. The computer restarts, and Windows loads and completes the installation. A username and a computer name are required. The computer name must be unique. Contact the instructor or lab assistant for a unique name, if necessary.

10. Contact the instructor for a password for the user account.

    Print the exact password to be used, with appropriate uppercase and lowercase letters.

    _____

11. Enter the password, enter a hint, and then click *Next*.

12. Enter the product key provided. Check with the instructor or lab assistant if you do not have one.

13. In the *Help Protect Your Computer and Improve Windows Automatically* dialog box, select the *Use Recommended Settings* option.

14. In the *Review Your Time and Date Settings* dialog box, select the appropriate time zone and date options. Click *Finish*.

Instructor initials: _____

15. Contact your instructor or lab assistant for the appropriate computer location. If the instructor or assistant is not available, select the *Work* option.

16. Click *Start*, and the Windows logon appears.

Instructor initials: _____

Lab 16.3 Windows 10 Installation

Objective: To install Windows 10 on a hard drive that does not have an existing operating system

Parts: A computer with the minimum hardware requirements for Windows 10

Windows 10 DVD, virtual image of the installation disc, or image on an eSATA or USB drive

Note: The screens may appear a little differently with different service packs.

Procedure: Complete the following procedure and answer the accompanying questions.

1. Configure the BIOS to boot from the optical drive, USB drive, or eSATA drive.

2. Insert or attach the Windows 10 installation media and turn on/restart the computer. The Windows Setup program starts automatically if the BIOS is configured correctly.

3. Select the appropriate regional options, such as language, time/currency, and keyboard/input method and click *Next*.

4. Select *Install Now* to start the Windows installation.

5. Enter the Windows product key given to you by the instructor. If you are reinstalling Windows, you can select the *I Don't Have a Product Key* option.

6. Select the proper edition of Windows. Check with the instructor if unsure. The edition must match the product key Windows version. Click Next.

7. Read the EULA (end user licensing agreement). Select (enable) the *I Accept the License Terms* checkbox and click *Next*.

8. Two installation options appear for Windows: to upgrade or to perform a custom installation. To install Windows as a clean install, click the *Custom: Install Windows Only (Advanced)* option.

9. When prompted for where to install Windows, select the *Drive Options (Advanced)* option.

10. Delete a partition, create a partition, and format a partition, as needed. When finished selecting the partition, click *Next*. If a RAID or SCSI driver is needed, install it at this point.

11. The computer restarts, and Windows loads and completes the installation. A username (or Microsoft account) and a computer name are required. The computer name must be unique. Contact the instructor or lab assistant for a unique name, if necessary.

Instructor initials: _____

12. Contact the instructor for a password/PIN for the user account.

Print the exact password to be used, with appropriate uppercase and lowercase letters.

_____

13. Enter the remaining settings (register a phone, One Drive, Cortana settings) per the instructor's directions.

14. Click *Accept*, and the Windows logon appears.

Instructor initials: _____

LAB 16

Lab 16.4 Windows 8/8.1 Upgrade

Objective: To become familiar with upgrading to Windows 8/8.1 from Windows 7

Parts: A computer with Windows 7 installed, Internet access, and Administrator rights

Windows 8/8.1 image disc or image on a flash drive or external drive

Procedure: Complete the following procedure and answer the accompanying questions.

1. Power on the computer that is to be upgraded and verify that Windows loads. Log in using the user ID and password provided by the instructor or lab assistant.

2. Download and burn a bootable Windows 8/8.1 DVD or have an image on a USB flash drive or external drive.

3. Before proceeding, it is recommended to back up any important data. If using a virtual machine, it is advised to create a snapshot that can be reverted to if you run into problems.

4. Review the Windows 8/8.1 minimum requirements to make sure the computer is compatible.

5. Insert the DVD into the computer and run the `setup.exe` file from the disc. You may be prompted to download updates by the installer; if so, download and install them.

6. When prompted, accept the licensing agreement for the installer.

7. When you are asked if you want to keep files, settings, apps, or nothing, select *Keep Files, Apps and Settings* and then click *Next*.

8. Review your selections. You should be installing a version of Windows 8 and keeping your personal files. If it looks correct, click *Install*; otherwise, click *Back* and change your selections.

9. The installation begins; keep in mind that it can take a few hours to complete and that during this process, the computer may reboot several times.

10. When the installation finishes, you are at a Windows 8/8.1 login screen.

11. Log in, and you are given the option to customize or use express settings for the new installation. Choose *Customize*.

12. Pick the settings you prefer.

13. Finish the customization process, and Windows finalizes its installation and takes you to your desktop.

Instructor initials: _____

Lab 16.5 Windows 10 Upgrade

Objective: To become familiar with upgrading to Windows 10 from Windows 8/8.1

Parts: A computer with Windows 8/8.1 installed, Internet access, and Administrator rights

Windows 10 image disc or image on a flash drive or external drive

Procedure: Complete the following procedure and answer the accompanying questions.

1. Power on the computer that is to be upgraded and verify that Windows loads. Log in using the user ID and password provided by the instructor or lab assistant.

2. Download and burn a bootable Windows 10 DVD.

3. Before proceeding, it is recommended to back up any important data. If using a virtual machine, it is advised to create a snapshot that can be reverted to if you run into problems.

4. Review the Windows 10 minimum requirements to make sure the computer is compatible.

5. Insert the DVD into the computer and run the `setup.exe` file from the disc. You may be prompted to download updates by the installer; if so, download and install them.

6. When prompted, accept the licensing agreement for the installer.

7. When you are asked if you want to keep files, settings, apps, or nothing, select *Keep Files, Apps and Settings* and then click *Next*.

8. Review your selections. You should be installing a version of Windows 10 and keeping your personal files. If it looks correct, select *Install;* otherwise, select *Back* and change your selections.

9. The installation begins; keep in mind it can take a few hours to complete and that during this process, the computer may reboot several times.

10. When the installation finishes, you are at a Windows 10 login screen.

11. Log in, and you are given the option to customize or use express settings for the new installation. Choose *Customize*.

12. Pick the settings you prefer.

13. Finish the customization process, and Windows finalizes its installation and takes you to your desktop.

Instructor initials: _____

Lab 16.6 Windows Registry Modification

Objective: To modify the Windows registry when given directions to do so

Parts: Computer with Windows 7, 8, 8.1, or 10 loaded

Notes: You must be an administrator or a member of the Administrators group to change registry settings. Sometimes, you are given directions by Microsoft to edit the registry to fix a problem. It is important that you follow the directions exactly as directed.

Procedure: Complete the following procedure and answer the accompanying questions.

1. Power on the computer and verify that Windows loads. Log on to the computer using the user ID and password provided by the instructor or lab assistant.

2. Open Windows Explorer (Windows 7) or File Explorer (Windows 8/8.1/10). Right-click any folder within *Documents*. If no folder exists, create one.

    Which editing options are available for a folder? (Select all that apply.)

    [Cut | Copy | Paste | Copy To Folder | Move To Folder | Delete | Rename | Send To]

3. Select the *Start* button (Windows 7) or right-click the *Start* button (Windows 8/8.1/10) > *Run* > type **regedit** > ⏎Enter > *Yes*.

4. Expand the Hkey_Classes_Root option by clicking the > (greater than sign) beside the option.

5. Scroll down to locate and expand AllFileSystemObjects. Note that items beginning with a character such as a . (period) appear before the alphabetized list of other objects.

6. Expand the shellex object and locate ContextMenuHandlers. Shellex is a shell extension key that lets you customize the Windows interface.

7. Right-click ContextMenuHandlers > *New* > *Key*. When the new folder (key) appears, type **Copy To** and press ⏎Enter. This registry modification adds a new option to the right-click menu called *Copy To*.

8. The Copy To object should still be selected in the left window. Double-click the *(Default)* name in the right panel. The *Edit String* window appears.

9. In the *Value Data* textbox, type the following value exactly as shown (the 0s are zeros):

    {C2FBB630-2971-11D1-A18C-00C04FD75D13}

    Click *OK*.

10. Verify that the change has occurred. Open *Windows Explorer/File Explorer* and right-click any folder.

    Does *Copy To Folder* appear as an option? [Yes | No]

    If not, redo the lab.

Instructor initials: _____

LAB 16

11. Return to the *Registry Editor* window. Using the same process, create another new key under `ContextMenuHandlers` and name the key *Move To*. The value data for the Move To key is as follows:

    {C2FBB631-2971-11D1-A18C-00C04FD75D13}

12. Use *Windows Explorer/File Explorer* to create two new folders. Copy a couple of files into each folder. Use the new *Copy To* and *Move To* options you just created.

13. Delete any folders/files that you have created.

14. To delete keys in Registry Editor, select the *Copy To* option in the left panel. From the *Edit* menu option, select *Delete* and select *Yes* when asked to verify. Delete the *Move To* key using the same process.

Instructor initials: _____

15. Close the *Registry Editor* window.

Lab 16.7 Windows 7 Backup

Objective: To back up files, including the operating system, if necessary, using the Backup and Restore utility

Parts: A computer with Windows 7 installed and Administrator rights

Procedure: Complete the following procedure and answer the accompanying questions.

Note: Even though only three files are backed up using this process, you can use the same process to back up the computer.

1. Create a new folder called *Stuff* under *Documents*.

2. Create three text files with any names and place them in the new *Stuff* folder.

3. Access the *System and Security* Control Panel *Backup and Restore > Set Up Backup* link. (Note that if the Backup and Restore link has already been accessed, the *Change Settings* link can be used to complete the lab.) > select a backup destination designated by the instructor or lab assistant > *Next* > select the *Let Me Choose* radio button > select *Next*.

    Note: You can use the *Let Windows Choose* radio button to back up the entire operating system and files.

4. Deselect all enabled checkboxes > expand *OS (C:)* by clicking the arrow beside it > expand *Users* > expand the username used to log in to the computer > expand *Documents* > select the *Stuff* folder to enable it for backup > *Next* > *Save Settings and Run Backup* button.

5. The backup executes. Show the instructor the completed backup.

Instructor initials: _____

6. Delete the *Stuff* folder and the three files contained within it.

Lab 16.8 Windows Update Utility

Objective: To configure a computer for Windows updates.

Parts: Computer with Windows 7, 8, 8.1, or 10 loaded and Internet access

Note: You must be an administrator or a member of the Administrators group to change Automatic Updates settings.

Procedure: Complete the following procedure and answer the accompanying questions.

1. Power on the computer and verify that Windows loads. Log on to the computer using the user ID and password provided by the instructor or lab assistant.

2. In Windows 7, click the *Start* button > *Control Panel* > *System and Security Windows Update* link.

    In Windows 8/8.1, right-click the *Start* button (or just search for the Control Panel using the *Search* charm) > *Control Panel* > *System and Security* link > *Windows Update* link > *Change Settings* link.

In Windows 10, click the *Start* button > *Settings* > *Update & Security*.

What option is currently selected?

_____

Which option do you think most large corporations would want as standard, and why do you think this?

_____

When was the last Windows update?

_____

3.   Close the *Windows Update* window.

4.   Click the *Cancel* button to close the *Automatic Updates* window.

Lab 16.9 Configuring Windows 7, 8, 8.1, and 10 for Ease of Access

Objective: To configure Windows 7, 8, 8.1, or 10 for customers who need a customized environment for visual, auditory, and physical reasons

Parts: Computer with Windows 7, 8, 8.1, or 10 installed

Procedure: Complete the following procedure and answer the accompanying questions. Note that not all steps are shown, and you must explore some settings based on the question asked.

1.   To access the Ease of Access Center in Windows 7, click the *Start* button > *Control Panel* > *Ease of Access* link. In Windows 8/8.1/10 locate and access the *Ease of Access* Control Panel utility.

2.   Select the *Let Windows suggest settings* link.

     What recommendations does Microsoft make available to someone at the workplace who has trouble seeing images on the screen because of the office lighting? Note that you have to make selections based on the scenario given to obtain this information. You do not have to select an option on each of the five screens that presents options. You should only select an option that relates to the scenario given. Click *Cancel* when you are done answering the question.

_____

_____

_____

3.   You should be back at the Ease of Access Center window.

4.   You should see the Make your computer easier to use section and the Explore All Settings section. Use *the Explore all settings* options to answer the questions.

     What is the purpose of the *Make the mouse easier to use* setting?

_____

     What is the purpose of the *Make it easier to focus on tasks* setting?

_____

     Which option do you think might be used on a Microsoft Surface tablet?

_____

5.   Return to the main *Ease of Access* Control Panel and reselect the *Let Windows Suggest Settings* link. You should be on the *Get recommendations to make your computer easier to use* window. If applicable, disable (uncheck) the *Lighting conditions make it difficult to see images on my monitor* checkbox.

6.   Select the *Images and text on TV are difficult to see (even when I'm wearing glasses)* checkbox. Click *Next* four times and then click *Done* to view Microsoft's recommendations.

     What options are recommended (checked) by Microsoft for this situation?

_____

_____

7.   In the *Change the color and size of mouse pointers* section, select the *Large Inverting* radio button. Select *Apply*.

8.   Move the mouse and open *Windows Explorer (Windows 7)/File Explorer* (Windows 8/8.1/10). Describe your experience.

_____

_____

Would office workers who do not have a visual impairment enjoy this feature?

_____

9.   Change the mouse pointer back to *Regular White*. Ensure that the *Turn on or off high contrast when left ALT + left SHIFT + PRINT SCREEN* is pressed, with all associated checkboxes enabled. Select *Apply*.

10. Hold down the left [Alt] key, and while keeping the key held down, press and hold the left [⬆Shift] key. While holding down both of these keys, press the [PrtSc] key ([Alt]+left [⬆Shift]+[Print Screen]). Release all three keys.

What audio signal do you hear?

_____

From information in the message, document how to disable the keyboard shortcut if these specific keys are used for another application.

_____

_____

11. Click *Yes*.

Describe the difference in screen appearance.

_____

Do you like the high contrast?

_____

12. Use the same keys again to disable the high-contrast setting. Click *Cancel* in the Recommended Settings window.

13. Reselect the *Get recommendations to make your computer easier to use* link. Remove the enabled option checkbox from the *Eyesight* window and click *Next*.

14. In the *Dexterity* window, select the *Pens and pencils are difficult to use* checkbox. Click *Next* or *Done* until you reach Microsoft's recommendations.

What option or options are recommended by Microsoft?

_____

What are toggle keys? What happens when a toggle key is pressed?

_____

15. Open *Notepad*. Notice the blinking cursor in the top-left corner.

16. Leave Notepad open and return to the *Recommended Settings* window. Notice the setting for *Set the thickness of the blinking cursor*. Change the thickness of the blinking cursor to **5**. Click *Apply*.

17. Return to *Notepad* and notice the difference in the blinking cursor.

18. Return to the *Recommended Settings* window and return the thickness to the default setting of **1** and click *Apply*. Close *Notepad*.

19. Return to the *Recommended Settings* window.

What is the Sticky Keys setting?

_____

_____

Who might benefit from the Sticky Keys setting?

_____

20. Enable (select) the *Set Up Filter Keys* link.

What is the Filter Keys feature?

_____

_____

What is the default amount of time the ⬆Shift key has to stay pressed to toggle on Filter Keys?

_____

By default, do you see a warning message, do you hear a tone, or do you get both a message and a tone when Filter Keys is active? [warning message | tone | both]

What is the Bounce Keys feature?

_____

What is the default time between keystrokes if the Bounce Keys feature is enabled?

_____

Is this setting adjustable? [Yes | No]

21. Click in the *Type text here to test settings* textbox. Type **hello**.

What happened?

_____

22. Click the *Set up repeat keys and slow keys* link.

23. Click in the *Type text here to test settings* textbox. Click and hold the Ⓗ key down until it appears in the textbox. Finish typing the word **hello** as a message. Note that in a virtualized environment, this option does not work. If you are in such an environment, simply write *virtualization used* in answer to the question below.

What indication did you get, in addition to seeing it appear in the textbox, that the letter "took"?

_____

Instructor initials: _____

24. Click *Cancel* to return to the *Set Up Filter Keys* screen.

What are the other settings this window offers?

_____

25. Click *Cancel* to return to the *Ease of Access Center*.

26. Return to the *Ease of Access* Control Panel utility and select the *Let Windows suggest settings* link. Return to the *Dexterity* window and clear the checkbox for the *Pens and Pencils Are Difficult to Use* option. Click *Next*.

27. On the *Hearing* window, select the *Conversations can be difficult to hear (even with a hearing aid)* checkbox. Click *Next* or *Done* until you reach the Microsoft recommendations.

What options are available?

_____

_____

28. Enable *Turn on visual notifications for sounds (Sound Sentry)*. Select the visual warning *Flash active window*. Click *Apply*. Leave that window open and access the *Hardware and Sound* Control Panel utility in a separate window. In the *Sound* section, select the *Change system sounds* link. On the *Sounds* tab, select a Windows notification that has a speaker beside it. Click the *Test* button.

Even if your computer does not have speakers, what visual clue do you get that a sound is being made? Note that this option may not function in a virtual environment; if you are in such an environment, simply write virtualization used in answer to the question below.

_____

29. Close the *Sound* window. Return to the *Recommended Settings* window. Remove the check from *Turn on visual notifications for sounds (Sound Sentry)*. Click *Apply*. Click *Cancel* to return to the Ease of Access Center.

30. Return to the *Ease of Access* Control Panel utility and select the *Let Windows suggest settings* link. Return to the Hearing window and disable the *Conversations can be difficult to hear (even with a hearing aid)* option. Click *Next* to advance to the Speech Options screen. Enable the *Other people have difficulty understanding me in a conversation (but not due to an accent)* option. Click *Next* or *Done* until you reach Microsoft's recommendations.

    What is Microsoft's recommendation?

    _____

31. Click the *Completing the questionnaire again* link. Return to the *Speech* page and enable the *I have a speech impairment* checkbox.

    Did this change Microsoft's recommendations? If so, what are the recommendations?

    _____

32. Return to the questionnaire and disable all options from the *Speech* page and click *Next* to advance to the Reasoning window. Select the *I have a learning disability, such as dyslexia* option. Click *Done*.

    What does Microsoft recommend for this type of person?

    _____

    _____

Instructor initials: _____

33. Click *Cancel*. Ensure that all Ease of Access options are disabled. Close the *Ease of Access Center* window.

Lab 16.10 Windows 7/8/8.1 System Restore Utility

Objective: To configure and use the System Restore utility

Parts: A computer with Windows 7, 8, or 8.1 installed and Administrator rights

Notes: You must be an administrator to perform System Restore. If System Restore has been disabled, this lab may have to be done over two class periods. One class period would be used to enable it and schedule a restore point, and the next class period to perform the system restore. Also note that an antivirus update or a Windows update might have to be reinstalled as a result of the system restore.

Procedure: Complete the following procedure and answer the accompanying questions.

1. Power on the computer and verify that Windows loads. Log on to Windows using the user ID and password provided by the instructor or lab assistant.

2. Hold down the ▇ key and press the Ⓡ key. In the Run box enter **rstrui** and click *OK*. An alternate way of bringing up System Restore is to type **rstrui** in the *Search* textbox.

3. In the System Restore window, read the beginning explanation of System Restore.

    What are two reasons that System Restore might be used?

    _____

    [T | F] System Restore does not affect personal data documents.

    [Yes | No] Can a recently installed application be affected by using the System Restore utility?

    [Yes | No] Is the System Restore process reversible?

4. Click the *Next* button. Note that if the Next button is grayed out, you may have to turn on system protection by clicking the *System Protection* link, selecting a drive, select *Configure*, enabling the *Turn on system protection* radio button, and clicking *OK* twice; then return to the *System Restore* window and click the *Next* button.

Are any restore points available? If so, list the latest one.

_____

5.   Create a restore point by using the *Create* button if one has never been created. Select the newest restore point (the one at the top of the list) and click *Next*.

What does Windows recommend creating if you have recently changed your Windows password?

_____

Instructor initials: _____

6.   Click *Finish* to confirm rolling back your system to an earlier time.

Under what conditions can the System Restore changes not be undone?

_____

_____

7.   Click *Yes* to the dialog message. The system restarts as part of the System Restore process.

Instructor initials: _____

8.   Log in to Windows and ensure that the system works.

9.   After the system has been restored to an earlier time, install any antivirus or Windows updates that have been affected by this system restore.

Lab 16.11 Windows 10 System Restore Utility

Objective: To configure and use the System Restore utility

Parts: A computer with Windows 10 installed and Administrator rights

Notes: You must be an administrator to perform System Restore. If System Restore has been disabled, this lab may have to be done over two class periods. One class period would be used to enable it and schedule a restore point, and the next class period to perform the system restore. Also note that an antivirus update or a Windows update might have to be reinstalled as a result of the system restore.

Procedure: Complete the following procedure and answer the accompanying questions.

1.   Power on the computer and verify that Windows loads. Log on to Windows using the user ID and password provided by the instructor or lab assistant.

2.   Windows 10 is the first operating system that has the System Restore utility, and it has it disabled by default. In order to use System Restore, system protection has to be enabled. Open the *System* Control Panel. Select the *System Protection* link from the left menu. The System Properties window opens with the System Protection tab open.

3.   In the *Protection Settings* window, notice that the C: drive has a protection status of off. Select the C: drive in the *Protection Settings* window and click the *Configure* button.

4.   In the *Restore Settings* section, enable the *Turn on system protection* radio button. Using the *Max Usage* slide bar, adjust the drive space allocated for restore points to approximately 15% of the drive. Click the *OK* button.

5.   On the *System Protection* tab, use the *Create* button to create a restore point. Name the restore point and click *Create*.

What did you name the restore point?

_____

What message did you get?

_____

Instructor initials: _____

6.   Click the *Close* button and then the *OK* button. Close the *System* Control Panel window.

7. Hold down the ▦ key and press the Ⓡ key. In the Run box, enter in **rstrui** and click *OK*. An alternate way of bringing up System Restore is to type **rstrui** in the *Search* textbox.

8. In the System Restore window, read the beginning explanation of System Restore.

What are two reasons that System Restore might be used?

_____

[T | F] System Restore does not affect personal data documents.

[Yes | No] Can a recently installed application be affected by using the System Restore utility?

[Yes | No] Is the System Restore process reversible?

9. Click the *Next* button.

Are any restore points available? If so, list the latest one. [Yes | No]

_____

_____

Instructor initials: _____

Using a Restore Point

10. To use a restore point and take a system back to an earlier point in time, select the newest restore point (the first one in the list) and then click *Next*.

Under what conditions can the System Restore changes not be undone?

_____

_____

11. Select *Yes* to continue. The system restarts as part of the System Restore process.

Instructor initials: _____

12. Log in to Windows and ensure that the system works.

13. Do not forget that after the system has been restored to an earlier time, you should install any antivirus or Windows updates that have been affected by this system restore. Click the *Close* button.

Lab 16.12 Upgrading a Hardware Driver and Using Driver Roll Back

Objective: To install an updated driver under the Windows operating system

Parts: A computer with Windows 7, 8, 8.1, or 10 installed and Internet access

Note: In this lab, a new driver is loaded, but then the old driver is reinstalled with the Roll Back Driver feature. The student must be logged in as a user with local Administrator rights to perform this lab.

Procedure: Complete the following procedure and answer the accompanying questions.

1. Turn on the computer and verify that the operating system loads. Log in to Windows using the user ID and password provided by the instructor or lab assistant.

2. Select an installed hardware device and locate an updated driver by using the Internet. Printers are a good choice. Download the driver to the hard drive. Note that some drivers may come in a compressed file and must be uncompressed before you can continue the procedure.

What device did you select to upgrade?

_____

What location (path, folder, desktop, and so on) was used to download the driver?

_____

Instructor initials: _____

Installing the Driver

3.   Open Device Manager.

4.   Expand the hardware category that contains the device being upgraded by clicking on the arrow beside the category.

5.   Right-click the device name and click the *Properties* selection.

6.   Select the *Driver* tab.

7.   Click *Update Driver* and select *Search Automatically for Updated Driver Software* to look not only on the computer for an updated driver but also search the Internet. Note that if a driver has been downloaded, use the *Browse My Computer for Driver Software* link to locate the downloaded driver.

Instructor initials: _____

Using Driver Roll Back

8.   Use *Device Manager*, right-click the device name again and select *Properties*.

9.   Click the *Driver* tab and click the *Roll Back Driver* button. Click the *Yes* button to roll back the driver. If the device driver has not been updated, driver rollback is be possible, and a message screen displays this fact.

Instructor initials: _____

10.   Close all windows and power off the computer properly.

Lab 16.13 Disabling a Hardware Driver

Objective:	To disable a driver under the Windows 7, 8, 8.1, or 10 operating system
Parts:	A computer with Windows 7, 8, 8.1, or 10 and a network adapter installed
Note:	The student must be logged in as a user with local Administrator rights to perform this lab. In this lab, a driver is disabled and then re-enabled. Sometimes Windows can install the wrong driver, in which case the driver must be disabled and then manually reinstalled.
Procedure:	Complete the following procedure and answer the accompanying questions.

1.   Turn on the computer and verify that the operating system loads. Log in to Windows using the user ID and password provided by the instructor or lab assistant.

2.   Using *Device Manager*, expand the *Network Adapters* category.

    What network adapter is installed in the computer?

_____

3.   Right-click a network adapter and select the *Disable* option.

    What message displays on the screen?

_____

4.   Click the *Yes* button.

    In Device Manager, how is a device that has its driver disabled displayed differently from any other device?

_____

5.   In *Device Manager*, right-click (or tap and briefly hold on) the same network adapter and select the *Enable* option. The device is re-enabled and appears normally in the window.

Instructor initials: _____

6.   Close the *Device Manager* window and all other windows.

Lab 16.14 Installing Hardware

Objective: To install a new hardware component under the Windows 7, 8, 8.1, or 10 operating system

Parts: A computer with Windows 7, 8, 8.1, or 10 installed

                  New device to install

                  Access to the Internet

Note: The student must be logged in as a user with local Administrator rights to perform this lab. In this lab, the Internet is used to obtain the device's installation instructions and latest device driver, and then the new hardware device is installed.

Procedure: Complete the following procedure and answer the accompanying questions.

1.   Log in using the user ID and password provided by your instructor or lab assistant.

2.   Using the Internet, locate the manufacturer's instructions for installing the device.

      Who is the device manufacturer?

      _____

3.   Using the Internet, locate the latest device driver that is compatible with the version of Windows being used.

      Does the device have an appropriate driver for the version of Windows being used? [Yes | No]

      What is the device driver version being downloaded?

      _____

4.   Connect the device to the computer using the proper installation procedures.

5.   Boot the computer. Usually, Windows automatically detects the new hardware and begins the *Found New Hardware* Wizard. If it does not present this wizard, look to see if the hardware device vendor supplied an installation program. If so, use that program to install the device. If no vendor-supplied installation program is available, use *Device Manager* or *Devices and Printers/Add a device* link to install the device. Install the device driver based on the device type and manufacturer's instructions.

      Did the Found New Hardware Wizard begin? [Yes | No]

6.   Test the device installation.

Instructor initials: _____

Lab 16.15 Installing and Removing Windows Components

Objective: To install and remove Windows 7, 8, 8.1, or 10 components

Parts: A computer with Windows 7, 8, 8.1, or 10 installed and Administrator rights

Procedure: Complete the following procedure and answer the accompanying questions.

1.   Turn on the computer and verify that the operating system loads. Log in to Windows using the user ID and password provided by your instructor or lab assistant. Ensure that the user ID is one that has Administrator rights.

Verifying and Installing Windows Features

2.   Open *Windows Explorer/File Explorer*, right-click (or tap and briefly hold on) *Computer/This PC*, and select *Properties*. Select the *System Protection* link. In Windows 10, you may have to enable system protection by clicking on the C: drive, select *Configure*, enable the *Turn on system protection* radio button, and select *OK*.

3.   Create a system restore point by clicking the *Create* button. In the description textbox type **class** followed by the current date. Click *Create*. A dialog box appears when the restore point has been successfully created. Click *OK*.

4.   Click *OK* in the System Properties window.

5. Access the *Programs* Control Panel utility and select the *Turn Windows features on or off* link in the Programs and Features section.

    List three enabled Windows features.

    _____

    List three Windows features that are turned off.

    _____

6. Notice that the Games option is controlled through this section if you are using Windows 7. Expand the *Games* option or another option that can be expanded.

7. Check with your instructor or lab assistant for a specific feature to turn on. One option would be to turn on the TFTP client if it is not enabled.

    Write the name of the program to be enabled.

    _____

8. Select the checkbox for the feature to be enabled and click *OK*. Note that enabling the feature might take a few minutes.

9. Re-access the *Turn Windows features on or off* link to verify that the feature now shows as enabled.

    Instructor initials: _____

10. Remove the check from the feature you just enabled and verify that the feature is removed successfully.

11. Access the *Programs* Control Panel utility. In the *Default Programs* section, select the *Set your default programs* link.

    What can be done from this window?

    _____

    _____

    _____

12. Select *Internet Explorer* or *Microsoft Edge* from the *Programs* list. Both of these are used as Internet browsers. Select the *Choose defaults for this program* link.

    List the extensions that are automatically opened by Internet Explorer or Microsoft Edge.

    _____

    _____

    List protocols that are automatically recognized from the address line in Internet Explorer or Microsoft Edge. Note that you might need to scroll down in order to see the protocols.

    _____

13. Click *Cancel* and *OK* to return to the Default Programs window.

14. Select the *Associate a file type or protocol with a program* link.

    List one program that does not have a program extension or protocol associated with it (that is, is listed as unknown in the *Current Default* column).

    _____

    _____

15. Leave this window open and create and save a Notepad document called **Superdog.txt**.

    Document the location where this document is saved.

    _____

16. Open *Windows Explorer* (Windows 7)/*File Explorer* (Windows 8/8.1/10) and locate the `Superdog.txt` file. In Windows 7, select the *Views* drop-down arrow. In Windows 8/8.1/10, select the *View* menu option.

What is the current view?

_____

17. Select the *List* view. Reselect the *View* menu option.

In Windows 7, select the *Organize* menu option > select *Folder and Search Options*. Select the *View* tab.

In Windows 8/8.1/10, select *Options* (located on the far right) > select the *Change folder and search options* link. Select the *View* tab.

What is the current setting for Hide extensions for known file types? [Enabled | Disabled]

18. Ensure that the *Hide extensions for known file types* option is disabled (unchecked). Select *OK*.

19. Return to *Windows Explorer/File Explorer* and ensure that the `.txt` extension is visible on the `Superdog.txt` filename. Right-click (or tap and briefly hold on) the `Superdog.txt` filename and select *Rename*. Rename the `.txt` extension to `.cas` (or your own initials, if they are not a common file extension). When the message window appears, select *Yes*.

How did the appearance of the file change?

_____

_____

20. Right-click (or tap and briefly hold on) the `Superdog` filename and select *Properties*.

What application does Windows assign to open the document?

_____

21. Click the *Change* button.

In Windows 7, notice that the *Always use the selected program to open this kind of file* checkbox at the bottom of the window is enabled. Select *Notepad* and click *OK*. Click *Apply* and *OK*.

In Windows 8/8.1/10, select the *More Options/More Apps* link. Select *Notepad* from the list.

22. Locate the `Superdog` file in Windows Explorer/File Explorer and double-click or double-tap the icon.

Does the file open? [Yes | No] If so, in what application?

Instructor initials: _____

23. Close the `Superdog` file. Return to the *Set Associations* window. Scroll down until you see the extension you used when you renamed the `Superdog` filename. Show your instructor or lab assistant the file extension.

Instructor initials: _____

24. Select the file extension in the list and click the *Change Program* button. Use the *Browse* button (Windows 7) or *More Options/More Apps* link (Windows 8/8.1/10) to find the WordPad application. In Windows 7, use the Search feature inside Browse, if necessary. When you find WordPad, select it and click *Open*. Click *OK*.

25. Return to *Windows Explorer/File Explorer*. Locate the `Superdog` file and double-click the icon.

Does the file open? [Yes | No] If so, in what application? Notepad

26. Close the file. Permanently delete the file by holding down the ⬆Shift key while pressing Del. Click *Yes* to permanently delete the file.

27. On your own, create another file that ends in the same file extension. Try to open it.

What happens?

_____

28. Close the file and permanently delete it.

29. Re-open the *System Restore* utility.

30. Select the *Choose a different restore point* radio button and click *Next*.

31. Select the *Class+Date* restore point that was created at the beginning of the lab and click *Next*. Click *Finish*. Read the message that appears and click *Yes*. The system restores the system to the time before this lab was started. The system reboots, and a dialog box appears, telling you whether the restore point was successful. Click *Close*.

32. Reopen the *Programs > Default Programs* Control Panel and select the *Associate a file type or protocol with a program* link.

33. Scroll through the list.

    Is the unique file extension used in this lab located in the list? [Yes | No]

34. Close the *all* windows.

Lab 16.16 Microsoft Management Console

Objective: To access and use the major utilities found in the Microsoft Management Console
Parts: A computer with Windows 7, 8, 8.1, or 10 installed and Administrator rights
Notes: You must be an administrator to utilize the Microsoft Management Console utilities.
Procedure: Complete the following procedure and answer the accompanying questions.

1. Power on the computer and verify that Windows loads. Log on to Windows using the user ID and password provided by the instructor or lab assistant.

2. To access Microsoft Management Console in Windows 7, click the *Start* button. In Windows 8, 8.1, or 10, right-click the *Start* button.

    In all operating systems select *Control Panel > System and Security* link > *Administrative Tools >* double-click the *Computer Management* option.

    Determine the subcategories for each of the major Computer Management sections. Document the subcategories in Lab Table 16.1.

LAB TABLE 16.1   Windows Computer Management console

Computer Management section	Subcategories
System Tools	
Storage	
Services and Applications	

3. Return to the *Computer Management* window and, if necessary, select the arrow beside *System Tools* to expand the section. If necessary, select the arrow beside *Shared Folders* to expand that section. Click the *Shares* folder. Shares are used when the computer is in a network environment. Other users on different computers can access resources on this computer. When networking is enabled, default administrative shares are created for each hard drive partition. Administrative shares can be easily identified by the $ (dollar sign) after the share name.

    List two default shares located on this machine. If none are available, document the fact.

    _____

4. If necessary, expand *Local Users* and *Groups* and click the *Users* folder.

    List the users shown in the Computer Management window.

    _____

5. To add a new user who will have access to this computer, click the *Action* menu option and select *New User*. Note that you may have to select the *More Actions* link to see this option. The New User window opens. Click the *Question Mark* icon located in the upper-right corner of the window. An arrow with an attached question mark appears as a pointer. Move the pointer to inside the *User Name* textbox and click. A Help box appears in Windows 7. Windows 8, 8.1, and 10 launch a web browser to technet.microsoft.com with a Knowledge Base article on users and groups.

6. In the *User Name* textbox, type **Jeff Cansler**. In the *Full Name* textbox, type **Jeffrey Wayne Cansler**. In the *Description* textbox, type **Brother**. In the *Password* and the *Confirm Password* textboxes, type **test**. Note that if a local policy is applied, you may have to strengthen this password to something like **Test1234%**. Ensure that the *User must change password at next logon* checkbox is disabled (not checked). Select the *User cannot change password* checkbox to enable this option. Select the *Create* button. Select the *Close* button. The Jeff Cansler user icon appears in the Computer Management window.

    Have a classmate verify the Jeff Cansler user icon. Have the classmate double-click the icon to verify your settings. Are the settings correct? If not, redo the previous step.
    [Yes | No]

    Classmate's printed name: _____

    Classmate's signature: _____

7. Log off the computer and log back on using the Jeff Cansler username with the password test (or the stronger password Test1234% if it was set).

    Did the log on process work correctly? If not, log back on and redo step 6. [Yes | No]

8. Log off the computer and log back on using the user ID and password given to you by the lab assistant or instructor (the original user ID and password). Access the *Computer Management* window and double-click the *Jeff Cansler* user icon. Select the *Member Of* tab.

    To what group does the Jeff Cansler user automatically belong?
    [Administrators | Power users | Staff | Users]

9. Click the *Add* button. The Select Groups window opens. In the *Enter the object names to select* textbox, type **Administrators** and click the *Check Names* button. Click the *OK* button. The information shown changes to the user, Jeff Cansler, belonging to both the Users and Administrator groups. Click the *Apply* button and then the *OK* button.

Instructor initials: _____

10. Re-open the Jeff Cansler user window and select the *Profile* tab.

    The *Profile* tab is used to specify a home directory for the user, run a logon script that sets specific parameters for the user, input a path that specifies where the user stores files by default, or input a shared network directory where the user's data is placed.

    The *Profile Path* textbox is where you type the location of the profile using a UNC. An example is \\users\profiles\jcansler.

    The *Logon Script* textbox is where you type the name of the logon script file, for example, startup.bat.

    The *Home folder local path:* textbox is where you type the full path for where the user's data is stored by default. An example is C:\users\jcansler. The *Connect* radio button is used to assign a network drive letter and specify the location of a network directory where the user's data is stored. An example is \\users\jcandata. Click the *Cancel* button to return to the Computer Management window. Notice that users that are disabled have a small down arrow on their icon.

    Are any users disabled? [Yes | No]

11. In the Computer Management window, select the *Groups* folder.

    List two default groups.

12. Double-click the *Administrators* group icon. The Administrators group has total control of the local machine.

   Are any users listed as part of the Administrators group? If so, list them.

   _____

   Fill in Lab Table 16.2 with the purpose of each group type. Use the *Help* menu item for more information than what is shown in the window.

   LAB TABLE 16.2   Windows User Groups

Group	Description
Administrators	
Backup operators	
Guests	
Users	

13. Exit Help and then click the *Users* folder located in the Computer Management window. Select the *Jeff Cansler* user icon. Click the *X* icon or click the *Action* menu item and select *Delete*. A message appears, asking if you are sure that you want to delete this user. Click the *Yes* button (twice if necessary).

14. Go into the *Administrators* group and verify that Jeff Cansler no longer appears there.

   Have a classmate verify that the Jeff Cansler user icon is deleted. Is the Jeff Cansler user icon deleted? If not, redo the previous step. [Yes | No]

   Classmate's printed name: _____

   Classmate's signature: _____

15. Select the *Device Manager* option located in the Computer Management window. This utility can also be accessed by typing **devmgmt.msc** in a Run box, in a Search textbox, or at a command prompt. Device Manager is used to access and manage hardware devices installed on the computer. It is also used to load new drivers and roll back to an older driver.

16. In the right panel, select the arrow by the computer name if the list is not already expanded. Expand the *Computer* category.

   Is this computer 32- or 64-bit based? [32-bit | 64-bit]

17. Expand the *Storage* category in the left pane. Select the *Disk Management* subcategory. The right pane displays information about each type of hard disk partition created on the drive. The top window shows information about each disk partition, including total capacity, file system, free space percentage, and so forth. The bottom windows show the drives and partitions in graphical form.

18. Right-click the first volume (usually C:) in the upper window and select the *Properties* option. An alternative method is to click the *Action* menu item and select *Properties*. The Disk Properties window opens.

19. On an NTFS partition, the *General* tab contains a *Disk Cleanup* button that can be used to clean up temporary files and delete applications not used, Windows components not used, log files, and old system restores.

    How much free space is on the selected drive?

    _____

    Which checkboxes are enabled? (Select all that apply.) [Compress this drive to save disk space | Allow files on this drive to have contents Indexed in addition to file properties]

20. Select the *Tools* tab.

    What tools are listed on the Tools tab?

    _____

    Match each the following tools with its associated task. Note that Windows 8/8.1/10 does not have the Backup tool on the *Tool* tab.

    _____ Backup   **a.** Scans the disk for damage

    _____ Error checking   **b.** Used to restore system files that have been saved

    _____ Defragmentation   **c.** Locates file clusters that are not consecutive (contiguous) and places the files in order

21. The Disk Management tool can create disk partitions, delete partitions, convert partitions to NTFS, create logical drives, and convert basic disks to dynamic disks. Click the *Cancel* button.

22. Expand the *Services and Applications* Computer Management category. Select the *Services* subcategory. A service is an application that runs in the background; you do not see it on the taskbar. The Services window is used to start, stop, pause, resume, or disable a service. You must be a member of the Administrators group to use this tool.

    List two services that start automatically and two services that require manual startup.

    _____

23. Double-click the *Computer Browser* service. The General tab is used to start, stop, pause, or resume a service (depending on its current state). The buttons in the Service status section are used to control these actions. The *General* tab is also used to set whether the service starts when the computer boots. Select the *Startup Type* down arrow to see a menu of startup options.

24. Close the *Service* window without making any changes to the service and close the *Computer Management* window.

    Instructor initials: _____

Lab 16.17 Exploring Windows Boot Options

Objective: To explore Windows 7, 8, 8.1, or 10 boot options that are used to troubleshoot startup problems

Parts: A computer with Windows 7, 8, 8.1, or 10 installed that has the capability to boot from a CD/DVD

               User ID that has Administrator rights

               Windows 7, 8, 8.1, or 10 DVD, operating system image, or virtual image

Note: In this lab, you boot without startup programs loaded, boot to Safe Mode, boot to Safe Mode with Command Prompt, boot to Enable Boot Logging and examine the `ntbtlog.txt` file, and boot to Recovery Console and examine commands using the command prompt. If the Windows DVD or image of the installation disc is not available, that one section could be skipped.

Procedure: Complete the following procedure and answer the accompanying questions.

1.   Turn on the computer and verify that the operating system loads. Log in to Windows using the user ID and password provided by your instructor or lab assistant.

Using Boot Options

2.   On Windows 7 restart the computer and press the ⒇F8⒈ key as the computer boots. If the *Advanced Boot Options* window does not appear, shut down the computer and restart. Press ⒇F8⒈ as the computer boots. The *Advanced Boot Options* menu appears. Select the *Safe Mode* option and press ⒇↵Enter⒈. Log in with an account that has administrator privileges.

On Windows 8, 8.1, or 10, select *Settings > Update and Recovery* (Windows 8)/*Update & Security* (Windows 10) > select *Recovery* from the left menu > in the Advanced startup section, select the *Restart Now Button* > select *Troubleshoot > Advanced Options > Startup Settings* > select the *Restart* button. After the restart, choose *Enable Safe Mode*.

When would a technician use the Safe Mode option as opposed to the Safe Mode with Command Prompt option?

_____

_____

_____

How does the look of the screen in Safe Mode differ from the look of the normal Windows desktop?

_____

_____

What Windows Help and Support topic automatically displays, if any?

_____

_____

How can you easily tell you are running in Safe Mode?

_____

3.   Access the *Administrative Tools* Control Panel link. Open *Computer Management*. Expand the *Services and Applications* category. Access the *Services* option.

4.   Quite a few services are automatic services that did not start in Safe Mode.

List two services that did not automatically start because Safe Mode was used.

_____

_____

5.   Close *Computer Management* and any Control Panel windows and restart Windows.

LAB 16

6. Re-access the *Advanced Boot Options (Windows 7)/Startup Settings (Windows 8/8.1/10)* menu. Refer to step 2, if necessary.

List the boot options available.

_____

_____

_____

_____

_____

Match each of the following definitions to the appropriate boot option:

_____ Safe Mode   **a.** Starts the system with minimum files and drivers, and only typed commands can be used

_____ Safe Mode with Command   **b.** Records the boot process into a text file that can later be
Prompt   viewed and used for troubleshooting

_____ Enable Boot Logging   **c.** Starts the system with minimal files and drivers, including the default video drivers

_____ Disable Automatic Restart   **d.** Allows a technician to have time to document an error that
on System Failure   occurs

7. Select the *Enable Boot Logging* option.

How does the desktop appear when using the Enable Boot Logging option?

_____

8. Use the *Search* function to locate and access the `ntbtlog.txt` file.

List two drivers that loaded properly.

_____

_____

List two drivers that did not load. Note that you may have to scroll through the list to see these.

_____

_____

Instructor initials: _____

9. Close all windows.

Recovery Environment

10. Insert the Windows installation disc into the optical drive or have the ISO on an external disk and power off the computer. Power on the computer. If prompted, press a key to start Windows from the disc. A menu appears, with a default option selected. Press [↵Enter]. If the computer does not boot from the Windows disc, the BIOS settings probably need to be adjusted.

11. Choose the appropriate language settings and click *Next*.

12. Select *Repair Your Computer*. In the options window on a Windows 7 computer, select the *Use recovery tools that can help fix problems starting Windows*; enable the *Select an operating system to repair* radio button. On a Windows 8 or 10 computer, select *Troubleshoot*.

13. Ensure that the operating system is selected and click *Next*.

List the recovery tool options.

_____

_____

Which option would be used to repair a system file?

_____

Which option would be used to check RAM?

_____

Which option do you think would be for advanced technicians?

_____

Which option configures the system to an earlier time, such as before a Windows update?

_____

Instructor initials: _____

14. Select the *Memory Diagnostic* link. Select the *Restart now and check for problems (recommended)* link. Do not press a key when the system reboots and gives the message Press a key to boot from CD or DVD.

List one status message.

_____

15. After the test executes and the computer reboots, as before, do not press any key, even when the message prompts to press a key to boot from a CD or DVD. After Windows reboots, log in again. Open *Event Viewer* by accessing the *System and Security* Control Panel > *Administrative Tools*. Double-click *Event Viewer* to open the tool.

16. Expand *Windows Logs*. Click the *System* Windows log. Right-click *System* and select *Find*.

17. In the *Find What* textbox, type the following:

    MemoryDiagnostics-Results

    Be careful that you type this exactly as shown and then click *Find Next*. The corresponding line is highlighted.

18. Close the *Find* window. Double-click the highlighted line to see the results of the memory diagnostic check. Select the *Details* tab.

What are the results shown in the friendly view?

_____

What event ID did Windows assign?

_____

19. Close all windows. Remove the Windows disc and return it to the instructor or lab assistant.

Lab 16.18 Windows System Configuration Utility

Objective: To use the System Configuration utility to troubleshoot boot problems

Parts: A computer with Windows installed

                User ID that has Administrator rights

Note: In this lab, create a shortcut to an application and then use the System Configuration utility to prevent it from loading. Explore various options that can be used in the System Configuration utility.

Procedure: Complete the following procedure and answer the accompanying questions.

1. Turn on the computer and verify that the operating system loads. Log in to Windows using the user ID and password provided by the instructor or lab assistant. Ensure that the user ID is one that has Administrator rights.

Creating an Application Shortcut in the Startup Folder

2. Use Windows Explorer/File Explorer to navigate to the following folder: `C:\Users\username\`
    `AppData\Roaming\Microsoft\Windows\Start Menu\Programs\Startup`. Note
    that the `username` is the name you used to log in to the computer. You may also have to adjust the
    Windows Explorer/File Explorer view so that hidden items (files and folders) are shown.

    In Windows 7, select the *Organize* drop-down arrow > select *Folder and Search Options* > select the
    View tab > select the *Show hidden files, folders, and drives* radio button > select *OK*.

    In Windows 8/8.1/10, select the *View* menu option > ensure that the *Show hidden files, folders, and
    drives* option is enabled.

3. In a separate window, use the *Search* feature to locate the original Notepad application (`notepad.`
    `exe`). Create a shortcut to the Notepad application and place it in the *Startup* folder located under the
    Programs folder (see step 2).

    Have a classmate verify your shortcut (especially that it is a shortcut and not a copy of the application
    or the application itself). Is the icon in the Startup folder a shortcut icon? [Yes | No]

    Classmate's printed name: _____

    Classmate's signature: _____

4. Restart the computer and verify that the Notepad program starts automatically when the computer
    boots. If it does not, redo the lab from the beginning.

Instructor initials: _____

System Configuration Utility

5. Hold down the ⊞ key and press Ⓡ; type **msconfig** and press ⏎Enter. An alternate method is to
    search for **msconfig**. The System Configuration utility window opens.

    What is the purpose of the System Configuration utility?

    _____

    What tabs are available in the System Configuration utility?

    _____

6. Click the *Diagnostic startup—Load basic devices and services only* radio button. Click the *Apply*
    button and then click the *OK* button. A System Configuration message box appears. Click the *Restart*
    button. When the computer restarts, log in with the same user ID used previously.

    Did the Notepad application automatically start?

    _____

7. Click *OK*. Return to the System Configuration (`msconfig`) utility and select the *Selective startup*
    radio button on the *General* tab. Checkboxes are now available so that you can select the startup files
    that are to be loaded the next time the computer boots. Select the *Load startup items* checkbox. Click
    the *Apply* button and then click *Close*. Click the *Restart* button and the system restarts. Log in using
    the same user ID and password as before.

    Did the Notepad application automatically start? Why or why not? [Yes | No]

    _____

8. Click *OK* if necessary. Return to the System Configuration utility and select the *Normal startup—
    Load all device drivers and services* option located on the *General* tab. Note that Windows
    automatically changes the radio button to the *Selective startup* option.

9. Select the *Startup* tab.

10. In Windows 7, select the *Shortcut to Notepad* checkbox to disable it > click *Apply* > click *Close*.

    In Windows 8/8.1/10, select the *Open Task Manager* link. In Windows 8/10, Task Manager (*Startup*
    tab) opens. In Windows 8/8.1/10, select *Notepad* and click the *Disable* button.

11.   Restart the computer. When the computer restarts, log in using the same user ID and click *OK*.

Did the Notepad application automatically start? Why or why not? [Yes | No]

_____

_____

Reopen the System Configuration utility to determine what is different about the General tab. Document your observations.

_____

_____

_____

Match each System Configuration utility tab to a characteristic. Note that not all characteristics are used. Each characteristic that does match a tab is used only once.

_____ General   **a.** Has an Advanced options button so that you can control the number of processors used to boot the system.

_____ Boot   **b.** Contains applications that begin every time the computer boots

_____ Services   **c.** Contains a section called Boot Loader that details operating system boot options

_____ Tools   **d.** Has an option to choose which boot files are processed

_____ Startup   **e.** Contains an Application Management option

                    f. Provides an easy way to launch System Restore and Registry Editor

12.   Select the *General* tab and select the *Normal startup* radio button > click *Apply* > click *Close* > click *Restart*. Log in using the same user ID as before.

13.   After the computer reboots, remove the shortcut to the Notepad application from the *Startup* folder.

Is the Notepad shortcut (and not the original application) deleted? [Yes | No]

Instructor initials: _____

Lab 16.19 Halting an Application Using Task Manager

Objective: To use Task Manager to halt an application

Parts: A computer with Windows 7, 8, 8.1, or 10 installed

Note: At times, it may be necessary to halt an application that is hung or stalled. Windows provides a method to accomplish this, through the Task Manager utility.

Procedure: Complete the following procedure and answer the accompanying questions.

1.   Turn on the computer and verify that the operating system loads. Log in to Windows using the user ID and password provided by the instructor or lab assistant. Ensure that the user ID is one that has Administrator rights.

2.   Open the Notepad utility.

3.   Open Task Manager by right-clicking in an empty space of the taskbar > select *Start Task Manager (Windows 7)/Task Manager (Windows 8/8.1/10)*. Note: You might have to select the *More Details* link to see the Task Manager data.

What type of things can you view from Task Manager?

_____

_____

4.   Select the *Applications* (Windows 7)/*Processes* (Windows 8/8.1/10) tab.

What applications, if any, are listed as open? Note that you might need to click the down arrow by the *More Details* option in Windows 8/10.

_____

Instructor initials: _____

5. Select the *Untitled—Notepad* (Windows 7)/*Notepad* (Windows 8//8.1/10) option and click the *End Task* button. Notepad closes.

    Could you close the Notepad application from within Task Manager? [Yes | No]

6. Close the *Task Manager* window.

Lab 16.20 Task Manager Features in Windows 8, 8.1, or 10

Objective: To use Task Manager technical features

Parts: A computer with Windows 8, 8.1, or 10 installed

Procedure: Complete the following procedure and answer the accompanying questions.

1. Turn on the computer and verify that the operating system loads. Log in to Windows using the user ID and password provided by the instructor or lab assistant. Ensure that the user ID is one that has Administrator rights.

2. Task Manager has more capabilities than ever before. To explore the tabs, open Task Manager and right-click the taskbar > select *Task Manager* (Windows 8/8.1/10). Note: You might have to select the *More Details* link to see the Task Manager data.

    Match each Task Manager tab to a characteristic. Each characteristic matches to only one tab, and all characteristics are used.

    _____ Processes   **a.** Shows the data usage of a particular application on a metered account

    _____ App history   **b.** Displays the impact an app has on the system when the system powers on

    _____ Users   **c.** Identifies which user is using a particular app or service and the PID

    _____ Services   **d.** Used to show what apps are open and the amount of CPU, memory, and disk space each one takes

    _____ Performance   **e.** When expanded, shows the apps a particular person has used

    _____ Startup   **f.** Shows the average response time of the hard disk

    _____ Details   **g.** Indicates whether a service is running or stopped

3. Select the *Startup* tab. This tab gives a technician great insight into apps used as part of the startup process and each one's impact on the startup process. One common complaint about computers today is the amount of time a device takes to boot. That time can be impacted by lengthy profiles and multiple profiles being applied in a corporate environment, but it is also impacted by apps and services during the startup process.

    Do any applications show a startup impact of high? If so, list one. [Yes | No]

Instructor initials: _____

4. Locate the Last BIOS time.

    What is the last BIOS time shown?

    _____

    What do you think is the significance of this value? You might want to search on the Internet, if possible, to see what the value is telling you.

    _____

    _____

5. Select the *Users* tab.

    A company has two shifts, and some employees use the same computer that a person on the previous shift used. Oftentimes to reduce boot times, the users will just log off but not power down the computer. Do you think if two users were logged onto the machine at the same time (but only one was actually using it), the Task Manager > Users tab would show both users? Why do you think this would be important to a technician? Be sure to answer both questions.

    _____

    _____

    _____

6. Open several apps and then select the *Processes* tab.

    Which category has the highest percentage of utilization? [CPU | Memory | Disk | Network | GPU]

    _____

    Why do you think this is the case on this particular computer?

    _____

    _____

Instructor initials: _____

7. Select the *App History* tab. A user has complained about computer performance. A technician has been using the App History tab to see the applications being used. The technician notices that the computer is a Windows 10 computer and some of the app statistics. For example, Cortana has used almost 23 minutes of CPU time and Microsoft Photos over 5 hours. The technician also noticed that the user had the Firefox browser up and states that this is the browser most often used, but Firefox is not shown in the Name list on the App History tab.

    Do you think that the values for each app are relevant to computer performance? Why or why not?

    _____

    _____

    Can the technician specify the point at which app date is collected on the App History tab? [Yes | No]
    If yes, how would a technician do that?

    _____

    _____

    Do you think that there is something wrong with the values shown on the App History tab since Firefox isn't showing up there? [Yes | No]
    Can you find any way that you might make it appear?

    _____

8. Use the *Options* menu option and select *Show History for All Processes*.

    Did anything change on the App History tab? [Yes | No]

    _____

    _____

Instructor initials: _____

9. Select the *Details* tab. By default, apps and services are listed in alphabetical order. You can click on the title of any column in order to view the items by that particular parameter. For example, click on the *Memory (private working set)* column name, and you see the apps listed, from the app that is currently using the most memory to the app that is using the least amount of memory.

    What app is using the most memory and appears at the top of the list?

    _____

10. Select the *PID* column name. PID stands for process ID. Each Windows process is assigned a unique number. Process IDs are used to stop an application using the `taskkill` command from the command line.

11. Select the *Name* column heading on the *Details* tab. A technician might use this to see if there are multiple instances of a particular application running. Note that multiple browser tabs would result in multiple instances of that particular browser being listed, with details about each tab. This is normal operation. A technician would also be interested in instances of an app being open that is not being used. This might be causing poor computer performance, and the particular app instance can be stopped.

12. Right-click on the name of any particular app.

    List an example of when a technician might use the *Set priority > High* option.

    _____

    _____

13. Right-click on the name of an app and select *Analyze wait chain*.

    What is the purpose of the Analyze wait chain function?

    _____

    _____

14. Click *Cancel*. Right-click on the name of an app again.

    Can you terminate the app from the context menu? [Yes | No]

    If yes, what option would you use? [End task | Set affinity | Create dump file]

15. Select the *Services* tab. Select the *Status* column header and scroll to the bottom to see all the services that have stopped.

    List any stopped service for which you are surprised that it is stopped or that it is a Windows service.

    _____

16. Close *Task Manager*.

Lab 16.21 Using Event Viewer

Objective: To use the Event Viewer program to troubleshoot problems

Parts: A computer with Windows 7, 8, 8.1, or 10 installed and a user ID that has Administrator rights

Note: In this lab, evaluate a computer event to see how to gather information using Event Viewer.

Procedure: Complete the following procedure and answer the accompanying questions.

1. Turn on the computer and verify that the operating system loads. Log in to Windows using the user ID and password provided by your instructor or lab assistant. Ensure that the user ID is one that has Administrator rights.

2. Event Viewer monitors and logs various events, such as when drivers and services load (or fail to load and have problems). Open the *System and Security* Control Panel utility > *Administrative Tools* > double-click *Event Viewer*. The Event Viewer window opens to the Overview and Summary window.

    How many total warning administrative events occurred on this computer?

    _____

3. In the left pane, expand the *Windows Logs* section > select *Security*. The most recent events are listed at the top. You might need to expand the window or reduce the size of the left and right panes in order to see the center pane better. Locate and double-click on the most recent event that shows as *Logon* in the *Task Category column*.

    From the General tab, what was the account name?

    _____

What time did the logon occur?

_____

Was the logon successful? In other words, did Event Viewer show this as an Audit Success or as an Audit Failure? [Yes | No]

_____

4. Close the security event Properties window. The Audit Success line in the center pane is still selected. In the right panel, select *Attach Task To This Event*. Type your first initial and last name as the name of the basic task (for example: `cschmidt`). Click *Next* on the following two windows.

   What three actions can be taken from this screen?

   _____

5. Click *Cancel*.

6. In the left panel, select the *Application* option from the *Windows Logs* category.

   What application caused the first event?

   _____

7. Select the *Windows Logs > Security* subcategory from the left panel.

   Scroll through the list of events logged and pay attention to the *Task Category* column. What type of task categories are most common?

   _____

   _____

   Does Windows log an event when a user logs off a Windows computer? [Yes | No]

8. Select the *Windows Logs > System* subcategory from the left panel. Double-click the first event listed. List the source of the first event.

   _____

9. Select the *Copy* button.

10. Open the *WordPad* application > access the *Edit* menu item > select *Paste*.

    What appeared in WordPad?

    _____

Instructor initials: _____

11. The event information can be saved as a text file and referenced later, especially when there is a problem. Close *WordPad* without saving the document. Close the *Event Properties* window.

12. In *Event Viewer*, expand *Applications and Services Logs*. Expand the *Microsoft* folder and the *Windows* folder. Expand the *TaskScheduler* to locate and click the *Operational* event log.

    What is the first informational TaskScheduler event logged? Note that on a virtualized machine, there might not be an event. If this is the case, just document that you were in a virtual environment as your answer.

    _____

13. Close *Event Viewer*.

Lab 16.22 Using Task Manager to View Performance

Objective:	To use the Task Manager program to evaluate basic computer performance
Parts:	A computer with Windows 7, 8, or 10 installed and user ID that has Administrator rights
Note:	In this lab, evaluate a computer event to see how to gather information using Event Viewer.
Procedure:	Complete the following procedure and answer the accompanying questions.

LAB 16

1. Turn on the computer and verify that the operating system loads. Log in to Windows using the user ID and password provided by the instructor or lab assistant. Ensure that the user ID is one that has Administrator rights.

2. Open Task Manager: Right-click the taskbar > select *Start Task Manager* (Windows 7)/*Task Manager* (Windows 8/8.1/10). *Note*: You might have to select the *More Details* link to see the Task Manager data. Click the *Performance* tab. The Performance tab is used to view CPU and memory usage in Windows 7, and in Windows 8, 8.1, and 10, the Performance tab also shows Disk and Ethernet (network) utilization.

3. Open *Notepad*, access the Internet, if possible, open a game, if possible, and start other applications.

    What happens to the CPU usage, as shown in Task Manager, as each application is opened?

    _____

    What is the memory usage?

    _____

    What is the total physical memory?

    _____

    How much memory is available?

    _____

Instructor initials: _____

4. Using Task Manager is a great way to see a snapshot of the status of two of the most important pieces of hardware, the CPU and RAM (even though the Task Manager application increases both the CPU and memory usage). If the CPU and memory utilization stay consistently high, you should add more RAM. If the CPU stays consistently level and at a high value, a more powerful processor is in order. Close all windows.

Lab 16.23 Performance and Reliability

Objective: To use Windows 7, 8, 8.1, or 10 tools to verify performance, measure reliability, and troubleshoot startup problems

Parts: Access to Windows 7, 8, 8.1, or 10 with a user ID that has Administrator rights

Procedure: Complete the following procedure and answer the accompanying questions.

1. Turn on the computer and verify that the operating system loads. Log in to Windows using the user ID and password provided by your instructor or lab assistant. Ensure that this user ID has full Administrator rights.

2. Access the *System and Security* Control Panel > *Administrative Tools* > double-click *Performance Monitor* > select the *Open Resource Monitor* link. The information shown on the *Overview* tab is known as the key table. It always contains a complete list of running (active) processes for the system. You can filter the data and look at the information more granularly by using the specific tabs.

3. Select the *CPU* tab. Notice the individual programs and processes listed in the *Processes* section. Select a particular process by selecting the checkbox by the process name. The top graph shows that particular process in relation to the total CPU usage.

    How many CPU threads are used by the Performance Monitor application?

    _____

4. Deselect any individual process(es) in the Processes section. Expand the *Services* section. Notice the last column: *Average CPU*. This column shows the average percentage of CPU consumption by a particular service.

    What service is taking the most CPU power?

    _____

5. Select the *Memory* tab. Notice the *Commit (KB)* column, which shows the amount of virtual memory reserved by Windows for a particular process.

List two processes and the amount of virtual memory used by the system for each process.

_____

_____

_____

6. Locate the *Working Set* column to see the amount of physical memory used by a particular process. Which process is using the most motherboard RAM?

_____

7. Select the *Disk* tab. Open any file and save it to a different location on the hard drive, if possible. Return to the *Disk* tab and notice the disk activity.

8. Select the *Network* tab. Connect to the Internet, if possible, then return to this tab. How many TCP connections are active?

_____

9. Close the *Resource Monitor* window and return to the *Performance Monitor* window.

10. Ensure that the top object, *Performance*, is selected in the left panel. Notice the *System Summary* section in the center of the right panel.

What is the available memory, in megabytes?

_____

Scroll down to see the *PhysicalDisk* component. What is the percentage of idle time?

_____

Locate the *Processor Information* section. What is the total percentage of processor time?

_____

11. Expand the *Monitoring Tools* object in the left panel. Select the *Performance Monitor* tool.

What is the default counter shown?

_____

12. Select the green plus symbol (+) from the graphical menu at the top of the chart. Scroll through the counters list until you locate and select the *PhysicalDisk* counter down arrow (⬇). Click once on the *Disk Reads/sec* counter. In the *Instances of selected object* window, select the number that corresponds to your primary hard drive partition. Click *Add*. Continue using the same process to add the following counters:

PhysicalDisk   Disk Writes/sec

LogicalDisk   % Free Space

Memory   Available Bytes

Memory   Cache Bytes

Processor   % Processor Time (All instances)

13. Click *OK*. If a message appears, saying that one of the counters is already enabled, click *OK*.

14. Allow the system to run at least two minutes. Do things on the computer during this time. Afterward, select the *Freeze Display* menu icon that looks like a pause button on a CD/DVD player ⏸.

15. Select the *Change graph type* drop-down menu item to *Histogram bar*. This is the third icon from the left on the graphic menu at the top of the graph. Select the *Available Bytes* counter.

What is the average number of available bytes of memory?

_____

16. Select the *Cache Bytes* counter row.

What is the maximum number of bytes in cache memory?

_____

Look at the bar graph. Which is higher: the number of disk reads per second or the disk writes per second?

_____

Instructor initials: _____

17. Change the graph type to the *Report* view.

Which one of these views do you think will be most used by a technician?

_____

_____

18. Close the *Performance Monitor* window.

19. In Windows 7, type **reliability monitor** in the *Search* textbox. Select the *View reliability history* link from the resulting list.

In Windows 8/8.1/10, search for **view reliability history** and select *View reliability history* from the resulting list.

Describe any event that the system considered important enough to potentially affect the computer reliability.

_____

20. Close all windows.

Lab 16.24 Windows Remote Desktop Connection

Objective: To configure a computer for remote access using the Remote Desktop tool

Parts: Two computers with Windows 7, 8, 8.1, or 10 loaded and connected to the same network

Notes: The Remote Desktop tool is disabled by default, and you can connect to (take over) computers running only Windows Professional, Enterprise, or Ultimate, but all Windows 7, 8, 8.1, and 10 versions can initiate the Remote Desktop connection.

                You must have the ability to create users on the remote computer or have a user ID already created and with a password assigned.

Procedure: Complete the following procedure and answer the accompanying questions.

1. Power on the computer that is to be accessed remotely and verify that Windows loads. Log in using the user ID and password provided by the instructor or lab assistant.

2. If both computers have a user ID with full Administrator rights and a password, this step can be skipped. Otherwise on both computers, access the *User Accounts* Control Panel utility > *Manage another account* > *Create a new account* link > type **tester** in the *New Account Name* textbox > select the *Administrator* radio button > click the *Create Account* button. Add a password by clicking the *tester* icon > *Create a password* link > in the *New password* textbox, type **tester** > in the *Confirm new password* textbox, type **tester** > click the *Create password* button. Close the User Accounts window. Log in using the tester account on both computers.

3. On both computers, open *Windows Explorer/File Explorer*. Locate and right-click the *Computer* item (*This PC* on Windows 8 and 10). Select *Properties*.

Document the full computer name for both computers. Note that it is very important to have the full computer name.

Computer 1

_____

Computer 2

_____

4. On both computers, select the *Remote settings* link. The *Remote* tab should be active.

    What is the current Remote Desktop setting? [Don't allow remote connections to this computer | Allow remote connections from computers running any version of remote desktop (less secure) | Allow connections only from computers running Remote Desktop with network level authentication (more secure) (Windows 7)/Recommended (Windows 8/8.1/10))]

    _____

5. On both computers in the Remote Desktop section, select the *Allow [Remote] connections from computers running any version of remote desktop (less secure)* radio button on Windows 7. On Windows 8, 8.1 and 10 uncheck the *Allow connections only from computers running Remote Desktop with Network Level Authentication (more secure)* option.

    What warning appears, if any?

    _____

6. If necessary, click *OK* on the message and click *OK* again. On both computers, access Windows Explorer/File Explorer (not the browser). In the left panel, select *Network*. A message at the top of the windows states that network discovery and file sharing are turned off and to click to change. Click inside that message and select *Turn on network discovery and file sharing > Yes, turn on network discovery and file sharing for all public networks*. Be sure to do this for both computers.

7. On computer 1, use the search function to search for `remote desktop connection` and select *Remote Desktop Connection.*

8. On computer 1 in the Remote Desktop Connection window, type the other computer's full computer name in the *Computer* textbox. Click *Connect.*

9. Enter a username/password. Click *Yes* on the request for a certification or if a certificate warning appears.

    What happened to the remote computer?

    _____

10. On computer 1 (that is controlling computer 2), add a new shortcut to the desktop of the remote computer. When finished, click the *Close* button (X) in the blue Remote Desktop panel located in the top center of the screen. Click *OK.*

11. Log in on the remote computer. Notice the new desktop shortcut.

Instructor initials: _____

    (Check for new desktop shortcut.)

12. Delete the newly installed desktop shortcut on the remote computer.

13. From computer 2, do the same procedure: Remote into computer 1, create a desktop shortcut on computer 1, release control of computer 1, and verify the desktop shortcut on computer 1.

Instructor initials: _____

    (Check for new desktop shortcut.)

14. Return all settings to the original configuration (refer to the step 4 answer).

15. Remove the tester user account from any computer if it was created.

Lab 16.25 Windows Task Scheduler

Objective: To become familiar with the Task Scheduler tool and the `at` command

Parts: Computer with Windows 7, 8, 8.1, or 10 installed and Administrator rights

Procedure: Complete the following procedure and answer the accompanying questions.

Using Task Scheduler

1. Search for **task** in the *Search* textbox and select Task Scheduler (Windows 7/10)/Schedule a Task (Windows 8) from the resulting list. Task Scheduler opens.

    Based on the information shown in the Overview of Task Scheduler pane, where are tasks stored?

    _____

2. In the *Actions* pane, select *Create Basic Task*. In the *Name* textbox, type your last name > *Next*. Notice that Trigger Action is highlighted, and Daily is the default task time > select the *One time* radio button > *Next* > set the time to start to be 5 Minutes from the current date and time > *Next*.

    What three actions can you take using this wizard?

    _____

3. Select the *Display a Message* radio button and click *Next*. In the Title textbox, type a brief description of this message, such as **Scheduled downtime**. In the Message textbox, type a respectable message that a technician might send. An example might be as follows: **Attention students, faculty, and staff. Our scheduled maintenance window will begin in 15 minutes. The server will be down for approximately 2 hours. Thanks for your patience.** Click the *Next* button.

4. Enable the *Open the Properties dialog for this task when I click finish* checkbox > click the *Finish* button. Note that in Windows 8, 8.1, or 10, you can no longer display a message or send an email by using Task Manager. If you are using Windows 8 or 10, skip to step 6.

5. Only in Windows 7, select the *Run whether user is logged on or not* radio button and click *OK*. Enter the proper username and password credentials.

6. Create another scheduled task that runs an application one time at a specific time. Show the instructor this task's credentials through the Task Scheduler Library and show the task working.

    Document the scheduled task and start time.

    _____

    _____

Instructor initials: _____

Lab 16.26 Windows Steps Recorder

Objective: To become familiar with the Steps Recorder app

Parts: Computer with Windows 7, 8, 8.1, or 10 installed

Procedure: Complete the following procedure and answer the accompanying questions.

1. From the *Search* textbox, type **steps recorder** and open the *Record steps to reproduce a problem* link (Windows 7)/*Steps Recorder* app (Windows 8/10). An alternate method is to run the **psr** command or locate the app through *Accessories*. The Steps Recorder app can be used to show a user how to do something or have a user capture the problem he or she is having to share it with you in order to provide more information. The recorder can record the screen and timestamp the recording, and comments can be added.

2. Select the down arrow by the question mark. Select *Settings*. Lab Table 16.3 shows the purpose of each option. Note that modifications to the Settings options are relevant only while the app is open. They return to the default once the app is closed and have to be changed again when the app is reopened.

LAB TABLE 16.3   Steps Recorder Settings options

Option	Description
Output File	The default location where recordings are saved.
Enable screen capture	The Yes option is the default, which captures what is shown on the screen. The No option is used to provide a text-based description and is commonly used if there is confidential or personal information shown on the screen.
Number of recent screen captures to store	The number can be lowered to save space or increased when more screen captures are needed.

What is the default number of screen captures to store? [5 | 10 | 15 | 25]

3. Click *OK*. Open one of your favorite Windows tools. If you can't think of one, open *Task Manager*.

4. In the *Steps Recorder* window, select *Start Record*.

What options do you have while recording? (Select all that apply.)

[Continue Recording | Delete Recording | Pause Record | Stop Record | Add Notation | Add Comment]

5. Select the *Add Comment* option. Point to an interesting area of the screen and drag the window to create a rectangle around that interesting area. In the *Highlight Area and Comment* textbox that appeared, type some words like **Help me!** then click *OK*.

6. Select the *Stop Record* option. The resulting window has the following main sections: Recorded Steps, Steps, and Additional Details, including the day, time, operating system, and applications being used.

7. Select *Review the recorded steps as a slide show*.

Is Microsoft PowerPoint required to view the recording? [Yes | No]

Describe how you think this option might be used in the corporate environment.

_____

_____

Instructor initials: _____

8. Use the *Close* box in the upper-right corner to close the Steps Recorder app. When prompted to save the recording, click *No*.

17 macOS and Linux Operating Systems Labs

Lab 17.1 Using the macOS Graphical User Interface

Objective: To work with the macOS graphical user interface, including the Dock, Finder, Mission Control, and widgets; the command line; and Time Machine

Parts: Computer with macOS

Procedure: Complete the following procedure and answer the accompanying questions.

1. Start by opening up a *Finder* window.

2. On the left side, you see a sidebar containing shortcuts to different parts of the file system. Right-click the *Applications* shortcut and select *Add to Dock*.

3. You should now have a new shortcut on the right side of the Dock.

   What happens when you click it?

   _____

4. This type of folder shortcut on the Dock isn't limited to just the Applications folder. You can use a similar shortcut with any folder, such as Downloads, Documents, and so on. You can drag and drop nearly anything to the Dock to create a shortcut.

   Creating a shortcut is a quick way to get access to your applications, but what other ways could you quickly access your applications?

   _____

5. To remove a Dock shortcut, either to a folder or application, simply drag it off the Dock, hold it with your cursor until it shows the word *remove* above it, and let go of it.

6. Open the System Preferences menu and go to the Mission Control Panel: *Finder > Applications > System Preferences > Mission Control*.

7. You see a section labeled Dashboard that is, by default, set to off. Change the option to *As Space* so that the dashboard appears in a separate space. Close the window.

8. Launch Mission Control (*Finder > Applications > Mission Control*). Click the window at the top labeled *Dashboard*.

9.   The dashboard area is for holding widgets, which are usually shortcuts, mini applications, or reminders. Select the + button at the bottom left and select *Stickies*. A sticky note appears, allowing you to save a message.

10.   Click the + button again, and you see a *More Widgets* button; click it.

11.   A browser window opens, allowing you to browse a repository of available widgets. Widgets are slowly being phased out of macOS, but many long-time users still use them.

Which useful widgets did you find on the Apple widget repository?

_____

Lab 17.2 Introduction to macOS System Preferences

Objective: To explore the macOS Settings option

Parts: Computer with macOS

Procedure: Complete the following procedure and answer the accompanying questions.

1.   Power on the computer with macOS and log in.

2.   On the Dock that runs along the bottom of the window, select the *System Preferences* icon (which has the gears on it). An alternative way of getting into System Preferences is to click on the Apple icon in the upper-left corner > *System Preferences*.

3.   Select the *Show All* button in order to see the configuration options.

4.   Locate the *Personal* section.

List three system preference icons located in the *Personal* section.

_____

_____

5.   Click once on the *General* icon.

What setting is the *General* icon used for?

a. to control how many recent items are shown in Documents

b. to show how much RAM is installed

c. to set an administrator password

d. to view installed devices and resources

6.   Select the left arrow to return to the main System Preferences window. Access the *Desktop & Screen Saver* settings. To change what the desktop looks like, ensure that the *Desktop* option at the top of the window is selected and choose either *Solid Colors* or *Desktop Pictures* from the left menu. Then choose the specific option in the right window.

7.   To select a specific screen saver (which is a best practice when you walk away from your desk for a moment), select the *Screen Saver* option from the top center of the window. Specific options are available to select on the left, and a preview displays in the right window.

What is the current setting for the screen saver to start after inactivity?

_____

8.   Use the left arrow to return to the main System Preferences window. Access the *Dock* settings. Here you can control where the Dock is located on the screen, how big it is, as well as specialized effects for how screens close.

9.   Use the left arrow to return to the main System Preferences window. Access the *Mission Control* settings. Mission Control dictates how open windows appear.

What keystroke is used to show the desktop?

_____

10. Use the left arrow to return to the main System Preferences window. Access the *Language and Text* settings. Across the top you see Language, Text, Region, and Input Sources.

11. Select the *Text* option so you see what typed characters will create special symbols, such as the registered trademark symbol, and whether the symbols are automatically inserted.

12. Select the *Input Sources* option from the top of the window. Notice all the inputs for different countries and character sets.

13. Use the left arrow to return to the main System Preferences window. Access the *Security & Privacy* settings.

    What is the current setting for requiring a password after the computer goes to sleep?
    [enabled | disabled]

14. Access the *FireVault* option at the top of the screen. This allows you to encrypt the hard drive.

15. Access the *Firewall* option at the top of the screen. In order to change these settings, you have to click the lock in the bottom-left corner. Go ahead and click the lock and enter the username and password required to make changes to the computer.

    What is the current setting for the firewall? [off | on]

16. If the firewall is currently off, select the *Turn On Firewall* option. Click the *Firewall Options* button. This is where you can block all incoming connections or put the computer in stealth mode. Click Cancel.

17. Select the *Advanced* button.

    What is the default setting to log out after inactivity?
    [15 minutes | 30 minutes | 60 minutes | 90 minutes]

    _____

18. Click the *OK* button to return to the Security & Privacy settings. If you turned on the firewall (refer to step 15), use the *Turn Off Firewall* button to disable it.

19. Select the *Privacy* option. You can enable location services here for any apps that use your location. You can also choose whether to automatically send information to Apple if a problem occurs. Click the lock in the bottom-left corner to lock the system and prevent further changes if it was locked when you started.

20. Use the left arrow to return to the main System Preferences window. Access *Spotlight*. These settings allow you to control where searches are performed first, second, and third.

21. Click the left arrow to return to the main System Preferences window. Locate the *Hardware* section of the System Preferences window. Here is where you can adjust the mouse for a left-handed person or adjust the tracking speed. You can also install a printer or see what print jobs are running.

22. Double-click the *Displays* icon. Select the *Color* option. Notice that this is where the *Calibrate* option is located.

23. Click the left arrow to return to the main System Preferences window. Notice the third section of icons in the *Internet & Wireless* section. Access *Network* settings. Here is where you can select and configure a wireless network or pair the laptop with a Bluetooth device.

24. Click the left arrow to return to the main System Preferences window. The *System* section allows you to configure the computer for another user through the *Users & Groups* icon, implement restrictions for younger children using the *Parental Controls* option, and set the correct time through the *Date & Time* icon.

25. Access the *Diction & Speech* settings. The *Dictation* option allows commands set up through the *Accessibility* option to work by being spoken (for example, "undo that"). The *Text to Speech* option at the top allows configuration of the system voice, the speed of the voice, and when certain things are announced.

26. Click the left arrow to return to the main System Preferences window. Review any options you like in the remaining Time Machine, Accessibility, and Startup Disk settings. (See Lab 17.3 for more on working with the Time Machine.)

27. Close the *System Preferences* window when you are finished by clicking the red circle (which has an X that appears when you hover over it) in the upper-left corner.

Lab 17.3 Using the macOS Terminal and Time Machine

Objective: To work with the macOS graphical user interface, including the Dock, Finder, Mission Control, and widgets; the command line; and Time Machine

Parts: Computer with macOS and a Time Machine backup drive

Procedure: Complete the following procedure and answer the accompanying questions.

1. Open the Terminal application by selecting *Finder > Applications > Utilities > Terminal.*

2. Type in the command **pwd**, and you see that you are located in the /Users/YOURUSERNAME directory.

3. Type the command **ls** to see what folders are in your current directory.

4. Navigate to the *Documents* folder.

   What command did you use to do this?

   _____

5. Create a blank file with the extension **.txt**. Name the file something unique that does not already exist.

   What command did you use to do this?

   _____

6. Run a Time Machine backup. If you do not have a Time Machine backup drive set up, you need to connect an external drive to the Mac. You will be prompted when connecting the new drive about whether you would like to use it for Time Machine; select *yes* and enable backups. After this is enabled, or if you already had backups enabled, you need to trigger a new backup. Open the Time Machine preferences by selecting *Finder > Applications > System Preferences > Time Machine.*

7. Enable (that is, place a check mark by) +* in the menu bar option.

8. In the right corner of the menu bar, click the circular clock icon and select Backup Now.

9. If this is the first time running a Time Machine backup, it may take a while to complete. You can check the status by clicking the same Time Machine icon in the menu bar. When it shows as completing a backup, return to the Terminal application.

10. Make sure you are still in the *Documents* folder and delete the file you created in step 5.

    What command did you use to do this?

    _____

11. Open a *Finder* window and navigate to the *Applications* folder. There should be a shortcut to it on the left side.

12. Double-click or tap and briefly hold the *Time Machine* icon. This should bring up the Time Machine interface, which is used to recover files.

13. In the Finder window select the *Documents* folder on the left side. Then go back to the most recent Time Machine backup by using the timeline on the right side. Select the file you created and deleted earlier and select *Restore.*

    Does the file appear in Finder after you click Restore? [Yes | No] If it does not, the Time Machine backup did not complete before you tried to delete the file.

Lab 17.4 Using Ubuntu Live DVD

Objective:　　To learn where to get Ubuntu and how to boot into a live DVD environment

Parts:　　Computer with a writable DVD drive and a blank DVD

Procedure:　　Complete the following procedure and answer the accompanying questions.

1. To start this exercise, first download an Ubuntu ISO file. The latest ISO can be downloaded from http://www.ubuntu.com/download/desktop. (For this exercise and chapter, we use a specific version of Ubuntu, but it is fine to download a newer version to follow along with this lab.)

2. After you download the image, burn it as a bootable image to your DVD. See the directions that follow for the operating system you are on to create the live DVD:

   > To create a bootable DVD from Windows 7, 8, or 10: Insert a blank DVD. Right-click the ISO image you downloaded and choose *Burn Disc Image*. From the Windows Disc Image Burner window, select the drive for the DVD burner and click *Burn*.

   > To create a bootable DVD from macOS: Insert a blank DVD. Launch *Disk Utility (Finder > Applications > Utilities > Disk Utility)*. Drag and drop the ISO file to the left pane in Disk Utility. Select the ISO file and then select *Burn* from the menu above. In the menu that appears, select the DVD drive and then select *Burn*.

3. After burning the DVD, keep the disc inside the optical drive and reboot the system.

4. As the system reboots, access the boot menu. To do this, press a special key or key combination, as delineated in Lab Table 17.1. If the keyboard shortcut listed does not work, research the manufacturer of your system on the Internet.

LAB TABLE 17.1　Boot menu shortcuts

System manufacturer	Key or key combination
Dell	F12
Lenovo	F8, F10, or F12
HP	Esc or F9
Asus	Esc or F8
Acer	Esc, F9, or F12
Macintosh	Option

5. When in the boot menu, boot from the DVD drive. (Make sure the DVD created in step 2 is inserted into the drive.)

TECH TIP

What to do if the system will not boot to the DVD

Make sure the DVD was created as a bootable disc. Boot back into the operating system, browse to the contents of the DVD, and make sure you see different files and folders on it. A common mistake is to burn the ISO file directly to the disc as if it were a regular data DVD. This will not create a bootable disc. The contents of the ISO file must be extracted onto the disc while the disc is being created.

6.   After the DVD loads, two options appear: Install Ubuntu and Try Ubuntu. Select the *Try Ubuntu* option to load the live DVD environment.

Were you able to boot to the live DVD? If so, show the instructor. Having the live DVD work properly is a requirement to advance to the next lab. If you cannot get it to work, consult with your instructor.

Instructor's initials: _____

Lab 17.5 Creating a Bootable Ubuntu USB Flash Drive Using macOS

Objective: To be able to create a bootable Linux-based flash drive

Parts: Computer with macOS installed

2 GB or higher flash drive (that will be wiped)

Access to the Internet or a downloaded Ubuntu ISO file

The free Etcher application or access to the Internet

Procedure: Complete the following procedure and answer the accompanying questions.

1.   Download an Ubuntu ISO file. The latest ISO can be downloaded from http://www.ubuntu.com/download/desktop.

2.   You will also need a free open source application called Etcher installed. It can be downloaded from https://etcher.io. You may have to enable the *App Store and Identified Developers* option in the *Allow Apps Downloaded From* section of the *Security & Privacy* system preferences. You may have to click the *Open Anyway* button on the same screen.

3.   Ensure that the USB flash drive does not contain any data that needs to be preserved and insert it into the Mac computer. Note that the contents of the flash drive will be erased as part of the process.

4.   Open the *Disk Utility* tool (by using Finder or Spotlight) and locate the USB drive. You may have to expand the external drives to see it.

5.   Select the flash drive from the left menu and select *Erase* from the top toolbar. Ensure that the format type is set to *MS-DOS (FAT)*.

What Disk Utility format types are available as options?

_____

Why do you think the Ubuntu ISO would require the MS-DOS (FAT) option?

_____

6.   Select the scheme type as *GUID Partition Map > Erase* button.

7.   Start the Etcher application and select the ISO file that was already downloaded. Select the flash drive as the target device by selecting *Flash*. (*Note*: If you receive a message that the disk is not readable, eject the drive. Do not select the Initialize option.)

8.   Reinsert the flash drive, if necessary, and restart the Mac while holding down the Option key. Select the *EFI Boot* option.

Did the system boot properly? [Yes | No]

Lab 17.6 Linux Command-Line Basics

Objective: To learn commands in the Linux environment

Parts: Computer with Ubuntu loaded, an Ubuntu Live CD (see Lab 17.4), or some version of Linux loaded

Procedure: Complete the following procedure and answer the accompanying questions.

1.   Log in with a username and password, as necessary.

2.   Open the *Terminal* application. The prompt shown on the screen shows your username, the name of the computer, and the current directory (if there is room).

3.   Type **pwd** to determine your current directory.

4.   Notice the time, which is usually displayed in the upper-right corner of the screen. To determine what time zone you are in, type the following commands:

date

timedatectl

5.   To find any files that have the word *timezone* in them, use the `locate` command:

locate timezone

6.   The `ls` command is used to list files that may be in the home directory. Items in blue are directories. Type the following command:

ls

7.   By default, hidden files do not display on the screen. You can add an option to the `ls` command to show them. Hidden files in Linux have filenames that begin with a period (.). Type the following to verify if there are any hidden files in the home directory:

ls -a

Were there any hidden files or directories?

_____

8.   To make a directory, type the following exactly as it is shown, including the capital letters CTS:

mkdir CTS1133

9.   To verify that the directory is there, use the `ls` command again by typing the following:

ls

10. To direct the operating system to move or change into that directory, you use the `cd` command. Type the following, ensuring that you type the letters `cts` in lowercase so you can see how the operating system handles this:

cd cts1133

What happened?

_____

11. Now type the command correctly and notice how the prompt changes:

cd CTS1133

12. To move back one directory to the home directory, you use the `cd  ..` command. Notice the space between the command `cd` and the two periods. You do not use a space like this in the Windows environment. Note that you can just type the `cd` command to return to the home directory no matter how many subdirectories down in the directory structure you are. For now, just move back one directory and type the following:

cd ..

13. Move back into the CTS1133 directory by using a command you have used previously in this lab.

How can you tell you are in the correct directory?

_____

14. From the CTS1133 directory, use the `touch` command to create a file (that is not going to have any information contained in it):

touch fileone

15. Use a command you have used earlier in this lab to verify that the file has been created.

What command did you use? [cd | cd .. | ls | touch]

16. Create a second file by copying the first file and renaming the file at the same time, using the `cp` command:

   `cp fileone mysecondfile`

17. Verify that there are now two files in the CTS1133 directory (fileone and mysecondfile).

18. Now use the `rm` command to remove a file. From the CTS1133 directory remove the mysecondfile file by typing the following command:

   `rm mysecondfile`

19. Use a command used previously in the lab to move back to the home directory.

   What command did you use? [cd | cd .. | ls | cp]

20. Use the `rmdir` command to remove a directory. Remove the CTS1133 directory by using the following command:

   `rmdir CTS1133`

   What happened?

   _____

21. Use a command previously used in this lab to move back into the CTS1133 directory. Once there, remove the file named fileone by using another command you have already used in this lab. Finally, return to the home directory and remove the CTS1133 directory.

   List each command used in this step.

   _____

   _____

   _____

   _____

22. Close the Terminal program.

Operating System Challenge

23. Access the system settings. There is commonly a desktop icon for this. Change the wallpaper to a different setting.

   What setting did you use?

   _____

24. See if there is a setting you can use to configure the mouse for a left-handed person.

   What setting did you use, if any?

   _____

Lab 17.7 Ubuntu Command-Line Challenge

Objective: To learn commands in the Ubuntu environment

Parts: Computer with Ubuntu loaded or an Ubuntu Live CD (see Lab 17.4)

Procedure: Complete the following procedure and answer the accompanying questions.

1. You must have successfully completed the Lab 17.5 to proceed with this lab.

2. While booted to the live DVD, open the *Terminal*.

   How did you open the Terminal?

   _____

   What is the current directory your Terminal session started in, and what command did you use to find out?

   _____

3. Notice that the time in the upper-right corner of the screen is likely different than your current local time. To find what time zone the system is set to, find the file named *timezone* and see what is written in it.

    How did you find the timezone file, and where was it located? What did it contain?

    _____

    List the commands you ran to install the application screen.

    _____

    _____

    _____

    _____

4. Use the **man page for apt-get** command to uninstall the screen utility.

    What command did you use?

    _____

18 Computer and Network Security Labs

Lab 18.1 Encrypting a File and Folder in Windows

Objective: To provide security for a particular file and folder, enable encryption using Windows 7, 8, or 10.

Parts: A computer with Windows 7, 8, or 10 that has at least one NTFS partition

Note: Two user accounts are needed and possibly created for this exercise: one account that encrypts a file and the other account to test the encryption. If two user accounts are not available, most of the lab can still be performed or a second user account can be added. This lab is best demonstrated with two accounts that have local administrator rights.

Procedure: Complete the following procedure and answer the accompanying questions.

1. Power on the computer and log on using the user ID and password provided by the instructor or lab assistant.

2. Access the Computer Management console by using the following directions, depending on the operating system used:

   In Windows 7, click the *Start* button > *System and Security* section of the Control Panel > *Administrative Tools* > double-click *Computer Management*.

   In Windows 8/10, search for and access *Administrative Tools* > double-click or tap and briefly hold on *Computer Management*.

3. Expand the *Storage* option and select *Disk Management*.

   How many disk partitions are available?

   _____

   Do any drive partitions use NTFS?

   _____

   If so, how many?

   _____

   Note that if no drive partitions use NTFS, this exercise cannot be completed.

4. Close the *Computer Management* window. Open *Windows Explorer/File Explorer*. Create a text file called *Security Test.txt* and save it in the *Documents* folder.

5. Right-click or tap and briefly hold the *Security Test.txt* file and select *Properties*. From the *General* tab, select the *Advanced* button.

6. Enable the *Encrypt contents to secure data* option > *OK*. Select the *Apply* button and the warning message shown in Lab Figure 18.1 appears.

LAB FIGURE 18.1   Windows encryption warning message

7. The default would be to encrypt the `Security test.txt` file and to encrypt the *Documents* folder. This is not what you want to do in this case, so select the *Encrypt the file only* radio button > *OK* > *OK*.

8. In *Windows Explorer/File Explorer*, click an empty spot in the right pane.

    Is there any indication that the file is encrypted? If so, what is it? Note that you might need to create an unencrypted file to answer this question.

    _____

9. In *Windows Explorer/File Explorer*, access the *Properties* window of the *Security Test.txt* file again. Select the *Advanced* button. From the *Advanced Attributes* window, select the *Details* button. If this is not available, ensure that you are on a file (and not a folder).

    What user(s) can access the encrypted file?

    _____

10. Notice the certificate thumbprint number to the right of the user. EFS can request a digital certificate from a CA (certificate authority) such as a server. If a digital certificate from a CA is not available, EFS can use a self-signed certificate.

    What are the first 16 hexadecimal digits used for the digital certificate?

    _____

    Compare these digits with the digits found by a fellow classmate. Are the digital certificates the same? If so, why do you think they are the same? If they are different, why do you think they are different?

    _____

11. Select the *Cancel* button on three different windows to exit the *Properties* window.

12. From *Windows Explorer/File Explorer*, open the *Security Test.txt* file, modify it, and save it.

    From Windows Explorer/*File Explorer*, does the file appear to still be encrypted?

    _____

13. Log off the computer and log on as a different user. If a different user does not exist, create one by using the *User Accounts* section of the Control Panel, if possible.

14. Use *Windows Explorer/File Explorer* to locate and open the *Security Test.txt* file located under the other username (commonly found at `C:\users\username\Documents`). Modify the file and save it, if possible.

Are there any problems opening, modifying, or saving the file?

_____

_____

_____

In one or more complete sentences, explain what happened and why you think it occurred this way.

_____

15. Log off the computer and log on as the original user.

16. Access the *Documents* folder and create a new folder called *Test*. Copy the *Security Test.txt* file into the new *Test* folder.

    Is the copied file encrypted in the *Test* folder?

    _____

17. Within the *Test* folder, create a new text file called *Security Test2.txt*.

    Is the newly created file encrypted?

    _____

Instructor initials: _____

18. Encrypt the *Test* folder using the default encryption setting *Encrypt the file and its parent folder (recommended)*.

    Does encrypting the folder change anything within the folder?

    _____

    If so, what does it change?

    _____

19. Within the *Test* folder, create and save a new file called *Security Test3.txt*.

    Is the newly created file encrypted?

    _____

20. Delete the *Security Test.txt*, *Security Test2.txt*, and *Security Test3.txt* files.

    Do you get any indication that the files were encrypted when they were deleted?

    _____

21. Permanently delete the *Test* folder and any files created in the *Documents* folder.

Lab 18.2 Using Windows 7/8/10 System Protection

Objective: To manually control the settings involved with system restore points using System Protection

Parts: A computer with Windows 7, 8, or 10 loaded with at least one NTFS partition

Note: This lab requires local administrator rights.

Procedure: Complete the following procedure and answer the accompanying questions.

1. Power on the computer and log on using the user ID and password provided by the instructor or lab assistant.

2. Access *Windows Explorer/File Explorer*. Right-click or tap and briefly hold on *Computer (Windows 7)/This PC (Windows 8/10)* > *Properties* > *System Protection* link > *System Protection* tab.

    In the *Protection Settings* section, document the available drives.

    _____

    Document whether protection is currently on or off for each of the available drives.

    _____

3.   Select *Configure*.

What options are available for *Restore Settings*?

_____

_____

_____

Microsoft says, "System Protection can keep copies of system settings and previous versions of files." Do you think this means system files, user data files, or both? Explain your reasoning.

_____

Thinking as a technician, which setting is optimum for most users?

_____

_____

What is one situation in which a technician would recommend the *Turn off system protection* option?

_____

4.   In Windows 7, ensure that the *Restore system settings and previous versions of files* radio button is selected.

In Windows 8/10, ensure that the *Turn on system protection* radio button is selected.

By default, Windows uses a maximum of 10% of the hard drive for system protection. However, the system enables you to adjust this amount in the Disk Space Usage section. Note that if you turn off system protection, you cannot use system restore points.

What is the current *Max Usage* setting?

_____

Describe a situation in which a technician would want to configure a machine for more than 10% of the hard disk space reserved for system protection.

_____

5.   Click *Cancel*.

On Your Own

6.   Create a system restore point.

Instructor initials: _____

7.   Close all windows.

Lab 18.3 Sharing a Folder in Windows 7

Objective: To share a folder and understand the permissions associated with a network share

Parts: Access to two Windows 7 computers with a user ID that has administrator rights

Procedure: Complete the following procedure and answer the accompanying questions.

1.   Turn on both computers and verify that the operating system loads. Log in to Windows 7 using a user ID and password that has full administrator rights and that is provided by your instructor or lab assistant.

2.   On the first computer, use Windows Explorer to create two subfolders within the *Documents* folder. Name the folders *READ* and *WRITE*.

3.   Within the *READ* folder, create a text document called *readme.txt*. Within the *WRITE* folder, create a text file called *changeme.txt*.

4. On both computers, determine the computer name by accessing the *System* section of the Control Panel. Determine the IP addresses of both computers by using the `ipconfig` command.

Document your findings.

Computer	Computer name	IP address
Computer 1		
Computer 2		

5. On both computers, access the *Network and Sharing Center* Control Panel link to document the current *Advanced Sharing Settings*.

Computer 1	Computer 2
Network discovery [On | Off]	Network discovery [On | Off]
Media streaming [On | Off]	Media streaming [On | Off]
Public folder sharing [On (read only, password required) | On (password required) | Off]	Public folder sharing [On (read only, password required) | On (password required) | Off]
Printer sharing [On | Off]	Printer sharing [On | Off]
File sharing connections [Use 128-Bit Encryption to Help | Enable File Sharing]	File sharing connections [Use 128-Bit Encryption to Help | Enable File Sharing]
Password protected sharing [Turn on password protected sharing | Turn off password protected sharing]	Password protected sharing [Turn on password protected sharing | Turn off password protected sharing]

6. On both computers, enable the following settings:
    > *File and printer sharing*
    > *Public folder sharing*
    > *Network discovery*

7. On both computers, use the *Folder Options* Control Panel > *View* tab > in the *Advanced Settings* window, locate the *Use Sharing Wizard (Recommended)* option.

What is the current setting for the *Use Sharing Wizard (Recommended)* option? [Enabled I Disabled]

_____

8. Ensure that the *Use Sharing Wizard (Recommended)* option is enabled. Apply changes as necessary. In Windows Explorer on the first computer, right-click the *READ* folder > *Properties* > *Sharing* tab.

Document the share network path that appears in the window.

_____

9. Select the *Advanced Sharing* button > enable the *Share this folder* checkbox > select the *Caching* button.

10. Select the *Configure Offline Availability for a Shared Folder Help* link.

What is the purpose of caching?

_____

_____

Is offline availability enabled by default for a shared folder? [Y I N]

What command can be used from a command prompt to configure caching options for a shared folder?

_____

11. Close the help window.

12. In the Offline Settings window, leave the default settings.

What is the default setting for offline access?

_____

13. Select *Cancel*. In the Advanced Sharing window, select the *Permissions* button. Notice that the Everyone group is listed by default.

Note: If you want to share with someone who is not listed, use the *User Accounts* Control Panel to create the account and then select that account name in the Permissions window.

If the local or domain policy requires a password, a password should be put on the user account. Best practice is to require passwords on all user accounts.

If the Everyone user account is selected and password protection is used, a user account is still needed to gain access.

What permissions are enabled by default for the Everyone group? [Full Control | Change | Read]

14. Click *OK* on the two windows and then click the *Close* button.

15. Open the *Computer Management* console. Expand *System Tools* and *Shared Folders*. Click *Shares* in the left pane. The READ share is listed in the right pane. If the share is missing, redo this lab from the beginning. Close the *Computer Management* window.

16. On the second computer, log on as the user given access in step 13 or use the user ID and password provided by the instructor or lab assistant.

17. On the second computer, open *Windows Explorer*. Select *Network* in the left pane. In the right pane, locate and double-click the name of the first computer.

Note: If the computer is not listed, click the *Start* button and in the *Search Programs and Files* text-box, type *computer_name* (where *computer_name* is the name of the first computer). Press ⏎Enter.

18. On the second computer, locate the *READ* share and the *readme.txt* document. Double-click the *readme.txt* file.

Does the file open? [Y | N]

19. Add a few words to the file. Click the *File > Save* menu option. Leave the filename the same and click the *Save* button. When asked if you want to replace the file, click *Yes*.

Does the file save? [Y | N]

20. Close the file and close the window that contains the file.

21. On the second computer inside the *Search programs and files* Start button option, type the share path documented in step 8 and press ⏎Enter. If an error occurs, check your typing or redo the steps to get a correct share path document in step 8.

What happens?

_____

22. Close the window. On the second computer, open *Windows Explorer*. Right-click *Computer* in the left pane and select *Map Network Drive*. Use the *Drive* drop-down menu to select a drive letter. In the *Folder* textbox, type the share path for the READ share documented in step 8. Click *Finish*. The share opens with the drive letter documented in the path at the top of the window. Note that you may have to expand the left pane to see the drive letter.

Instructor initials: _____

23. On the second computer, again access *Windows Explorer* and locate the drive letter that was just mapped to a network drive. Because Windows share paths can be lengthy, a common practice is to use a mapped network drive for the share.

    How can you easily identify mapped drive letters in Windows Explorer (besides a quite high drive letter, in some cases)?

    _____

24. Close all windows on the second computer.

25. In Windows Explorer on the first computer, right-click the *WRITE* folder > *Properties* > *Sharing* tab.

    Document the share network path that appears in the window.

    _____

26. Select the *Advanced Sharing* button > select the *Share this folder* checkbox.

27. Select the *Permissions* button.

28. Select the correct username or group and select the *Change* > *Allow* checkbox. Click *OK* on two windows and then click the *Close* button.

29. On the second computer, locate the *changeme.txt* document that is shared from the first computer.

30. Modify and save the *changeme.txt* file.

31. On the first computer, open the *changeme.txt* file. Close the file.

    IS the file changed? [Y | N]

Instructor initials: _____

32. On the second computer, try changing the name of the *changeme.txt* file.

    Can you change the name of the *changeme.txt* file? [Y | N]

33. Verify whether the filename changed on the first computer.

    Des the filename change on the first computer? [Y | N]

    If so, what is the new name?

    _____

34. On the second computer, right-click the *WRITE* folder and select *Always available offline*.

    What indication is given that a folder is available offline?

    _____

    Can a particular file be given this same attribute? [Y | N]

35. Disconnect the second computer from the network by removing the network cable from the network adapter.

36. From a command prompt on the second computer, ping the first computer using the IP address documented in step 4.

    Des the ping succeed? [Y | N]

37. With no network access, open the *WRITE* folder and access the *changeme.txt* file. Modify the file and save it.

38. Reconnect the second computer to the network.

39. From the first computer, access the *WRITE* folder.

    Are the document changes saved on the first computer when the second computer is disconnected from the network? [Y | N] Once you determine the answer, close the file.

40. On the second computer, again access the *changeme.txt* file and try to permanently delete the file.

    Can you permanently delete the *changeme.txt* file? [Y | N]

41. On the first computer, create a subfolder under the *READ* folder. Name the folder *SUB_READ*. Create a text file in the *SUB_READ* folder called *sub_file.txt*.

42. On the second computer, locate and right-click the *SUB_READ* shared folder. Select *Properties*.

    What attributes does this folder have? [Read-only | Hidden | None]

43. On the second computer in *Windows Explorer*, locate the *sub_file.txt* file. Select *Properties*.

    What attributes, if any, are enabled by default? [Read-only | Hidden | None]

44. Click *Cancel*. Try to modify the *sub_file.txt* file.

    Can you change the *sub_file.txt* file? [Y | N]

Instructor initials: _____

45. On the second computer, remove the mapped drive (and any drive that you created on your own) by using *Windows Explorer* to locate the mapped drive letter under *Computer* in the left pane. Right-click the mapped drive and select *Disconnect*.

46. On the first computer, permanently delete the *READ* and *WRITE* folders and all files and subfolders contained within them.

47. On the first computer, put the *Advanced Sharing Settings* options back to the original configuration, as documented in step 5. Put the *Use Sharing Wizard* back to the original setting, as documented in step 7. Show your lab partner the documented settings and the current configuration. Have your lab partner use the following table to document that the computer has been put back to the original configuration.

Computer 1 (permanently deleted folders/sharing settings)
Printed name of lab partner
Signature of lab partner

48. On the second computer, put the *Advanced Sharing Settings* options back to the original configuration, as documented in step 5. Put the *Use Sharing Wizard* back to the original setting, as documented in step 7. Show your lab partner the documented settings and the current configuration. Have your lab partner use the table that follows to document that the computer has been put back to the original configuration.

Computer 2 (permanently deleted folders/sharing settings)
Printed name of lab partner
Signature of lab partner

49. On both computers, delete any user accounts that have been created. *Note:* You must be logged in as an administrator to delete user accounts.

Lab 18.4 Sharing a Folder in Windows 8/10

Objective: To share a folder and understand the permissions associated with a network share

Parts: Access to two Windows 8 or 10 computers with a user ID that has administrator rights

Note: You must have a password assigned to the login account for this lab to work.

Procedure: Complete the following procedure and answer the accompanying questions.

1. Turn on both computers and verify that the operating system loads. Log in to Windows 8 or 10 using an account that has full administrator rights and that is provided by your instructor or lab assistant.

2. On the first computer, use *File Explorer* to create two subfolders within the *Documents* folder. Name the folders *READ* and *WRITE*.

3. Within the *READ* folder, create a text document called *readme*. Within the *WRITE* folder, create a text file called *changeme*.

4. On both computers, determine the computer name by accessing the *System* section of the Control Panel. Determine the IP addresses of both computers by using the `ipconfig` command.

    Document your findings.

Computer	Computer name	IP address
Computer 1		
Computer 2		

5. On both computers, if the IP address starts with the number 169, use the *Network and Sharing Center* section of the Control Panel > *Change Adapter Settings* > right-click or tap and briefly hold the Ethernet wired NIC icon > *Properties* > double-click or double-tap *Internet Protocol Version 4 (TCP/IPv4)* > select the *Use the Following IP Address* radio button. Assign IP addresses as follows:

Computer 1	Computer 2
IP address: **192.168.10.11**	IP address: **192.168.10.12**
Subnet mask: **255.255.255.0**	Subnet mask: **255.255.255.0**

    Apply the changes to the IP address if necessary.

    Does the address have to be manually assigned on Computer 1? [Yes | No]

    Does the address have to be manually assigned on Computer 2? [Yes | No]

6. On both computers, access the *Network and Sharing Center* Control Panel link to document the current *Advanced Sharing Settings*. Do this for the current profile as well as the other profiles. You can tell which option is the current profile by looking for the profile that has the words *(Current Profile)* beside it.

	Computer 1	Computer 2
Private profile		
Network discovery [On	Off]		
Network discovery *Turn on automatic setup of network connected devices* suboption [Enabled	Disabled]		
File and printer sharing [On	Off]		
HomeGroup connections [Allow Windows to Manage HomeGroup Connections	Use User Accounts and Passwords to Connect to Other Computers] *Note:* This option might not be available in Windows 10 in version 1803 and higher.		
Guest or Public profile		
Network discovery [On	Off]		
File and printer sharing [On	Off]		
All Networks profile		
Public folder sharing [On	Off]		

	Computer 1	Computer 2
Public folder sharing [On | Off]		
Media streaming [On | Off]		
File sharing connections [Use 128-bit Encryption to Help Protect File Sharing Connections | Enable File Sharing for Devices That Use 40- or 56-bit Encryption]		
Password protected sharing [On | Off]		

7. On both computers, enable the following settings:

   Private profile:

       Network discovery: **On**

       Network discovery *Turn on automatic setup of network connected devices* suboption: **enabled**

       File and printer sharing: **On**

       HomeGroup connections: *Use user accounts and passwords to connect to other computers:* **enabled**

   Guest or Public profile:

       Network discovery: **On**

       File and printer sharing: **On**

   All Networks profile:

       Public folder sharing: **On**

       Media streaming: **Off**

       File sharing connections: **Use 128-bit encryption**

       Password protected sharing: **Off**

8. After signing off and back on as directed on both computers, use both computers to search for and access the *Folder Options* (Windows 8)/*File Explorer Options* (Windows 10) section of the Control Panel > *View* tab > in the *Advanced Settings* window, locate the *Use Sharing Wizard (Recommended)* option.

   What is the current setting for the *Use Sharing Wizard* option? [Enabled | Disabled]

9. Ensure that the *Use Sharing Wizard* option is enabled. Apply changes as necessary. In File Explorer on the first computer, right-click or tap and briefly hold on the *READ* folder > *Properties* > *Sharing* tab.

10. Select the *Advanced Sharing* button > enable the *Share this folder* checkbox > select the *Caching* button.

   What is the purpose of caching?

   _____

   _____

   Is offline availability enabled by default for a shared folder? [Y | N]

   What command can be used from a command prompt to configure caching options for a shared folder? Note that you may have to refer to Chapter 15 to answer this question.

11. In the *Offline Settings* window, leave the default settings.

What is the default setting for offline access?

_____

12. Select *Cancel*. In the *Advanced Sharing* window, select the *Permissions* button. Notice that the Everyone group is listed by default.

Notes: If you want to share with someone who is not listed, use the *User Accounts* section of the Control Panel to create the account; then select that account name in the Permissions window.

If the Everyone user account is selected and password protection is used, a user account is still needed to gain access.

What permissions are enabled by default for the Everyone group? [Full Control | Change | Read]

13. Select *OK* on two consecutive windows.

Document the share network path that appears in the window.

_____

14. Select the *Close* option at the bottom. While still working on Computer 1, open the *Computer Management* console. In the left window, expand *System Tools* and *Shared Folders*. Select *Shares* in the left pane. The READ share (along with other shares) should be listed in the right pane.

Is the READ share present? [Yes | No]

If the share is missing, redo this lab from the beginning. Close the *Computer Management* window.

15. On the second computer, open *File Explorer*. Select *Network* in the left pane. In the right pane, locate and double-click or double-tap the name of the first computer.

Notes: If the computer does not show in the list, search for **computer_name** (where *computer_name* is the name of the first computer). Press ⏎Enter.

16. On the second computer, locate the *readme.txt* document within the *READ* share. Double-click or double-tap the *readme.txt* file to open it.

Does the file open? [Y | N]

17. Add a few words to the file. Select the *File > Save* menu option. Leave the filename the same and select the *Save* button. When asked if you want to replace the file, select *Yes*.

Is the file saved? [Y | N]

18. Select *OK*. Close the file and close the window that contains the file. Note that you cannot save it.

19. On the second computer, in the *Search* textbox, type the share path documented in step 13 and press ⏎Enter. If an error occurs, check your typing or redo the steps to get a correct share path documents in step 13.

What happened?

_____

20. Close the window. On the second computer, open *File Explorer*. Right-click or tap and briefly hold on the words *This PC* in the left pane and select *Map network drive*. Use the *Drive* drop-down menu to select a drive letter. In the *Folder* textbox, type the share path for the READ share documented in step 13. Select *Finish*. The share opens with the drive letter documented in the path at the top of the window.

Instructor initials: _____

21. On the second computer, again access *File Explorer* and locate in the left pane the drive letter that was just mapped to a network drive. Note that you may have to expand the left window by moving the pointer over the dividing line between the left and right panes. When the pointer changes to a double arrow, click and move the line to the right. Because Windows share paths can be lengthy, a common practice is to use a mapped network drive for the share.

    How can you easily identify mapped drive letters in File Explorer (in addition to a quite high drive letter, in some cases)?

    _____

22. Close all windows on the second computer.

23. In *File Explorer* on the first computer, locate the *WRITE* subfolder of *Documents*. Right-click or tap and briefly hold on the *WRITE* folder icon > *Properties* > *Sharing* tab.

24. Select the *Advanced Sharing* button > enable the *Share this folder* checkbox.

25. Select the *Permissions* button.

26. Select the correct username or group and enable the *Change Allow* checkbox. Select *OK* on two consecutive windows.

    Document the share network path that appears in the window.

    _____

27. Select the *Close* option at the bottom. On the second computer, using any of the techniques previously demonstrated, locate the *changeme.txt* document located on Computer 1.

28. Modify the text inside the file and save the *changeme.txt* file.

29. On the first computer, open the *changeme.txt* file.

    Is the file changed? [Y | N]

30. On the second computer, try changing the name of the *changeme.txt* file to *changeme2.txt*.

    Can you change the name of the *changeme.txt* file? [Y | N]

31. Verify whether the filename changed on the first computer.

    Does the filename change on the first computer? [Y | N]

    If so, what is the new name?

    _____

Instructor initials: _____

32. On the second computer, right-click or tap and briefly hold on the *WRITE* folder and select *Always available offline*.

    What indication is given that a folder is available offline?

    _____

    Can a particular file be given this same attribute? [Y | N]

33. Disconnect the second computer from the network by removing the network cable from the network adapter or disabling the network card. You may have to research how to do this if you do not remember how.

34. From a command prompt on the second computer, ping the first computer by using the IP address documented in step 4 (or step 5 if it was manually assigned).

    Does the ping succeed? [Y | N]

35. With no network access on the second computer, use Computer 2 to open the *WRITE* folder and access the *changeme2.txt* file. Modify the file and save it.

36. Reconnect the second computer to the network or re-enable the NIC.

37. From the first computer, access the *WRITE* folder.

    Are the document changes saved on the first computer when the second computer was disconnected from the network? [Y | N]

38. On the second computer, again access the *changeme2.txt* file and try to permanently delete the file.

    Can you permanently delete the *changeme.txt* file? [Y | N]

39. On the first computer, create a subfolder under the *READ* folder. Name the folder *SUB_READ*. Create a text file in the *SUB_READ* folder called *sub_file.txt*.

40. On the second computer, locate and right-click or tap and briefly hold on the *SUB_READ* shared folder. Select *Properties*.

    What attributes does this folder have? [Read-only | Hidden | Archive | Compress | Encrypt | None]

41. On the second computer in *File Explorer*, locate the *sub_file.txt* file. Select *Properties*.

    What attributes, if any, are enabled by default?

    [Read-only | Hidden | Archive | Compress | Encrypt | None]

42. Select *Cancel*. Try to modify the *sub_file.txt* file.

    Can you change the *sub_file.txt* file? [Y | N]

Instructor initials: _____

43. On the second computer, remove the mapped drive (and any drive that you created on your own) by using *File Explorer* to locate the mapped drive letter under *This PC* in the left pane. Right-click the mapped drive and select *Disconnect > Yes*. Close *File Explorer*.

44. On the first computer, permanently delete the *READ* and *WRITE* folders and all files and subfolders contained within them.

45. On the first computer, put the *Advanced Sharing Settings* options back to the original configuration, as documented in step 6. Put the *Use Sharing Wizard* back to the original setting, as documented in step 8. If you manually configured an IP address in step 5, return the computer to the *Obtain an IP Address Automatically* setting. Show your lab partner the documented settings and the current profile configuration. Have your lab partner use the table that follows to document that the computer has been put back to the original configuration.

Computer 1 (permanently deleted folders/sharing settings)
Printed name of lab partner
Signature of lab partner

46. On the second computer, put the *Advanced Sharing Settings* options back to the original configuration, as documented in step 6. Put the *Use Sharing Wizard* back to the original setting, as documented in step 8. If you manually configured an IP address in step 5, return the computer to the *Obtain an IP Address Automatically* setting. Show your lab partner the documented settings and the current configuration. Have your lab partner use the table that follows to document that the computer has been put back to the original configuration.

Computer 2 (permanently deleted folders/sharing settings/IP address)
Printed name of lab partner
Signature of lab partner

Lab 18.5 Creating a Local Security Policy for Passwords

Objective: To provide additional security by requiring certain password parameters as a local computer security policy

Parts: A computer with Windows 7 Professional

Procedure: Complete the following procedure and answer the accompanying questions.

Notes: Local administrator rights are required for this lab. The computer should be part of a workgroup, not a domain. However, even though domain policy requirements override local policy, the lab may still work as written.

1.   Power on the computer and log on using the user ID and password provided by the instructor or lab assistant.

2.   Access the Local Security Policy console by selecting the *Start* button > *Control Panel* > *System and Security* > *Administrative Tools* > double-click *Local Security Policy*.

3.   Expand the *Account Policies* option.

   What two options are available?

   _____

4.   Select the *Password Policy* subcategory. Lab Table 18.1 details these options.

LAB TABLE 18.1   Windows *Password Policy* option descriptions

Option	Description
Enforce password history	Specifies the number of unique and new passwords that must be used before an old password can be reused.
Maximum password age	Specifies the number of days a password has to be used before it has to be changed.
Minimum password age	Specifies the smallest number of days for which a user can use the same password.
Minimum password length	Specifies the fewest characters required for the password. The fewest characters the password can be is zero. The more characters required, the better the security. A common setting is 7 or 8; 14 characters is the most you can require in this setting.
Password must meet complexity requirements	Sets higher standards for the password, such as not being the same as the username, being six characters or more, or requiring uppercase and lowercase letters, numerals, and symbols such as # or !.
Store passwords using reversible encryption for all users in the domain	Specifies whether passwords are stored using reversible encryption. Reversible encryption is used only if an application uses a protocol that requires knowledge of a user password for authentication purposes.

   Use Lab Table 18.2 to document the current settings.

LAB TABLE 18.2   Current *Password Policy* settings

Option	Current setting
Enforce password history	
Maximum password age	
Minimum password age	
Store password using reversible encryption for all users in the domain	
Minimum password length	
Password must meet complexity requirements	

5. Change the password policy settings to the options shown in Lab Table 18.3.

LAB TABLE 18.3 New *Password Policy* settings

Option	New setting
Enforce password history	One password remembered
Minimum password Length	Eight characters
Passwords must meet complexity requirements	Enabled

6. Create a new user account by clicking the *Start* button > *User Accounts* Control Panel > *Manage another account* link > *Create a New Account* link > type **Teststudent** for the new account name and ensure the *Standard user* radio button is selected > *Create Account* button. The Teststudent icon appears in the window. Select the *Teststudent* icon > *Create a password* link > in the *New password and confirm new password* textboxes, type **student123%**. In the Type a password hint textbox, type **student one two three** percent. Click on the Create password button.

    What indication is given that a policy is in place?

    _____

7. Log off as the current user. Log in as *Teststudent* with the password of **student123%**.

    What message appears upon logon?

    _____

8. Log off as *Teststudent* and log back in using the original user account.

9. Return to the *Local Security Policy* console. Expand *Local Policies* and select *Audit Policy*.

    What is the current setting for Audit Account Logon Events?

    [No Auditing | Success | Failure | Success and Failure]

    List three other items that can be audited.

    _____

    _____

10. Double-click the *Audit Account Logon Events* option. The two options are Success and Failure, and both options can be enabled. Success logs every time someone logs in to the computer. Failure logs every failed logon attempt. Enable both the *Success* and *Failure* checkboxes > *Apply* button > *OK* button.

11. Log off as the current user and log in as *Teststudent*, typing the password as **Tester?1** (which is an incorrect password—but use it anyway).

    What message appeared?

    _____

12. Click *OK* and this time type the correct password, **student123%**. Log off as *Teststudent*. Log back on as the original computer user.

13. To see events that have been enabled and logged, click the *Start* button *Control Panel* > *System and Security* > *Administrative Tools* > *Event Viewer* > expand the *Windows Logs* category on the left > select *Security*. Scroll down to select a line that shows as an *Audit Failure*. Note that you may need to expand the *Keywords* section by moving the pointer over the dividing line between the *Keywords* header and the *Date and Time* column header. When the pointer changes to a bar with two arrows extending from the bar, click and drag the bar to the right to expand the *Keywords* section. Look for a lock graphic instead of a key on the left.

14. Notice that when you select a security event, information about that event shows in the bottom window.

     What event number was the audit failure?

     _____

     Does the General tab show the computer name for the violation? [Yes | No]

Instructor initials: _____

15. Close *Event Viewer*. Return to the *Security Policy* console. Set the *Audit Account Logon* events setting to the original setting (refer to step 9).

     Have a classmate verify your setting and print and sign his or her name on your answer sheet.

     Classmate's printed name _____

     Classmate's signature _____

16. Configure the *Password Policy* settings to their original configuration (refer to step 4).

     Have a classmate verify your settings and print and sign his or her name on your answer sheet.

     Classmate's printed name _____

     Classmate's signature _____

17. Expand *Local Policies*. Select the *User Rights Assignment* option. Use Lab Table 18.4 to document the current settings for various options.

LAB TABLE 18.4   Windows *User Rights Assignment* settings

Option	Current setting
Access this computer from the network	
Allow logon through remote desktop services	
Deny logon locally	
Force shutdown from a remote system	
Generate security audits	
Load and unload device drivers	
Take ownership of files or other objects	
Restore files and directories	
Shut down the system	

18. Select the *Security Options* in the left pane. Use Lab Table 18.5 to document the current settings for various security options used by companies.

LAB TABLE 18.5   Windows *Security* settings

Option	Current setting
Accounts: Administrator account status	
Accounts: Guest account status	
Accounts: Rename administrator account	
Devices: Allow to format and eject removable media	
Devices: Prevent users from installing printer drivers	

Option	Current setting
Interactive logon: Message text for users attempting to log on	
Interactive logon: Prompt user to change password before expiration	
Interactive logon: Require smart card	
Network access: Let everyone permissions apply to anonymous users	
Network access: Shares that can be accessed anonymously	
Network security: Force logoff when logon hours expire	
Shutdown: Allow system to be shut down without having to log on	

Instructor initials: _____

19. Close the Security Policy console. Access *User Accounts* and remove the *Teststudent* user account.

Have a classmate verify your setting and print and sign his or her name on your answer sheet.

Classmate's printed name _____

Classmate's signature _____

20. Close the *User Accounts* window and reboot the computer.

Lab 18.6 Creating a Local Security Policy for Passwords in Windows 8/10

Objective: To provide additional security by requiring certain password parameters as a local computer security policy

Parts: A computer with Windows 8 Professional or 10 Professional or higher loaded

Notes: Local administrator rights are required for this lab. The computer should be part of a workgroup, not a domain. However, even though domain policy requirements override local policy, the lab may still work as written.

Procedure: Complete the following procedure and answer the accompanying questions.

1. Power on the computer and log on using the user ID and password provided by the instructor or lab assistant.

2. Access the Local Security Policy console by accessing the *Administrative Tools* Control Panel > double-click on *Local Security Policy*.

3. Expand the *Account Policies* option in the left pane.

What two options are available?

_____

4. Select the *Password Policy* subcategory. Lab Table 18.6 details these options.

LAB TABLE 18.6   Windows *Password Policy* option descriptions

Option	Description
Enforce password history	Specifies the number of unique and new passwords that must be used before an old password can be reused.
Maximum password age	Specifies the number of days a password has to be used before it has to be changed.
Minimum password age	Specifies the smallest number of days for which a user can use the same password.
Minimum password length	Specifies the fewest characters required for the password. The fewest characters the password can be is zero. The more characters required, the better the security. A common setting is 7 or 8; 14 characters is the most you can require in this setting.
Password must meet complexity requirements	Sets higher standards for the password, such as not being the same as the username, being six characters or more, or requiring uppercase and lowercase letters, numerals, and symbols such as # or !.
Store passwords using reversible encryption for all users in the domain	*If enabled, passwords are stored using reversible encryption. Used only if an application uses a protocol that requires knowledge of a user password for authentication purposes.*

Use Lab Table 18.7 to document the current settings.

LAB TABLE 18.7   Current *Password Policy* settings

Option	Current setting
Enforce password history	
Maximum password age	
Minimum password age	
Minimum password length	
Password must meet complexity requirements	

5.   Change the password policy settings to the options shown in Lab Table 18.8.

LAB TABLE 18.8   New *Password Policy* settings

Option	New setting
Enforce password history	One password remembered
Minimum password length	Eight characters
Passwords must meet complexity requirements	Enabled

6.   Select the *Account Lockout Policy* subcategory. Lab Table 18.9 details these options.

LAB TABLE 18.9   Windows *Account Lockout Policy* option descriptions

Option	Description
Account lockout duration	Indicates the number of minutes someone is locked out if a password is mistyped. A value of 0 requires an administrator to unlock it. Requires the *Account Lockout Threshold* to be configured.
Account lockout threshold	Indicates the number of failed logon attempts that can cause a user account to be locked. A value of 0 will never lock out a user, no matter how many times he mistypes his password.
Reset account lockout counter after	Indicates the number of minutes that have to pass before the logon attempt counter is reset to 0 bad logon attempts. Requires the *Account Lockout Threshold* option to be configured.

7. Minimize the *Local Security Policy* console. Create a new user account by using the following directions, based on whether you use Windows 8 or Windows 10:

   Windows 8: Access *Settings > Accounts >* select the *Other Accounts* link from the left pane > in the *Manage Other Accounts* section, select the *Add an Account* link > type **Teststudent** for the username and **Student234%** as the password > type **student 234 percent** in the *Password Hint* textbox > select the *Next* button > *Finish*.

   Windows 10: Access *Settings > Accounts >* select the *Family & Other Users* link from the left pane > in the *Other Users* section, select the *Add Someone Else to This PC* link > type **Teststudent** for the username and **Student234%** as the password > type **student 234 percent** in the *Password Hint* textbox > select the *Next* button.

8. Log off as the current user. Log in as *Teststudent* and a password of **Student234%**.

   What message appears upon logon?

   _____

9. Try to access the *Local Security Policy* console Administrative Tools option.

   Can the *Teststudent* user change the password policy? [Yes | No]

10. Log off as *Teststudent* and log back in using the original user account.

11. Return to the *Local Security Policy* console. Expand *Local Policies* and select *Audit Policy*.

    What is the current setting for Audit Account Logon Events?

    [No Auditing | Success | Failure | Success and Failure]

12. Double-click the *Audit account logon events* option. The two options are Success and Failure, and both options can be enabled. Success logs every time someone logs in to the computer. Failure logs every failed logon attempt.

    What are the current settings?

    Success [Enabled | Disabled]

    Failure [Enabled | Disabled]

13. Enable both the *Success* and *Failure* checkboxes > *Apply* button > *OK* button.

14. Log off as the current user and log in as Teststudent but using the password **CatchMe123** (which is an incorrect password—but use it anyway).

    What message appears upon logon?

    _____

15. Select *OK*. Log in as *Teststudent* and the correct password, **Student234%**.

16. To see events that have been enabled and logged, such as the ones just set as the local policy, access the *Administrative Tools* Control Panel > *Event Viewer* > expand the *Windows Logs* category on the left and select *Security*.

   Can the Teststudent user access Event Viewer details that were enabled in the local security policy? [Yes | No]

17. Log off as *Teststudent*. Log back on as the original computer user.

18. Access the *Administrative Tools* Control Panel > *Event Viewer* > *Security* option in the left pane > expand the *Windows Logs* category on the left and select *Security*. Scroll down to select a line that shows as an *Audit Failure*. Note that you may need to expand the *Keywords* section by moving the pointer over the dividing line between the *Keywords* header and the *Date and Time* column header. When the pointer changes to a bar with two arrows extending from the bar, click and drag the bar to the right to expand the *Keywords* section. Look for a lock graphic instead of a key on the left.

19. Notice that when you select a security event, information about that event appears in the bottom window.

   What event number is the audit failure?

   _____

   Does the General tab show the computer name for the violation? [Yes | No]

   Instructor initials: _____

20. Close *Event Viewer*. Return to the *Local Security Policy* console. Set the *Audit Account Logon Events* setting to the original setting (refer to step 11).

   Have a classmate verify your setting and print and sign his or her name on your answer sheet.

   Classmate's printed name _____

   Classmate's signature _____

21. Configure the *Password Policy* settings to their original configuration (refer to step 4).

   Have a classmate verify your password policy settings by printing and signing his or her name.

   Classmate's printed name _____

   Classmate's signature _____

22. In the *Local Security Policy* window, expand *Local Policies*. Select the *User Rights Assignment* option. Use Lab Table 18.10 to document the current settings for various commonly used options.

LAB TABLE 18.10   Windows *User Rights Assignment* settings

Option	Current setting
Access this computer from the network	
Allow log on through Remote Desktop Services	
Deny log on locally	
Force shutdown from a remote system	
Generate security audits	
Load and unload device drivers	
Restore files and directories	
Shut down the system	
Take ownership of files or other objects	

23. Select the *Security* options in the left pane. Use Lab Table 18.11 to document the current settings for various options.

LAB TABLE 18.11 Windows *Security* settings

Option	Current setting
Accounts: Administrator account status	
Accounts: Guest account status	
Accounts: Rename administrator account	
Devices: Allow to format and eject removable media	
Devices: Prevent users from installing printer Drivers	
Interactive logon: Message text for users attempting to log on	
Interactive logon: Prompt user to change password before expiration	
Interactive logon: Require smart card	
Network access: Let everyone permissions apply to anonymous users	
Network access: Shares that can be accessed anonymously	
Network security: Force logoff when logon hours expire	
Shutdown: Allow system to be shut down without having to log on	

Instructor initials: _____

24. Close the *Security Policy* console. Access *User Accounts* and remove the *Teststudent* user account by selecting the account name > *Delete the account* link > *Delete files* > *Delete account*.

   Have a classmate verify your setting and print and sign his or her name on your answer sheet.

   Classmate's printed name _____

   Classmate's signature _____

25. Close the *User Accounts* window and reboot the computer.

Lab 18.7 Using Windows Defender in Windows 7

Objective: To use System Configuration and Windows Defender to troubleshoot problems related to booting and spyware

Parts: Computer with Windows 7 installed

   User logon that has administrator rights

Note: In this lab, you explore various options that can be used within the System Configuration and Windows Defender windows. If the computer has a third-party security suite such as Norton or McAfee that has antispyware or anti-malware, the Windows Defender application may not be enabled.

Procedure: Complete the following procedure and answer the accompanying questions.

1.   Turn on the computer and verify that the operating system loads. Log in to Windows.

2.   Open *Windows Explorer*. From the *Organize* menu option > *Folder and search options* > *View* tab.

What is the current setting for the Hidden files and folders section? (Don't show hidden files, folders, or drives I Show hidden files and folders)

_____

What is the current setting for the *Hide extensions for known file types* option? [Enabled I Disabled]

What is the current setting for the Hide protected operating system files (Recommended) option? [Enabled I Disabled]

3.   Configure the following Windows Explorer settings:
     > *Show hidden files, folders, and drives* radio button—enabled (checked)
     > *Hide extensions for known file types*—disabled (unchecked)
     > *Hide protected operating system files (recommended)*—disabled (unchecked)

Click *Yes* (if prompted) > *Apply* > *OK*. Close *Windows Explorer*.

4.   Open the *Start* menu and in the *Search programs and files* textbox, type **defender** > click *Windows Defender*. If a note appears, saying that Windows Defender is turned off, select the *Click here to turn it on* option. If needed, obtain updates before continuing.

Was Windows Defender disabled? [Yes I No]

5.   Select the *Tools* menu option > *Options*.

What actions are defined from this window?

_____

_____

6.   Select the *Tools* menu option > *Quarantined items*.

List any software that Windows Defender has prevented from executing.

_____

7.   Select the *Tools* menu option > *Allowed items*.

List any software that is not monitored by Windows Defender.

_____

What happens if an item is removed from the list? How did you find this information?

_____

_____

_____

Instructor initials: _____

8.   Select the *Tools* menu option > *Options* > *Real-time protection* from the left pane.

Is Real-time protection enabled? [Yes I No]

What options are available besides enabling real-time protection?

_____

9.   Select *Excluded file types* from the left pane.

What file extension is given as an example of a file type to exclude?

_____

10. Select the *Advanced* option from the left pane.

What type of scanning is enabled? [Scan Archive Files I Scan Email I Scan Removable Drives I Use Heuristics I Create Restore Point]

_____

What will a machine do if it uses heuristics?

_____

11. Select *Administrator* from the left pane.

    What two options are configured here?

    _____

12. Return *Windows Defender* to its original state (refer to step 4).

13. Return Windows Explorer to the original settings (refer to step 2).

14. Show the instructor that the settings have been reconfigured to the original settings.

Instructor initials: _____

15. Close the *Windows Defender* window.

Lab 18.8 Using Windows Defender in Windows 8/10

Objective: To be able to use System Configuration and Windows Defender to troubleshoot boot and spyware problems

Parts: Computer with Windows 8/10 installed

            User logon that has administrator rights

Note: In this lab, you will explore various options that can be used within the System Configuration and Windows Defender windows. If the computer has a third-party security suite such as Norton or McAfee that has antispyware or anti-malware, the Windows Defender application may not be enabled.

Procedure: Complete the following procedure and answer the accompanying questions.

1. Turn on the computer and verify that the operating system loads. Log in to Windows.

2. Open *File Explorer* > *View* tab > *Options* > *Change folder and search options* > *View* tab.

   What is the current setting for the Hidden files and folders section? [Do not show hidden files and folders | Show hidden files and folders]

   What is the current setting for the *Hide extensions for known file types* option? [Enabled | Disabled]

   What is the current setting for the *Hide protected operating system files (Recommended)* option? [Enabled | Disabled]

3. Configure the following File Explorer settings:
   > *Show hidden files, folders, and drives* radio button—enabled (checked)
   > *Hide extensions for known file types*—disabled (unchecked)
   > *Hide protected operating system files (Recommended)*—disabled (unchecked)

4. Access the *Windows Defender* Control Panel. If a note appears, saying that Windows Defender is turned off, select the *Click here to turn it on* option. If needed, obtain updates before continuing.

   Was Windows Defender disabled? [Yes | No]

5. Examine the *Home* tab.

   What actions are defined from this window?

   _____

   _____

6. Select the *History* tab > select the *Quarantined Items* option. Click the *View details* button.

   List any software that Windows Defender has prevented from executing.

   _____

7. Select the *History* tab > select the *Allowed Items* option is selected. Click the *View details* button.

   List any software that is not be monitored by Windows Defender.

   _____

8. Select the *Settings* link.

    Is real-time protection enabled? [Yes | No]

    Is cloud protection available? [Yes | No]

    What options are available besides enabling real-time protection?

    _____

    _____

    _____

9. In Windows 8, select the *Advanced* option from the left pane. For Windows 10, skip to step 11.

    What type of scanning is enabled? [Scan Archive Files | Scan Email | Scan Removable Drives | Use Heuristics | Create A Restore Point | Allow All Users to View the Full History Results]

10. In Windows 8, select *MAPS* from the left pane.

    What is the purpose of MAPS?

    _____

11. Return *Windows Defender* to its original state (refer to step 4).

12. Return *File Explorer* to its original settings (refer to step 2).

13. Close all windows.

Lab 18.9 Sharing Files with Windows 8/10 Public Folders

Objective: To be able to access a file from another computer that has been shared through a Windows 8/10 public folder

Parts: Two Windows 8 or 10 computers on a wired or wireless network

Procedure: Complete the following procedure and answer the accompanying questions.

1. Ensure that the two computers have IP addresses on the same network (so you will be able to ping between the computers).

2. On both computers, make a shortcut on the desktop to the *Public* folder. The public folder is commonly located at `C:\Users\Public`.

3. On Computer 1, create a text document and put it in the *Public Documents* subfolder.

    What did you name the text document?

    _____

4. Ensure that both computers are visible from File Explorer by accessing the *Advanced sharing settings* from the *Network and Sharing Center* Control Panel and turning on *Network discovery* and File and print sharing. Turn off *Password-protected sharing*.

5. Ensure that both computers can share files using the public folder by enabling the *Turn on sharing so anyone with network access can read and write files in the Public folders* option found in the *All Networks* profile.

6. From the second computer, access and change the text document.

    Are you able to change the document across the network? [Yes | No] If not, redo the lab.

Instructor initials: _____

Lab 18.10 Configuring a Secure Wireless Network

Objective: To be able to configure a secure wireless AP (access point) or router and attach it a wireless client

Parts: One wireless access point or router

A computer with an integrated wireless NIC or a wireless NIC installed as well as an Ethernet NIC

One straight-through cable

Procedure: Complete the following procedure and answer the accompanying questions.

1. Obtain the documentation for the wireless AP or router from the instructor or the Internet.

2. Reset the wireless AP or router as directed by the wireless device manufacturer.

   Document the current Ethernet NIC IPv4 setting. [DHCP | Static IP Address]

   If a static IP address is assigned, document the IP address, subnet mask, default gateway, and DNS configuration settings.

   _____

3. Attach a straight-through cable from the computer's Ethernet NIC to the wireless AP or router.

4. Power on the computer and log on, if necessary.

5. Configure the computer with a static IP address or DHCP, as directed by the wireless device manufacturer.

6. Open a web browser and configure the wireless AP or router with the following parameters:
   > Change the default SSID.
   > Disable SSID broadcasting enabled for this lab.
   > Configure the most secure encryption and authentication supported by both the wireless NIC client and the wireless AP or router.
   > Change the default password used to access the wireless AP or router.

   Document the settings after you have configured them:

   SSID:

   _____

   SSID broadcasting disabled? [Yes | No]

   _____

   Password for wireless device access:

   _____

   Type of security used:

   _____

7. Save the wireless AP or router configuration.

8. Disconnect the Ethernet cable.

9. Enable the wireless NIC and configure it for the appropriate SSID.

10. Configure the wireless NIC for a static IP address or DHCP, as directed by the wireless AP/router manufacturer.

11. Open a web browser and access the wireless AP or router. If access cannot be obtained, troubleshoot as necessary or reset the wireless AP or router to the default configuration and restart the lab.

    What frequency (channel) is being used by the wireless AP or router and the wireless NIC for connectivity?

    _____

12. Show the instructor the connectivity.

Instructor initials: _____

13. Open a command prompt and type `netsh wlan show settings` to see the wireless network settings.

14. Reset the wireless AP or router to the default configuration settings.

15. Reset the computer(s) to the original configuration settings.

Instructor initials: _____

Lab 18.11 Configuring Windows 7, 8, or 10 with a DNS Server IP Address

Objective: To be able to configure a DNS server IP address on an Ethernet adapter

Parts: Windows 7, 8, or 10 computer with administrator access

Procedure: Complete the following procedure and answer the accompanying questions.

1. Sign into the computer and access the Network Connections section of the Control Panel.

2. Right-click on the *Ethernet* connection > *Properties*.

3. Double-click on the *Internet Protocol Version 4 (TCP/IPv4)* option.

   Document the current Ethernet NIC IPv4 settings.

   [DHCP (*Obtain an IP address automatically* radio button) | static IP address (*Use the following IP address* radio button)]

   [DHCP-provided DNS server (*Obtain DNS server address automatically* radio button) | static DNS server address (*Use the following DNS server addresses* radio button)]

   _____

   If a static IP address or DNS server address is assigned, document the IP address, subnet mask, default gateway, and DNS configuration settings.

   _____

4. Because a DNS server might be down, might be under attack, or might have been hacked, you might be required to manually configure a DNS server IP address. In this case, select the *Use the Following DNS Server Addresses* radio button.

5. In the *Preferred DNS Server* textboxes, type the IP address **208.67.222.222**, which is an OpenDNS server address hosted by Cisco Systems, Inc. > *OK*.

6. Open a web browser and access a web page that probably hasn't been used before. Some suggested ones are ThinkGeek.com, uncommongoods.com, and goodreads.com.

   Are you able to access at least one different website by using the new DNS server setting? [Yes | No]

Instructor initials: _____

7. Return to the Ethernet connection and set it back to the settings documented in step 3. Ensure that you click OK in order to save the settings.

8. Open a web browser and access a web page that probably hasn't been used before. Some suggested ones are brainyquote.com, wired.com, and codinggame.com.

   Are you able to access at least one different website by using the original DNS server setting? [Yes | No]

   Are you able to tell the difference in the speed of the access using the new DNS server setting compared to the original setting ? [Yes | No]

To receive your 10% off
Exam Voucher, register
your product at:

www.pearsonitcertification.com/register

and follow the instructions.